KNOWLEDGE AND BELIEFS IN MATHEMATICS TEACHING AND TEACHING
DEVELOPMENT

The International Handbook of Mathematics Teacher Education

Series Editor:

Terry Wood
Purdue University
West Lafayette
USA

This *Handbook of Mathematics Teacher Education*, the first of its kind, addresses the learning of mathematics teachers at all levels of schooling to teach mathematics, and the provision of activity and programmes in which this learning can take place. It consists of four volumes.

VOLUME 1:
Knowledge and Beliefs in Mathematics Teaching and Teaching Development
Peter Sullivan, *Monash University, Clayton, Australia* and Terry Wood, *Purdue University, West Lafayette, USA* (eds.)
This volume addresses the "what" of mathematics teacher education, meaning knowledge for mathematics teaching and teaching development and consideration of associated beliefs. As well as synthesizing research and practice over various dimensions of these issues, it offers advice on best practice for teacher educators, university decision makers, and those involved in systemic policy development on teacher education.
paperback: 978-90-8790-541-5, hardback: 978-90-8790-542-2, ebook: 978-90-8790-543-9

VOLUME 2:
Tools and Processes in Mathematics Teacher Education
Dina Tirosh, *Tel Aviv University, Israel* and Terry Wood, *Purdue University, West Lafayette, USA* (eds.)
This volume focuses on the "how" of mathematics teacher education. Authors share with the readers their invaluable experience in employing different tools in mathematics teacher education. This accumulated experience will assist teacher educators, researchers in mathematics education and those involved in policy decisions on teacher education in making decisions about both the tools and the processes to be used for various purposes in mathematics teacher education.
paperback: 978-90-8790-544-6, hardback: 978-90-8790-545-3, ebook: 978-90-8790-546-0

VOLUME 3:
Participants in Mathematics Teacher Education: *Individuals, Teams, Communities and Networks*
Konrad Krainer, *University of Klagenfurt, Austria* and Terry Wood, *Purdue University, West Lafayette, USA* (eds.)
This volume addresses the "who" question of mathematics teacher education. The authors focus on the various kinds of participants in mathematics teacher education, professional development and reform initiatives. The chapters deal with prospective and practising teachers as well as with teacher educators as learners, and with schools, districts and nations as learning systems.
paperback: 978-90-8790-547-7, hardback: 978-90-8790-548-4, ebook: 978-90-8790-549-1

VOLUME 4:
The Mathematics Teacher Educator as a Developing Professional
Barbara Jaworski, *Loughborough University, UK* and Terry Wood, *Purdue University, West Lafayette, USA* (eds.)
This volume focuses on knowledge and roles of teacher educators working with teachers in teacher education processes and practices. In this respect it is unique. Chapter authors represent a community of teacher educators world wide who can speak from practical, professional and theoretical viewpoints about what it means to promote teacher education practice.
paperback: 978-90-8790-550-7, hardback: 978-90-8790-551-4, ebook: 978-90-8790-552-1

PREFACE

It is my honor to introduce the first *International Handbook of Mathematics Teacher Education* to the mathematics education community and to the field of teacher education in general. For those of us who over the years have worked to establish mathematics teacher education as an important and legitimate area of research and scholarship, the publication of this handbook provides a sense of success and a source of pride. Historically, this process began in 1987 when Barbara Jaworski initiated and maintained the first Working Group on mathematics teacher education at PME. After the Working Group meeting in 1994, Barbara, Sandy Dawson and I initiated the book, *Mathematics Teacher Education: Critical International Perspectives,* which was a compilation of the work accomplished by this Working Group. Following this, Peter de Liefde who, while at Kluwer Academic Publishers, proposed and advocated for the *Journal of Mathematics Teacher Education* and in 1998 the first issue of the journal was printed with Thomas Cooney as editor of the journal who set the tone for quality of manuscripts published. From these events, mathematics teacher education flourished and evolved as an important area for investigation as evidenced by the extension of JMTE from four to six issues per year in 2005 and the recent 15th ICMI Study, *The professional education and development of teachers of mathematics.* In preparing this handbook it was a great pleasure to work with the four volume editors, Peter Sullivan, Dina Tirosh, Konrad Krainer and Barbara Jaworski and all of the authors of the various chapters found throughout the handbook.

Volume 1, *Knowledge and Beliefs in Mathematics Teaching and Teaching Development,* edited by Peter Sullivan, examines the role of teacher knowledge and beliefs. This important aspect of mathematics teacher education is at present the focus of extensive research and policy debate globally. This is the first volume in the series and is an excellent beginning to the handbook.

REFERENCES

Jaworski, B., Wood, T., & Dawson, S. (Eds.) (1999). *Mathematics teacher education: Critical international perspectives.* London: Falmer Press.

Sullivan, P. & Wood, T. (Eds.). (2008). *International handbook of mathematics teacher education: Vol. 1. Knowledge and beliefs in mathematics teaching and teaching development.* Rotterdam, the Netherlands: Sense Publishers.

Wood, T. (Series Ed.), Jaworski, B., Krainer, K., Sullivan, P., & Tirosh, D. (Vol. Eds.) (2008). *International handbook of mathematics teacher education.* Rotterdam, the Netherlands: Sense Publishers.

Terry Wood
West Lafayette, IN
USA

PETER SULLIVAN

KNOWLEDGE FOR TEACHING MATHEMATICS

An Introduction

This introduction to Volume 1 of the Handbook draws on some teachers' answers to prompts about a particular mathematics question to highlight the challenge and complexity of describing the knowledge that mathematics teachers need in order to be able to teach. It points the way to the various chapters in the volume that provide theoretical and practical perspectives on the many dimensions of this knowledge for teaching.

VOLUME 1 OVERVIEW

This volume presents research and theoretically informed perspectives on *Knowledge and Beliefs in Mathematics Teaching and Teaching Development*. The chapters together address the "what" of mathematics teacher education, meaning knowledge for mathematics teaching and teaching development and consideration of associated beliefs. As well as synthesising research and practice over various dimensions of these issues, the volume offers advice on 'best practice' for teacher educators, university decision makers, and those involved in systemic policy decisions on teacher education.

There are four sections. The first, about mathematics discipline knowledge for teaching, contains chapters on mathematics discipline knowledge from both East Asian and Western perspectives, with separate chapters addressing primary/elementary teacher education and secondary teacher education, along with a chapter on approaches for assessing this mathematics knowledge of prospective teachers. The second section describes ways of thinking about how this mathematical knowledge is used in teaching. It includes chapters on pedagogical content knowledge, on knowledge for and about mathematics curriculum structures, the way that such knowledge can be fostered with practising teachers, on a cultural analysis of mathematical content knowledge, and on beliefs about mathematics and mathematics teaching. The third section outlines frameworks for researching issues of equity, diversity and culture in teaching mathematics. The fourth section contains a description of an approach to methods of researching mathematics discipline knowledge of teachers.

This introduction is not an attempt to summarise the chapters. (I encourage you to read a perceptive description of the various chapters and their emphases, along with insights into ways of progressing thinking about knowledge for teaching, in the review chapter written by John Mason). Nor is this introduction an overview of

P. Sullivan and T. Wood (eds.), Knowledge and Beliefs in Mathematics Teaching and Teaching Development, 1–9.

the various dimensions of knowledge that teachers might be expected to have. The different sections on the volume illustrate those. Nor is it a summary of the respective research perspectives or ways of viewing knowledge for teaching. The abstracts and the respective chapters do that.

Rather, this introduction argues that the issues of teacher knowledge and belief are important and complex. It presents a rationale for anyone with an interest in mathematics teacher education to read the volume. To begin, I describe why teacher knowledge matters, then through a particular mathematics question present three perspectives on the knowledge needed for teaching mathematics, and finally consider what this means for teacher education.

TEACHER KNOWLEDGE MATTERS

The challenge of describing succinctly the knowledge required for teaching is reflected in the debate within the mathematics education community on key issues and characteristics of effective mathematics teaching. On one side of the debate, there is substantial support for a need to intertwine conventional discipline-based learning with physical, personal and social dimensions, and the imperative to develop expertise relevant for demands of global economy and the nature of thinking required. As an example, there are explicitly stated demands in Australian curriculum documents, such as: students should demonstrate useful mathematical and numeracy skills for successful general employment and functioning in society, and develop understanding of the role of mathematics in life, society and work, as well as developing flexible and creative approaches to solving problems. Those on this side of the debate recommend that students work on questions illustrating the usefulness of mathematics and those that foster creativity and engagement. The other side of the debate takes a more explicitly mathematical perspective with attention to the principles, patterns, processes, and generalisations that have conventionally formed the basis of the mathematics curriculum. It can be assumed that proponents of this side of the issue would anticipate teachers using classroom experiences that focus students' attention onto the mathematics.

It is stressed that this debate is far from academic. Schools in Western contexts, at least, are confronting serious challenges from disengaged students (e.g., Russell, Mackay, & Jane, 2003), with the implication that more interesting, functionally relevant tasks can enhance engagement (see Klein, Beishuizen, & Treffers, 1998). At the same time, there is a serious decline in the number of students entering university level mathematics courses (at least in the countries where the debate rages), threatening international competitiveness and innovation, fostering calls for more mathematical rigour at secondary level. As society, commerce, technology and more or less everything else is becoming more complex, to understand the complexity and contribute to developments requires an understanding of mathematics, and not only the formal processes, but also the power of generalisation, the nature of problem solving, and the demands for creativity, adaptability and the on-going nature of learning.

Essentially this debate is about the nature of discipline knowledge and the nature of learning, and is evidenced in various countries such as through the "Math Wars" in the United States (Becker & Jacobs, 1998) and in other disciplines, such as in the concerns about the teaching of reading in Australia (Reid & Green, 2004).

In any case, advances in technology make everyday living, the work environment, and mathematics itself more, not less, important and complex; future citizens need to be better educated than previous generations. For a better educated population we need teachers who can cope with this increased complexity, and so the knowledge that teachers bring to their classrooms matters. Again this knowledge is not just about the formal processes that have traditionally formed the basis of mathematics curriculums in schools and universities but the capacity to adapt to new ways of thinking, the curiosity to explore new tools, the orientation to identify and describe patterns and commonalities, the desire to examine global and local issues from a mathematical perspective, and the passion to communicate a mathematical analysis and world view.

LOOKING AT A MATHEMATICS QUESTION FROM THREE PERSPECTIVES

To illustrate the complexity and challenge of identifying the expected knowledge for teaching mathematics, three perspectives on the knowledge needed for teaching are described in the context of a particular mathematics question that I, with Doug Clarke (see Chapter 6, this *Handbook,* this volume) and Barbara Clarke (see Chapter 10, this *Handbook,* volume 3), asked of several teachers. As part of a survey we gave to teachers, one question invited teachers to respond to a prompt that sought insights into the extent to which they could describe the content of a particular mathematics question or idea, and the ways that they might convert the question to a lesson.

Knowing the Mathematics

The first part of the prompt to the teachers in the survey, including the mathematics question was as follows:

The following is a description of an idea that might be used as the basis of a lesson

$$\text{Which is bigger } \frac{2}{3} \text{ or } \frac{201}{301} ?$$

Suppose hypothetically I, as a mathematics teacher, might consider using this question as the basis of a lesson. The first step is to work out the answer. If I am not sure that I can work out the answer, then I probably will not use the question. There are, of course a number of ways of finding the answer, and these are categorised as one of two types:

3

Type A: Algorithmic

This type of response includes converting both denominators to 903, and either by cross multiplying or by converting the respective fractions to equivalent fractions with the denominator of 903, the fractions can then be directly compared.

A different approach, that could also be termed algorithmic, would be to convert the fractions to decimals, possibly using a calculator, and then comparing the decimal representations. Note that this is actually harder than it looks in that the decimals to be compared are 0.6677774086 and 0.666666667, which is possibly more complex for the target students than the original task.

Type B: Intuitive

This would include methods such as realising that the real comparison is $\frac{200}{300}$ and $\frac{201}{301}$. Since this is complex, a simpler comparison can be made, such as $\frac{2}{3}$ and $\frac{3}{4}$ where 1 has been added to the numerator and denominator, which clearly makes the second fraction larger. This can then be tried with different examples, and an inference made about the original comparison

Another method was described by Doug Clarke who had posed the question to some teachers in the U.S. One of them answered:

> We could think of 200/300 as a basketball player's free throw success rate, as 200 successful throws out of 300. In moving to 201/301, the basketball player has had one more throw, which was successful. His average must therefore have improved, and so 201/301 must be larger.

A third approach is directly intuitive. I have posed the question to both students and teachers, and it is interesting that many give the correct answer, but cannot explain their correct answer. For them it is actually intuitive or obvious that the second is larger. It is not for me.

Mathematics teacher educators hope that all mathematics teachers would be able to solve the question by at least one or more of the algorithmic methods. Clearly we would also hope that mathematics teachers would at least consider that intuitive type methods might be possible in this case, perhaps prompted to consider this possibility by the unusual numbers in the fractions. For both algorithmic and intuitive approaches, the knowledge required is mathematical and is not specific to teachers or teaching. We would expect that mathematicians, for example, would give more accurate and more diverse intuitive solutions than the general population, and probably more than would teachers.

Mathematical Knowledge for Teaching

Many of the authors in this volume refer to the work of Deborah Ball exemplified by the research reported by Hill, Rowan, and Ball (2005) exploring what they call mathematical knowledge for teaching which includes what they term specialised content knowledge. In the case of the question, given above, this mathematical knowledge for teaching includes the process of teachers working out how to use such a question in their teaching. For this, among other things, teachers need ways to describe what is needed to solve the question. For this, specialised knowledge is needed. In our project, we asked teachers (referring to the above question):

> If you developed a lesson based on this idea, what mathematics would you hope that the students would learn?

The fundamental concept can be described as comparing fractions, with the question offering opportunities for students to seek alternate or intuitive strategies, as well as considering formal approaches to comparisons, such as finding a common denominator or converting to decimals.

We asked 107 primary and junior secondary teachers to articulate what they saw as the content by responding to the above prompt. Many responses were disappointing, ranging from vague to inaccurate. Table 1 summarises their replies. The first category, where the respondents were able to describe what the question was about, was acceptable. The other categories, whether teachers had a limited and inaccurate view (for example, a number of teachers wrote "place value"), or a vague view (for example, one teacher wrote "What a fraction is. Fractions are just another way to write a number where they are used in everyday life"), did not convey that they understood the focus or potential of the question.

Table 1. Categorisation of responses describing the content of the question (n = 107)

	No. of responses
Students learn various ways of comparing	38
A single specific concept (not comparing)	39
General and only vaguely related multiple concepts	30

Only a little over one third of the teachers were able to specify the content of the question in a meaningful way, and there was little difference in the proportion of primary and junior secondary teachers in this category, perhaps confirming that responding to this prompt requires more than the ability to answer the question.

To be effective, teachers would need to be able to identify specific concepts associated with a question so that they can match it to curriculum documents, can talk to other teachers about it, and maybe even explain the concepts to the students. We would not, for example, expect teachers to have the specialised knowledge of researchers on ways that the learning of fraction concepts develops, for example. But we would expect teachers to be able to match a question they had seen, such as the one above, with curriculum documents or other literature.

The knowledge to do this is not just the mathematics, which is clearly a prerequisite, but is about the curriculum, the language used, connections within the curriculum, what make this question unexpectedly difficult, and even more general knowledge about strategies such as "make the problem simpler".

Mathematics Knowledge, Mathematics Knowledge for Teaching, and Pedagogy

Once teachers are confident that they can answer the question, and they have the words to describe what the question is about, there is the challenge of converting the question to a learning experience for their students. Most chapters in this volume draw on the notion, from Shulman (1986), of pedagogical content knowledge. Thankfully, most of the chapters explore the subtlety of the construct, and elaborate its meaning and implication for teacher learning. It is unfortunate that the term has often be used to include everything other than specialised mathematical knowledge, but the following chapters seek to elaborate the nature of this aspect of teachers' knowledge. In the survey mentioned above, the notion of teachers' pedagogical content knowledge was explored through the following prompt (also relating to the above question):

Describe, briefly, a lesson you might teach based on this idea.

We had hoped to see descriptions of lessons that would allow students to see that there were various ways to solve the task, and ideally teachers would plan specifically to allow students to explore the task in their own way at some stage. The categories used for their responses are presented in Table 2, along with the numbers of teachers responding in each category:

Table 2. Categorisation of the lessons based on the question (N=107)

	Responses
A teacher-centred lesson, incorporating a specific strategy for teaching the task	20
Student-centred, perhaps using a meaningful example, emphasising student generation of strategies and discussion (or the process)	14
Real life or concrete examples but only vaguely related to the concepts	38
Teacher-centred but with a general strategy not specific to the task	9
Nothing or don't know	23

Around 19% of the hypothetical lessons could be described as good traditional teaching, with a higher proportion of the secondary teachers (25%) than primary (16%) in this category. Given that the teachers identified an appropriate focus for the task, such lessons have a good chance of producing useful learning for those students. Nevertheless, such teachers may well miss key opportunities that the above question offers. For example, the fact that the question can be solved in different and non-algorithmic ways is itself powerful learning for students, and yet this traditional approach can create the impression that there is just one way.

About 13% of the lessons were of the "reform" style (the second category), with similar percentages of both primary and secondary teachers. Assuming that the teachers implement their hypothetical lesson effectively, this would be likely to foster learning, utilising the potential of the question.

The other hypothetical lessons do not create confidence that these teachers can transform a mathematics question into an effective mathematics lesson. For example, 35% of the hypothetical lessons could be described as meaningless use of relevant or real life examples. This is not what an emphasis on relevance is intended to achieve. Taken at face value, it could be suspected that most students would not learn effectively during such lessons in that the connection between the representations and the concepts may be difficult for students to ascertain for themselves.

It should be noted that the responses perhaps underestimate the potential of teachers to respond to the prompts. The prompts were part of a larger survey, although it is noted that the teachers were not rushed, and there was no advantage in finishing quickly. It is also possible that the teachers did not know how much detail we sought; the responses were therefore categorised leniently.

WHAT THIS MEANS FOR TEACHER KNOWLEDGE

It seems that the key focus of the debate should not be so much on traditional versus reform. Indeed, a well structured traditional lesson explicitly teaching a process for answering the above question, followed by structured practice, may well result in productive learning, so long as the teacher is aware that there are multiple ways of approaching the question. Nor should the debate focus on utility versus high level mathematics. Even though many teachers commented on the difficulty of identifying a practical context, the question is focused on the development of a mathematical idea, and perhaps a way of working. So a focus on mathematics does not detract from learning that can be adaptable and transferable. The debate should focus on identifying what teachers need to know to teach mathematics well. This is clearly complex and multidimensional.

To illustrate this complexity, the steps in a reform lesson based on the above question require sophisticated actions by teachers. For example, in the "reform" category of lesson in the above table, there are a number of key stages. Anne Watson and I (Chapter 5, this *Handbook,* Volume 2) describe these stages through a generic description of a lesson that might be suitable for such a question:

> Teacher poses and clarifies the purpose and goals of the question. If necessary, the possibility of student intuitive responses can be discussed.
> Students work individually, initially, with the possibility of some group work. Based on students' responses to the task, the teacher poses variations. The variations may have been anticipated and planned, or they might be created during the lesson in response to a particular identified need. The variations

might be a further challenge for some, with some additional scaffolding for students finding the initial task difficult.

The teacher leads a discussion of the responses to the initial question. Students, chosen because of their potential to elaborate key mathematical issues, can be invited to report the outcomes of their own additional explorations.

The teacher finally summarises, with the students' input perhaps, the main mathematical ideas.

The elements of this lesson all require specific actions by the teachers and therefore specific knowledge.

CONCLUSION

Overall these three perspectives – knowledge of mathematics, knowledge for teaching mathematics, and knowledge of pedagogy – on the one question given above highlight the challenge of specifying the knowledge and beliefs required for effective mathematics teaching. For example, among other things, we would expect teachers to be able to:
– answer the above question correctly;
– anticipate that intuitive methods are possible;
– use relevant language to describe the content represented by the question;
– match the content to the curriculum.
We anticipate that teachers would also:
– appreciate the difficulties that students generally, and their students in particular might experience;
– be aware that lessons can be structured so that the learning is the product of students' exploration, as distinct from listening to explanations;
– know how to pose tasks;
– know to stand back, and to wait before offering guidance;
– assess student learning; and
– conduct effective discussion and reviews.
And these qualities have not even started to explore the complexity of knowledge about pedagogy, student management, interpersonal relationships, historical perspectives, cultural influences and differences, social disadvantage, linguistic challenges, and so on.

While it is necessary that teachers know the relevant mathematics, this is clearly not sufficient. There is much more, and the challenge for mathematics teacher educators is to find ways to describe the scope and depth of knowledge. In the following chapters you will find information about ways of researching such knowledge and beliefs, ways of describing the knowledge, and ways of working with prospective and practising teachers to increase their knowledge for mathematics teaching.

REFERENCES

Becker, J. P., & Jacobs, B. (1998). 'Math War' developments in the United States (distributed by e-mail).

Hill, H. C., Rowan, B., & Ball, D. L. (2005). Effects of teachers' mathematical knowledge for teaching on student achievement. *American Educational Research Journal, 42*, 371–406.

Klein, A. S., Beishuizen, M., & Treffers, A. (1998). The empty number line in Dutch second grades: *Realistic* versus *gradual* program design, *Journal for Research in Mathematics Education, 29*, 443–464.

Reid, J., & Green, B. (2004). Displacing method(s)? Historical perspectives in the teaching of reading. *Australian Journal of Language and Literacy, 27*(1), 12–26.

Russell, V. J., Mackay, T., & Jane, G. (2003). *Messages from MYRAD (Middle Years Research and Development) – Improving the middle years of Schooling,* IARTV.

Shulman, L. S. (1986). Those who understand: Knowledge growth in teaching. *Educational Researcher, 15*, 4–14.

Peter Sullivan
Faculty of Education
Monash University
Australia

SECTION 1

MATHEMATICS DISCIPLINE KNOWLEDGE
FOR TEACHING

MIKE ASKEW

1. MATHEMATICAL DISCIPLINE KNOWLEDGE REQUIREMENTS FOR PROSPECTIVE PRIMARY TEACHERS, AND THE STRUCTURE AND TEACHING APPROACHES OF PROGRAMS DESIGNED TO DEVELOP THAT KNOWLEDGE

This chapter examines the research evidence for the sort of mathematics discipline knowledge that primary teachers might need in order to teach effectively and improve student learning. One conclusion is that, despite the wealth of research into this domain, the exact nature of such mathematical knowledge is still not clear, and the evidence for the impact on learning outcomes is equivocal. I argue that instead of trying to set out the mathematical content for prospective teachers, teacher education might be better directed at helping teachers develop a certain mathematical sensibility. I also go on to argue that trying to draw distinctions between content knowledge and pedagogical content knowledge may no longer be helpful.

INTRODUCTION

Concern about the mathematical knowledge of primary (elementary) teachers is not recent. Over a century ago Dewey (1904, 1964) argued that teachers need to be familiar with the nature of inquiry in particular domains. (I am taking 'primary' as schooling for children aged five to 11, and shall use the terms primary and elementary as interchangeable.). But it was not always thus.

In medieval universities no distinction was made between knowledge of a discipline and knowing how to teach it – if you knew the former, it was assumed that you would be able to teach it (McNamara, Jaworski, Rowland, Hodgen, & Prestage, 2002). Today, apprenticeship models of learning still draw no distinction between being an expert crafts-person and being able to induct an apprentice into the craft. With the introduction of schooling for greater numbers of children, however, a separation of knowing and teaching evolved. Discipline knowledge, rather than taken as a given, begins to be problematised. Teaching moved from being part of ongoing practices within disciplines; teaching became a practice in its own right. This meant the need to impart knowledge *about* disciplines that one was not necessarily part *of*. Knowing (doing) and teaching were severed.

P. Sullivan and T. Wood (eds.), Knowledge and Beliefs in Mathematics Teaching and Teaching Development, 13–35.

Once this separation of knowing and teaching, of content and pedagogy occured, then questions about the extent and form of the discipline knowledge for teaching emerge.

Common sense suggests that an effective teacher of mathematics would need to have understanding of the discipline, so it is hardly surprising that researchers are interested in the mathematics that primary teachers may need to know. But is common sense correct? The evidence for exactly what primary teachers (both prospective and practising) do need to know about mathematics is still debated. In this chapter I explore something of the current state of this debate and suggest some directions that the argument may go.

Although the overall focus of the chapter is on prospective teachers much of the research in this area has explored the mathematics of practising teachers. So I also draw on this research. Partly for pragmatic reasons: the research on prospective primary school teachers is less extensive than that on practising teachers. Partly for theoretical reasons: looking at what experienced primary teachers need to know may help clarify what might need to be addressed with prospective teachers. My gaze thus encompasses studies both of prospective and practising teachers.

Two thousand and eight seems an opportune time to be taking stock of the research into the mathematical subject knowledge of primary teachers, as the field might be considered to have recently 'come of age', if one takes 1986 as a birth-date. Marking 1986 is not arbitrary. First, that year marks the publication of what is possibly the seminal paper on knowledge for teaching, Lee Shulman's 'Those who understand: knowledge growth in teaching' (Shulman, 1986). Also published that year was the 3rd Edition of the *Handbook of Research on Teaching* (Wittrock, 1986). Connolly, Clandinin, and He (1997, p. 666) note that in that edition of the Handbook there are only two, relatively minor, references to research into teacher knowledge and suggest that since then the field has 'exploded'. Since 1997 this explosion has not diminished: this chapter is necessarily selective of the literature.

As well has the huge expansion of studies over the last 20 years or so, another significant change continues to foreground the importance of teacher subject knowledge. In many parts of the world, there has been increasing political and policy involvement in the setting out and defining of the subject knowledge for teaching generally and mathematics specifically (Poulson, 2001). Defining and codifying of subject knowledge for teaching is taken by many policy makers as central to improving standards of pupil learning. In England, for example, much policy effort and public funding has gone into attempts to improve teachers' subject knowledge: centrally determined curricula have been set out for teacher educators to follow, prospective teachers have had their subject knowledge 'audited'; and online teacher tests of 'numeracy' have been developed. It is worth asking whether research findings warrant such efforts.

PRIMARY TEACHERS: THE CASE FOR DISCIPLINE KNOWLEDGE?

Elsewhere in this volume Kaye Stacey, and Shiqi Li and colleagues present the case for mathematics subject knowledge and secondary school teachers; and

Yeping Li and colleagues do the same for primary level teachers. As I argue below the evidence for the importance of subject knowledge in primary schools is more equivocal.

Across the studies into teacher knowledge, two particular questions recur:

What is the relationship between teachers' mathematics subject knowledge and the teaching and learning of mathematics in primary schools?

What sort of mathematics subject knowledge do primary school teachers need to know?

In a fully rational world the second question would only be addressed once the first had been answered. But, if as indicated, common-sense suggests that there must be a relationship between discipline knowledge and the ability to teach, then work can proceed on the second question prior to the first being answered. And indeed, despite mixed answers to the first question, work continues unabated on the second. For example, in a major study into young children learning mathematics. Kilpatrick and colleagues (National Research Council, 2001) address these questions in reverse order, looking first at 'knowledge of mathematics' and then 'teachers' mathematical knowledge and student achievement' (pp. 372–377). With regard to knowledge of mathematics, the authors claim that content knowledge is 'the cornerstone of teaching for proficiency' and

improving teachers' mathematical knowledge and their capacity to use it to do the work of teaching is crucial in developing students' mathematical proficiency. (p. 372)

Just over a page later, however, in examining the links between teacher content knowledge and student achievement, the same writers report:

For the most part, the results have been disappointing: Most studies have failed to find a strong relationship between the two." (p. 373)

A North American review of research asked what kind of subject matter preparation is needed for prospective teachers (Wilson, Floden, & Ferrini-Mundy, 2001). Drawing on rigorous selection for inclusion of studies, the authors could only find seven studies, four of which included mathematics and of these four only one addressed the mathematics subject knowledge of elementary teachers (Darling-Hammond, 2000). Wilson and her colleagues report that the conclusions from these studies in establishing the impact of discipline knowledge are contradictory and "undermine the certainty often expressed about the strong link between college study of a subject matter area and teacher quality" (p. 6).

It is unusual to find a paper on teachers' subject knowledge that does not pay homage to Shulman's work on forms of knowledge for teaching. Less often acknowledged is the cautiousness that Shulman and his colleagues' expressed over generalising the range of their work to primary school teachers (Grossman, Wilson, & Shulman, 1989; Shulman, 1987; Wilson, Shulman, & Richert, 1987). In his 1987 paper, Shulman expresses his *belief* that findings from the research carried out with secondary school teachers may well apply to primary teachers, but was "reluctant to make that claim too boldly" (p. 4). A little later, Grossman and colleagues (1989) point out that there are considerable differences between teaching only one subject in secondary schools and the demands of teaching several subjects in primary schools and that imputing implications from their work in secondary schools 'for elementary school teaching should be drawn cautiously' (p. 28).

Despite such caveats, one thing is clear from the research evidence: many prospective and practising primary teachers have, or express, a lack of confidence in their mathematical knowledge. Wragg, Bennett, and Carré (1989) surveyed teachers from 400 primary schools in Great Britain and found a self-reported lack of confidence in their knowledge of the mathematics required to teach the national curriculum (although these same teachers expressed an even greater lack of confidence about science). Other research by the same team assessed prospective teachers' knowledge of mathematics (and other subjects) at the beginning and end of their teacher education. For many their knowledge was limited both times.

In a study of teaching 4- to 7-year-olds, Aubrey (1997) found that teachers claimed not to have extensive knowledge of mathematics. Many other studies have found similar results (Bennett & Turner-Bisset, 1993; Rowland, Barber, Heal, & Martyn, 2003; Simon & Brown, 1996).

What such studies, particularly, but not exclusively from the USA and UK, established is a *deficit* model of teachers' knowledge, leading to at least two impacts. Firstly, focusing on what primary teachers did not know fanned the flames of a 'crisis' in the knowledge base of the teaching forces. Even now, findings are couched in terms of the negative: Stacey, Helme, Stienle, Baturo, Irwin, and Bana (2003) report that 'only 80% of the sample tested as experts' (p. 205). While it might be reasonable to expect 100% to be proficient, at 80% the pot is certainly much more full than empty. Secondly, it was imputed that improving teachers' subject knowledge would necessarily improve teaching and learning (Askew, Brown, Rhodes, Wiliam, & Johnson, 1997a; Brown, Askew, Baker, Denvir, & Millett, 1998). However, such a conclusion needs to be treated cautiously.

With colleagues (Askew & Brown, 1997; Brown et al., 1998) I have argued that while there may be evidence that teachers lack subject knowledge when this is assessed outside the context of the classroom: whether or not this is a hindrance in practice is more difficult to establish. For example, in our study of effective teachers of numeracy (number sense) we observed only two occasions where teachers appeared to be hampered by a lack of mathematical knowledge, out of 86 mathematics lessons observed in total. We concluded that while some teachers of younger children may have real problems with their understanding of subject knowledge, it was not clear how much this actually impacted on their effectiveness (Askew et al. (1997a, p. 59).

Bennett and Carre (1993) found that prospective primary teachers who were mathematics specialists did display greater subject knowledge than those specialising in other areas (music and early years). However when they observed all these prospective teachers actually teaching they found little difference in their practices that distinguished the mathematics specialists from the non-specialists teaching mathematics. These observations took place whilst the teachers were still in training so we do not know if there was a longer term impact of the mathematics specialists' greater subject knowledge. It may be that novice teachers share a common set of concerns, irrespective of their subject specialism. Concerns centred around becoming familiar with the curriculum, planning lessons, managing 30 or more children, and building productive classroom relationships. Such concerns initially may over-ride attention to the particularities of subject content; in moving from being novice teachers to experienced ones, specialised content knowledge may begin to have an impact.

Nevertheless, it would seem that a certain threshold of discipline knowledge is necessary for effective teaching. Whilst a major longitudinal study carried out in the 1960s could find no association between teachers' study of higher level mathematics and their students' achievement, the director later argued that teachers need to attain a certain level of mathematical understanding, but that beyond a certain level further study of mathematics did not lead to increased student gains (Begle, 1979). A later study found associations between student attainment and the number of mathematics courses that their teachers had studied, but only up to a certain number of courses (although this was with secondary teachers, there is no reason to suppose the results would be different for primary) (Monk, 1994).

A major difficulty in establishing the impact of discipline knowledge is the means by which teachers' mathematical knowledge has been identified and quantified. Until recently studies have often relied on proxies such as highest level of formal qualification in mathematics or courses taken rather than looking 'inside the black box' at the mathematics that teachers actually draw on when teaching.

The fact that such proxies have not demonstrated a link between subject matter knowledge and teaching expertise or pupil outcomes is hardly surprising as there are at least two problems.

Firstly, the assumption that examination results are an accurate reflection of someone's level of understanding. Success on formal mathematics examinations may be attained through a base of procedural rather than conceptual understanding, and it may be that is the view of mathematics that such 'successful' teachers develop. This conjecture is supported by research we carried out in England. Observations of lessons conducted by teachers with higher formal mathematical qualifications did tend to be more procedural in their content. These same teachers, in interview, expressed difficulty in understanding why some pupils had problems with mathematics. Further, there was a slight negative association between the gains over the course of a year that the pupils made on a specially designed number assessment and the highest level of mathematical qualification of their teachers: the higher the level of qualification, the lower the gains the pupils made (Askew, Brown, Rhodes, Wiliam, & Johnson, 1997b).

Secondly, even if qualifications are an accurate measure of understanding, are they the ones that teachers will need to draw on in the classroom? As discussed below, it is only recently that researchers have begun to try and 'unpack' the knowledge specifically needed from primary teaching.

To summarise, there is agreement in the literature on prospective and practising primary teachers' mathematical knowledge in the conclusion that a certain lack of knowledge of mathematics is associated with less successful teaching and lower student attainment.

The flip-side of this argument – that more subject knowledge is linked to better teaching and learning – is less well established. In part this is a result of the proxies used as measures to examine subject knowledge. More recent studies have begun to examine more closely the nature and content of discipline knowledge needed by primary teachers, and it is to these that I now turn.

DISCIPLINE KNOWLEDGE: FROM WHETHER TO WHAT?

In this section I look at ways that various writers have classified mathematics discipline knowledge for primary teachers. The work of Ball and her colleagues has been particularly influential in the study of the mathematics for teaching and most classifications bear strong resemblances to frameworks that they have set out. For example, in an early work, Ball (1990) argues for attention to the distinction between knowledge *of* mathematics – the various meanings attached to different representations and associated procedures. Alongside this, teachers also need to have knowledge *about* mathematics – the means by which 'truth' is established within the discipline. This distinction echoes Lampert's (1986) separation of procedural and principled knowledge, the former involving 'knowing that', and includes the rules and procedures of mathematics ('knowledge of mathematics' in Ball's terms). Principled knowledge is more conceptual – the knowing why of mathematics. Other similar distinctions are between the substantive (facts and concepts) and the syntactic (nature of knowledge growth in the field through inquiry and, in the case of mathematics, proof) (Shulman, 1986).

Even earlier was Skemp's (1976) setting out of instrumental or relational understanding. As is often the case, a dominant metaphor here is that of a map. For Skemp, instrumental understanding was analogous to being given step-by-step instructions for getting from A to B; many people's understanding of traditional algorithms would be described as instrumental. Relational understanding is more akin to having a map; so if one gets lost then one has the wherewithal to figure out the way back to the right path.

Thompson, Philipp, Thompson, and Boyd (1994) discuss the difference between calculational and computational, although this distinction is more akin to beliefs about the curriculum than about mathematical knowledge per se. It could be perfectly possible for a teacher to have a rich and varied understanding of the mathematics curriculum and yet still hold that learning basic computational skills is the goal of primary mathematics teaching.

The work of Grossman, Wilson, and Shulman (1989) is based around three dimensions (Thompson et al., 1994) rather than two. Like later writers they stress the importance of understanding the organising principles of a discipline, and also factual knowledge and central concepts.

Distinctions between conceptual/procedural, instrumental/relational and so forth seem reasonable, but closer examination reveals some difficulties. Suppose a teacher knows how to carry out a multiplication algorithm accurately but cannot articulate how it works. Is the ability to correctly carry out the calculation any less 'conceptual' than being able to explain how it works? Much of mathematics relies on procedural fluency, so there is a danger in perceptions of conceptual 'good', procedural 'bad'.

Also, looking at the mathematics that teachers draw on in mathematics lessons could be as much a measure of their beliefs about the role of mathematics in the curriculum as about their knowledge of mathematics per se. For example, researchers have identified teachers with good understanding of mathematics but who still adopted 'transmission' style teaching approaches rather than work on crafting student explanations (D. Ball, 1991; D. L. Ball, 1991).

Thus a number of distinctions have been drawn up which are now largely taken as descriptive most notably between discipline knowledge and pedagogical knowledge. Within discipline knowledge the distinction is made between 'facts, concepts and procedures' – the established cannon of mathematical knowledge – and the way that the community of mathematicians has come to establish this knowledge. Within pedagogic knowledge there is a similar separation of knowledge of how to teach particular mathematical topics (didactics) and knowledge of how the individual learner might develop understanding (psychology). In Davis and Simmt's (2006) terms these are assumed distinctions between established/dynamic and collective/individual. They argue that the distinctions between 'formal disciplinary knowledge and instructional knowledge ... between established collective knowledge and dynamic individual understandings ... are inherently problematic' (p. 293). I return to this point later.

Despite the prevalence of the claims for there to be (at least) two sides to the coin of mathematics subject knowledge, surprisingly little attention has been paid to setting out the range of procedural/factual knowledge that it might be reasonable for primary teachers to know. This aspect appears, by and large, to be taken for granted: either this is the bulk of subject knowledge that teachers have learned through their own mathematics education or they gain it through teaching and becoming familiar with such knowledge as embodied in curriculum materials.

Our own research at King's College, London, supports the conjecture that procedural knowledge of mathematics is not the issue. As part of a five-year longitudinal study of teaching and learning numeracy in primary schools (the *Leverhulme Numeracy Research Programme*, Millett, Brown, & Askew, 2004), we interviewed a group of teachers about a variety of mathematics problems. Their responses indicated that they could, on the whole, arrive at correct answers. But when it came to probing the rationales behind their answers, it became clear that their solutions were based on instrumental/procedural approaches. The difficulty here is not that teachers were unable to reach correct answers, but that they were not able to generalise from their answers.

Where attention has turned to looking in detail at the content of teachers' subject knowledge the focus is often on the *quality* of understandings rather than the actual *content* of them. As Freudenthal (1975) expressed it, it may be that more nuanced understandings are required. Ball and Bass (2003) similarly argue that mathematics-for-teaching knowledge is not a case of knowing more than or to a greater 'depth' than that expected of students; it needs to be qualitatively different.

Ma (1999) expresses qualitative difference through her construct of 'profound understanding of fundamental mathematics' (PUFM) such understanding being exhibited by the Chinese teachers in her study, whilst the USA teachers presented knowledge that was lacking in conceptual underpinning and 'unconnected'. Powerful though Ma's evidence is, it still only partially sets out what such PUFM might look like. Her detailed qualitative work addresses a small number of the topics in the primary mathematics curriculum. And the teachers involved in Ma's study were specialist mathematics teachers and so not representative of the majority of primary school teachers.

Nevertheless, the metaphor of teachers needing to have 'connected' mathematical knowledge resonates through other research. Our study of effective teachers of numeracy in primary schools engaged teachers in constructing 'concept maps' of understanding number (Novak & Gowin, 1984). In interviews, we asked teachers to list as many topics in learning about number in the primary years as they could. Each topic was noted on a separate 'stickie'. The teachers then 'mapped' these out onto a larger sheet of paper. Once the locations of these topic 'landmarks' had been chosen, the teachers drew arrows connecting topics: arrows could be one or two headed to indicate directions of links, and topics could have multiple connections. Finally, and importantly, they were asked to label the arrows to provide concise descriptions of the nature of the connections.

We analysed the completed concept maps in terms of the numbers of connections identified, the range of the connections and the quality of the descriptions of the links. We found that there was a strong association between the complexity of the maps that teachers produced and the average gains in scores that their classes attained on a numeracy assessment over the course of a year. Where teachers had more 'connected' maps, the gains for classes were higher (Askew et al., 1997a). Writing recently, Hough, O'Rode, Terman, and Weisglass (2007) look at how concept maps can also be used with prospective teachers to help them think about connections in mathematics.

Like our study, Ma's conclusions about teachers' knowledge are based on interviews rather than observation of actual classroom practice. Ball and her colleagues have turned to taking an approach more grounded in practice by looking at the demands made in classrooms (Ball, Hill, & Bass, 2005). For example, by looking in detail at the standard algorithm for long multiplication they draw out the knowledge of language and representations that teachers may need in teaching the algorithm.

Will working on areas such as those identified by Ball et al. improve teaching? It may be that the mathematical behaviours demonstrated by effective teachers are still proxies for something else – a mathematical sensibility – that cannot be reduced to a list of mathematical topics. And transfer across the curriculum is an issue. For example, an item from the Ball research asks teachers to judge which of several 'non-standard' vertical algorithms would work for any multiplication. If teachers are able to answer this correctly, does that indicate a similar ability to unpack non-standard methods for, say, division?

One of the few reports to set out the actual range of subject knowledge that prospective elementary school teachers might be expected to be confident in is the report of the Conference Board of the Mathematical Sciences (2001). In terms of number and operations, the authors' argue that

> Although almost all teachers remember traditional computation algorithms, their mathematical knowledge in this domain generally does not extend much further. … In fact, in order to interpret and assess the reasoning of children learning to perform arithmetic operations, teachers must be able to call upon a richly integrated understanding of operations, place value, and computation in the domains of whole numbers, integers, and rationals. (p. 58)

When it comes to adumbrating the learning needed, there is little that looks different to what one might find in a typical primary mathematics syllabus. Teachers, for example, are expected to develop 'a strong sense of place value in the base-10 number system' which includes 'recognizing the relative magnitude of numbers' (p. 58). Readers are left to decide for themselves exactly what constitutes a 'strong sense'.

Part of the problem here is the codification of networks of knowledge into discrete lists of points (death by a thousand bullet points). Working with a group of teachers to elicit the range of representations that might be grouped together as multiplication, Davis and Simmt (2006) conclude that 'multiplication was not the sum of these interpretations. … we conjecture that access to the web of interconnections that constitute a concept is essential for teaching' (p 301). They challenge attempts to delineate and list the elements of mathematical knowledge:

> What is multiplication? has no 'best' or 'right' answer. Responses, rather, are matters of appropriateness or fitness to the immediate situation. The underlying notion of adequacy that is at work here stands in contrast to the pervasive assumption that mathematical constructs are unambiguous and clearly defined. (p. 302)

Formulating content lists is prey to another difficulty: the assumption that the traditional curriculum will continue to be the bedrock of primary mathematics. That central to the curriculum is 'children learning to perform arithmetic operations' and, as Ball, Hill, and Bass. (2005) assert, that they need to be 'able to use a reliable algorithm to calculate an answer' (p.17). Some curricula, for example in Australia, have already tossed the 'reliable algorithm' for long division onto the curriculum scrap-heap, with the view that new technologies have produced more efficient and reliable methods for carrying out such calculations. It may be the case that other algorithms are regarded similarly in the future. Assuming that the primary curriculum will not (need not?) change very much in the near future may become a self-fulfilling prophecy if too much effort goes into specifying the knowledge that teachers need to know.

Rather than acquire a 'body' of mathematical knowledge, perhaps primary teachers need something else – a mathematical sensibility – that would enable them to deal with existing curricula but also be open to change.

A FRAMEWORK FOR WORKING WITH PROSPECTIVE TEACHERS

Rather than expecting primary teachers to enter the profession knowing all the discipline knowledge that they might ever need to draw on, is it more reasonable to expect them to learn new aspects of the discipline, as and when they need to? As Sullivan (2003) argues 'so long as teachers have the orientation to learn any necessary mathematics, and the appropriate foundations to do this, then prior knowledge of particular aspects of content may not be critical' (p. 293).

How then might we encourage this sort of orientation? What sort of foundations might it need? At the risk of adding to an already burgeoning number of frameworks for considering mathematics subject knowledge for teaching, I set out what I consider to be key elements for prospective primary teachers. My starting point is adapted from Whitehead (1929, reprinted 1967). He argues that the curriculum should be a process, a cycle of exploration and inquiry, a blend of 'romance, precision and generalization' (p. 17). Whitehead suggested that these three elements should, to an extent, follow each other in that order; I look at them in the order of precision, generalization and romance. To illustrate my arguments I draw on examples from the domain of multiplicative reasoning.

Precision

The Oxford English Dictionary definition of precision involves being 'definite, exact, accurate and free from vagueness'. Accuracy is thus part of precision but not the whole of it. Accuracy does, however, provide a starting point for considering of precision, and accuracy is arguably the part of the mathematics curriculum with which most primary teachers are most familiar. Indeed for many it is the main purpose of the mathematics curriculum: getting right answers (and, unfortunately for some learners, getting them right quickly). It is also part of the curriculum dear to the hearts of policy makers. Any perceived attempts to diminish this aspect of the curriculum are met with cries of lowering of standards and 'fuzzy' teaching. Hence the continuing debate in some parts of the world on whether or not 'standard algorithms' should be taught.

But accuracy without insight is limiting. As discussed earlier, as part of a large, longtitudinal study (Millett, Askew, & Simon, 2004) my colleagues and I interviewed 12 teachers about a number of mathematical tasks. In the main, they were able to find accurate answers to the tasks. But their approaches to finding answers revealed a lack of insight into how and why correct answers can come about. A question we asked about factors and divisibility illustrates the difficulty.

Inscribed in the English national curriculum for mathematics is the expectation that children are taught rules of divisibility. We presented the teachers a selection of numbers and asked them to figure out which digits were divisors of each of the numbers (calculators were available). For example, they had to decide which digits were factors of 165. The teachers all were confident that 165 would not be divisible by 2, or 4 ("it's odd") and that ending in 5 meant it was divisible by 5. They knew that there was a rule for checking divisibility by 3, although some needed help to recall it.

However, deciding whether or not 6 was a factor of 165 was not immediately apparent to them. Ten of the twelve teachers needed to carry out dividing by 6 to check whether or not there was a remainder. Asked whether knowing that 165 was not divisible by 2 could help in deciding if 6 was a factor, they reasoned along the lines of "no, because the fact that it was divisible by 3 might have made 6 a factor".

The final number we presented was $3^2 \times 5^2 \times 7$. This time, all 12 teachers had to multiply the product out to 1575 and then check each digit in turn. When they had established that 3, 5, 7 and 9 were factors we asked whether, looking back at the original number, they might have been able to predict any of these results. No, was the general response. The sense of why they could not have predicted this outcome was summed up by the teacher who said: "No, because you never know that the way the 3s, 5s and 7 were multiplied together may have led to it being divisible by, say, 2."

None of the teachers appeared particularly surprised at the result that having started with a combination of 3s, 5s and 7 the only factors to emerge were 3, 5, 7 and 9. These teachers displayed a marked lack of curiosity about the connection between the initial product and their answers. This issue of being mathematically curious is one that I return to below.

But precision is more than accuracy. For instance teachers need to be aware of the importance of precise language in describing mathematical action. In a lesson observed as part of this same research programme, a teacher was modelling division with a class of 8- and 9-year-olds. She had a number of children standing holding empty boxes and was modelling how many boxes would be filled if 7 cubes from 42 were put into each box; the model was of division as quotition (measurement). However, throughout the modelling the teacher kept up a running commentary about how the cubes were being 'shared out' amongst the boxes: the language of division as partition. While problems like 'How many bags are needed to put 42 apples into bags of 7?' and "How many apples will be in each bag if 42 are shared between 7 bags?' can both ultimately be represented by 42   6, children are likely initially to solve these in different ways. Teachers need to appreciate the need for precision and not muddling the two models through inappropriate marrying up of words and actions.

Generalization

Without awareness of the move into the general, teaching and learning primary mathematics is unlikely to move beyond an emphasis on getting correct answers.

For example, consider exploring with children whether or not the equation

$$45 \times 24 = 90 \times 12$$

is true or not.

Working from a base of precision, one way to answer this is to test it out; calculating the product on each side of the equation will reveal the equation to be correct. Inspection of the numbers involved may suggest a connection between them. This could be tested out with other similar examples, arriving at a conjecture that doubling one number and halving the other preserves the answer. This empirical approach to generalising does not establish why the conjecture holds true, or whether or not it will continue to hold. And it does not provoke curiousity into whether or not this can be generalised further – would trebling one number and 'thirding' the other also work? A generalisation is reached, but it is a rule-without-reason.

Consider, instead, modelling this with an array. I appreciate that some readers may think that this strays into the realm of pedagogic-content knowledge here, rather than content knowledge. Arrays provide a powerful model for examining the structure of multiplication and so, I suggest, are as much part of content knowledge as pedagogic. A few simple diagrams, as shown in Figure 1, with an open array quickly establishes the veracity of the equation.

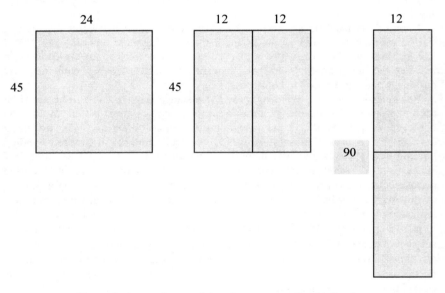

Figure 1: Arrays for examining the structure of multiplication.

This analytic approach to generalising (Schmittau, 2003) goes beyond the 'specialise (through lots of examples) generalise model' to seeing the general-in-the-specific. It is a precise argument, but not based on the precision of answers. The move to the general is a short one – the actual dimensions of the rectangles are immaterial and the argument can, literally, be seen to hold whatever dimensions are used to label the sides. Generalising is an adjunct to precision.

But the use of the array goes beyond establishing the specific result. It opens up the possibility of other constructions: do we only have to slice our rectangle into two pieces? What about three slices? Or four? Curiosity is opened up.

Romance

Mathematics has beauty and romance. It's not a boring place to be, the mathematical world. It's an extraordinary place; it's worth spending time there. (Marcus du Sautoy, Professor of Mathematics, University of Oxford)

Beauty maybe considered a quality pertaining to the other – the quality of mathematics that gives pleasure. Or it may be in the eye of the beholder – how the subject finds beauty in mathematics. Whichever, there is a 'distance' between subject and object. Beauty can be admired from afar. Romance, however, implies intimacy, a certain reciprocity, an entering in to a relationship *with* the other. *Care* and *curiosity* are elements of entering into a romantic relationship with another person that I suggest can be applied to romance with mathematics.

Romance and Care
Noddings (1992) questions whether it is too anthropomorphic to talk of caring for an abstract discipline like mathematics. Her basic position is that of establishing caring relationships, so a caring relationship with mathematics may indeed be problematic, and that 'strictly speaking, one cannot form a relation with mathematics' (p. 20). After all, how can mathematics care 'back'? Yet, she argues, we can talk meaningful about caring for mathematics, that 'oddly, people do report a form of responsiveness from ideas and objects. The mathematician Gauss was "seized" by mathematics' (p. 20). And Bertrand Russell is said to have described mathematics as his chief source of happiness.

Noddings goes on to argue that

teachers should talk with students about the receptivity required in caring about mathematics. People can become engrossed in mathematics, hear it "speak to them," be seized by its puzzles and challenges. It is tragic to deprive students of this possibility. (Noddings, 1992, p. 152)

Initial education for prospective teachers often engages them in mathematical inquiry. But to what extent does such work engross, seize or challenge teachers with mathematics? Davis and Simmt (2003) suggest that a common purpose of engaging teachers in mathematical inquiry is predominantly pedagogical, so that teachers are better placed to model to students 'what it means to engage with mathematical problems and processes'. This, they argue is problematic because treating teaching as

a modelling activity seems to be rooted in the assumption of radical separations among persons in the classroom. The teacher models, the learner mimics, but their respective actions are seen to be separable and to spring from different histories, interests and so on. (Simmt, Davis, Gordon, & Towers, 2003)

In my experience of engaging teachers in mathematical inquiry, they talk not so much in terms of how the experience will help them model for their students but more of re-entering the experience of being a learner – the joys and frustrations of engaging in such work. The emphasis is still individualistic with a focus on the learner experience rather than the mathematics. Either response – modelling or empathy - not only separates teachers and students, it enable teachers to maintain a distance from the mathematics. The focus of mathematical inquiry with primary school teachers needs to be on the mathematics.

Building on Noddings' work I add the distinction between caring *for* and caring *about*. It probably is unreasonable to expect all primary school teachers to care for mathematics – people develop different appetites for different subjects. But they do, I think, have a duty to care about mathematics: to recognise and acknowledge the role that mathematics has played and continues to play in shaping the world we live in. One step in promoting caring about is the development of curiosity.

Romance and Curiosity
When a National Curriculum was first established in England, funding was provided for many primary teachers to engage in 20 days of mathematical professional development. Local funding for this was conditional on teachers working on their discipline knowledge. As the 20 days released from school were spread over two terms there was sufficient time to establish relationships with teachers that allowed for working on aspects of mathematics that they might usually shy away from.

On one such course that I conducted, the following incident occurred towards the end when the teachers and I had got to know each other quite well. Working on a particular inquiry I had given out some calculators. One of the teachers, Ursula, called me over.

"My cheap calculator that I bought at a garage has got a $1/x$ button on, so why doesn't this expensive one?"

"Well, it does," I replied " it's that x^{-1} button."

This seemed an opportunity to explore powers and so I stopped everyone to go through an argument as to why x^{-1} is equated with $1/x$.

While the teachers' nods during my explanation suggested that they were following my argument, afterwards there was a lot of muttering at Ursula's table.

"Is there anything you are not clear about?' I enquired.

"No, we follow your argument," Ursula replied. "But we were just saying to each other, 'why would anyone ever want to do that in the first place?'"

This incident has stayed with me over the years, acting as a touchstone for several issues. First it highlights that teachers' emotional relationship with mathematics cannot be separated from their intellectual, cognitive, knowledge of the subject. This was a group of teachers who had begun to work with the mathematics intellectually – they were willing to 'play the game' of developing mathematical ideas with me. But they were not engaged with the game in the sense of deriving satisfaction from the pleasure of playing it, as evidence by the asking of why would anyone want to do that. Hodgen (2004) highlights the importance of desire and imagination in developing and transforming teachers' relationships with mathematics.

We talk about engagement with mathematics as if the playing around with ideas in and of itself is sufficient to make teachers and pupils want to carry on with the play. As Simmt, Davis, Gordon, and Towers (2003) put it, teachers have an 'obligation' to be curious about mathematics. Prospective teachers are encouraged to be curious about students' responses to mathematics but this needs to be counterbalanced with a curiosity about mathematics itself. Visiting a class recently, the teacher, in slightly exasperated terms, asked me 'why, just when you think the children have got it, they can just as easily lose it?' When I asked to elaborate on what the 'it' was, she talked of a boy who could correctly say whether or not a number up to 8 was odd or even, but had answered that nine was also even. I suspected that he may have over-generalised and, sure enough when I asked him why he thought nine was even, he demonstrated how nine tallies could be set out into three 'even' (that is, same sized) sets. Part of being curious here is about being interested in the pupil's thinking, but there is also the curiosity of wondering if it is possible to construct a mathematics where nine could be considered even. Such mathematical curiosity, when present 'compels teacher attendance to student articulations, it opens up closed questions, and … can trigger similar contributions from learners' (Simmt et al., 2003, p. 181).

Simmt and her colleagues go on to argue that 'curiosity is not an innate proclivity, but can be learned, to some extent at least' and that this learning of curiosity comes about through collective activity – a theme I return to in the final section.

One of the delicious aspects of entering into a new romantic relationship is finding out about the history of the other. Being curious about the history of mathematics is another aspect of subject knowledge that I would argue is necessary.

Knowledge of the history of mathematics can help teachers appreciate that there is no one single story, no 'truth' of the way that mathematics has developed. For example the story of 'Pascal's' triangle challenges the popularly held belief that mathematics is the result of individual activity and inspiration. Although key theories are attributed to individuals – Newton Pascal, Pythagoras – these individuals were part of ongoing communities, collectives. Not only did they stand on the shoulders of giants, they rubbed shoulders with their peers. The development of mathematics is a collective endeavour.

The story of the development of mathematics as one of the emergence and invention of ideas, either to solve problems or simply through 'playing' with mathematical objects, may challenge dominant views of the linearity of learning mathematics. This perspective may help teachers to appreciate that there is no 'truth' about the way that students learn mathematics. As Davis and Sumara argue the distinction between established knowledge (the curriculum) and knowledge that learners are developing or product versus process may not be the most appropriate distinction. That the actual distinction may be more a matter of scale than quality: it's the time span of development that is different rather than the substance of the knowledge per se (Davis & Sumara, 2006). Appreciating the history of mathematics problematises the distinction between the established canonical body of knowledge and the tentative knowledge of learners

A commonly held misconception amongst students of history is that the discipline is simply about the chronological listing of events. In contrast, historians are more concerned with states of being than lists of events. This view of history also has implications for the mathematics classroom. Teaching mathematics is commonly perceived as a series of lessons covering a collection of mathematical topics. Perhaps we should be attending more (or at least equally) to what 'states' we want our classrooms to be in to allow for the emergence of mathematics.

This points to the need to shift the discussion away from the individualistic view of teachers, to a recognition that knowledge and learning is collective rather than individual. We have to shift the attention away from the *what* of mathematics subject knowledge that teachers 'need' to the *why* of what are they learning about the way that they do mathematics. What does it mean to part of a community of mathematicians rather than an isolated acquirer of mathematical knowledge? Before examining this question, I look at some of the theoretical and epistemological stances that might underpin much of the work in this area to date. Through making these explicit, directions for future work begin to emerge.

DISCIPLINE KNOWLEDGE: DISCOVERED OR CREATED?

An issue arising from early work into subject matter knowledge was a lack of theorising of how discipline knowledge might inform and come to be played out in practice. As Leinhardt and Smith point out, there was a lack of problematising the issue of transfer: "No one asked how subject matter was transformed from the knowledge of the teacher into the content of instruction" (Leinhardt & Smith, 1985, p. 8). But this assumes that there are different knowledge 'packages' to be transported and transformed. It is built upon an objectivist epistemology.

Shulman's models of knowledge has elements of an objectivist epistemology: knowledge comprises objects located in the minds of individual teachers. While philosophers of mathematics question an objectivist epistemology of mathematics (Ernest, 1998) research that continues to treat subject knowledge as object may fix us in a teacher-centred pedagogy, with the assumption that the main source of learning comes about through the pre-exisiting knowledge of the teacher.

Davis and Simmt (2006) argue that the practices of research mathematicians involve creating concise expressions of mathematics, through 'compressing' information. Teachers, in contrast, have the opposite task and need to be "adept at prying apart concepts, making sense of the analogies, metaphors, images, and logical constructs that give shape to a mathematical construct" (p. 301).

Ball and Bass (2000) regard this ability to 'unpack' mathematics as an aspect of pedagogical content knowledge. This raises the question of how easy and/or necessary it is to separate discipline knowledge from pedagogic knowledge. If mathematical constructs are shaped through "analogies, metaphors, image, and logical constructs" then are these part of pedagogical content knowledge or part of subject knowledge? And does it matter?

The answer comes down to a philosophical position on the epistemology of mathematics. If one believes that there are idealised mathematical forms that exist independently of representations, illustrations, examples and so forth, that there is a signifier/signified distinction (Walkerdine, 1988), then such 'unpacking' (or re-packaging) is going to be seen as a pedagogic skill. If, on the other hand, one views mathematics as a 'language game' (Wittgenstein, 1953) only brought into being through representations, illustrations, examples and not existing outside these, then this is an aspect of subject knowledge as much as pedagogic.

As McNamara (1991) argues, all mathematics is a form of representation. Similarly, I have questioned whether attempts to classify different types of teacher knowledge and to separate these from beliefs is possible, or desirable, as all such propositional statements are brought into being through discourse and any classification into discrete categories can only be established within social relations (Askew, 1999).

Thus distinctions between subject knowledge, pedagogic knowledge, semantic/syntactic, product/process can be regarded as the being constructed within the discourse of research literature, rather than being discovered as independently existing 'objects. In line with Vygotsky's observation, psychology creates the very objects that it investigates.

> The search for method becomes one of the most important paradoxes of the entire enterprise of understanding the uniquely human forms of psychological activity. In this case, the method is simultaneously prerequisite and product, the tool and the result of the study. (Vygotsky, 1978, p. 65)

Vygotsky thus challenges the view that the method of inquiry in psychology is separate from the results of that inquiry, the traditional 'tool for result' position (Newman & Holzman, 1993). Instead

> As "simultaneously tool-and-result", method is practiced, not applied. Knowledge is not separate from the activity of practicing method; it is not "out there" waiting to be discovered through the use of an already made tool. … Practicing method creates the object of knowledge simultaneously with creating the tool by which that knowledge might be known. Tool-and-result come into existence together; their relationship is one of dialectical unity, rather than instrumental duality. (Holzman, 1997, p. 52)

Tool-and-result means that no part of the practice can be removed and looked at separately. Like the classic vase and faces optical illusion neither the faces nor the vase can be removed and leave the other. There is no mathematical discipline knowledge that can be removed from the way that it has been studied and looked at separately. There is no content knowledge separate from pedagogic knowledge.

There is simply the practice of working together on the problem. This 'practice of method' is entire in itself and '(t)he practice of method is, among other things, the radical acceptance of there being nothing social (-cultural-historical) independent of our creating it' (Newman & Holzman, 1997, p. 107).

The most important corollary of the 'practice of method' is, for Newman and Holzman the priority of creating and performing over cognition: "We are convinced that it is the creating of unnatural objects–performances–which is required for ongoing human development (developing)" (Newman & Holzman, 1997, p. 109).

In a similar vein, Adler (1998) refers to knowing being a dynamic and contextualised process, in contrast to 'knowledge' as more static and abstract. The key distinction here is that knowing is only manifested in practice, and unfolds within a social practice. The dynamics of this unfolding are different from those of 'testing' teachers' subject knowledge in contexts that differ greatly from being in the classroom: one-to-one interviews, multiple choice questions and so forth. We might question the assumption that knowledge can be 'retrieved' outside the context in which it is used: there is no retrieval, there is only practice.

Tool-and-result presents a double challenge to the research on teacher subject knowledge: firstly that the research itself constructs objects of knowledge, and, secondly, that knowledge in classrooms emerges within ongoing discourse. Vygotsky's theory dissolves the notion that teachers 'carry' a store of mathematical knowledge that they 'apply' in classrooms, and which mediates between the established cannon of mathematical knowledge and the emergent mathematics of the classroom.

Davis and Simmt (2006) argue that constructed distinctions along the lines of product and process are not helpful and that, from a complexity perspective, the accepted cannon of codified mathematical knowledge and the emergent mathematical understandings of learners are 'self-similar'. This does not mean that either is reducible to the other, but any difference between the two is more a matter of scale than quality. Arguing that 'learning' needs to be extended beyond being regarded as only happening in the heads of individuals, Davis and Simmt consider mathematics as a learning system. Any distinction between discipline knowledge and knowledge of how learners develop mathematical understanding is a matter of timescale: mathematical discipline is only relatively stable in comparison to mathematics in classrooms. It becomes impossible to separate subject knowledge from pedagogic knowledge: "we must consider *both* teachers' knowledge of established mathematics *and* their knowledge of how mathematics is established as inextricably intertwined" (Davis & Simmt, 2006, p. 300, original emphasis).

This is not to argue for a shift to a view of 'learner-centred' classrooms. As Davis points out the question is not one of whether or not classrooms are learner-centred or teacher-centred but whether or not they are mathematics centred. The argument for primary school teachers to engage in mathematical activity may be more to do with helping them better understand how mathematical knowledge is established than with the substance of discipline knowledge that they actually acquire.

FROM THE INDIVIDUAL TO THE COLLECTIVE

Finally I examine whether the enterprise of looking at /for prospective primary teachers' subject knowledge needs to move in different directions. To move away from the individualistic/cognitive focus that dominates so much of the literature towards a collective/situated perspective. That classrooms are constituted as they are with a single teacher to a large group of students is an historically contingent norm rather than a necessary condition for the organisation of teaching and learning. As such, the location of the 'problem' of discipline knowledge within the heads of individual teachers is a result of this contingency. Rather than continuing to seek to solve the problem by working on what is 'in' teachers heads perhaps a more productive approach is to look to how schooling is constituted, to accept that the knowledge of mathematics for teaching, particularly in primary schools, is likely to be distributed across a group of teachers and to work with this.

Although studies of classroom communities have begun to take social, situated and collective perspectives (Lerman, 2000), studies of teachers' subject knowledge remain, by and large, within the paradigm of individual cognition. Even those studies that have begun to look at the mathematics knowledge that teachers actually use in classrooms are still driven by a desire to 'extract' such knowledge from its history and context, and codify and canonise it.

Adler (1998) argues that learning to become a mathematics teacher means becoming able to talk within the discourses of mathematics teaching and to talk about such discourses. Thus there is more than simply learning new knowledge and such talk needs to be developed through collective engagement.

Much of the research into subject knowledge is predicated (tacitly) on the assumption that it is necessary for one individual (the teacher) to be able to make sense of another individual's (the pupil) cognitions. With a shift to recognising the importance of the social in developing individual understandings, this 'head-to-head' model is only part of the picture. Perhaps even the focus on individual pupils needs to be questioned: "The 'learning system' that the teacher can most directly influence is not the individual student, but the classroom collective" (Davis & Simmt, 2003, p. 164)

If the classroom collective rather than the individual student should be the focus of the teacher, then should the teaching collective rather than the individual teacher be the focus of the researcher? This is as much a political question as a theoretical one. It is notable that teacher development in places like the USA and UK focuses on the development of the individual, in line with the dominant political culture of 'self-actualisation'. Other traditions of development, for example lesson study in Japan (Lewis, 2002) already attend more to the collective than the individual.

Attending to the distributed nature of discipline knowledge means paying greater attention to the communities within which teachers are located. Millet, Brown, and Askew (2004), examine the importance of the professional community of teachers within schools. Some of the schools tracked over five years in the course of the *Leverhulme Numeracy Research Programme* were able to able successfully to 'share' mathematical expertise through setting up teams of teachers with collective responsibility for mathematics across the school.

Other research studying the effectiveness of 90 primary school teachers in teaching mathematics, I and colleagues (Askew et al., 1997b) identified one school where the pupil gains over the course of a year on an assessment of numeracy were consistently high across all classes. This was despite the fact that not all teachers in the school demonstrated particularly strong discipline knowledge. One factor that we conjecture contributed to these consistent gains was the strength of support provided by two teachers who shared the responsibility for mathematics across the school and who had complementary strengths. One had a strong mathematical background gained through studying a science degree. The other had studied the psychology and pedagogy of primary mathematics over several years of ongoing involvement in professional development.

One claim arising from the research into teacher knowledge is that lack of subject knowledge leads to over-reliance on textbooks in the classroom. It may be that rather than lack of subject knowledge, use of textbooks is the result of teachers seeking 'surrogate' classroom partners. In the absence of another adult being physically present in the room, the voice of the textbook may provide the next best thing. The issue may not be one of helping individual teachers become better 'equiped' to scale the peaks of mathematics lessons, but acknowledging their need for fellow climbers.

This is not to deny the place of the individual, but to recognise that individual cognition is part of a wider network. As Davis and Simmt express it:

> mathematical knowing is rooted in our biological structure, framed by bodily experiences, elaborated within social interactions, enabled by cultural tools, and part of an ever-unfolding conversation of humans and the biosphere. (p. 315)

It seems there is plenty to keep researchers in this field going for many more years yet.

REFERENCES

Adler, J. (1998). Lights and limits: Recontextualising Lave and Wenger to theorise knowledge of teaching and of learning school mathematics. In A. Watson (Ed.), *Situated cognition and the learning of mathematics*. Oxford: Centre for Mathematics Education Research. University of Oxford, Department of Educational Studies.

Askew, M. (1999). *Teachers, orientations and contexts: Repertoires of discourse in primary mathematics*. Unpublished doctoral thesis. King's College, University of London, London.

Askew, M., & Brown, M. (1997). *Effective teachers of numeracy in UK primary schools: teachers' beliefs, practices and pupils' learning*. Paper presented at the European Conference on Educational Research (ECER 97), Johann Wolfgang Goethe Universitat, Frankfurt am Main.

Askew, M., Brown, M., Rhodes, V., Wiliam, D., & Johnson, D. (1997a). *Effective teachers of numeracy: Report of a study carried out for the Teacher Training Agency.* London: King's College, University of London.

Askew, M., Brown, M., Rhodes, V., Wiliam, D., & Johnson, D. (1997b). The contribution of professional development to effectiveness in the teaching of numeracy. *Teacher Development, 1*(3), 335-355.

Aubrey, C. (1997). *Mathematics teaching in the early years: An investigation of teachers' subject knowledge.* London: Falmer.

Ball, D. (1990). The mathematical understandings that prospective teachers bring to teacher education. *The Elementary School Journal, 90*(4), 449–466.

Ball, D. (1991). Teaching mathematics for understanding: What do teachers need to know about subject matter? In M. Kennedy (Ed.), *Teaching Academic Subjects to Diverse Learners.* New York: Teachers College Press.

Ball, D. L. (1991). Research on teaching mathematics: Making subject matter part of the equation. In J. Brophy (Ed.), *Advances in research on teaching, Vol II. Teachers' knowledge of subject matter as it relates to their teaching practice.* Greenwich, CT: JAI press.

Ball, D. L., & Bass, H. (2000). Interweaving content and pedagogy in teaching and learning to teach: knowing and using mathematics. In J. Boaler (Ed.), *Multiple perspectives on mathematics teaching and learning* (pp. 83-104). Westport, CT: Ablex Publishing.

Ball, D. L., & Bass, H. (2003). *Toward a practice-based theory of mathematical knowledge for teaching.* Paper presented at the Proceedings of the 2002 annual meeting of the Canadian Mathematics Education Study Group, Edmonton, AB.

Ball, D. L., Hill, H. C., & Bass, H. (2005). Knowing mathematics for teaching: Who knows mathematics well enough to teach third grade, and how can we decide? *American Educator, Fall 2005*, 14–17, 20–22, 43–46.

Begle, E. G. (1979). *Critical variables in mathematics education: Findings from a survey of the empirical literature.* Washington DC: Mathematical Association of America and National Council of Teachers of Mathematics.

Bennett, N., & Carre, C. (Eds.). (1993). *Learning to Teach.* London: Routledge.

Bennett, N., & Turner-Bisset, R. (1993). Case studies in learning to teach. In N. Bennett & C. Carre (Eds.), *Learning to yeach.* London: Routledge.

Brown, M., Askew, M., Baker, D., Denvir, H., & Millett, A. (1998). Is the National Numeracy Strategy research-based? *British Journal of Educational Studies, 46*(4), 362–385.

Conference Board of the Mathematical Sciences. (2001). *The mathematical education of teachers.* Washington DC: American Mathematical Society and Mathematical Association of America.

Connolly, F. M., Clandinin, D. J., & He, M. F. (1997). Teachers' personal practical knowledge on the professional knowledge landscape. *Teaching and Teacher Education, 13*(7), 665-674.

Darling-Hammond, L. (2000). Teacher quality and student achievement: A review of state policy evidence. *Education Policy Analysis Archives.*

Davis, B., & Simmt, E. (2006). Mathematics-for-teaching: An ongoing investigation of the mathematics that teachers (need to) know. *Educational Studies in Mathematics, 61*, 293–319.

Davis, B., & Sumara, D. (2006). *Complexity and education: Inquiries into learning, teaching and research.* Mahah, NJ & London: Lawrence Erlbaum Associates.

Dewey, J. (1964). The relation of theory to practice in education. In R. Archambault (Ed.), *John Dewey on education* (pp. 313–338) (original work published in 1904). Philadelphia: University of Pennsylvania.

33

Ernest, P. (1998). *Social constructivism as a philosophy of mathematics*. New York: State University of New York Press.

Freudenthal, H. (1975). *Mathematics as an educational task*. Dordrecht, the Netherlands: Reidel.

Grossman, P. L., Wilson, S. M., & Shulman, L. E. (1989). Teachers of substance: Subject matter knowledge for teaching. In M. C. Reynolds (Ed.), *Knowledge base for the beginning teacher*. New York: Pergamon.

Hodgen, J. (2004). Identity, motivation and teacher change in primary mathematics: A desire to be a mathematics teacher. *Proceedings of the British Society for Research into Learning Mathematics, 24*(1).

Hough, S., O'Rode, N., Terman, N., & Weissglass, J. (2007). Using concept maps to assess change in teachers' understandings of algebra: A respectful approach. *Journal of Mathematics Teacher Education, 10*, 23–41.

Lampert, M. (1986). Knowing, doing, and teaching multiplication. *Cognition and Instruction, 3*(4), 305-342.

Leinhardt, G., & Smith, D. A. (1985). Expertise in mathematics instruction: Subject matter knowledge. *Journal of Educational Psychology, 77*(3), 247–271.

Lerman, S. (2000). The social turn in mathematics education research. In J. Boaler (Ed.), *Multiple perspectives on mathematics teaching and learning* (pp. 19–44). Westport, CT: Ablex Publishing.

Lewis, C. C. (2002). *Lesson study: A handbook of teacher-led instructional change*. Philadelphia, PA: Research for Better Schools Inc.

Ma, L. (1999). *Knowing and teaching elementary mathematics: Teachers' understanding of fundamental mathematics in China and the United States*. Mahwah, New Jersey: Lawrence Erlbaum Associates.

McNamara, D. (1991). Subject knowledge and its application: problems and possibilities for teacher educators. *Journal of Education for Teaching, 17*(2), 113–128.

McNamara, O., Jaworski, B., Rowland, T., Hodgen, J., & Prestage, S. (2002). *Developing mathematics teaching and teachers: A research monograph*. Retrieved 15/1/08, from http://www.maths-ed.org.uk/mathsteachdev/

Millett, A., Askew, M., & Simon, S. (2004). Reponses of teachers to a course of intensive training. In A. Millett, M. Brown & M. Askew (Eds.), *Primary mathematics and the developing professional* (Vol. 1, pp. 127–154). Dordrecht/Boston/London: Kluwer Academic Publishers.

Millett, A., Brown, M., & Askew, M. (Eds.). (2004). *Primary mathematics and the developing professional* (Vol. 1). Dordrecht/Boston/London: Kluwer Academic Publishers.

Monk, D. H. (1994). Subject area preparation of secondary mathematics and science teachers adn student achievement. *Economics of Education Review, 13*, 125–145.

National Research Council. (2001). *Adding it up: Helping children learn mathematics*. Washington DC: National Academy Press.

Newman, F., & Holzman, L. (1993). *Lev Vygotsky: Revolutionary scientist*. London: Routledge.

Noddings, N. (1992). *The challenge to care in schools*. New York and London: Teachers College Press.

Novak, J. D., & Gowin, D. B. (1984). *Learning how to learn*. New York, NY: Cambridge University Press.

Poulson, L. (2001). Paradigm lost? Subject knowledge, primary teachers and education policy. *British Journal of Educational Studies, 49*(1), 40–55.

Rowland, T., Barber, P., Heal, C., & Martyn, S. (2003). *Prospective primary teachers' mathematics subject knowledge: Substance and consequence.* Paper presented at the British Society for Research into Learning Mathematics.

Schmittau, J. (2003). Cultural-historical theory and mathematics education. In A. Kozulin, B. Gindis, V. S. Ageyev & S. Millar, M. (Eds.), *Vygotsky's educational theory in cultural context.* Cambridge: Cambridge University Press.

Shulman, L. S. (1986). Those who understand: knowledge growth in teaching. *Educational Researcher, 15,* 4–14.

Shulman, L. S. (1987). Knowledge and teaching: foundations of the new reforms. *Harvard Educational Review, 57,* 1–22.

Simmt, E., Davis, B., Gordon, L., & Towers, J. (2003). Teachers' mathematics: Curious obligations. *Paper presented at the Proceedings of the 2003 Joint Meeting of PME and PMENA* (pp. 175-182). Honolulu, HI: Centre for Research and Development Group University of Hawaii.

Simon, S., & Brown, M. (Cartographer). (1996). *Teacher beliefs and practices in primary mathematics.*

Skemp, R. (1976). Relational understanding and instrumental understanding. *Mathematics Teaching, 77,* 20–26.

Stacey, K., Helme, S., Steinle, V., Baturo, A., Irwin, K., & Bana, J. (2003). Preservice teachers' knowledge of difficulties in decimal numeration. *Journal of Mathematics Teacher Education, 4,* 205–225.

Sullivan, P. (2003). Editorial: Incorporating knowledge of, and beliefs about, mathematics into teacher education. *Journal of Mathematics Teacher Education, 6,* 293–296.

Thompson, A. G., Philipp, R. A., Thompson, P. W., & Boyd, B. A. (1994). Calculational and conceptual orientations in teaching mathematics. In D. B. Aichele & A. F. Coxford (Eds.), *Professional development for teachers of mathematics (1994 yearbook).* Reston VA: The National Council of Teachers of Mathematics, Inc.

Vygotsky, L. S. (1978). *Mind in society.* Cambridge, MA: Harvard University Press.

Walkerdine, V. (1988). *The mastery of reason: Cognitive development and the production of rationality.* London: Routledge.

Whitehead, A. N. (1929, reprinted 1967). *The aims of education and other essays.* New York The Free Press.

Wilson, S. M., Floden, R., E, & Ferrini-Mundy, J. (2001). *Teacher preparation research: Current knowledge, gaps, and recommendations. An executive summary of the reseach report.* Washington, WA: University of Washington, Center for the Study of Teaching and Policyo. Document Number.

Wilson, S. M., Shulman, L. S., & Richert, A. E. (1987). '150 different ways' of knowing: Representations of knowledge in teaching. In J. Calderhead (Ed.), *Exploring teachers' thinking* (pp. 84–103). London: Cassell.

Wittgenstein, L. (1953). *Philosophical investigations* (translated by G. E. M. Anscombe). Oxford: Blackwell.

Wittrock, M. (Ed.). (1986). *Handbook of research on teaching.* New York: Macmillan.

Wragg, E. C., Bennett, S. N., & Carre, C. G. (1989). Primary teachers and the National Curriculum. *Research Papers in Education, 4*(3), 17–45.

Mike Askew
Department of Education and Professional Studies
King's College
London, UK

YEPING LI, YUNPENG MA, AND JEONGSUK PANG

2. MATHEMATICAL PREPARATION OF PROSPECTIVE ELEMENTARY TEACHERS

Practices in Selected Education Systems in East Asia

Providing prospective elementary school teachers with adequate preparation in mathematics is undoubtedly important, but the respective emphases remain contested. This chapter summarises extensive information from our study undertaken to examine and review the practices in mathematical preparation of prospective elementary teachers in six selected education systems in East Asia, with detailed information collected from Mainland China and South Korea. To further our understanding of the possible effectiveness of teacher preparation programmes in East Asia, we also investigated prospective elementary school teachers' beliefs and knowledge in elementary school mathematics together with teacher educators' opinions about mathematical preparation of elementary school teachers in the case of Mainland China and South Korea. It was found that many variations are evidenced in programme set-up and curriculum structure for preparing elementary school teachers both across and within the six education systems. Nevertheless, mathematics is generally seen as an important subject in elementary teacher preparation programmes in all six education systems. The performance of prospective teachers sampled in Mainland China and South Korea also supports the perception that prospective elementary teachers in East Asia have a strong preparation in mathematics content knowledge. Furthermore, it seems that teacher educators in Mainland China and South Korea still seek to provide even more training in mathematics, especially in school mathematics, for prospective elementary teachers. The culture of valuing mathematical preparation in elementary teacher education programmes presents a salient feature of these education systems in East Asia.

INTRODUCTION

It is well recognised that teachers and their teaching are key to the improvement of students' mathematics learning (e.g., National Commission on Teaching and America's Future [NCTAF], 1996; National Council of Teachers of Mathematics [NCTM], 1991; Sowder, 2007). Educational research over the past decades, especially in the United States, has seen a dramatically increased emphasis on preparing and developing teachers who will take the main role in providing high quality classroom instruction (e.g., Sikula, 1996; Townsend & Bates, 2007). Yet, a

P. Sullivan and T. Wood (eds.), Knowledge and Beliefs in Mathematics Teaching and Teaching Development, 37–62.

recent review of research literature on mathematics teacher preparation indicates that we still do not know much about the effects of prospective teacher preparation in content and methods on their classroom instruction (Wilson, Floden, & Ferrini-Mundy, 2001). Nor is it clear to teacher educators which courses prepare prospective teachers to help them take up the challenge of developing effective mathematics instruction (e.g., Ball, Hill, & Bass, 2005). As issues related to mathematics teacher preparation are not restricted to specific regions; worldwide efforts to improve teacher education programmes have led to the increased interest in learning about teacher education practices in other education systems, especially those that have consistently produced students with high achievement in school mathematics (e.g., Silver & Li, 2000; Stewart, 1991).

Over the past decades, students in East Asia have attracted mathematics educators' attention worldwide for their superior performance in mathematics as documented in several large-scale international comparative studies (e.g., Beaton, et al, 1996; Lapointe, Mead, & Askew, 1992; Mullis, Martin, Gonzalez, & Chrostowski, 2004). Efforts to search for possible contributing factors led to a great deal of interest in examining mathematics teachers and their teaching practices in East Asia (e.g., Ma, 1999; Stigler & Hiebert, 1999). Existing cross-national studies have revealed remarkable differences between Japan, Hong Kong and the United States in mathematics classroom instruction (Hiebert, et al., 2003; Stigler & Hiebert, 1999), as well as differences between Mainland China and the United States in teachers' knowledge of mathematics for teaching (e.g., An, Kulm, & Wu, 2004; Ma, 1999). In particular, Ma's study (1999) revealed that Chinese elementary teachers had a profound understanding of the fundamental mathematics they teach, whereas U.S. counterparts lacked a strong knowledge base in mathematics. As argued by Ma (1999), the results provide a partial explanation for what contributed to Chinese students' achievement in school mathematics, and are in alignment with current understanding that teachers and their teaching are key to the improvement of students' learning (e.g., NCTAF, 1996; NCTM, 1991). Paradoxically, according to Ma (1999), Chinese elementary teachers actually received less formal education, in terms of the number of years spent before entering the teaching profession, than their U.S. counterparts. The apparent cross-national discrepancy between teachers' knowledge and the number of years training they received in China and the United States remains open to multiple interpretations. One possible explanation is that Chinese teachers had better opportunities to continue to improve their mathematics knowledge for teaching over the years. At the same time, it is also unclear whether Chinese elementary teachers might enjoy a better start than their American counterparts upon the completion of their teacher education programmes. Much remains to be understood about teacher education practices in China, as well as other education systems in East Asia, that prepare teachers who eventually take a primary role in developing classroom instruction that helps generate students' high achievement in school mathematics.

The value of exploring and understanding teacher education practices in an international context was recognised many years ago. As early as 1953, the

International Council on Education for Teaching (ICET) was founded with a fundamental purpose of assisting the improvement of teacher education around the world. Through its world assemblies, ICET published proceedings on teacher education in different education systems (e.g., Klassen & Collier, 1972; Klassen & Leavitt, 1976). Similar efforts can also be seen in recent years (e.g., Britton, Paine, Pimm, & Raizen, 2003; Cheng, Chow, & Mok, 2004; Eraut, 2000; Tisher & Wideen, 1990). Studies on teacher education policy and practices focused on various aspects of teacher education programmes including features and changes over different periods of time. However, not until a few years ago, there were few efforts to explore mathematics teacher education practices in an international context (e.g., Jaworski, Wood, & Dawson, 1999; Li & Lappan, 2002; Silver & Li, 2000). Across education systems, different perspectives and approaches used in the preparation of elementary mathematics teachers are especially interesting. Different from the preparation at the secondary school level where mathematics teachers are normally content specialists, elementary school teachers are typically responsible for teaching all different content subjects in one education system but not in another. Cross-system variations in the practices of assigning elementary teachers instructional responsibility can be taken as a profound factor in influencing teachers' instructional practices, their professional development, and subsequent students' learning in different systems. At the same time, cross-system variations in assigning elementary teachers instructional responsibility can presumably suggest possible differences existed in preparation requirements provided to prospective elementary teachers across systems. Thus, an understanding of preparation requirements for elementary school teachers in other systems should provide a unique opportunity for teacher educators to learn possible alternative practices for improving teacher preparation.

This chapter reviews current practices of prospective elementary school teacher preparation in several selected education systems in East Asia, including Hong Kong, Japan, Mainland China, Singapore, South Korea, and Taiwan. Although it is still not clear what courses prospective elementary school teachers should take, it is now generally recognised that teachers' *mathematical knowledge* for teaching is essential to effective classroom instruction (e.g., Ball, Hill, & Bass, 2005; RAND Mathematics Study Panel, 2003). It thus becomes the focus of this chapter to examine and discuss the practices in mathematical preparation of elementary (mathematics) teachers in these selected education systems in East Asia.

In particular, we examine the programme structure in mathematics course offerings for prospective elementary school teachers with detailed information collected from Mainland China and South Korea. To further our understanding of the possible effectiveness of teacher preparation programmes in East Asia, we also investigate prospective elementary school teachers' beliefs and competence in elementary school mathematics together with teacher educators' opinions about mathematical preparation of elementary school teachers in the case of Mainland China and South Korea. Correspondingly, we took various approaches in our data collection. In addition to the collection and analysis of documents that relate to teacher preparation programmes in East Asia from literature and online resources, we also carried out surveys with a sample of prospective elementary school teachers and some mathematics teacher educators in Mainland China and South Korea. The results thus allow us to develop a better understanding of relevant practices in elementary teacher preparation in East Asia.

This chapter is organised in four parts. In the first part, we provide contextual information about these six selected education systems in East Asia. We intend to establish whether elementary school teachers are content specialists or generalists and what requirements may be in place for becoming elementary school teachers across these education systems. Secondly, programme features for elementary teacher preparation are examined and discussed, with special attention to curriculum requirements in mathematics content training across these selected education systems. Detailed information related to programme requirements is exemplified through the case study of Mainland China and South Korea. Thirdly, we examine and discuss prospective elementary teachers' beliefs and knowledge in school mathematics based on the data collected from Mainland China and South Korea. In the last part, teacher educators' perceptions of the effectiveness of elementary teachers' mathematics preparation in Mainland China and South Korea are taken as insiders' views to discuss possible advantages and disadvantages of elementary teacher preparation practices in East Asia.

ELEMENTARY TEACHERS IN SELECTED EDUCATION SYSTEMS IN EAST ASIA

General Characteristics of Six Selected Asian Education Systems and Their Cultural Contexts

The selected six education systems in East Asia, Hong Kong, Japan, Mainland China, Singapore, South Korea, and Taiwan, share some broad similarities. Apart from the well-known fact that students in all these education systems achieve well on large-scale international examinations in mathematics, they are all centralised education systems. In particular, the school mathematics curriculum framework is set up at the system level, and it serves as a guideline for school mathematics curriculum and instructional activities at all grade levels. Additionally, school textbooks used in these Asian education systems are required to bear an approval from a system-level authority. Moreover, these educational systems share the same cultural roots. Although there are a variety of ethnic groups living in some education systems such as Hong Kong, Mainland China, Singapore, and Taiwan, some education researchers have argued that there is a "Confucian Heritage Culture" (CHC) in this region (e.g., Bond, 1996; Wong, 2004). Confucius is a legendary figure in the Chinese history, whose thoughts in morals, government, and education have been influential in forming Chinese culture. There are some salient values, as summarised by Bond (1996) from relevant studies, common to the CHC regions in East Asia. Such common values include hierarchy, discipline and a strong achievement orientation.

Although the six selected education systems share some broad similarities in student schooling and mathematics education (e.g., Schmidt, McKnight, Valverde, Houang, & Wiley, 1997), they differ in many other aspects, such as geographic locations, economy, language, and political system. For example, Hong Kong and Singapore were both British colonial territories (Brimer, 1988; Hayhoe, 2002; Thomas, 1988). Therefore, English is an official language in both Hong Kong and Singapore, especially for government and trade. Although Hong Kong began to adopt Mandarin as its official language with the return of sovereignty to China in 1997, this change may take a long time (Adamson & Lai, 1997). Because of the role played by the English language and the influence of non-Confucian (i.e., Western) culture, many educational practices in Hong Kong and Singapore may be more like those in the West than is the case with Mainland China's practices. Likewise, educational researchers documented similarities and differences in schooling between Japan and Mainland China (e.g., Tobin, Wu, & Davidson, 1989); mathematics classroom instruction between Japan and Taiwan (e.g., Stigler, Lee, & Stevenson, 1987); and teacher preparation between Hong Kong and Japan (e.g., Grossman, 2004). Therefore, the selection of these six Asian education systems provides an adequate basis to examine and understand possible variations in elementary teacher preparation in East Asia.

Who Teaches Elementary School Mathematics and How to Become a Teacher?

Elementary school teachers take different instructional responsibilities across these six education systems in East Asia. While elementary school teachers in Mainland China are often assigned to focus their teaching on a main subject (e.g., Chinese, mathematics), elementary school teachers in the other five education systems teach many different school subjects. Table 1 summarises elementary teachers' instructional responsibilities in these six education systems.

Table 1. Some general characteristics related to elementary teachers in East Asia

System	H. K.	Japan	M. China	Singapore	S. Korea	Taiwan
Subject taught	3 or more subjects	All subjects	1 or 2 subjects	2–4 subjects	All subjects	3 or more subjects
Position qualification	Certificate	Certificate & exam	Certificate	Programme studies	Certificate & exam	Certificate & exam
Years of education	Varied	4 years	Varied	Varied	4 years	4 years

In Table 1 one can see that the assignment of elementary teachers' instructional responsibilities has a wide spectrum of variation across these six systems. In the case of Mainland China, elementary school teachers are prepared to be capable of teaching all content subjects at the elementary school levels as needed. This preparation is reflected in the programme requirements for prospective elementary school teachers, except special training programmes provided in music, art, physical education and English. In reality, the exact teaching assignment varies depending on the size of the schools. Typically, elementary school teachers are assigned to teach one main subject as a focus area, especially in large schools. In small and/or rural schools, elementary school teachers can be expected to teach one

41

main subject like mathematics, plus one or two other subject areas such as art, physical education, or music. In contrast, teachers in Japan and South Korea are required to teach all subjects at the elementary school level (Park, 2005). [1] It seems to be in-between for elementary teachers in Hong Kong, Singapore and Taiwan, where teachers often need to teach three or more subjects. The teachers' instructional assignments in some education systems, such as Singapore and Taiwan, are also different due to different perspectives of various school subjects in that system. For example, specialist teachers are required in Singapore for art, music, physical education or mother tongue languages (i.e., Chinese). All other elementary school teachers are expected to teach English, mathematics and either science or social studies or perhaps all four (Lim-Teo, 2002). Likewise, in Taiwan, about one third of elementary teachers are specialist teachers for courses like art, music, or science. The remaining elementary teachers are responsible for teaching all subject areas to their classes (Lin, 2000; Lo, Hung, & Liu, 2002). In contrast, mathematics is taken as a main school subject with a similar status as the mother-tongue language in Mainland China. Thus, elementary schools in Mainland China emphasise the quality of mathematics instruction and assign teachers to teach mathematics as a focus subject area.

In order to become an elementary school teacher in these six education systems, it is consistent that a teacher certificate is required. Certainly, other variations exist for some specific requirements. In particular, Singapore is a city-nation and has a unique situation, where the Ministry of Education is the only entity that recruits prospective teachers for education and is also the only employer that provides all graduates jobs at different schools (Lim-Teo, 2002). As the education is provided by the only National Institute of Education (NIE) that works closely with Singapore Ministry of Education, the quality of prospective elementary teacher preparation is closely monitored through programme studies at NIE. Hong Kong, in a sense similar to Singapore, imposes no additional certification requirements beyond successful completion of preparation programme study (Wang, Coleman, Coley, & Phelps, 2003).

In Japan, South Korea, and Taiwan, successful completion of teacher preparation programme studies at specific institutions is only one necessary step to possibly become employed as a teacher. In addition to the teacher certificate, prospective teachers are also required to take and pass specifically designed exams for regular employment. Such requirements are especially important in these systems because teaching is a highly sought after position. For example, being a teacher is traditionally valued and respected in South Korea. In comparison with other jobs, teaching is popular partly because of its security and stability. Once a person becomes a teacher, he/she can teach for a long period of time without dismissal. As a result, top students from high schools often intend to become prospective elementary school teachers. Up until the early 1990s, a graduate from

---

[1] Note that there are also some exceptions in South Korea where some subjects such as physical education, music, art, and English are assigned to specific teachers. The number of specific teachers is determined by the size of the schools, and the subjects are dependent upon the conditions of the schools and the preference of the specific teachers. Such specific teachers are not necessarily content specialists.

one of the 13 specific universities in South Korea could have become an elementary school teacher without taking any examination, and served for the specific province in which that university is located. Since then, however, the policy of no examinations has been changed so that every graduate has to pass a national examination to be an elementary school teacher. Correspondingly, there is no limitation for a prospective teacher to apply for a teaching position in other provinces regardless of the location of his/her graduating university. As a result, the competition is becoming intense, especially for those who want to be a teacher in popular cities such as Seoul.

In Mainland China, a teacher certificate system was initiated in 1996 and began its implementation in 2000. According to the Teacher's Act released in 1993, the minimum requirement for being qualified as an elementary school teacher is the completion of a 3-year programme of study at a normal school that admits junior secondary school graduates. As reported in the 2006 National Statistics Bulletin Board for Educational Development (Ministry of Education, Mainland China, 2007), 98.87% of all 5,587,600 elementary teachers met this minimum requirement.

Although the requirement of a teacher certificate is quite consistent across these education systems, more variations can be observed in terms of the years of preparation needed for obtaining a certificate both across and within these education systems. Comparatively, it is now common practice in Japan, South Korea, and Taiwan that prospective teachers take a four year B.A. or B.Sc. programme study. In the other three education systems, there are still mono-technical institutions like normal schools or junior normal colleges that offer 2-4 year preparation programmes. In Singapore, it is still a common practice to offer 2-year Diploma of Education programmes for high school or polytechnic graduates together with the one-year Postgraduate Diploma in Education (Primary) programme and the regular 4-year B.A. or B.Sc. programmes. In Hong Kong, Japan, Mainland China, and Taiwan, there has been a move to upgrade elementary teacher preparation to 4-year B.A. or B.Sc. programmes and to become an open system where teacher preparation can be offered not only in normal colleges but also in comprehensive universities. Japan took such a step much earlier than Hong Kong (Grossman, 2004; Leung & Park, 2002), and then Taiwan in 1994 (Lin, 2000) and Mainland China in 1999 (Department of State, Mainland China, 1999). For example, as reported in the newspaper of China Education (2006), from 1999 to 2005, the number of normal schools for junior secondary school graduates decreased from 815 to 228, the number of junior normal colleges that offer 5 (or '3+2') or 3 years teacher preparation programmes decreased from 140 to 58, and the number of normal universities and comprehensive universities that offer 4-year B.A. or B.Sc. teacher preparation programmes increased from 87 to 303. Thus, while 4-year B.A. or B.Sc. preparation programmes have become more and more popular across these education systems in East Asia, other programmes that offer fewer years preparation are still in existence. To reflect different preparation that prospective elementary teachers have received, teacher certificates are often provided with some differentiations in different education systems.

ELEMENTARY TEACHER PREPARATION IN EAST ASIA

General Features of Elementary Teacher Preparation Programmes in East Asia

In contrast to the centralised administration of school mathematics curriculum, teacher preparation programmes show many more variations both across and within these education systems in East Asia. While the variations are understandably large between teacher preparation programmes for elementary school level and ones for secondary school level, programmes for elementary teacher preparation alone present many different pictures both across and within these education systems. According to a classification system used by Park (2005), teacher education programmes can roughly be classified along two dimensions: (1) the type of university (i.e., mono-purpose institutes that focus on teacher preparation versus comprehensive universities) where elementary teacher education programmes are typically housed in an education system, and (2) the nature of programmes where prospective elementary teachers are required to complete: an integrated programme of study or post-baccalaureate training in education for those who have received their Bachelor degree in a subject content field. This two-dimensional classification system led Park (2005) to provide a general sketch of elementary and secondary school teacher preparation programmes in East Asia. In particular, the majority of elementary teacher preparation programmes are integrated programmes in nature and housed in mono-purpose institutions in Hong Kong, Japan, Mainland China, South Korea and Taiwan. Whereas in Singapore, it has both integrated programmes and post-baccalaureate diploma in education programmes for elementary teacher preparation that are housed in the only teacher education institution, National Institute of Education (NIE), as part of a comprehensive university (Lim-Teo, 2002).

The two-dimensional classification framework used by Park (2005) is helpful to a certain degree for understanding the structure of elementary teacher preparation programmes in different education systems, but it does not reflect some rich variations in existing elementary teacher preparation programmes that have evolved over time in East Asia. For example, some of the elementary school teachers are educated through teacher education programmes offered in comprehensive universities in Hong Kong, Japan, and South Korea, but especially more in Mainland China and Taiwan. Depending on how well elementary teacher education programmes can serve the needs in different systems and cultural contexts, elementary teacher education programmes have been undertaking different development trajectories over the years. In the case of South Korea, the structure of elementary teacher preparation programmes has been fairly stable over the past decade. There are 11 unique national universities specialising in preparing only elementary school teachers who teach from grade 1 to grade 6. These 11 universities are spread out across the nation, located in a main city per province. In addition, there are two comprehensive universities that also offer an elementary teacher preparation programme. One is the national university specialising in teacher education ranging from preschool through elementary to secondary education. The other is a private comprehensive university that offers not only teacher education programmes but also other programmes such as business and engineering. Compared to various programmes for preparing secondary school mathematics teachers offered by a lot of national and private universities (see Chapter 3 by Shiqi Li and colleagues in this volume), the system of preparing elementary school teachers is rather uniform and stable in South Korea.

Quite different from the case of South Korea, elementary teacher preparation programmes in Mainland China have experienced some dramatic structural changes over the past decades at the levels of both institution and programme. Historically, all elementary school teachers were prepared exclusively through normal schools. These are typically 3-year mono-technical institutions that admit junior secondary school graduates who are interested in becoming elementary school teachers and pass an entrance examination. This type of programme dominated elementary teacher preparation in Mainland China from the late 1970s to the late 1990s. Over the years, there has been gradual upgrading of teacher preparation programmes with the start of junior normal colleges offering 5 (or 3+2) or 3-year preparation programmes in the mid of 1980s and 4-year B.A. or B.Sc. preparation programmes in universities in 1998. Currently, all three types of preparation programmes are in co-existence, but with rapid changes to upgrade elementary teacher preparation into 4-year B.A. or B.Sc. programmes. As of the end of 2002, it took less than four years for Mainland China to have a total of 130 normal and comprehensive universities that offer such a B.A. or B.Sc. programme in elementary teacher preparation (Huang, 2005).

Programme Requirements in Mathematics for Elementary Teacher Preparation

The variations evidenced in preparation programmes both across and within these six education systems inevitably lead to variations in programme requirements for elementary teacher preparation. Apparently, different types of teacher education programmes existing in an education system would reflect different curriculum requirements. For example, there are three different types of elementary teacher preparation programmes available in Mainland China:

(1)   3-year programmes offered by normal schools (N. S.);
(2)   5 (i.e., '3+2') or 3-year programmes offered by junior normal colleges (J. N. C.); and
(3)   4-year B.A. or B.Sc. programmes offered by normal or comprehensive universities (N./C. U.).

In Table 2, the structure and requirements are summarised for preparing elementary teachers in these three types of programmes.

Table 2. Curriculum requirements of different types of programmes in Mainland China

Programmes	N. S. 3 years	J. N. C. 3+2 years	J. N. C. 3 years	N./C. U. 4 years
Gen. education	16.1%	14.5%	22.3%	varied
Edu. major	11.5%	9.5%	17.1%	varied
Content subjects	50%	44.7%	14.9%	varied
Selectives	8.6%	15%	32.8%	varied
Edu. activities	13.8%	16.3%	12.9%	varied

In Table 2, we adapted a course structure that can roughly accommodate different types of elementary teacher preparation programmes. Normal schools provide 3-year preparation programmes for junior secondary school graduates. The programmes offer a common curriculum to all prospective teachers. Chinese and mathematics are two main subjects with 17.5% and 16.4% course hours of the whole curriculum, plus a methods course each in Chinese and mathematics respectively. Mathematics content courses basically cover fundamental theories of elementary mathematics and what students typically need to learn in high school such as elementary functions, analytical geometry, and introduction to calculus. Junior normal colleges are the type of mono-purpose institutes that provide either a 5-year preparation programme for junior secondary school graduates or a 3-year program for secondary school graduates. For those junior secondary school graduates who enrol in the 5-year preparation programme, the first three years are used in a way similar to completing the typical three year secondary school study and followed by two more years' study in the programme. Thus, the 5-year preparation programme is also termed '3+2'. Both the 5-year and 3-year preparation programmes offer subject specifications beyond the common curriculum for all prospective teachers. In the 5-year programme, prospective teachers typically need to take five mathematics content courses (e.g., algebra, geometry, mathematical analysis) and one methods course as part of their common curriculum.

For those majoring in mathematics education, they need to take three more courses in mathematics: probability and statistics, mathematical thinking and method, and analytical geometry. Adding these mathematics courses brings the percentage of course hours in mathematics total to about 22%. In the 3-year programme, only one mathematics course and one methods course are required in the common curriculum. For those majoring in mathematics and science, prospective teachers typically need to take five more mathematics courses. Adding the mathematics courses required in common curriculum, prospective teachers majoring in mathematics education are required to take about 26.5% course hours in mathematics. The Ministry of Education in Mainland China provided curriculum guidelines for the programmes offered in both normal schools and junior normal colleges, but not yet for the 4-year B.A. or B.Sc. programmes. Thus, more variations exist in such newly developed 4-year programmes housed in normal or comprehensive universities.

Even within the same type of preparation programmes in an education system, it can be the case that there are large variations across institutions. Again in the case of Mainland China, the curriculum structure and requirements of 4-year B.A. or B.Sc. programmes can be classified into three sub-categories. The classifications are mainly based on the orientation in preparing elementary teachers as generalists or content specialists. See Table 3 for the curriculum structure and average course requirements obtained from several normal universities representing each of the three sub-categories: integrated, middle ground, having a focus area. (Note: the results presented in the following table may not add to 100% due to rounding errors.)

Table 3. Sample curriculum of three different 4-year preparation models in Mainland China

Programme	N./C. U.		
	Integrated	Mid ground	Focus area
Gen. education	32.2%	30%	33.8%
Edu. major	31.4%	17.6%	21.7%
Content subjects	23.9%	41.1%	33.9%
Edu. activities	12.4%	11.2%	10.5%

As shown in Table 3 programmes in these three sub-categories have a similar curriculum structure, consisting of four components: general education courses; education major courses; content subject courses; and educational activities including student teaching and thesis. But there are many more variations in terms of the type and number of specific courses required. For the 'integrated' sub-category, the programme provides elementary teacher preparation as a whole and prospective teachers need to take courses in different subject areas. In contrast, the programme in the 'focus area' sub-category provides prospective elementary teachers choices of subject focus areas such as mathematics. The subject specification automatically leads to more content course requirements in a specific subject. The programme in the 'mid ground' sub-category basically provides grouped subject orientation. It typically includes two general subject orientations: science oriented and humanity oriented. The specific course structure and the number of courses provided vary from institution to institution. Across these programmes, the total credit hours required can range from 150 to 197.

Understandably, the variations within a specific education system are not consistent across different education systems. Mainland China may be taken as a case with the most variations in terms of many different aspects, especially at the time when the system is undertaking some fundamental changes to upgrade its teacher education. Comparatively, other education systems have a smaller scale of variation. For example, in Taiwan, it is generally required that 4-year B.A. or B.Sc. preparation programmes need to have at least 148 credit hours. Among the 148 credit hours, 97 credit hours are required for courses in the categories of general knowledge, basic subject, and professional education. These are the common course requirements for all prospective teachers who may plan to teach in any subject areas. The remaining 51 credit hours are for courses in the focus area of prospective teachers' own choice. The structure is similar to the sub-category of 'focus area' programme in Mainland China (see Table 3). For the mathematics education major, prospective teachers are expected to take additional mathematics courses in Calculus, Algebra, Analysis, as well as mathematics education courses such as Study of Elementary School Mathematics Curricula (Lo, Hung, & Liu, 2002). Although there are some variations in terms of specific curriculum content and courses required across institutions, these are all minor variations under the same curriculum guidelines.

The case of South Korea is in between in terms of variations. Prospective elementary school teachers in South Korea have the option of choosing one school subject area, such as mathematics or music, as a focus area during their four year programme study. They can also choose general elementary education or computer education as their focus area, even though they are not specific school subjects. In fact, the universities offering elementary teacher education programmes are structured with departments according to different focus areas. Most of these universities have departments of moral education, Korean language education, social studies education, mathematics education, science education, physical education, music education, fine arts education, practical arts education, elementary education, English education, and computer education.

Because elementary school teachers in South Korea need to teach every school subject, prospective elementary school teachers are required to take the same courses with only the exception of their focus areas. In general, the total credit hours required for a bachelor degree is about 145 and the credit hours for the focus area is 21. In other words, about 85% of the course requirements are the same for any prospective elementary school teacher. With regard to requirements common in mathematics, elementary teacher education programmes consist of the liberal arts courses and the major courses. Among the liberal art courses, prospective teachers take a compulsory course (2-3 credit hours) dealing with the foundations or basics of mathematics. Among the major courses, prospective teachers take 2 to 4 compulsory courses (4-7 credit hours) in mathematics.

The most common courses are (Elementary) Mathematics Education I with 2 credit hours and (Elementary) Mathematics Education II with 3 credit hours. The former mainly deals with overall theories (including the national mathematics curriculum) related directly to teaching elementary mathematics, whereas the latter covers how to teach elementary mathematics tailored to multiple content areas such as number and operations. The course of Mathematics Education II often requires prospective teachers to analyse elementary mathematics textbooks and to practise teaching through mock instruction. Most institutions also offer elective courses in mathematics for the category of the liberal arts courses and the major courses. Taken together, a minimum of three courses or 6 credit hours in mathematics are required for all prospective elementary teachers. All of these mathematics-bound courses are offered by the department of mathematics education in each institution, except in the two comprehensive universities where both elementary and secondary teacher education programmes are provided. Across institutions, there are some variations in terms of the number of credit hours required in mathematics and names used to call different mathematics courses. For example, Mathematics Education I may be called Theory of Teaching Elementary School Mathematics or Understanding of Elementary Mathematics Education. Likewise, Mathematics Education II may be called Practice of Teaching Elementary School Mathematics or Practice of Elementary Mathematics Education or even structured as three sub-courses in one of the eight institutions surveyed. But in essence, these course requirements are remarkably similar across institutions.

As seen in Table 1, elementary school teachers may teach many different school subjects in all these education systems, except in Mainland China where teachers' instructional responsibility is often focused on a main school subject like mathematics. In general, one may expect that in-service teachers' instructional responsibility in different education systems would be consistent with the training that prospective teachers receive. As illustrated in the above discussion, this is often not the case. For example, in Mainland China where practising teachers often need to have a focus teaching subject, teacher preparation programmes were traditionally set up to offer virtually the same curriculum of studies to all prospective elementary teachers in normal schools with 3-4 year programmes for junior secondary school graduates. This situation began to change when junior normal colleges were introduced with more years of preparation and selection of a focus subject area (National Education Committee, Mainland China, 1995; Ministry of Education, Mainland China, 2003). The new 4-year B.A. or B.Sc. preparation programmes started in 1999 in Mainland China also have many more variations as the system does not yet have a uniform curriculum. In contrast, elementary teachers in other education systems need to teach many different school subjects. However, teacher preparation programmes in these education systems often require prospective teachers to have a focus area through their studies.

Instructional and Assessment Approaches Used in Mathematics Content and Methods Courses for Prospective Elementary Teachers

Prospective teachers' learning is influenced not only by what they learn (i.e., course content) but also by the way they are taught (i.e., instructional approaches used in programme courses). As there is limited information available about instructional approaches used in courses for prospective teachers in East Asia, we conducted a survey with mathematics teacher educators in some selected institutions in Mainland China and South Korea. Several questions in the survey were specifically designed to ask mathematics teacher educators about the instructional and assessment formats used in mathematics content and methods courses for prospective elementary teachers. They were also asked about their opinions on any changes needed for instructional and assessment methods.

In Mainland China, although instructional and assessment methods used can vary from one instructor to another, some common features are prevalent. Answers from 20 mathematics teacher educators in 10 institutions indicated that lectures are the dominant method used in teaching mathematics content courses, with 19 out of

20 respondents indicating that lectures are used all the time or most of the time. The result is consistent with other observations in Mainland China (e.g., Chen, 2003; Liu, 2005). Moreover, our survey also shows that most respondents indicated that they sometimes used the methods of cooperative learning and self-exploratory in mathematics content course instruction. In comparison, there are more different methods used in teaching mathematics methods courses. While 13 out of the 20 respondents indicated that lectures are used all the time or most of the time, many others reported the use of case analysis, cooperative learning, and mock teaching. When asked whether any changes in instructional methods would be needed, more than 50% respondents indicated that changes are needed for methods course instruction but not for content courses. Many teacher educators preferred to include more case analyses to make connections with classroom instruction in methods course instruction. The results suggest that Chinese mathematics teacher educators would like to see more changes in methods course instruction but feel comfortable with the dominant use of lecture in teaching mathematics content courses. With regard to assessment formats, our survey results indicate that written tests and homework assignments were the most commonly used methods in both mathematic content and methods courses in Mainland China. Some teachers also reported the use of term papers and topic study as assessment approaches in both types of mathematics courses. Similar to the results reported for instructional methods, mathematics teacher educators saw the need for a change in assessment approaches more in the methods course but not in the content courses. In particular, suggestions were made to adopt multiple assessment approaches, emphasise the knowledge application in instruction, use mock teaching, and analyse textbooks. When asked how best to prepare prospective elementary teachers in mathematics methods courses in terms of both content covered and instructional approaches used, many teacher educators indicated the need to connect theory learning and instructional practices, follow curriculum changes in elementary mathematics, and use the instructional case analysis method.

In South Korea, our survey results were obtained from eight mathematics teacher educators representing eight national universities out of the 13 institutions that have elementary teacher preparation programmes. The survey results present a picture that shares some similarities with the case in Mainland China. Although the formats for teaching both mathematics content and methods courses also varied from one respondent to another, the overall tendency of instructional formats of mathematics content and methods courses was a lecture-oriented style with an estimated use of more than 60% of the time for the content courses and 40% to 75% of the time for the methods courses. More instructional methods were reported in use for the methods courses, which includes the use of presentation, cooperative learning, individual and group activities, seminar, and mock teaching. Likewise, the overall tendency of assessment formats was reported to use written tests in more than 70% of the time in conjunction with a few homework assignments for the content course, and in more than 50% of the time in conjunction with homework assignments and presentations for the methods course. When asked about any changes needed in instructional and assessment approaches used in the mathematics content courses, the answers included the use of more cooperative learning or projects, the design of interesting teaching materials, engaging students in classroom instruction activities, and the use of various assessment methods beyond written test and homework assignments. In comparison, there were more and different suggestions made for possible changes in the methods course. Some teacher educators insisted on the connection between the methods course instruction and elementary school mathematics classrooms. Beyond teaching general theories mainly by lecture, suggestions were made to analyse in detail the national mathematics curriculum and a series of elementary mathematics textbooks and to let prospective teachers experience know how to teach elementary mathematics as realistically as possible. Other suggestions include encouraging peer discussions among prospective teachers themselves, providing constructive feedback for each mock teaching, and using multiple teaching models applicable to elementary mathematics classrooms. With regard to the opinion about how to best prepare prospective elementary teachers in mathematics methods courses in terms of both content covered and instructional approaches used, the common answer was a combination of profound understanding of elementary mathematics contents (or big ideas) and experience of using multiple teaching models.

PROSPECTIVE ELEMENTARY TEACHERS' BELIEFS AND KNOWLEDGE IN MATHEMATICS: SAMPLE RESPONSES FROM CHINA AND SOUTH KOREA

Given that students in East Asia often performed well in international examinations of school mathematics, it may be reasonable to assume that prospective teachers in these high-achieving education systems should also be well prepared in mathematics and ready to teach. However, there have been some uncertainties over the years about the quality of prospective teacher preparation in Mainland China (e.g., Fang & Paine, 2000), Singapore (see Lim-Teo, 2002), and Taiwan (e.g., Lo, Hung, & Liu, 2002). To gain a better understanding of prospective elementary teachers' beliefs and knowledge in mathematics, we thus developed and conducted a survey in Mainland China and South Korea.

The survey contains two main parts with five items for each part. Part 1 contains items on prospective teachers' knowledge of elementary mathematics curriculum and their beliefs in their preparation and mathematics instruction. Part 2 has five items that assess prospective elementary school teachers' mathematics knowledge and pedagogical content knowledge on the topic of division of fractions. Most items were taken from a previous study (Li & Smith, 2007), with some items adapted from school mathematics textbooks and others' studies (e.g., Hill, Schilling, & Ball, 2004; TIMSS 2003; Tirosh, 2000). Given the limited page space we have here, only a few items from each part and prospective teachers' responses to these questions are included to provide a glimpse of prospective teachers' beliefs and knowledge in mathematics.

In Mainland China, the survey was given to both junior and senior prospective elementary teachers in 10 institutions. Five institutions are normal universities or colleges that offer 4-year B.A. or B.Sc. preparation programmes, and the other five are junior normal colleges that offer 5 (i.e., '3+2') or 3 years programmes for junior secondary school graduates and secondary school graduates respectively. 361 responses were collected and used for data reporting, with 50.4% of responses from junior normal colleges and 49.6% from normal universities/colleges. In South Korea, the survey data was collected from 291 seniors in three universities that all offer 4-year B.A. or B.Sc. preparation programmes. These 291 seniors included those with mathematics education as their focus area, and ones with their focus areas in other subjects. Due to the sampling difference across these two education systems, the results reported here are not for comparison purposes and should not be taken as reflecting the overall situation in these two education systems. A thorough data analysis and detailed reporting is needed before a cross-system comparison can possibly be made.

Prospective Teachers' Knowledge in Elementary Mathematics Curriculum and Beliefs about Their Own Knowledge Preparation

The following three items (note: only part of items 2 and 3 are included here) were included in Part 1. In general, responses from sampled prospective teachers in both Mainland China (361 respondents) and South Korea (291 respondents) show that prospective teachers often do not feel over-confident with their knowledge and readiness to teach elementary school mathematics. The results present a picture of sampled prospective teachers' self-confidence in two Asian education systems, which is quite different from the high confidence displayed by a sample of prospective teachers in the United States (Li & Smith, 2007). (Note: the results presented in the following tables may not add to 100% due to rounding errors.)

1. How would you rate yourself in terms of the degree of your understanding of the National Mathematics Syllabus?
       (a) High   *(b)* Proficient
       (c) Limited   *(d)* Low

Table 4. Percent of Sampled Prospective Teachers' Self-rating of the Degree of their Curriculum Understanding

	High	Proficient	Limited	Low
Mainland China	3%	13%	60%	24%
South Korea	2%	18%	66%	14%

It can be seen in Table 4 that many sampled prospective teachers in both Mainland China and South Korea did not think that they know their national mathematics syllabus well. In particular, there are only 16% of sampled prospective teachers in Mainland China and 20% of those in South Korea self-rated with either "high" or "proficient" understanding of their national mathematics syllabus. Consequently, 84% of sampled prospective teachers in Mainland China and 80% in South Korea self-rated with either "limited" or "low" understanding of their national mathematics syllabus.

2. The following list includes some topics that are often included in school mathematics. Choose the response that best describes whether primary school students have been taught each topic.
   (a) Mostly taught before grade 5
   (b) Mostly taught during grades 5-6
   (c) Not yet taught or just introduced during grades 5-6
   (d) Not included in the National Mathematics Syllabus
   (e) Not sure

   ( ) Addition and subtraction of fractions
   ( ) Multiplication and division of fractions
   ( ) Representing decimals and fractions using words, numbers, or models

Table 5. Percent of Sampled Prospective Teachers' Choices about the Curriculum Placement of Three Content Topics

	Topic: Addition and Subtraction of Fractions				
	Choice (a)	Choice (b)	Choice (c)	Choice (d)	Choice (e)
M. China	**71%***	26%	2%	0%	1%
S. Korea	**79%**	18%	1%	0%	2%
	Topic: Multiplication and Division of Fractions				
	Choice (a)	Choice (b)	Choice (c)	Choice (d)	Choice (e)
M. China	20%	**67%**	8%	2%	3%
S. Korea	34%	**61%**	3%	1%	2%
	Topic: Representing Decimals and Fractions with Words, Numbers, or Models				
	Choice (a)	Choice (b)	Choice (c)	Choice (d)	Choice (e)
M. China	**42%**	24%	11%	7%	17%
S. Korea	**64%**	18%	4%	3%	11%

Note (*): Bold means the correct choice for the topic in that education system.

Table 5 presents a diverse picture for both Mainland China and South Korea. The results show that the majority of sampled prospective teachers in both Mainland China (71%) and South Korea (79%) know that the topic of "addition and subtraction of fractions" is taught before grade 5 in elementary mathematics curriculum. It becomes less certain to these sampled prospective teachers that the topic of "multiplication and division of fractions" is taught between grades 5-6 in Mainland China (67%) and South Korea (61%). For the topic of "representing decimals and fractions using words, numbers, or models", a high percentage of sampled prospective teachers in South Korea (64%) knew the correct placement of this topic in elementary school mathematics, but a smaller percentage of those sampled prospective teachers in Mainland China (42%) knew its correct placement and some of them (17%) were not sure. The result suggests that using non-numerical representations such as visual representations may not be a familiar area to many prospective teachers in the Chinese sample.

3. Considering your training and experience in both mathematics and instruction, how ready do you feel you are to teach the following topics?
    (a) Very ready
    (b) Ready
    (c) Not ready

    ( ) Primary school mathematics in general
    ( ) Number – Representing decimals and fractions using words, numbers, or models
    ( ) Number – Representing and explaining computations with fractions using words, numbers, or models

Table 6. Percent of sampled prospective teachers' choices of their readiness to teach elementary school mathematics

Primary school mathematics in general			
	Choice (a)	Choice (b)	Choice (c)
M. China	13%	72%	15%
S. Korea	6%	80%	14%
Number – representing decimals and fractions using words, numbers, or models			
	Choice (a)	Choice (b)	Choice (c)
M. China	13%	52%	36%
S. Korea	7%	71%	22%
Number – representing and explaining computations with fractions using words, numbers, or models			
	Choice (a)	Choice (b)	Choice (c)
M. China	12%	44%	44%
S. Korea	6%	70%	23%

Table 6 shows that the majority of sampled prospective teachers in South Korea felt that they are ready to teach the three topics specified (80%, 71%, and 70% respectively). Much smaller percentages of those in South Korea felt that they are very ready to teach these three topics (6%, 7%, and 6%, respectively), and some would not feel confident (14%, 22%, and 23% for each of these three topics, respectively). The results from sampled prospective teachers in Mainland China present a different picture. In particular, a higher percentage of prospective teachers felt that they are very ready to teach these three topics (13%, 13%, and 12% respectively). However, only about 15% felt that they are not ready to teach primary school mathematics in general, relatively high percentages of sampled prospective teachers felt that they are not ready to teach the other two topics with the use of different representations (36% and 44%, respectively). The results may well relate to what has been reported in Table 5, where more than 50% of respondents were unclear about the curriculum placement of the topic of 'representing decimals and fractions using words, numbers, or models'. The results may also relate to the fact that both juniors and seniors from two different types of institutions (i.e., junior normal colleges and normal universities) were included in this survey result from Mainland China. Consequently, the results from Mainland China contain relatively smaller percentages of sampled prospective teachers who would think that they are ready to teach these three topics as specified.

Prospective Teachers' Knowledge in Elementary Mathematics: Division of Fractions

Division of fractions is a difficult topic in elementary school mathematics (e.g., Ma, 1999), not only for school students but also for teachers (e.g., Li, 2008; Li & Smith, 2007). By focusing on this content topic, we developed a survey with test items that aim to assess prospective teachers' mathematics content knowledge and pedagogical content knowledge on this topic. In particular, the following two items were included in part 2 of our survey (note: only part of item 4 is included here, and the items are numbered here in terms of the sequence of items included in this chapter). In general, sampled prospective elementary teachers in both Mainland China (361 respondents) and South Korea (291 respondents) were quite successful in solving division of fraction items that assess teachers' mathematics knowledge. But the results from answering items targeted on teachers' pedagogical content knowledge present two quite different pictures in Mainland China and South Korea. Such differences are likely beyond sampling differences and can possibly relate to the different training provided for prospective elementary teachers in these two education systems.

4. Solve the following problems (no calculator). Be sure to show your solution process.

(1). Say whether $\dfrac{9}{11} \div \dfrac{2}{3}$ is greater than or less than $\dfrac{9}{11} \div \dfrac{3}{4}$ without solving. Explain your reasoning.

In the case of Mainland China, about 94% of the sampled prospective teachers provided the correct answer (i.e., the first numerical expression is greater than the second one). And the remaining 6% did not get the correct answer. Out of those getting the correct answer, about 64% did not carry out computations. The common explanations are (a) "If the dividend is the same, the smaller the divisor, the larger the quotient; the larger the divisor, the smaller the quotient." and (b) "2/3 is smaller than 3/4". And many respondents provided both reasons. The remaining 36% did the computation to reach the correct answer.

In South Korea, about 95% of the sampled prospective elementary teachers answered correctly. They mentioned, "If the divisor is the smaller (and the dividend is the same), the result of the division is bigger". Some respondents demonstrated the fact that 2/3 is smaller than 3/4 in words (68%) or by drawing (5%). Others demonstrated using the common denominator 12, in words (9%) or by drawing (3%). About 5% of these teachers answered correctly used an analogy with natural numbers. There were about 5% of the sampled prospective teachers who answered incorrectly or did not answer at all. They either made a mistake on which fraction is bigger between 2/3 and 3/4, or did not infer correctly on what would be the result of division if the divisor was the smaller.

5. How would you explain to your students why $\dfrac{2}{3} \div 2 = \dfrac{1}{3}$? Why $\dfrac{2}{3} \div \dfrac{1}{6} = 4$?

(item adapted from Tirosh, 2000.)

For the sample prospective teachers in Mainland China, about 88% provided valid explanations for dividing a fraction by a natural number. However, the dominant explanation was based on the algorithm, "dividing a number equals to multiplying its reciprocal" (64%). The other 24% were dominated by explanations such as "dividing a whole into three equal parts, each part should be 1/3, so two parts should be 2/3. 2/3 ÷ 2 means to equally divide 2/3 into 2 pieces, thus one piece should be 1/3", or "The half of 2/3 is 1/3". Similar patterns of success rates and explanation were observed with the second fraction division computation. In particular, about 82% of respondents provided valid explanations but the majority explained directly in terms of the same algorithm, that is, flip and multiply (73%). The other 9% provided their explanations mainly as "dividing a whole into six equal parts, each part is 1/6, four parts should be 4/6. In other words, 4/6 contains four 1/6. Thus, 4/6 ÷ 1/6 = 4. Because 4/6 equals 2/3, so 2/3 ÷ 1/6 = 4." A few students also tried to draw a picture such as a circle to help with their explanations. Some others either provided incomplete solutions or misunderstood the problem as to explain why 2/3 ÷ 2 is smaller than 2/3 ÷ 1/6.

In the case of South Korea, about 98% of prospective teachers provided valid explanations with regards to dividing a fraction by a natural number. They came up with various methods such as drawing (45%), using manipulative materials (10%), using the meaning of division and/or fractions (8%), finding the common denominator (6%), number lines (6%), and using word problems (5%). In addition, about 15% of the respondents provided explanations in more than two ways. Only about 3% of the respondents predominately employed the algorithm of "flip and multiply". In contrast, about 88% of the sampled prospective teachers provided valid explanations with regards to dividing a fraction by a fraction. They again came up with various methods such as drawing (33%), finding the common denominator (23%), number lines (5%), using manipulative materials (5%), using the meaning of division (3%), using the relationship between fractions (1%), and using word problems (1%). Note that the percentage of respondents finding the common denominator was dramatically increased from 6% to 23%, whereas the percentage of respondents using manipulative materials was decreased from 10% to 5%. Although drawing was still the preferred approach, about 4% experienced difficulty and failed. For instance, an area model was drawn to represent $2/3 \times 1/6$ instead of $2/3 \div 1/6$. Finally, about 10% of these prospective teachers used the "flip and multiply" algorithm as providing an explanation for the second division computation.

MATHEMATICAL PREPARATION OF ELEMENTARY TEACHERS: SAMPLE CHINESE AND KOREAN TEACHER EDUCATORS' VIEWS

Teacher preparation programmes are a moving target with constant changes in the structure and curriculum requirements. Such changes or needs for changes in an education system can be perceived quickly by its insiders but not outsiders of that system. We thus included some questions in our survey for mathematics teacher educators from Mainland China and South Korea to learn their views about mathematical preparation of elementary teachers in these two systems respectively.

As discussed previously, Mainland China is in the process of restructuring and upgrading its teacher preparation programmes. Three different types of elementary teacher preparation are currently in existence and there are many variations across institutions even for the same type of 4-year B.A. or B.Sc. preparation programmes. The existing variations led to different perceptions held by different mathematics teacher educators in Mainland China. Nevertheless, many teacher educators thought that prospective teachers were serious about teaching and were willing to learn. Some thought that prospective teachers had adequate training in collegiate mathematics and developed their abilities in analysing and solving problems.

At the same time, however, many teacher educators thought that some prospective teachers did not have solid training in basic but important school mathematics. The differences between these teacher educators' views are in line with sampled prospective teachers' self-rating where about 13% of prospective teachers felt that they are very ready to teach primary mathematics in general and about 15% felt not ready (see Table 6). Finally, many teacher educators thought that it is necessary to help prospective teachers connect their mathematics learning with current elementary mathematics curriculum reform and instruction. In fact, about 84% of 361 prospective teachers surveyed in Mainland China self-rated with either "limited" or "low" understanding of the national mathematics syllabus.

In South Korea, all prospective elementary school teachers need to take one course (2-3 credit hours) where they learn the basics of mathematics, and then take two more courses of about 5 credit hours where they learn not only general theories and curriculum related to teaching elementary mathematics, but also teaching methods related to different mathematics content topics. With these course studies in mathematics, most of the teacher educators in the survey thought that prospective teachers still do not have enough mathematical training for their future teaching career. At the same time, they admitted that it is difficult for prospective teachers to have enough background knowledge in each school subject, mainly because elementary school teachers need to teach every subject. Nevertheless, teacher educators expected that prospective teachers should have appropriate knowledge preparation in their focus area. Some teacher educators provided a cautionary note that the courses should be tailored to prospective elementary school teachers so that the mathematics contents should be different from those for secondary mathematics teachers. It was emphasised by sampled teacher educators that mathematics content courses should be designed in a way to help prospective teachers deepen their understanding of mathematics content taught in elementary school, not sophisticated university level mathematics such as algebra or analysis as a discipline, and to foster their pedagogical content knowledge.

Most of the teacher educators surveyed in South Korea also thought that all prospective teachers should have more opportunities to learn mathematics content and method, partly because mathematics is one of the most important subjects in elementary school and it is taught more hours per week than other subjects such as social studies or music. With the perceived lack of sufficient mathematics content and method courses, most teacher educators expected prospective teachers' competence in mathematics to be average or below average. Some teacher educators worried about prospective teachers' lack of profound understanding of basic but important mathematical concepts. Others thought that prospective teachers would have confidence in elementary mathematics content, but not in collegiate mathematics (i.e., the compulsory course in the category of liberal arts courses). In fact, according to the mathematics knowledge survey, about 86% of the 291 sampled prospective teachers indicated that they are either ready or very ready to teach elementary school mathematics in general (see Table 6), given their education received in both mathematics content and method. At the same time, many teacher educators underlined the strengths of current teacher preparation in that prospective elementary teachers learn how to teach every subject. In particular, the comprehensive programmes help prospective teachers make good connections among multiple subjects for developing an inter-disciplinary approach, and have good understanding of children and general pedagogical knowledge.

CONCLUSION

Discussions presented previously show many variations in programme set-up and curriculum structure for preparing elementary school teachers both across and within these six education systems. Although there is a trend for all of these education systems to improve and upgrade their elementary teacher preparation, different development trajectories have been undertaken in different system contexts. Specific curriculum structure of teacher preparation is also influenced by different factors, including the type of degrees awarded and the orientation placed in preparing generalists or subject specialists. Nevertheless, mathematics is generally seen as an important subject in elementary teacher education in all these six education systems. Our preliminary survey results obtained from sample prospective teachers in Mainland China and South Korea also support the perception that prospective elementary teachers in East Asia have a strong preparation in mathematics content knowledge. However, it seems that teacher educators still seek to provide even more training in mathematics, especially in school mathematics, to prospective elementary teachers.

At the beginning of the chapter, we mentioned some cross-national studies (e.g., An, Kulm, & Wu, 2004; Ma, 1999) that has led to the ever-increasing interest in learning more about teacher education practices in East Asia. In particular, Ma's study suggested that the Chinese elementary school teachers in her sample demonstrated their profound understanding of fundamental elementary mathematics they teach. However, our preliminary survey results do not seem to support the hypothesis that prospective elementary teachers in Mainland China may have strong preparation in pedagogical content knowledge. Although the sample of practising teachers in Ma's study is different from the sample of prospective teachers in our survey, the results obtained from our survey can safely suggest that the training provided to prospective teachers will not automatically lead to the profound understanding of school mathematics demonstrated by practising teachers in Ma's study. It is thus possible, as Ma (1999) pointed out, that the Shanghai teachers' profound understanding of fundamental mathematics in her sample resulted from being subject specialists in teaching and having opportunities to study the teaching materials intensively together with other teachers that occurs after leaving their teacher preparation programme.

ACKNOWLEDGEMENTS

We would like to thank Xi Chen, Dongchen Zhao, and Shu Xie for their assistances in the process of preparing this chapter. We are also grateful to all the survey participants in Mainland China and South Korea for sharing their time and efforts.

REFERENCES

Adamson, B., & Lai, W. A. (1997). Language and the curriculum in Hong Kong: Dilemmas of triglossia. *Comparative Education, 33*, 233–246.

An, S., Kulm, G., & Wu, Z. (2004). The pedagogical content knowledge of middle school mathematics teachers in China and the U.S. *Journal of Mathematics Teacher Education, 7*(2), 145–172.

Ball, D. L., Hill, H. C., & Bass, H. (2005, Fall). Knowing mathematics for teaching: Who knows mathematics well enough to teach third grade, and how can we decide? *American Educator*, 14–17, 20–22, 43–46.

Beaton, A., Mullis, I., Martin, M., Gonzalez, E., Kelly, D., & Smith, T. (1996). *Mathematics achievement in the middle school year: IEA's Third International Mathematics and Science Study (TIMSS)*. Boston, MA: TIMSS International Study Center, Boston College.

Bond, M. H. (1996). Chinese value. In M. H. Bond (Ed.), *The handbook of Chinese psychology* (pp. 208–226). Hong Kong: Oxford University Press.

Brimer, M. A. (1988). Hong Kong. In T. N. Postlethwaite (Ed.), *The encyclopedia of comparative education and national systems of education* (pp. 332–338). Elmsford, NY: Pergamon Press.

Britton, E., Paine, L., Pimm, D., & Raizen, S. (Eds.) (2003). *Comprehensive teacher induction.* Dordrecht, the Netherlands: Kluwer Academic Publishers.

Chen, W. S. (2003). Teaching reform of primary education discipline from the perspective of the mathematics accomplishments of primary school teachers. *Journal of Jimei University, 4,* 95–96. [in Chinese]

Cheng, Y. C., Chow, K. W., & Mok, M. M. C. (Eds.) (2004). *Reform of teacher education in the Asia-Pacific in the new millennium – Trends and challenges.* New York, NY: Springer.

China Education (2006). Looking at teachers on teacher's day: Team building of our secondary and elementary teachers gets to a new height, September 9, 2006, p. 5.

Department of State, Mainland China. (1999). *The agenda for revamping education in the 21ˢᵗ century. Beijing, China:* Author.

Eraut, M. (Ed.) (2000). Design of initial teacher education. *International Journal of Educational Research, 33*(5).

Fang, Y.-P., & Paine, L. (2000). Challenges and dilemmas in a period of reform – Preservice mathematics teacher education in Shanghai, China. *The Mathematics Educator, 5*(1/2), 32–67.

Grossman, D. L. (2004). Higher education and teacher preparation in Japan and Hong Kong. *Nagoya Research on Higher Education, 4,* 105–126. Retrieved September 10, 2007, from http://www.cshe.nagoya-u.ac.jp/publications/journal/no4/08.pdf

Hayhoe, R. (2002). Teacher education and the university: A comparative analysis with implications for Hong Kong. *Teaching Education, 13*(1), 5–23.

Hiebert, J., Gallimore, R., Garnier, H., Givvin, K.B., Hollingsworth, H., Jacobs, J., et al. (2003). *Teaching Mathematics in seven countries: Results from the TIMSS 1999 Video Study* (NCES 2003-013). U.S. Department of Education. Washington, DC: National Center for Education Statistics.

Hill, H.C., Schilling, S. G., & Ball, D.L. (2004). Developing measures of teachers' mathematics knowledge for teaching. *Elementary School Journal, 105,* 11–30.

Huang, W.-D. (2005). A comparative study on undergraduate course plans of primary education. *Curriculum, Teaching Material and Method, 2,* 79–84 [in Chinese].

Jaworski, B., Wood, T., & Dawson, S. (Eds.), (1999). *Mathematics teacher education: Critical international perspectives.* Philadelphia, PA: Falmer Press.

Klassen, F. H., & Collier, J. L. (Eds.) (1972). *Innovation now! International perspectives on innovation in teacher education.* Washington, D.C.: International Council on Education for Teaching.

Klassen, F. H., & Leavitt, H. B. (Eds.), (1976). *International perspectives of teacher education: Innovations and trends.* Washington, D.C.: International Council on Education for Teaching.

Lapointe, A. E., Mead, N. A., & Askew, J. M. (1992). *Learning mathematics.* Princeton, NJ: Educational Testing Service.

Leung, F., & Park, K. (2002). Competent students, competent teachers? *International Journal of Educational Research, 37,* 113–129.

Li, Y. (2008). What do students need to learn about division of fractions? *Mathematics Teaching in the Middle School, 13,* 546–552.

Li, Y., & Lappan, G. (Eds.) (2002). Developing and improving mathematics teachers' competence: Practices and approaches across educational systems. *International Journal of Educational Research, 37*(2).

Li, Y., & Smith, D. (2007). Prospective middle school teachers' knowledge in mathematics and pedagogy for teaching – The case of fraction division. In J. H. Woo, H. C. Lew, K. S. Park, & D. Y. Seo (Eds.), *Proceedings of the 31ˢᵗ Conference of the International Group for the Psychology of Mathematics Education* (Vol. 3, pp. 185–192). Seoul, the Republic of Korea: Psychology of Mathematics Education.

Lim-Teo, S. K. (2002). Prospective preparation of mathematics teachers in the Singapore education system. *International Journal of Educational Research, 37*, 131–143.

Lin, P.-J. (2000). Two approaches of assisting teachers in adjusting to curriculum reform in Taiwan. *The Mathematics Educator, 5*(1/2), 68–82.

Liu, C.-G. (2005). On the reconstruction of the training model of the primary education. *Journal of Nanjing Xiaozhuang College, 2*, 59–60 [in Chinese].

Lo, J.-J., Hung, C.-C., & Liu, S.-T. (2002). An analysis of teacher education reform in Taiwan since 1994 and its potential impact on the preparation of mathematics teachers at the elementary school level. *International Journal of Educational Research, 37*, 145–159.

Ma, L. (1999). *Knowing and teaching elementary mathematics: Teachers' understanding of fundamental mathematics in China and the United States.* Mahwah, NJ: Lawrence Erlbaum Associates.

Ministry of Education, Mainland China. (2003). *Three-year program curriculum plan for preparing elementary school teachers.* Beijing, China: Author [in Chinese].

Ministry of Education, Mainland China. (2007). *2006 National statistics bulletin board for educational development* [in Chinese]. Retrieved September 7, 2007 from http://www.moe.edu.cn/edoas/website18/level3.jsp?tablename=1068&infoid=29052

Mullis, I.V.S., Martin, M.O., Gonzalez, E.J., & Chrostowski, S.J. (2004). *Findings from IEA's trends in international mathematics and science study at the fourth and eighth grades.* Chestnut Hill, MA; TIMSS & PIRLS International Study Center, Boston College.

National Commission on Teaching and America's Future. (1996). *What matters most: Teaching for America's future.* New York: Teachers College Press.

National Council of Teachers of Mathematics. (1991). *Professional standards for teaching mathematics.* Reston, VA: Author.

National Education Committee, Mainland China, (1995). *Program plan in junior normal colleges for preparing elementary school teachers.* Beijing, China: Author [in Chinese].

Park, K. (2005, August). *Mathematics teacher education in East Asian countries – From the perspectives of pedagogical content knowledge.* Plenary lecture given at ICMI regional conference – The Third East Asia Regional Conference on Mathematics Education, Shanghai, China. Retrieved on September 5, 2007, from http://www.math.ecnu.edu.cn/earcome3/Plenarylecture.htm

RAND Mathematics Study Panel. (2003). *Mathematical proficiency for all students: Towards a strategic development program in mathematics education.* Santa Monica, CA: RAND Corporation MR-1643.0-OERI.

Schmidt, W. H., McKnight, C. C., Valverde, G. A., Houang, R. T., & Wiley, D. E. (1997). *Many visions, many aims (Vol. 1): A cross-national investigation of curricular intentions in school mathematics.* Dordrecht, the Netherlands: Kluwer Academic Publishers.

Sikula, J. (Ed.) (1996). *Handbook of research on teacher education.* (2nd edition). New York, NY: Macmillan.

Silver, E. A., & Li, Y. (2000). Understanding professional preparation and development of mathematics teachers in different education systems: An introduction. *The Mathematics Educator, 5*(1/2), 1–4.

Sowder, J. T. (2007). The mathematical education and development of teachers. In F. K. Lester, Jr. (Ed.), *Second handbook of research on mathematics teaching and learning* (pp. 157–223). Charlotte, NC: Information Age Publishing and the National Council of Teachers of Mathematics.

Stewart, D. K. (1991). Teacher education in countries around the world: Studies in the ERIC data base. *Journal of Teacher Education, 42*, 350–356.

Stigler, J. W., & Hiebert, J. (1999). *The teaching gap – Best ideas from the world's teachers for improving education in the classroom*. New York, NY: The Free Press.

Stigler, J. W., Lee, S.-Y., & Stevenson, H. W. (1987). Mathematics classrooms in Japan, Taiwan, and the United States. *Child Development, 58*, 1272–1285.

Thomas, R. M. (1988). Singapore. In T. N. Postlethwaite (Ed.), *The encyclopedia of comparative education and national systems of education* (pp. 594-597). Elmsford, NY: Pergamon Press.

Tirosh, D. (2000). Enhancing prospective teachers' knowledge of children's conceptions: The case of division of fractions. *Journal for Research in Mathematics Education, 31*(1), 5–25.

Tisher, R. P., & Wideen, M. F. (Eds.) (1990). *Research in teacher education: International perspectives*. Bristol, PA: The Falmer Press.

Tobin, J. J., Wu, D. Y. H., & Davidson, D. H. (1989). *Preschool in three cultures: Japan, China, and the United States*. New Haven, CT: Yale University Press.

Trends in International Mathematics and Science Study [TIMSS 2003]. *TIMSS contextual background questionnaires for teacher, grade 8, mathematics*. Retrieved October 26, 2006 from http://timss.bc.edu/timss2003i/PDF/T03_TeacherMath_8.pdf

Townsend, T., & Bates, R. (Eds.) (2007). *Handbook of teacher education: Globalisation, standards and professionalism in times of changes*. New York, NY: Springer.

Wang, A. H., Coleman, A. B., Coley, R. J., & Phelps, R. P. (2003). *Preparing teachers around the world*. Princeton, NJ: Educational Testing Service.

Wilson, S. M., Floden, R. E., & Ferrini-Mundy, J. (2001). *Teachers preparation research: Current knowledge, gaps and recommendations*. A research report prepared for the U.S. Department of Education by the Center for the Study of Teaching and Policy in collaboration with Michigan State University.

Wong, N-Y. (2004). The CHC learner's phenomenon: Its implications on mathematics education. In L. Fan, N-Y. Wong, J. Cai, & S. Li (Eds.), *How Chinese learn mathematics: Perspectives from insiders* (pp. 503–534). Singapore: World Scientific.

Yeping Li
Department of Teaching, Learning, and Culture
Texas A&M University, U. S. A.

Yunpeng Ma
School of Education
Northeast Normal University, P. R. China

JeongSuk Pang
Department of Elementary Education
Korea National University of Education, South Korea

LI SHIQI, HUANG RONGJIN, AND SHIN HYUNYONG

3. DISCIPLINE KNOWLEDGE PREPARATION FOR PROSPECTIVE SECONDARY MATHEMATICS TEACHERS

An East Asian Perspective

This chapter presents and compares the structure and content of programmes for the preparation of prospective secondary mathematics teachers in China and Korea. It describes the structure of the programmes, presents samples of the actual programmes, and outlines some characteristics of innovative courses. It provides readers with a sense of the depth expected in the respective programme elements, and allows consideration of the respective perspectives on the discipline preparation expected of teachers in China and Korea, and the balance of this discipline preparation with other programme elements.

INTRODUCTION

The phenomenon that East Asian students have consistently outperformed their counterparts in mathematics in many international comparative studies (Mullis, Martin, Gonzalez, & Chrostowski, 2003; OECD, 2003) has aroused policy makers and researchers' interests in exploring the underlying reasons (Leung, 2005; Leung & Park, 2002; Park & Leung, 2003). In view of the fact that students learn most of their mathematics through their teachers, it is reasonable to explore mathematics teacher education in these countries. In examining the teacher education system in East Asia, it was found that there are diversities in terms of the mechanisms for preparing teachers. Some systems provide an integrated approach such as acquiring a teacher certificate through a four-year bachelor degree programme through a comprehensive university such as in Korea or Chinese Taipei (Taiwan), or through a Normal Institute as in Mainland China. While some systems adopt an end-on approach such as after completing a bachelor degree and then taking a one- or two-year PGCE (Post Graduate Certificate in Education) programme as in Hong Kong or Japan. Each model has its own strengths and weaknesses with regards to acquiring the subject knowledge and pedagogical knowledge (Leung, 2003; Park, 2005). Furthermore, based on a close examination of mathematics teacher preparation in East Asia from a pedagogical perspective, Park (2005) called for the need for a proper balance between discipline knowledge and the pedagogy needed to transform it. Some studies indicated there are remarkable differences in pedagogical knowledge between Chinese and U.S. mathematics teachers (An, Klum, & Wu, 2004; Ma, 1999), and that these differences come from practising teachers' learning communities (Ma, 1999; Wang & Paine, 2003). Undoubtedly,

P. Sullivan and T. Wood (eds.), Knowledge and Beliefs in Mathematics Teaching and Teaching Development, 63–86.

prospective teacher programmes and mechanisms play a crucial role in teacher professional development which is explored in the East Asia teacher education system. In this chapter, we provide a detailed examination of prospective mathematics teacher education systems and the core curricula of these programmes, underlining principles of designing and teaching these courses in Mainland China and Korea. Through this lens, we hope to offer an East Asian points of view on preparing prospective secondary mathematics teachers.

THE STRUCTURE OF MATHEMATICS TEACHER EDUCATION PROGRAMMES

This section outlines the structure of programmes for prospective mathematics teachers in China, and then in Korea.

Mathematics Teacher Education in China

Since adopting the "nine-year compulsory education system" in 1978, teacher education has become a daunting task. Through approximately 20 years of efforts, a three-staged process of "normal" education has been established and has made significant contribution to educating teachers from elementary to secondary level in China. It means: (1) primary school teachers are trained in secondary normal schools; (2) junior high school teachers are trained in three-year teacher colleges; and, (3) senior high school teachers are trained in four-year teacher colleges and normal universities. However, with the rapid development of the economy and technology in China, it has been an urgent agenda to upgrade and foster teachers' quality. In order to meet this challenge, the Ministry of Education (1998) documented an action plan for revitalising education in the 21st century. Two projects were launched; one is referred to as the "Gardener Project" and aims to establish continuing teacher education systems for practising teachers. Meanwhile, the Ministry of Education (1999) enacted *a decision on deepening education reform and whole advancing quality education* in which comprehensive universities and non-normal universities were encouraged to engage in educating elementary and secondary teachers. This meant that the privilege of normal universities for teacher education changed. The Ministry of Education (2001) put forward a process to perfect an open teacher education system based on the existing normal universities and supported by other universities, and to integrate prospective teacher preparation and practising teachers' professional development. Through five years of research, teacher education has shown some changes:
(1) integration of education of prospective and practising teachers;
(2) opening of teacher education in all qualified universities rather than just normal universities;
(3) forming a new three-staged teacher education: where primary school teachers are trained in the three-year teacher colleges or four-year teacher colleges; the junior and senior high school teachers are trained in four-year teacher colleges and normal universities, and some of the senior high school teachers are required to

attain postgraduate level studies. In order to achieve this feature, the Academic Degree Committee of the Ministry of Education set a special degree, called a Professional Degree of Master of Education (PDME), for school teachers.

The candidates are only required to sit for the Joint Examination given by the related universities, and do not need to take the National Postgraduate Entrance Examination. Their study is 2-4 years duration part-time, however, it is necessary to study at university full time for one year accumulatively (23 credit points) and present a teaching-related dissertation at the end. Furthermore, in order to allow some non teaching experienced candidates who could be school teachers to obtain PDME, a new model, called 4+2 (which means four-years undergraduate course and two-years postgraduate course) has been successfully utilised by Beijing Normal University since 2003. (Gu, 2006)

In 2004, there were more than 400 institutes conducting teacher education programmes and around 280 of them were teacher education universities or colleges. It was also found that one third of graduates who became teachers were from non-teacher education institutes (Yuan, 2004). This proportion has steadily increased in recent years. In addition, there is now a flexible and encouraging accreditation system for teacher recruitment in China. University degree holders who wish to become school teachers and can pass some related examinations, usually pedagogy, psychology and subject didactics, in order to be a secondary school teacher.

Mathematics Teacher Education in Korea

Education of Teachers
In Korea, there are three kinds of bodies that exist for educating prospective teachers. In this section, 'teacher' means 'prospective teacher'.

Teacher education universities are the typical bodies for educating teachers. Every graduate of these is offered the teaching certificate. There are three types of universities for teacher education.
- Universities only for educating elementary school teachers. There are 11 such national universities. Ewha Woman's University, which is not only for educating teachers, but is the unique private university that is for educating elementary school teachers.
- Colleges only for educating secondary teachers. Many universities (national and private) have a college for educating secondary teachers.[1]

---

[1] In fact, there are 31 departments of mathematics education in Korea. Ewha Woman's University educates elementary teachers as well as secondary teachers.

- Korea National University of Education (KNUE) is the only university which educates teachers for all levels of schools: kindergarten, primary and secondary schools.

There are also some programmes in general universities. The department of mathematics of general universities is not for teacher preparation. Usually, however, these departments do have some students who want to become teachers. A small portion of them are selected. They take the required pedagogical courses including field experience. At graduation, they are given the teaching certificate.

There are also many graduate schools of education. Many are mainly for professional development for practising teachers, but some educate prospective teachers. The students in these programmes are mathematics majors. They take required pedagogical courses including field experience. At graduation, they are given the teaching certificate and a Master Degree of education.

Employment of Teachers

Any candidate achieving a teaching certificate needs to pass a national examination, called Teachers Employment Test (TET), to be a classroom teacher of national or public schools. The TET consists of two phases. The first phase is a paper examination. The questions on the test can be categorised into three areas: mathematics (50%), mathematics education (20%), and general education (30%). If an examinee is successful in the first phase, she/he can join the second phase. The second phase varies depending on the provincial education bureau. The performance and teaching ability of the teacher is the main concern of this phase. If successful in the TET, it is possible to enter the classroom as a teacher after a short period of orientation organised by each provincial education bureau. The TET has serious impact on the curriculum of teacher educating institutes. Park (in preparation) gives more detailed information of the TET.

It has recently been announced that the TET will consist of three phases from 2009. Through the first phase which will be mainly a paper examination, double the necessary number of teachers will be selected. At the second phase, which will be mainly comprehensive writing on mathematics and pedagogy, 130% will be selected. The final phase will vary depending on the provincial education bureau. However, the aptitude and teaching ability will be checked through an in-depth interview and field test.

MATHEMATICS TEACHER EDUCATION PROGRAMMES

This section outlines the content of programmes for prospective secondary mathematics teachers in China and Korea.

Programmes for Preparing Secondary Mathematics Teachers in China

Outline of Curriculum Development
Due to historical reasons, from 1949 Mainland China was modelled after the

former Soviet Union (Soviet Russia), including the education system. Thus, mathematics teacher education was heavily influenced by Russian mathematics philosophy, mathematics curriculum, and pedagogy of mathematics (Zhang & Wang, 2000). These influences on the evolution of mathematics education in Mainland China are mainly reflected in the following aspects: (1) regarding mathematics as an abstract, rigorous and wide application subject as suggested by Aleksandrov et al. (1964). Thus, logical deduction and formal mathematical operations have been emphasised in mathematics education until now. (2) The aim of education is "to transmit the most stable knowledge accumulated over thousands of years" to young generations, advocated by Russian educationalist Kailofu (1951). This is in line with the Chinese notion of teaching which is "to transmit, instruct, and disabuse" (师说 师者，所以传道受业解惑也). Thus, teacher-centred and whole classroom lecture has dominated classroom teaching at primary and secondary schools in Mainland China.

(3) Providing a strong advanced mathematics content knowledge and study of primary mathematics is necessary for prospective teachers.

In the 1950s, there were three compulsory advanced mathematics courses (called the "Old Three Advances"), *advanced algebra, analytical geometry and mathematical analysis* which are quite difficult for freshmen who have not learnt primary calculus at secondary school, particularly in learning the $\varepsilon-\delta$ definition of limit. However, through learning these three advanced mathematics courses, the students were trained in rigorous logical reasoning and mathematical literacy which lays a sound foundation of mathematics for their future career as secondary mathematics teachers. In the 1960s, the mathematics courses were extended to include some pure mathematics courses such as functional analysis, abstract algebra, and applied mathematics such as probability and statistics, partial differential equations, operation research, and computation methods. Thus, it was a key development of mathematics education in normal universities and has shaped the direction of further development. However, Mainland China has suffered from two political movements "The Great Leap Forward" (1957-1961) and "Cultural Revolution" (1966-1977) in which the education system was seriously damaged. Through some policies around 1980, the mathematics curriculum returned to that in the 1960s. Advanced algebra, analytical geometry and mathematical analysis as "old three advanced ones" were recognised as dominant courses, and function analysis, abstract algebra and topology were selected as "new three advanced mathematics courses". Thus, the mathematics content knowledge was further emphasised in the mathematics education in normal universities. In the late 1980s, related computer science courses became compulsory, and, in the 1990s, mathematical modelling, mathematics experiments and mathematics education technology became optional courses in departments of mathematics. Since then, modern technology and modern mathematics and mathematics education ideas have become important influences on the mathematics education in Mainland China.

Reformed Curriculum for Mathematics Education

After the 1990s, with the advancement of mathematical sciences and information technology, mathematics education has been challenged in many ways in China. Theoretically, with the rapid development of information technology, 'doing' mathematics is no longer a business of using "one paper, one pencil and a brain" and teaching mathematics is not a matter of using chalk and board. It is mathematical modelling, mathematics experiments, and mathematical education technology which have come to the forefront of mathematics education. Mathematics is not only a tool for training the mind and expressing other subjects, but also comes to the fore by producing direct economic effect. With the integration of mathematical theory and mathematical technology, the functions of mathematics have been extended widely. Thus the ideas of mathematics education have to be changed from a traditional and static notion to a constructive and dynamic one. In addition, with the expansion of recruitment of students at universities during the 1990s, and the diversity of employment opportunities for mathematics graduates, the quality of the students in mathematics departments has unavoidably fallen. Meanwhile, the curricula at secondary schools were condensed and adjusted, some advanced mathematics such as calculus, probability and statistics, vectors and matrices, and mathematical modelling were included in the secondary mathematics curricula. Both internal and external factors have forced normal universities to undertake certain reforms to meet the challenges. Through a four-year study, a report was written on the curriculum reform in mathematics departments at normal universities (Zhang & Wang, 2000). The report claimed that the aims of mathematics education at normal universities were basically to train prospective mathematics teachers and to prepare students for further research or quantitative fields. As a consequence, it is necessary to focus on mathematical content knowledge in the department of mathematics. In addition, when emphasising mathematics subject matter knowledge, it is also important to keep one eye on studying primary mathematics with updating ideas. Moreover, it is more important to update the ideas on mathematics and mathematics education. Zhang and Wang (2000) suggest that mathematics curriculum at the department of mathematics should follow the following principles: (a) less and more refined foundation courses, (b) broader and concise specialisation courses, (c) multiple optional courses, and (d) high quality mathematics education courses. The curriculum schedules in the department of mathematics at different normal universities are diverse. The following Tables 1, 2, 3 and 4 outline programmes for mathematics major undergraduate students at East China Normal University:

Table 1. Required courses

Required Courses. Sub-total: 83 credit points (cps)			
Analytic geometry and higher algebra	10	C- Language	3
Calculus and mathematical analysis	14.5	General physical	6
Ordinary differential equation	3	General psychology	2
Partial differential equation	3	Pedagogy	3

Probability and statistics	4	Mathematics didactics	3
Abstract algebra	3	Educational technology	2
Differential geometry	3	Teacher's spoken language	1
Complex function theory	3	Teaching practice	6
Mathematical experiment	2.5	Thesis	8
Mathematical modelling	3		

There is a trend to provide students with more flexible choices in courses and specialisations. For example, at East China Normal University, according to students' interests and requirements, they are streamed into three optional majors: mathematics education, foundation mathematics, and applied mathematics. The following outlines some electives:

Table 2. Elective courses with some limitations

One series from two. Sub-total needed: 11 cps

Pure mathematics series		Applied mathematics series	
Higher algebra in depth	2	Linear programming	2.5
Real function theory	3	Computational approach	3.5
Functional analysis	3	Statistical approach	2
Topology	3	Control theory	3

Table 3. Elective courses with some limitations

Three from six. Sub-total needed: 6 cps

Ordinary differential equation in depth	2	Introduction to mathematics education	2
Classical geometry	2	Assessment of mathematics education	2.5
Galois theory (Abstract algebra in depth)	2.5	Elementary mathematics in depth	2.5

Table 4. Free elective courses

Elective courses. Sub-total needed: 20 cps

Mathematics education series		Pure mathematics series		Computational & applied series	
Modern mathematics and school mathematics	2	Overview of modern mathematics	1	Numerical solution of differential equation	2
Elementary number theory	2	Calculus on manifold	2	Finite element method	2
Mathematics curriculum theory	2	Algebraic curves	2	Matrix theory	2
Philosophy and history of mathematics	2	Complex function theory in depth	2	Applied partial differential equation	2
Problem solving and mathematical competition	2	Modular theory and representation of group	2	Environmental mathematics modelling	2
GSP and course ware	2	Lie algebra	2	Biomathematics	2
Methodology of mathematics	2	There are other series in mathematics and other courses in general			

The preparation of prospective mathematics teachers (i.e., in the department of mathematics at normal universities) exhibits the following characteristics:

(a) providing prospective teachers with a foundation in profound mathematics knowledge and high advanced mathematics literacy;
(b) emphasising review and study of primary mathematics. It was believed that a profound understanding of primary mathematics and strong ability of solving problems in primary mathematics were crucial to being a qualified mathematics teacher at secondary schools. Due to the tradition of examination-oriented teaching, a high level of problem solving ability is necessary for a qualified teacher;
(c) teaching practicum is limited. A six-week teaching practicum can only provide prospective teachers with a preliminary experience of teaching in secondary schools.

This reflects a belief that a solid mathematics base is vital for teacher preparation. Furthermore, higher mathematics courses are taken as a priority and privilege since prospective teachers will have less chance to learn them in their career lives. It is a main aim to foster prospective teachers with a bird's eye view of understanding elementary mathematics deeply rather than immediately connecting to what they will teach in schools, though there are special courses such as Modern Mathematics and School Mathematics, and Elementary Mathematics in Depth which connect higher mathematics to elementary mathematics. In contrast with the rigid requirement of mathematics, it is hoped that graduates learn teaching skills from their practical teaching when they become teachers. In fact, their professional development is strongly supported by a well-organised teacher continuing education (Huang, 2006). It is worth mentioning that every secondary school year in China has two semesters and each has 18 weeks for teaching and two for examinations (a 2 credit-point course means 18 periods of 90 minute lessons), much longer than most countries. Longer semesters provide prospective teachers sufficient time to acquire enough mathematical and pedagogical knowledge and to understand them in depth.

Programmes for Preparing Secondary Mathematics Teachers in Korea

Number theory, linear algebra, abstract algebra, analysis, complex analysis, differential geometry, topology, probability and statistics, discrete mathematics, and mathematics education are the compulsory courses for prospective teachers in Korea. Usually, the teacher education departments also offer more advanced courses for the ones mentioned above as well as some independent courses such as set theory and the history of mathematics. Even though the contents of the courses are partially influenced by the TET, they depend on the tradition and the faculty members of each institute. Each institute for teacher education has its own curriculum and content.

In Korea, there are two types of professors at teacher education departments. Some are specialists of mathematics, and others are specialists of mathematics education. Usually each group has not much interest in the others' work. In other words, mathematicians only teach mathematics, and education specialists only teach education related topics without much interest in mathematics at university level. It is the students' duty to digest these two areas of knowledge to come up with the useful knowledge which will be needed for their future careers as mathematics teachers. However, it has been recently pointed out that this paradigm of teacher education is not effective. In fact, in 2005, the Korea Research Foundation launched a project to develop curriculum and teaching/learning materials for the departments of mathematics education at the various teacher education universities. Some products include:

(1) suggestions for developing curriculum for mathematics departments of teacher education universities;

(2) extended syllabi of 26 key courses for mathematics department of teacher education universities. Each syllabus consists of approximately 100 pages of description;

(3) a list of approximately 300 non-professional books which are recommended for prospective or practising teachers of mathematics;

(4) a list of approximately 200 web-sites which are recommended for prospective or practising teachers of mathematics.

In particular, the syllabi have been developed according to the following suggestions which are proposed in the final report of the project:

(1) To help students to understand the foundation of mathematics.

(2) To help students know and utilise the effectiveness and usefulness of mathematics and eventually use and enjoy mathematics in real life.

(3) To help students integrate all branches of mathematics and to connect each course with school mathematics.

(4) To stimulate the intellectual interest of students to induce self investigation.

(5) To incorporate technology in some courses.

(6) To show a teaching programme (or model).

The following is an example of the proposed course schedules for the department for educating secondary school mathematics teachers. The number of credits of all courses is three.

Table 5. Proposed course schedules

Year	Courses for the First Semester	Courses for the Second Semester
1	Calculus I	Calculus II
	Set Theory	Discrete Mathematics
	Linear Algebra and Its Applications	Number Theory and Its Applications
2	Geometry I	Geometry II
	Analysis I	Analysis II
3	Abstract Algebra I	Abstract Algebra II
	Differential Equations	Complex Analysis
	General Topology	Differential Geometry
	Probability and Statistics	Applied Mathematics
	Foundations of Mathematics Education	Teaching and Learning of Mathematics
		Field Experience I
4	Algebra for School Mathematics	Analysis for School Mathematics

Geometry for School Mathematics	Probability and Statistics for School
History of Mathematics for School Teachers	Mathematics
Problem Solving in Mathematics	Philosophy of Mathematics for School
Field Experience II	Teachers
	School Mathematics and Modern Mathematics
	Assessment in Mathematics

The courses for seniors are designed to actively incorporate pedagogy into mathematics. However, this proposal has not yet been effectively implemented in many departments. For this proposal to be successfully implemented it would need to be recommended that it be connected with the TET.

CHARACTERISTICS OF INNOVATIVE COURSES

To illustrate the dynamic nature of course development, the following sections presents examples of some innovative course in both China and Korea.

Selected Innovative Courses in China

In order to meet the reform of mathematics curriculum for preparing secondary mathematics teachers, some organisations are editing relevant textbooks to meet the special needs of mathematics school teachers. For example, the Higher Education Press has published a series of textbooks for mathematics teacher education, such as Mathematical Analysis, Higher Algebra and Analytical Geometry, Theory of Real Variable Function, Theory of Complex Variable Function, Introduction to Mathematics Education, Research on Secondary School Algebra, Research on Secondary School Geometry, Research on Secondary School Probability and Statistics, and Mathematics Education Technology etc. The following will describe and discuss some specific courses in terms of their design principles, organisation and features to demonstrate the characteristics of these reform-oriented courses at East China Normal University.

Course 1. Higher Algebra and Analytical Geometry
Analytical geometry and higher algebra are two courses for freshmen at the department of mathematics at teacher-training universities and colleges in China. The analytical geometry course taught at universities mainly consists of three-dimensional topics while the higher algebra course usually includes two parts: linear algebra and polynomial theories.

Since the late 1990s, some professors at the East China Normal University have developed a new course titled Higher Algebra and Analytical Geometry, which integrated the two traditional courses of Higher Algebra and Analytical Geometry (Chen, 2000). The rationale of designing the new course is that linear algebra, as the main content of higher algebra, has a profound geometric underpinning, while analytical geometry aims to study geometry problems with algebraic methods. As a result, the two courses are internally connected in terms of the mathematical ideas and methods. In an interview, Professor Chen Zhijie, an algebraist, the chief designer of the courses, presented the following information about the background and some unique features of the newly designed course.

Historically, the development of algebra and geometry are tightly related and mutually supported side by side. The relationship between these two areas can be described as algebra providing the research methods for geometry while geometry providing visual representations of algebra. The latter one is more important than the former for future teachers. It was suggested that looking for a visual background from the perspective of geometry is helpful for students to understand abstract algebraic concepts. Many examples demonstrate that if an algebraic abstract concept can be visually presented by geometrical representations, students can get a deeper understanding of the concept and be more motivated of the study in general. Such a new course is intended to foster students' abilities of analysing and solving problems in integrated ways with algebra and geometry.

One of the considerations of the integrated course is that, in practical teaching, there are some difficulties in teaching higher algebra and analytic geometry separately. Usually, the two courses are taught in parallel in the first semester at the department of mathematics. There are many overlapping related concepts between these two courses. Sometimes, the instructors of analytic geometry had to mention some new concepts, which would be formally taught later in a higher algebra course. Such a paradox may be due to the traditional artificial split of these courses.

Based on this understanding, the attempt to integrate these two courses has relied on the geometric meaning of algebraic concepts. For example, in order to help students get a visual perception of a vector in concrete vector space, the 3-dimensional vector algebra is introduced first, and then, the concept of n-dimension vector space is introduced subsequently. Thus, students could be successful in learning n-dimensions of vector spaces based on the learning of 3 dimensions of vector space.

Another example is the concept of the function of the determinant is introduced through calculating the directed volume of a parallel polyhedron which is formed by n vectors. This not only allows students to have an impressive perception of the geometric meaning of determinant, but also makes the definition of determinant as the alternating sum of the products of terms more obvious. This treatment provides the determinant of the product of matrices with a geometric explanation and further makes the determinant of matrix product equal to the product of determinants of matrices more visible

In the same way, the concept of linear mapping is introduced before the definition of the matrix operations. Based on the one to one correspondent relationship between linear mapping and the matrix operations, operations of linear mapping can be used for defining relevant operations of matrices. So the properties of matrix operations and the properties of linear mapping can be justified at the same time, only one of them needs to be proved carefully. Thus the geometric meaning of matrices is manifest implicitly.

In the process of curriculum reform, the problems of reselecting and reorganising the topics need to be considered. After some necessary adaptation, most of content of linear algebra was maintained in the new course. However, the content of analytical geometry was tailored, and reshaped to a certain extent. Since spatial visualisation is vital for students' mathematical development in general, and for multivariate calculus in particular, the methods of drawing spatial graphs, the intersection of curved surfaces and its projection on the coordinate plane etc. are kept, though they may not be tightly related to some content in linear algebra. The mechanical proving of geometry theorems which is built on the theories of polynomials of several indeterminates should be introduced.

It is important for prospective mathematics teachers to learn that the truth of plane geometry proposition could be proved by programming methods which can be realised with the help of some specific software. In order to discuss mechanical proof of the geometry theorem, some traditional topics in both analytic geometry and higher algebra were condensed, or deleted.

The main content of this new course is as follows:

Chapter 1 Vector algebra
Chapter 2 Determinant
Chapter 3 Linear equation system and linear subspace
Chapter 4 Rank of matrix and the operations of matrices
Chapter 5 Linear space and Euclidean space
Chapter 6 Common curved surfaces in geometry space
Chapter 7 Linear transformation
Chapter 8 Functions of linear space
Chapter 9 Coordinate transformation and point transformation
Chapter 10 Polynomial of one indeterminate and integer factoring
Chapter 11 Polynomial of several indeterminates
Chapter 12 Polynomial matrix and Jordan canonical form
Chapter 13 Discussion and application of Jordan canonical form

Course 2. Mathematical Analysis

Mathematical analysis is always regarded as one of the most important courses for mathematics majors at university. This course lasts three semesters (one and a half years), six periods in each week including four periods of formal classes and two periods of problem-solving classes. The course is thought to be of more importance because it includes many important mathematical concepts which form the basis for learning other courses of the mathematics major. Moreover, it provides students with a valuable opportunity to develop their conceptual thinking and rigorous deductive reasoning ability. As a result, the course maintains a higher demand for students' learning. For example, most of the important concepts are introduced systematically, and nearly all of the theorems are proved formally and rigorously. Higher cognitive level problems are assigned to students as homework. These requirements may imply the basic belief of mathematicians that mathematical analysis has a long history so that it is a classical and well-developed course. It is unnecessary to reform it substantially. So the course still keeps most of the content, as well as the structure and features, over the last 25 years. Only a few parts are modified.

However, based on many years of teaching experience, nearly all instructors of the course have realised that it is not easy for freshmen students to master so much new knowledge, especially in their first semester in which calculus with one variable is taught. In order to help students learn this content easily and meaningfully, some examination of the content has been done, but the rigorous demands of the relevant content are still maintained. The topic of real number continuity in calculus is provided as a typical example.

There is a group of six theorems in the topic of real number, including the Heine-Borel theorem, the rest of interval theorem, Cauchy criterion for convergence, monotone convergence theorem etc., as well as the proofs of equivalence. From the perspective of mathematicians, the topic about completeness theory of real number is a core in calculus, especially the related proofs. Although there are difficulties for students to understand these theorems and proofs, it is certain that they are crucial for mathematics majors. In fact, this topic is waived at some universities while it is taught in a traditional way at others. How to cope with such a topic was an issue at ECNU more than 20 years ago, and the reform has been conducted carefully. Now the teaching of some topics is treated in a special way to reduce the difficulties but the course still keeps the essential content consistent.

Traditionally, this topic was introduced just after the topics of the limit of series and function. Now, it is delayed and taught after all the chapters of differential theories. In the new textbook, the six theorems and the proofs of equivalence are still formally introduced. Instructors may teach them in several classes and one or two of the proofs remain as students' home work. Therefore, even though some students who are not able to fully understand and master all of the proofs, at least they will know a set of theorems and the rigorous equivalent proofs between them. It is important for prospective teachers to know and believe that any mathematics propositions have to be proved mathematically, which may influence their teaching in schools.

Course 3. History of mathematics and its implications for mathematics education
Since the late 1980s, the history of mathematics is an elective course for mathematics education programmes in many normal universities. The teaching content was selected by the teachers who teach the course because there was no unified syllabus and textbook available. The majority of the universities used the teaching materials they developed themselves, while there were several institutes adopting the Chinese version of *An Introduction to the History of Mathematics* by Eves (1986). From the 1990s, more and more normal universities have adopted a textbook, entitled *A History of Mathematics* by Wenlin Li (1999). Traditionally, the teaching of the history of mathematics aims to introduce the history without paying attention to its connection with pedagogy of mathematics at secondary school level. Thus, the usefulness of this course is not so satisfactory for teacher education. In order to improve the appropriateness of mathematics history at normal universities, by adopting research findings of history and pedagogy of

mathematics (e.g., Fauvel & Mannen, 2000), some major adjustments of mathematics history courses have been made recently, and following aspects are emphasised:

1. Through many historical cases, the importance of the history of mathematics in cultivating students' attitudes and values is discussed.
2. The history of mathematics as instructional resources, and relevant historical topics in high school mathematics are described, such as the concept of function, trigonometric formulas, arithmetical and geometrical sequences, the binomial theorem, complex numbers, mathematical induction, the volume of the sphere, conic sections, classic probability, etc.
3. Teaching designs based upon the history of mathematics, directly or indirectly, are introduced, such as teaching of linear equations, quadratic equations, system of linear equations, application of similar triangles, complex numbers, trigonometric formulae (e.g. Wang, 2006, 2007; Zhang, 2007) and so on.
4. More attention is paid to historical parallelism (or the historical-genetic principle), which implies that an individual's mathematical understanding processes can be illuminated by the historical developments of mathematical ideas. Many famous mathematicians have paid keen attention to the importance of this issue since the end of the last century and have conducted empirical studies on the historical parallelism, i.e., symbolic algebra (Harper, 1987), actual infinity (Moreno & Waldegg, 1991), the concept of plane (Zormbala & Tzanakis, 2001), the concept of angle (Keiser, 2004), the limit of functions (Juter, 2006). Further empirical studies on relevant concepts such as imaginary numbers, infinite set, functions, tangent of curve (e.g., Wang et al., 2005, 2006) are described in the course.
5. There are 11 historical topics in Optional Course 3 in the new curriculum at senior high school. Some of them are: Ancient Greek mathematics; Ancient Chinese mathematical treasures; Development of Calculus – epoch-marking mathematical achievements; puzzle problems for thousands of years – solution of Galois; Cantor's set theory; Development of random and probability thinking; Development of modern mathematics in China, etc. Thus, this course values both the history of mathematics and its implications for mathematics teaching at secondary schools through historical case studies for the new school curriculum reform.

Below are two cases as examples.

Case 1: Linear equations with one unknown. In the section "Teaching designs based upon the history of mathematics", the concept of linear equations with one unknown was introduced through solving relevant historical problems classified under the following types: arithmetic operation problems; cooperation problems; journey problems; fixed sum problems; and remainder problems. Through solving these problems in turn, the development of the concept of linear equations with one unknown was reconstructed. Two examples of these problems are as follows:

Example 1. (1) Alice, Bonnie, and Jessica can make 300, 250 and 200 bricks per day respectively. How long will it take for them working together to make 1500 bricks?

(2) If Alice works one day, and Bonnie and Jessica work together with her, how long will it take to finish this task? Let the number of days be x, establish the equation with x respectively (Cooperation problem, adapted from *The Greek Anthology* (Paton, 1979).

Example 2. (1) It takes 5 days for the first ship to sail from place A to B and 7 days for the second ship to sail from place B to A. If the two ships start the voyage from A and B respectively at the same time, in how many days will they meet each other? (2) If the second ship has sailed for two days before the first ship starts its voyage, in how many days will they meet each other? Let the number of days be x, create the equation with respect to x. (Journey problem, adapted from the Nine Chapters on the Mathematical Art [Guo, 2004] and Liber Abaci Siegler, 2002).

Based on the previous problems, and historical origins, the concept of linear equations with one unknown was introduced. The main aim of this design is to help students experience the process of creating linear equation with one unknown to solve problems with situations from daily life, and to introduce the concept of linear equations. On the one hand, through solving relevant historical problems, students realise the necessity of learning the concept and stimulate the motivation of learning; on the other hand, through re-constructing the historical sequences, the learning is based on the students' knowledge preparation, and cognitive appropriateness, from easy to more difficult.

Case 2. Introduction of imaginary numbers. In the same section of "Teaching designs based upon the history of mathematics", the history of the development of complex numbers is introduced. Usually, the concept of the imaginary number is introduced through solving the equation $x^2 + 1 = 0$, but it does not motivate students and convince them of the necessity of learning the topic. Therefore, the Leibniz problem (McClenon, 1923) is used to introduce this topic as follows:

Thus far, students have explored the real number system. Then, are there any numbers different from real numbers? Please explore the following problem:

Given $x^2 + y^2 = 2$, $xy = 2$, find: (1) $x + y = $? (2) the values of x and y.

We can find the values of $x - y$ ($\pm\sqrt{6}$), but we cannot find the real value of x and y. The existence of $x - y$ assures us that x and y must exist, but they are not real numbers. What are they? Let us take a closer look at the nature of x and y. Based on the equation $x + y = \sqrt{6}$ and $xy = 2$, we can regard x and y as two roots of a quadratic equation with one unknown. But there is no real root with regard to this equation. It is necessary to introduce a new type of number in order to solve this problem. The key to solving this problem is to express the roots when the discriminate is negative. Therefore, the necessity of introducing the imaginary numbers has been dealt with properly.

Course 4. Modern Mathematics and School Mathematics
From the late 1980s, many teacher education universities in China have developed a series of special courses for prospective mathematics teachers. The aim of these

courses is to strengthen the connection between higher mathematics students learnt at university and the mathematics they will teach at school. Generally, learning higher mathematics will give an overall view of elementary mathematics. However, mathematics teacher educators believe that it is foundational and more helpful for prospective teachers to make some implicit connections between higher mathematics and elementary mathematics. For example, the underlying differences and conceptual development relationship between finite additivity of the concepts of length/area in elementary geometry and denumerably additivity of the concept of measurement in real function theory. Making sense of accurate and detailed connections will promote future teachers to understand allowing them to teach elementary mathematics with understanding and flexibly.

At the Department of Mathematics at ECNU, a course titled Modern Mathematics and School Mathematics has been delivered for more than 15 years. Though it is an optional course, the majority of students who want to become mathematics teachers have taken this course.

The main content of the course is:

- Set theory as mathematics language: A brief history of set theory, its language, open sentence and quantifiers, power set concepts, calculation in sets, and the Z-F Axioms in set theory
- Relations and functions: The Cartesian product, relations abstracted from real life, the representations of relations, equivalent relations and functions as a special relation
- Mapping and its applications: The mapping and drawer principle, permutations, combinations and mapping, the computation formula of the number of surjections, the perspectives of mapping as scientific method
- Quotient set and congruence: Models of quotient sets, algebraic calculations, problem solving with remainders and language
- Mathematical induction: The Peano Axiom and mathematical induction principle, ordered set and well-ordered set, the equivalence between induction axiom and well-ordered axiom
- Number systems: The principle of the extension of number systems, the system of N, Z, Q, R, C, 4-tuple and 8-tuple numbers etc.
- Polynomial ring and factoring: The ideal subring, highest common factor, Euclidean algorithm, and prime factoring
- The three great problems in geometric construction: The criterion of construction with a ruler and compass, extension field, and the three great problems in geometric construction
- Set algebra and propositional calculus: The shortcomings of traditional logic, algebra and set algebra, proposition and compound of proposition, qualifier and predicate
- Vector geometry and mechanical proving in elementary geometry: Vector space, creating a geometric model, the algebraic definition of an angle, and brief introduction of mechanical proving,
- Geometry foundations and geometric models: Euclidean elements, Hilbert axiomatic theory and geometry, hyperbolic geometry and elliptic geometry,

Erlangen Programme, transformation groups and geometry, projective geometry and its applications in school mathematics
- Length and area: Length axiom and area axiom, the area of a triangle and convex polygons, and measurement
- Topology in brief: Local and global properties, topology space, Brouwer fixed point theorem, definition of dimension and fractal dimensions.

This course introduces many different kinds of relationships between higher and elementary mathematics. Most of the content discusses the relationships between relevant concepts, such as the quotient set and congruence, ideal and common factors, mapping, relations and functions, extension field and three great problems in geometric construction, Peano Axiom and the mathematical induction principle, set algebra and propositional calculus, etc. When teaching related topics or concepts in secondary schools, teachers may call on their backgrounds from advanced mathematics perspectives and use such knowledge to teach students with profound understanding. Other kinds of relationships may not be so obvious and direct, but they may imply certain strategies or thinking skills, for example, relationships between vector geometry and mechanical proving, hyperbolic/elliptic geometry and Euclidean geometry, fractal dimension and plane/solid geometry etc. Realising these kinds of relationships may broaden prospective teachers' visions and also foster their mathematics thinking capabilities and problem solving skills.

Selected Innovations in Korea

The following outline some innovations in the Korean system.

1. Directions of textbook development
The general direction of developing textbooks is to present mathematics as a story combined with pedagogy. Based on the proposed curriculum, the *Korea Society of Mathematical Education* has decided to publish a series of textbooks for mathematics teachers.
  (1) Textbooks for mathematical courses
The following four (Vol.1 through Vol. 4) books were published.
1: Abstract Algebra for Secondary School teachers
2: Mathematics Education at Kindergarten.
3: Algebra for Elementary School Teachers. The main portion of elementary school mathematics is algebra. An independent course of algebra is required for all elementary prospective teachers. This is a proposed textbook for the course.
4: Set Theory for School teachers. This book can be used at universities for educating secondary school mathematics teachers as well as at universities for educating elementary school mathematics teachers.

The following four books (Vol. 5 through Vol. 8) are scheduled to appear in March of 2008.

5: Real Analysis for Secondary School Teachers

6: Number Theory for Secondary School Teachers. Cryptographic content is included. Secure key distribution, coin flipping by telephone, and digital signature are some of the examples which are covered during the course.

7: Mathematics for Elementary School Teachers. This book is being written by two authors, a mathematician and an education specialist.

8: Teaching Materials for Secondary School Teachers. The scheduled content of this book is: the value of mathematics, the beauty of mathematics, the power of mathematics, probability, symmetry, dimension, and modesty of mathematics.

The following two books are scheduled to be developed during 2008.

9: Linear Algebra for Secondary School Teachers. Coding Theory is included. Syndrome decoding schemes and cyclic codes are some of the examples which are covered during the course.

10: Physics for Mathematics Teachers: The role of mathematics in electromagnetic theory, relativity theory and quantum mechanics is briefly explained. The principal equations (Maxwell's equations, for example) in each theory are the main topics.

The following books and more will be developed in the future..

11: Geometry for Secondary School Teachers

12: Probability and Statistics for Secondary School Teachers

13: Topology for Secondary School Teachers

14: History and Philosophy of Mathematics – For School Mathematics Teachers

(2) Textbooks for pedagogical courses

Books on mathematics curriculum, psychology, and teaching methods respectively, will be developed.

2. A detailed description

The text *Abstract Algebra for Secondary School Teachers* is used as an example. This book is used for two semesters (Abstract Algebra I and Abstract Algebra II). It consists of two parts, and each part is for a semester course. Each course consists of 45 class hours, and each class hour is for 50 minutes duration. The first part is on algebraic structures. Three structures of group, ring, and vector space are mainly discussed. The second part is on the applications of algebraic structures. The field of constructible numbers, the Galois Theory, and the construction of regular polygons are the main themes. The main content is:

(1) The course is focused on 3 algebraic structures: group, ring, and vector space. The basic examples are Z, Q, R^2, R^3, $Mat_2(R)$, Q[x], R[x]. The definitions, examples, and basic properties of these algebraic structures are introduced in parallel. The parallel discussion which is one of the characteristics of the book is to help prospective teachers to have an overall understanding of algebraic structures.

(2) This course is neither for group theory nor for ring theory. Understanding

important algebraic structures through basic examples and school mathematics is the main purpose.

(3) Substructures (subgroup, subring, and subspace), quotient structures (with normal subgroup and ideal), and direct products (sums) are introduced in parallel. Some concepts (e.g., subset, partition by an equivalence relation, Cartesian product, nZ, Z_n, and matrix and determinant) in set theory, number theory, and linear algebra are mentioned.

(4) The homomorphism and linear mapping are introduced in parallel. Various functions (e.g., function in set theory and continuous functions in calculus) are mentioned.

(5) Lagrange Theorem is proved. Students compare the theorem with the following facts;

In set theory, $|X \cup Y| = |X| + |Y| - |X \cap Y|$.

In linear algebra, $\dim(X + Y) = \dim X + \dim Y - \dim(X \cap Y)$.

In ring (field) theory, $[L : F] = [L : K][K : F]$ for $F \leq K \leq L$.

(6) The basic properties of maximal ideals are proved and some finite fields (of order 4, 8, 9) are constructed. The prime fields Z_p, p: prime, are mentioned.

(7) Some topics which need number theory, group theory, and ring theory are discussed.

(8) Field extension and constructible numbers are studied briefly. The co-work of algebra and geometry is explained.

(9) Some students will take the advanced course (Abstract Algebra II). The course mainly deals with Galois Theory. To be ready for the course the students will be given some homework.

Some features of the book are the following. It is pointed out that commutativity, associativity, and distributive property are deeply connected with finiteness and convergence. The following examples are presented.

(1) Check the associativity and commutativity in the series:

$$1 - 1 + 1 - 1 + \cdots + 1 - 1 + \cdots$$

(2) Discuss the following argument:

$$\lim_{n \to \infty} \frac{1 + 2 + \cdots + n}{n^2}$$
$$= \lim_{n \to \infty} \left(\frac{1}{n^2} + \frac{2}{n^2} + \cdots + \frac{n}{n^2} \right)$$
$$= \lim_{n \to \infty} \frac{1}{n^2} + \lim_{n \to \infty} \frac{2}{n^2} + \cdots + \lim_{n \to \infty} \frac{n}{n^2}$$
$$= 0.$$

(3) Discuss the following argument:

(i) If we let $x = 0.999\ldots$, then $10x = 9.999\ldots$, so $9x = 9$, thus $x = 1$.

This book also discusses the co-work of algebra and geometry through the

following topics.
(1) Some examples in analytic geometry.
(2) Erlangen Programme by Felix Klein.
(3) A proper picture explaining the equality: $(a + b)^2 = a^2 + 2ab + b^2$.
(4) Construction of numbers.
(5) Proper pictures explaining the following equalities:

$$1 + \frac{1}{2} + \frac{1}{2^2} + \frac{1}{2^3} + \cdots = 2,$$

$$1 + \frac{1}{4} + \frac{1}{4^2} + \frac{1}{4^3} + \cdots = \frac{4}{3}.$$

This book proposes various types of problems. Essays, performance assessment, and group projects are some of the examples. Some students may want to study abstract algebra more deeply. This book is not deep and broad enough. Some additional mathematical books are recommended.

3. Course management
Each course has been designed to provide the necessary pedagogical content knowledge to prospective teachers. It seems to be inevitable for each course to be managed tightly. It seems to be helpful for some supplementary books to be recommended during the course. The following books (translated into Korean) are helpful for the course.
 · Fermat's Last Theorem (S. Singh 1997).
 · The Man Who Loved Only Numbers (P. Hoffman 1998).
 · My Brain Is Open (B. Schechter 1998).
 · Knowing and Teaching Elementary Mathematics (L. Ma 1999).
 · Mystery of Aleph (A. D. Aczel 2000).
 · The Elegant Universe (B. Greene 1999).
 · Beautiful Mind (S. Nasar 1998).
 · In Code (S. Flannery & D. Flannery 2000).
 · Flatland (E. Abbott, Annotated by I. Stewart 2002).

Some students might read some of the above books as they take the previous courses. This course is mainly offered through mathematical lectures. It is recommended to give three or four lectures through PowerPoint which are specially designed for providing pedagogical knowledge. A special web site is devoted to this course. Various materials for further readings or in-depth study are provided here.

CONCLUSION

From the aforementioned descriptions and analysis, we can summarise that there are similarities and differences between the cases in China and Korea with respect to the programmes offered for prospective teachers, as well as the mechanism of educating and recruiting mathematics teachers. On the basis of the curriculum framework in China and Korea, both traditional and innovative programmes emphasise the foundation of mathematics subject knowledge in terms of its systematic structure, and demand for logical reasoning. These features are echoed in other studies. For example, the Glenn commission (U.S. Department of Education, 2000) put forwarded that "High quality teaching requires that teachers have a deep knowledge of subject matter". But, the ways to reflect such a belief in practice depend on the specific context found in different countries.

In the reform-oriented mathematics courses in the case of China, it seems that much of the endeavour taken was to make difficult advanced mathematics knowledge easier for prospective teachers to understand (e.g., the case of Higher Algebra and Analytic Geometry, and Mathematical Analysis), but the original aim is to maintain the difficulty level of the mathematics content. These mathematics courses pay less attention to exploring the implications for teaching secondary school mathematics; however, there are other courses offered students as a compensation or remedy, such as Modern Mathematics and School Mathematics, Research on Secondary School Algebra, Research on Secondary School Geometry, Research on Secondary School Probability and Statistics, which specifically deal with the connection between higher and elementary mathematics. The course on the history of mathematics plays an additional role to help future teachers deal with elementary mathematics topics from a mathematical historical perspective.

The innovative mathematics courses in the case of Korea are integrated and devote much attention to both: internal connections between higher mathematics and relevant elementary mathematics, and connections between mathematics and pedagogy of teaching relevant content. Given that teacher preparation programmes tend to work in a zero-sum game environment where additional preparation in mathematics results in decreased preparation in some other areas such as pedagogy (Jermey et al., 2003), Korean innovative courses attempt to adopt an integrated approach to connect subject knowledge and pedagogy pertaining to the learning and teaching of specific mathematics content. This effort is well supported by Kant's words, "pedagogy without mathematics is empty, mathematics without pedagogy is blind" (cited from Park, 2005). Thus, the mathematics content and pedagogy should be emphasised properly.

The practice in China may imply that mathematicians there still value the mathematical structure and nature of mathematics subject matter, and hope to provide students a refined and profound mathematics foundation, with a broad and concise mathematics background, and further try to help students to master mathematics more easily and properly. At the same time, they leave the responsibility of connecting higher mathematics to elementary mathematics and the responsibility of providing high quality mathematics pedagogical knowledge for mathematics educators. However, mathematicians in Korea seem to realise it is their responsibility to make the connection between higher and elementary mathematics explicit and teach subject content knowledge for teaching school mathematics.

These reformed curricula are new and only implemented during the past years, therefore there is no empirical data demonstrating intended results. But some initial responses from prospective teachers and instructors of those courses are positive. It is certain that these reformed programmes for prospective mathematics teachers will have promising influences on mathematics teacher education in the future.

ACKNOWLEDGEMENT

The chapter was supported by Eastern China Normal University (ECNU) 985 project funded by China Ministry of Education. The authors would like to thank Professors Chen Zhijie, Pang Xuecheng and Wang Xiaoqin at ECNU for their help and references.

REFERENCES

Aleksandrov, A. D., Kolmogorov, A. N., & Lavrent'ev, M. A. (1964). *Mathematics: Its content, methods, and meaning* (S. H. Gould & T. Bartha, Trans.). Cambridge, MA: M.I.T. Press,

An, S., Kulm, G., & Wu, Z. (2004). The pedagogical content knowledge of middle school mathematics teachers in China and the U.S. *Journal of Mathematics Teacher Education, 7*, 145–172.

Chen, Z. (2003). *Higher algebra and analytic geometry* [in Chinese]. Beijing: China Higher Education Press & Berlin: Springer-Verlag.

Eves, H. (1986). *An introduction to the history of mathematics* [Chinese version] Taiyuan, China: Shanxi People Press.

Fauvel, J., & van Maanen, J. (2000). *History in mathematics education.* Dordrecht, the Netherlands: Kluwer Academic Publishers.

Fauvel, J. (1991). Using history in mathematics education. *For the Learning of Mathematics, 11*(2), 3–6.

Gu, M. (2006). The reform and development in teacher education in China. Keynote speech at the First International Forum on Teacher Education. Shanghai, China. Retrieved February, 4, 2008 from http://www.icte.ecnu.edu.cn/EN/show.asp?id=547

Guo, S. (2004). *Collected collation of the nine chapters on the mathematical arts* [in Chinese]. Shenyang, China: Liaoning Education Press.

Harper, E. (1987). Ghosts of Diophantus. *Educational Studies in Mathematics, 18*, 75–90.

Huang, R. (2006). Tension and alternative of in-service secondary mathematics teacher profession development in China. *Proceedings of the Second International Forum on Teacher Education* (pp. 162–179). October 25–27, 2006, Shanghai, China.

Jeremy, A. K., Duane, A. C., & Kimberly, A. B. (2003). The role of mathematics teachers' content knowledge in their teaching: A framework for research applied to a study of student teachers. *Journal of Mathematics Teacher Education, 6*, 223–252.

Juter, K. (2006). Limits of functions as they developed through time and as students learn them today. *Mathematical Thinking and Learning, 8*, 407–431.

Keiser, J. M. (2004). Struggles with developing the concept of angle: Comparing sixth-grade students' discourse to the history of angle concept. *Mathematical Thinking and Learning, 6*, 285–306.

Kairov, I. A. (1951). *Theory of education* [in Chinese] (Y. Sheng, Trans.). Beijing: People's Education Press.

Leung, F. K. S. (2003). Issues concerning teacher education in the East Asian region. *Asia-Pacific Journal of Teacher Education Development, 6*(2), 5–21.

Leung, F. K. S., & Park, K. (2002). Competent students, competent teachers? *International Journal of Educational Research, 37*(2), 113–129.

Leung, F. K. S. (2005). Some characteristics of East Asian mathematics classrooms based on data from the TIMSS 1999 Video Study. *Educational Studies in Mathematics, 60*(2), 199–215.

Li, W. (1999). *A history of mathematics* [in Chinese]. Beijing: China Higher Education Press, Berlin: Springer-Verlag.

Ma, L. (1999). *Knowing and teaching elementary mathematics: Teachers' understanding of fundamental mathematics in China and the United States.* Mahwah, NJ: Lawrence Erlbaum Associates.

McClenon, R. B. (1923). A contribution of Leibniz to the history of complex numbers. *American Mathematical Monthly, 30*, 369–374.

Ministry of Education, P.R.China (1998). *An action plan for vitalizing education to face the 21 century* [in Chinese]. Retrieved February, 6, 2008 from http://www.moe.edu.cn/edoas/website18/level3.jsp?tablename=208&infoid=3337 (?)

Ministry of Education, R.P. China (1999). *Decision on deepening education reform and whole advancing quality education* [in Chinese].Retrieved February, 6, 2008 from http://www.edu.cn/20011114/3009834.shtml.

Ministry of Education, R.P. China (2001). Agenda *on the reform and development of the basic education by state department of P. R. China* [in Chinese]. Retrieved February, 6, 2008 from http://www.edu.cn/20010907/3000665.shtml.

Moreno, L., & Waldegg, G., (1991). The conceptual evolution of actual mathematical infinity. *Educational Studies in Mathematics, 22,* 211–231.

Mullis, I. V. S., Martin, M. O., Gonzalez, E. J., & Chrostowski, S. J. (2004). *International mathematics report: Findings from IEA's trends in International Mathematics and Science Study at the fourth and eighth grades.* Boston: TIMSS & PIRLS International Study Center, Boston College.

OECD (2003). *Learning for tomorrow's world: First results from PISA 2000.* Paris: Organisation for Economic Co-operation and Development.

Park, K. (2005, August). Mathematics teacher education in East Asian countries from the perspective of pedagogical content knowledge. Plenary lecture at EARCOME 3 (The Third East Asia Regional Conference on Mathematics Education).Shanghai, China.

Park, K. (in preparation). Mathematics teacher education in Korea, In F. K. S. Leung & Y. Li (Eds.), *Mathematics curriculum and teacher education in East Asia.* Rotterdam, the Netherlands: Sense Publishers.

Park, K., & Leung, F. K. S. (2003). Factors contributing to East Asian students' high achievement in mathematics: The case of Korea. *The Mathematics Educator, 1,* 7–19.

Paton, W. R. (1979). *The Greek anthology with an English translation.* Cambridge, MA: Harvard University Press.

Siegler, L. E. (2002). *Fibonacci's Liber Abaci: A translation into modern English of Leonardo Pisano's book of Calculation.* New York: Springer-Verlag.

U.S. Department of Education (2000). Before it's too late: A report to the nation from the national commission on mathematics and science teaching for the 21st century. Washington, DC: Author.

Wang, J., & Paine, L. (2003). Learning to teach with mandated curriculum and public examination of teaching as contexts. *Teaching and Teacher Education, 19,* 75–94.

Wang, X., Fang, K., & Wang, C. (2005). Justification of the historical-genetic principle from a test. *Journal of Mathematics Education, 14*(3), 30–33 [in Chinese].

Wang, X., & Zhou, B. (2006). Senior middle school students' understanding about actual mathematical infinity. *Journal of Mathematics Education, 15*(4), 90–93 [in Chinese].

Wang, X. (2006). Teaching design of the concept of quadratic equation from the viewpoint of HPM. *Mathematics Teaching in Middle Schools, 12,* 50–52 [in Chinese].

Wang, X. (2007). Teaching design of the concept of system of linear equations with two unknowns from the viewpoint of HPM. *Mathematics Teaching in Middle Schools, 5,* 48–51 [in Chinese].

Yuan, Z. D. (2004). A transition from normal education to teacher education, *China Higher Education, 5,* 30–32 [in Chinese].

Zhang, D., & Zhou, Y. (1990). *Modern mathematics and school mathematics* [in Chinese]. Shanghai: Shanghai Education Publishing House.

Zhang, X. (2007). The derivation of the addition formula: An example of integrating the history of mathematics in mathematics teaching. *Mathematics Teaching, 2,* 42–44 [in Chinese]

Zhang, X., & Wang, X. (2007). Teaching design of complex numbers from the viewpoint of HPM. *Mathematics Teaching in Middle Schools, 6,* 4–7 [in Chinese].

Zormbala, K., & Tzanakis, C. (2001). The concept of the plane in geometry: Elements of the historical evolution inherent in modern views. Retrieved February, 4, 2008 from http://www.icme-organisers.dk/tsg17/Tzanakis-Zorbala.pdf.

Li Shiqi
Department of Mathematics
East China Normal University
Shanghai
China

Huang Rongjin
Department of Teaching, Learning and Culture
Texas A & M University
U.S.A.

Shin Hyunyong
Department of Mathematics Education
Korea National University of Education
Korea

KAYE STACEY

4. MATHEMATICS FOR SECONDARY TEACHING

Four Components of Discipline Knowledge for a Changing
Teacher Workforce

This chapter addresses the mathematics required for teaching in secondary
schools, from early adolescence to preparation for university. The chapter works
from a vision of good mathematics learning which values working from reasons
not just rules, and being able to use whatever mathematics has been learned for.
solving problems within and beyond mathematics. Four components of
mathematical knowledge are needed for teaching: (i) knowing mathematics in a
way that has special qualities for teaching; (ii) having experienced mathematics in
action solving problems, conducting investigations and modelling the real world;
(iii) knowing about mathematics including its history and current developments;
and (iv) knowing how to learn mathematics. The chapter includes a short survey of
teacher certification requirements in some western countries, and also reviews
some reports that highlight shortages of well-qualified mathematics teachers. The
policy responses to this situation relate to certification requirements, as well to the
adequate provision for practising teachers of experiences that address all four
components of discipline knowledge for teaching mathematics.

INTRODUCTION

This chapter addresses the mathematics required for teaching in secondary schools.
In the chapter, I consider secondary school as being for students aged
approximately 11 to 18 and primary school for students aged approximately 5 to
11. This chapter is concerned with preparation of teachers who will teach a broad
spectrum of secondary mathematics through the middle and upper years of
secondary school. Secondary school encompasses a very wide range of
mathematics learning, from the early adolescent years when some students are still
struggling with ideas of whole number place value up to the highest levels of
school achievement when some students are prepared to enter the most demanding
university mathematics courses. This wide range of mathematical content and
student achievement necessitates a breadth of teaching tasks which in turn requires
a broad range of mathematical knowledge for teaching. Given that other chapters in
this volume deal with mathematics knowledge for teaching from an Asian
perspective, this chapter is concerned with 'western' countries although a
comprehensive review cannot be attempted because of the large variety of

P. Sullivan and T. Wood (eds.), Knowledge and Beliefs in Mathematics Teaching and Teaching
Development, 87–113.

arrangements for teacher education and of school systems. I hope that the examples chosen serve to illustrate challenges and opportunities in many western countries. The term 'mathematics' is generally used to apply broadly to the mathematical sciences, including pure and applied mathematics, statistics, operations research, and parts of computer science.

In the past in many countries, mastery of the subject matter has been regarded as the only requirement to be a teacher. Aldrich (1990) notes that for much of English history the accepted method of preparation for teaching in a grammar school or public school or university was holding a master's degree from Oxford or Cambridge. Learning to teach was by an informal apprenticeship and teaching was often a family trade. Shulman (1986) notes that no distinction was made between content and pedagogy: those who knew the subject matter well were assumed to be able to teach it. Later, when university education departments were established, they generally prepared primary teachers since content knowledge was still regarded as sufficient for secondary teachers. Aldrich (1990) supports this by noting that even in 1925 there were 4602 students in university education departments in England preparing for primary teaching, but only 917 students preparing for secondary teaching.

Today, teacher education is seen to address several types of knowledge and skills and it is common to follow Shulman (1986) to describe these as content knowledge, general pedagogical knowledge, pedagogical content knowledge and knowledge of various aspects of the education setting (including knowledge of the learners, curriculum, educational contexts, purposes and values). This chapter is principally concerned with content knowledge, but since the purpose of this content knowledge is to teach, there is inevitably a blending with pedagogical content knowledge. Indeed in her study of pedagogical content knowledge (PCK), Chick (2007) found strict separation was unhelpful and so developed a framework for PCK with three components: (i) 'clearly PCK'; (ii) general pedagogical knowledge specifically applied in a content context (e.g., knowledge of what area of applications might be most motivating for students); and (iii) content knowledge in a pedagogical context (e.g., deep understanding of content, ability to deconstruct or connect content). This chapter considers the content knowledge that supports all three of these parts of PCK, with a specific emphasis on the development of content knowledge and content knowledge in a pedagogical context.

Those who use mathematics professionally learn to apply mathematical thinking to fields of endeavour such as engineering, finance or meteorology, and their work is characterised by a productive interplay between their knowledge of mathematics and their knowledge of the field of application. It is the same with teaching; we can think of mathematical knowledge being applied to the task of teaching with a productive interplay between what the teacher knows about mathematics and what the teacher knows about students and curriculum. Mathematical knowledge is applied to solve the real problems of teaching when teachers analyse a task to identify sources of difficulty, select an example with certain properties, identify the important pre-requisite knowledge for a topic and make connections between topics and engage in many other aspects of the work of teaching. These are the special skills, at the interface between mathematics and teaching, which teachers uniquely need. In this chapter I address the content knowledge needed to support these skills.

Anyone who reflects on what mathematics teachers should know does so in relation to two things – the mathematics that students should learn at school, and the most important features of mathematics as an activity. I believe that a good mathematics education engages all students at every level in age-appropriate activities that develop:
– knowledge of facts
– fluency and accuracy in routine procedural skills;
– deep conceptual understanding;
– understanding of the major applications of mathematics;
– ability to communicate using clear and precise mathematical language;
– ability to tackle non-routine problems systematically;
– ability to apply what has been learned to solve problems in real world contexts;
– ability to conduct investigations using mathematics;
– logical reasoning and a conception of the nature of proof;
– practical ability for measuring, estimating, drawing and constructing;
– sensible use of calculators and computers;
– appreciation of the dynamic role of mathematics in society and the processes by which mathematics grows;
– confidence and a productive disposition, which inclines one to see mathematical activity as useful and worthwhile.

This list does not specify the content of mathematics learning, but it express an orientation to the processes and outcomes of learning any mathematics, which values working from reasons not just rules and being able to use whatever mathematics has been learned for solving problems within and beyond mathematics. The list is in broad agreement the U.S. report *Adding It Up* (Kilpatrick, Swafford & Findell, 2001) which lists five strands of mathematical proficiency (conceptual understanding, procedural fluency, strategic competence, adaptive reasoning, productive disposition) although with a stronger emphasis on applications and problem solving outside mathematics. I take these orientations and values to apply to all mathematics education – in school and in the preparation of teachers.

This chapter begins with a short survey of the mathematical knowledge required to be a fully qualified mathematics teacher in several western countries. I then discuss in turn several different aspects of the content knowledge needed for teaching, which are widely recognised in the literature as important. These are:
– Knowing mathematics
– Experiencing mathematics in action
– Knowing about mathematics
– Knowing how to learn mathematics
In the final section, I will discuss how the recommendations given in earlier sections, which outline an ideal answer to the question 'what mathematics should mathematics teachers know?' are affected by the reality in many countries of a

decline in the availability of well-qualified teachers. The chapter concludes with some questions for the future.

TEACHER CERTIFICATION REQUIREMENTS AROUND THE WORLD

For certification as a secondary mathematics teacher, educational jurisdictions require studies in mathematics and in education and usually specify the amount of university-level study of content knowledge rather than its nature and characteristics. INCA, the internet archive reviewing curriculum and assessment frameworks that is sponsored by the United Kingdom's Qualifications and Curriculum Authority (HREF1) provides summary data on the professional education typically required of secondary teachers, including mathematics teachers, in a range of countries. INCA divides teacher training into 'concurrent' where teacher education is combined with a degree which results in the award of a Bachelor of Education or similar; 'combined' where there is a joint degree in education and a specific subject; 'consecutive', where a programme of professional education training is undertaken after an undergraduate degree and 'on-the job training'. Almost without exception, prospective teachers are required to gain a background in their discipline area(s) and to study education but there are differences in the balance between discipline content knowledge and pedagogical knowledge. It is the case that specifications for teacher certification apply to all secondary teachers; there are no special requirements listed for mathematics teachers. However, it is sometimes the case that upper secondary teachers (those of students about 15-18 years old) are required to undertake more discipline study than lower secondary teachers.

It is not possible to give a thorough review of the requirements for certification as a teacher of secondary mathematics, because of the substantial variation within and between countries. For example, while the United Kingdom, the Netherlands, Australia, Canada, New Zealand and the United States of America all endorse both the concurrent model and the consecutive model, the total time required to complete the qualification varies between 3 and 6 years. Germany, Hungary, Sweden, and Switzerland, Japan and Korea endorse the concurrent model. Italy and Spain have consecutive models. Stephens (2003) discusses the variety of courses offered in USA, Australia, the Netherlands and Japan in detail.

There is also a variety of institutions where teacher education is conducted. For example, the German Education server (HREF2) states that teacher training is divided into two parts, first studying at a university, and then practical pedagogical training. Teacher training courses are offered at universities, technical universities, pedagogical universities and art and music colleges while the pedagogical training in terms of a preparatory service takes place in school practical seminars and training schools.

Most countries specify only the amount of mathematics (and other subjects) to be studied for qualification as a teacher. In the UK, according to Goulding, Hatch, and Rodd (2003), most secondary mathematics teachers complete a one year Post Graduate Certificate of Education which follows a degree. These candidates are required to have at least 50% mathematics or content strongly related to mathematics within their undergraduate degree. This is spelt out in broad terms in the UK "Qualifications to teach" (HREF3) as "Teachers should have a secure knowledge and understanding of the subject(s) they are trained to teach. For those qualifying to teach secondary pupils, this knowledge and understanding should be at a standard equivalent to degree level". Spain provides something of a contrast because while their teachers are required to undertake general then professional studies the particular discipline which may be the focus of their undergraduate general degree may not be linked to the subject they intend to teach. To become a secondary mathematics teacher, it is not necessary for the candidate's general degree qualification to have been in mathematics (HREF1). The requirements for initial teacher training in the UK are further described by McNamara, Jaworski, Rowland, Hodgen, and Prestage (2002), including the introduction of the "Numeracy Skills Test" for all primary and secondary teachers (not just mathematics teachers) by the central Teacher Training Agency as part of a wide-reaching standards agenda. They also conduct audits of the mathematics content of teacher training courses.

France is an example of a system that has stronger national agreement on the content of mathematics that prospective teachers should study. In writing about the French requirements for mathematics teachers, Robert and Hache (2000) draw attention to the strong emphasis placed there on the teachers' personal knowledge of mathematics. To qualify as a mathematics teacher in France students undertake five years of training beginning at University and with final two years at IUFM (Institut Universitaire de Formation des Maîtres). In the first three years, prospective mathematics teachers are expected to study a standard undergraduate mathematics syllabus including classical linear algebra, real analysis, topology, differential and integral calculus and options such as probability, complex analysis or numerical analysis. The first year at IUFM is again devoted to mathematics, preparing for a highly competitive theoretical examination with written and oral components. The written paper covers problems from the mathematics topics that students are expected to have covered during their university studies (analysis, topology and functional analysis, integration and differential calculus, groups, rings, and linear algebra, geometry) while the oral examination focuses on topics from the later part of the high school curriculum. Henry (2000) notes that this year helps students consolidate their knowledge and reorganise it for teaching. This theme of knowledge being reorganised for teaching is also evident in initiatives that are described in later sections. Clearly France expects a high level of uniformity in the students' undergraduate mathematics programmes. Only in the fifth year is there any consideration of what the profession will involve. Robert and Hache (2000) observe that in the French system it is accepted that a thorough knowledge of mathematics is the most important ingredient for teaching. They observe that there is a need for teachers to be able to do mathematics themselves but also to take account of the students. Despite their years of study in mathematics, it is not uncommon for teachers to have difficulty in presenting mathematics in such a way that links are formed and students in their class are enabled to appreciate the structure of mathematics.

In the United States there is no uniform specification by teacher certification agencies of the mathematics which should be studied by prospective secondary teachers. In some institutions the academic home for studies in both mathematics discipline and methods is in the mathematics department. In others they are separated, although the effects of this are not well studied (Graham, Li, & Curran Buck, 2000). The USA endorses both the concurrent and consecutive models but in either case the range and depth of mathematics studied may vary. To provide guidance, the Conference Board of the Mathematical Sciences (CBMS) (2001), which is associated with both the Mathematical Association of America and the American Mathematical Society, put forward the following general recommendations regarding the mathematics curriculum and instruction for prospective teachers. They state that an aim is "to convince faculty that there is more intellectual content in school mathematics instruction than most realise, content that teachers need to understand well" (p. 3).

– Recommendation 1. Prospective teachers need mathematics courses that develop a deep understanding of the mathematics they will teach.
– Recommendation 2. Although the quality of mathematical preparation is more important than the quantity, the following amount of mathematics coursework for prospective teachers is recommended. Prospective high school teachers of mathematics should be required to complete the equivalent of an undergraduate major in mathematics, that includes a 6-hour capstone course connecting their college mathematics courses with high school mathematics.
– Recommendation 3. Courses on fundamental ideas of school mathematics should focus on a thorough development of basic mathematics ideas. All courses designed for prospective teachers should develop careful reasoning and mathematical 'common sense' in analysing conceptual relationships and in solving problems.
– Recommendation 4. Along with building mathematical knowledge, mathematics courses for prospective teachers should develop the habits of mind of a mathematical thinker and demonstrate flexible, interactive styles of teaching.

The CBMS report also lists mathematics topics that they believe should be studied by prospective secondary mathematics teachers, which are discussed below. In parallel with their assertion, strongly backed by extensive research of the mathematics requirements embedded within teaching tasks, they recommend a stronger focus on topics related to school mathematics than might usually be expected in university studies and attention, in Recommendation 4, to the atmosphere within which this content is delivered. This is in contrast to the regulations for certification in nearly all the countries discussed, where the requirements for being a teacher specify the *amount* of mathematics to be studied but are prescriptive about neither the content of the courses nor the teaching methods and attitudes developed by these courses.

KNOWING MATHEMATICS

In this section and the three following, I discuss the mathematical discipline studies for teaching. This first section discusses the content; the next section discusses how it is essential for mathematics teachers to have experienced doing mathematics through open investigations and modelling the real world. In this regards it is often the case that good mathematics learning for prospective teachers is not different from good mathematics learning for other undergraduates. In the next two sections, I discuss what teachers should know about mathematics as a discipline and how they need to be able to continue to learn mathematics independently.

There is no question that teachers need a sound understanding of mathematics for teaching in secondary schools, but there are important questions of how much, what topics, and what should be the qualities of their mathematical knowledge. As noted elsewhere, most jurisdictions specify only how much mathematics (or any other discipline area) a secondary teacher requires for certification. In this section, we discuss what topics and what qualities this knowledge should have. Before leaving the question of quantity of mathematics teaching however, I note that the specification of some study of university level mathematics indicates several values – that teachers should have strengthened their mathematical knowledge and skills beyond what is needed at the school level, that they should know more than their students, and that they should have some perspective on where school mathematics leads. It is also worthwhile noting that there is an assumption that those who have completed school mathematics know its content well. This assumption is reassessed below: students learning mathematics as mathematically immature adolescents are unlikely to have experienced it with the richness and perspective required for teaching.

Commentaries and opinions on the mathematics that teachers should know reflect ideals of what constitutes good school mathematics and what constitutes good mathematical practice in a wider sense. Regardless of one's philosophical stance on the nature of mathematics, it is abundantly clear that the existing and ideal school and university curricula and the values about mathematics itself that people hold are socially constructed, with the result that recommendations for teacher education vary from time to time and place to place, always expressing what is seen as the ideal. In the era of the 'new mathematics' in school curricula and Bourbaki formalism amongst mathematicians, for example, people valued a highly logical approach to mathematics where even school children drew on set theory and definitions of fundamental objects to deduce their properties. As another example, from Cyprus, Stylianides, Stylianides, and Philippou (2007) document prospective teachers' knowledge of proof by mathematical induction. The article assumes that all mathematics teachers should have mastered various forms of proof and should be able to give their students rich experiences related to proof. Whilst I would like this to be true in my own country, many fully qualified mathematics teachers in Australia have little understanding of proof. It is also the case that proof and verification currently play a very small part in Australian school mathematics. The 1999 TIMSS video study (Hiebert et al., 2003), for example, found practically no instances of proof or deduction in large random samples of Grade 8 lessons from Australia, USA and the Netherlands, although instances of proof were prominent in Japan.

The most prominent recent recommendations of mathematical knowledge for teaching have been given by the Conference Board for the Mathematical Sciences (CBMS, 2001) in the USA. Here I discuss only their recommendations for high school teachers (grade levels 9–12). The CBMS report begins by reviewing research that shows that beyond a threshold, having taken additional subject matter courses has only a small effect on teachers' effectiveness. They take this as a challenge to rethink teacher education so that what prospective teachers learn will indeed increase their effectiveness in the classroom in the future. As a consequence they recommend emphasising the underlying nature of the subject matter, a deep understanding of the subject in a way that is organised for teaching, and awareness of historical, cultural and scientific roots to mathematical ideas and techniques. They consider that recent changes in areas of application of mathematics caused a broadening of school mathematics to include more statistics and discrete mathematics and the use of new technologies opened up new opportunities for both teaching strategies and content to be studied. Consequently, they conclude that future teachers need to know more mathematics than before, somewhat different mathematics than before, and to experience learning it in a new way for themselves.

The CBMS report outlines the content of a mathematics major for prospective teachers. In doing this, it is mindful that mathematics departments may not have the student numbers to warrant special programmes for teachers. As a consequence they have to consider whether the mathematical knowledge required by prospective teachers is quite different to that required by students pursuing other mathematics-related professions. Although they initially state that it is quite different, they later propose that the recommendations for prospective teachers, which outline a major study broader than before and with stronger connections to school mathematics and with use of modern technology, may well serve today's US undergraduates better than traditional majors. They note that mathematics courses which traditionally aimed at preparing students for graduate school work in mathematics must now serve a much wider constituency including mathematics majors not planning graduate work, and undergraduates with other major studies, such as engineering or science.

The broad content of the CBMS recommended university major is organised around five themes of the high school curriculum: algebra and number theory, geometry and trigonometry, functions and analysis, statistics and probability, and discrete mathematics and computer science. The report gives an explanation of the special role and emphasis of each of these areas in the education of teachers. They recommend use of new technology, and note that prospective teachers need to understand the differences between electronic calculation to advance learning, human computation to advance learning, and electronic computation as a practical expedient, as well as learning to use a wide range of mathematical software (e.g., CAS, school-level technology such as graphics calculators and dynamic geometry) and learning some computer-related mathematics and the basics of computer science. In setting out proposed content for each of the courses, the principle that university study of mathematics should illuminate high school mathematics is strong. This is in agreement with Cooney and Wiegel's (2003) Principle 2 that prospective teachers should explicitly study and reflect on school mathematics. For example, in algebra and number theory suggested exercises are to explain how operations of school algebra link with formal axiomatic principles and to justify each step of a common procedure (such as solving a quadratic equation) with field or ring properties. The geometry and trigonometry course is used to demonstrate the nature of axiomatic reasoning, and uses computer graphics and robotics as applications to strengthen students' understanding of modern areas of application and use of technology. Looked at from the British mathematics tradition, the proposed major seems to be lacking an emphasis on the major applications of mathematics, especially relating to partial differential equations. There are also some personal favourite topics of mine that are omitted. For example, I would like to include the study of complex analysis because it gives a strong sense of how the real number line is embedded in the complex plane and because it explains the difficulties with the definitions of log and power functions for negative and fractional numbers; difficulties that impinge on high school mathematics. These examples serve to show the increasing pressure on curriculum time in the mathematics major. The enormous growth in mathematical sciences over the last century is necessarily changing the face of both undergraduate and school mathematics and the place of every component needs to be regularly reassessed.

Although the CBMS report claims that their mathematics major designed for teachers may serve other undergraduates better than a traditional major in mathematics, they also recognise that teachers need some knowledge of mathematics that is unique to teaching. The main need is to assist prospective teachers to make insightful connections between the advanced mathematics they are learning and school mathematics. They recommend that this can be done within each course, but it can also be done by offering a capstone course, taught jointly with mathematics educators. Extensive suggestions for the contribution of each of the five themes to the capstone course are given. For example, linking to the functions and analysis theme, the report suggests that the capstone course looks at the concept of function as a unifying theme in mathematics, examines the role of computers as tools for graphing and computation, examines relations between exploration and proof, and offers some experience of mathematical modelling. Other suggestions include historical perspectives on the development of the idea of function from a 'formula' to a 'mapping' and the cognitive difficulties that modern students experience in making this same transition, examining the use of graphing technology in teaching calculus, and drawing connections between the functions used in different branches of mathematics including probability distributions and log-log plots. How all of this material, with more from the other four themes, could fit within the one capstone course is not addressed. The squeeze on time in the mathematics major comes not only from the expansion of mathematics, but also from the growing appreciation of the need for connections to school mathematics.

Other moves to reform undergraduate education have also found good alignment between the needs of prospective teachers and the needs of the new population of undergraduates now in universities. Pierce, Turville, and Giri (2003) report on the process of review of mathematics courses in an Australian mathematics department where a significant proportion of mathematics majors are prospective teachers. They report that the review was a challenging and reinvigorating process, requiring analysis of what mathematicians valued, but also coming to see their teaching from the students' viewpoints. They argued "mathematical thinking, key skills and conceptual understandings were valued, so too was the exposure of students to various branches of mathematics and their applications. What we needed was to approach this learning from the students' perspective" (p. 155). Their review set goals for knowledge of mathematics, experience of the process of doing mathematics ("reason mathematically, communicate and solve problems"), and for knowledge about mathematics ("understand and appreciate the role of mathematics and its applications in the real world"). They also specified goals related to career development ("Education students should form a positive view of their potential careers as mathematics teachers") and goals related to improving their experience of learning mathematics ("incorporate up-to-date teaching technology and utilise methods that enhance student learning"). Pierce et al. (2003) adopted a thematic approach to their new curriculum, and planned for the use of realistic problems to introduce the need for theory. They gave courses non-traditional and enticing names such as "Logic and Imagination". Practical activities and current technologies were used to enhance the process, and the assessments were chosen to cater for different learning styles and to encourage a range of different skills of communication and analysis. In accordance with the results of many other investigations, surveys revealed that their earlier students often had a narrow perception of mathematics, focussing on routine processing, and so their reinvigorated curriculum for mathematics teachers (and other students) also aimed to heighten enthusiasm for mathematics by using engaging topics in both learning and assessment. The use of new technologies was one tool they used to change undergraduate students' perceptions. In particular they wanted to use new technologies to emphasise a view of mathematics as description and explanation, rather than mathematics as rules for symbol manipulation. Pierce et al. (2003) found that these changes resulted in an increase in both initial enrolments and retention rates, increasing awareness of the relevance of mathematics for other disciplines and every day life, reduction in mathematics anxiety, increasing interest in mathematical thinking and an improved understanding of mathematics. Initiatives such as this may produce teachers with better understanding--although of a possibly more limited curriculum--and with more enthusiasm for mathematics. In turn, by increasing mathematics enrolments, it may produce more mathematics teachers.

Attitudes to and Beliefs about Mathematics

Initiatives such as that of Pierce et al. (2003) and the capstone course of CBMS intend to create more a more productive disposition towards mathematics in future teachers. There is a large literature (reviewed, for example, by Cooney and Wiegel, 2003) which shows that teachers' attitudes to, and beliefs about, mathematics influence their teaching. Some of these attitudes and beliefs are inconsistent with the reform vision of mathematics set out above, especially as they are often dominated by the view of teaching and learning mathematics by 'rules without reasons'. As Lachance and Confrey (2003) observe, teacher reform efforts are often "attempting to get teachers to think about and to teach mathematics in ways which they have never experienced as learners" (p. 110). It is clear that all mathematics education, at school and within teacher education, contributes to the attitudes and beliefs that teachers bring to with them to their work and hence to those that they impart to students. Teacher education that supports the implementation of a better form of mathematics teaching will itself need to demonstrate the characteristics of that mathematics teaching.

It is important, though, to remember that there is not only one good way to teach mathematics and that there are different valid views of what is most important about mathematics. Kendal and Stacey (2001) studied two experienced teachers in one school who were incorporating computer algebra systems into their introductory calculus teaching. They incorporated this new technology into their pedagogy in different ways, consistent with their different beliefs and understandings about mathematics. The different conceptions of mathematics influenced their particular choices while using technology, their emphasis, and how to incorporate the graphical and symbolic algebra capabilities of the calculator into their lessons. In turn, these choices affected what their students learned. Although both classes achieved almost identical overall achievement, they showed quite different strengths. One teacher enjoyed the exactness of mathematics and especially liked the capability of the computer algebra system to give exact answers (e.g., fractions, square roots). He privileged the teaching of mathematical procedures, to which he added new technology procedures. His class was better at recognising how differentiation could be applied to solve a problem. The other teacher privileged conceptual understanding of mathematical ideas supported by extensive use of technology graphing and consequently his students were superior at interpretation of mathematics.

It is also important to recall that teachers will move beyond their own preferences in the interest of students. Teachers' own beliefs about mathematics can be mediated by beliefs about students and their needs, especially as their experience of students and teaching grows. Good teachers aim to give the best education for every individual student, regardless of their mathematical talent and approach to school work, and this can override the teacher's personal preferences. An excellent example of this was provided in a recent project (Stacey, Stillman & Pierce, no date) where we worked with teachers in six schools to enhance students' achievement and engagement through using real world problems and new technology. At the end of an interview Meryl, one teacher in the project, explained that she used the project activities to teach in a way different to her own preferences because she judged doing so was in the interests of her students:

> Personally I like algebra. If I could choose to teach children where I don't need to have activities, where I don't need do a lot of modelling or real life problems, I would. I would just do the 'boring' algebra. I enjoy that most. But the percentage of students in a normal cohort who would gain from that is just a minor part. The majority gain more from this approach.

The Quality of Knowledge

The above discussion has focussed mostly on what teachers should know. However, it is well established that for this content knowledge to be effective for teaching, it requires certain characteristics. Shulman (1986) listed aspects such as the amount and organisation of knowledge, understanding the structures of the subject matter and how truth and falsehood are established, and being able to explain why a proposition is regarded as true, why it is worth knowing and how it relates to other propositions within and beyond the discipline. Many subsequent studies have shown that these characteristics are often lacking even in prospective teachers who have strong undergraduate mathematics backgrounds (see, for example, Ball, 1990; Goulding, Hatch, & Rodd, 2003). Concerns to ensure content knowledge has such characteristics lie behind proposals such as the CBMS capstone course.

There is a growing body of research which aims to measure some of these qualities of teachers' subject matter knowledge. Connectedness is one that has received considerable prominence in recent literature. Chinnappan and Lawson (2005) present a framework which enabled them to characterise teachers' content knowledge and content knowledge for teaching. They demonstrated how to map teachers' content knowledge and their knowledge for teaching one topic (in this case in geometry) in a way which revealed and began to quantify the connectedness of that knowledge. This draws on research which shows that knowledge structures which are more comprehensive and more internally and externally connected are more likely to be useful in problem solving. In this case the 'problem solving' is the act of teaching itself. Their maps revealed qualitative and quantitative differences in the connectedness of knowledge of two well-qualified and experienced secondary mathematics teachers. Further developments in research on measuring the qualities of teachers' knowledge bases will help us understand which differences and which magnitudes of differences impact upon teaching effectiveness.

EXPERIENCING MATHEMATICS IN ACTION

The most influential argument for teachers to experience the process of doing mathematics was put forward by Polya (1962) in his books on how to solve mathematical problems and his exposition of problem solving heuristics. Polya's work was inspired by his "concrete, urgent, practical aim: to improve the preparation of high school mathematics teachers" (p. vii) and so along with case studies of interesting problems and their solutions, he provided a section on "hints for teachers and teachers of teachers" (p. 209) drawn from his own teaching experiences. Writing in the era of the 'new math', Polya found the issue of what content should be offered to prospective high school teachers and to their students too controversial for agreement, but he proposed that knowledge of the process of doing mathematics was something upon which experts would agree.

> Our knowledge about any subject consists of *information* and of *know how*. If you have genuine *bona fide* experience of mathematical work on any level, elementary or advanced, there will be no doubt in your mind that, in mathematics, know-how is more important than mere possession of information. Therefore, in the high school, as on any other level, we should impart, along with a certain amount of information, a certain degree of *know-how* to the student. What is know-how in mathematics? The ability to solve problems – not merely routine problems but problems requiring some degree of independence, judgment, originality, creativity. [...] The teacher should know what he is supposed to teach. He should show his students how to solve problems – but if he does not know, how can he show them? The teacher should develop his students' know-how, their ability to reason; he should recognise and encourage creative thinking – but the curriculum he went through paid insufficient attention to his mastery of the subject matter and no attention at all to his know-how, to his ability to reason, to his ability to solve problems, to his creative thinking. Here is, in my opinion, the worst gap in the present preparation of high school mathematics teachers. To fill this gap, the teachers' curriculum should make room for creative work at an appropriate level (p. vii).

Polya's recommendations for teaching teachers about mathematical problem solving and investigation have been the basis of much subsequent work. He recommended problems that did not require much knowledge beyond high school mathematics, but did require concentration and judgement. His book was organised around strategies for problem solving, illustrated by problems chosen to highlight the strategies. He also advised that prospective teachers should reflect on the classroom use of such problems. He therefore supplemented the 'look back' phase of doing mathematics (where problem solvers reflect on the mathematical solution) by an additional didactically-oriented phase. Polya's basic ingredients for teaching problem solving of experience, strategies and reflection have formed the basis of many subsequent endeavours, including those of Schoenfeld (1985), and Mason, Burton, and Stacey (1982).

Since the time of Polya, explicit attention to the process aspects of mathematics has been evident as a goal in teacher preparation courses. This is evident, for example, in two of the 3 principles that Cooney and Wiegel (2003, p. 806) recommend for mathematics for prospective teachers:

– Principle 1: Preservice teachers should experience mathematics as a pluralistic subject.
– Principle 2: Preservice teachers should explicitly study and reflect on school mathematics.
– Principle 3: Preservice teachers should experience mathematics in ways that support the development of process-oriented teaching styles.

Experiencing mathematics as a pluralistic subject (Principle 1) includes (among other things) experiencing mathematical investigation and problem solving, and Principle 3 calls for prospective teachers to be supported in making such experiences a reality for their own students. Recently, Ryve (2007) found that 6 of 28 teacher education institutions in Sweden had a specific course directed to problem solving, although he noted different foci. Some courses emphasised the mathematical aspects of the tasks with which the prospective teachers engage. Others dealt with problem solving tasks in relation to the secondary school students' learning and behaviour. Others emphasised aspects of the problem solving process, such as interpretations of answers, multiple solutions etc. Other important differences are whether a course sets out to examine only problems challenging to school students or aims to extend prospective teachers' own problem solving, giving them a taste of the genuine problem solving experience which they aim to provide for school students. In my opinion, some attention to the latter (teachers' own experience of doing mathematics) is essential in order to equip them to provide rich experiences for school students. Stacey (2005), using examples from Singapore and three western countries, documents how the goal of teaching children to be better problem solvers (teaching for problem solving) has now generally been supplanted by the intention of 'teaching through problem solving' where students encounter new material about standard topics through investigations. They are expected to acquire problem solving and investigative approaches implicitly. It is my opinion that this approach is unlikely to give student teachers the explicit knowledge of the process of doing mathematics that they require for teaching it well, and that there is a need to provide prospective teachers with supported experience of doing mathematics at their own level, with discussion of strategies and reflection on successful elements.

Ryve (2006) also notes the importance of studies which examine the different character of courses that are provided in teacher education. It is hoped that such studies might extend the primarily quantitative discussions of how much mathematics prospective teachers should learn, to examining qualitatively the nature of their participation in those courses and consequently how their views of mathematics could be extended. The literature provides many examples of how prospective teachers' views and approaches to solving mathematical problems are limited. Van Dooren, Verschaffel, and Onghena (2003) examined secondary prospective teachers solving algebraic and arithmetic word problems. The secondary teachers had good content knowledge, but their habits and attitudes whilst problem solving were stereotyped and some were not open to look for the alternative methods which their future pupils may use. They characterised the prospective teachers, at both the beginning and end of their teacher preparation, as tending to have routine expertise rather than *adaptive expertise*. They concluded that prospective teacher education needed to promote experiences of doing mathematics that encouraged flexible thinking and created a well-organised body of professional knowledge.

Despite the agreement that all mathematics students, and especially teachers, should have direct experience of the processes of mathematical discovery, investigation and application, the history of its implementation has been anything but smooth, in teacher education as well as in schools and universities. Burkhardt and Bell (2007), for example, describe the development of problem solving in UK school mathematics over more than a century. They highlight the many different interpretations of problem solving, from mathematical research by professionals; to the solution of 'riders' where knowledge of theorems and proofs is adapted to a novel problem situation; to conducting open investigations such as finding which numbers are not sums of consecutive numbers; to modelling the real world; to teaching for functional numeracy and mathematical literacy (as defined by OECD, 2003). They highlight the gap between the goals for having students' experience any of the above forms of problem solving and the understanding by school systems of the nature of the change required and the conditions under which it could really be achieved. It is likely that the situation is similar in teacher education, with a mismatch of goals and reality.

Burkhardt and Bell's article also draws attention to the fact that there is a lot more to the 'experience of doing mathematics' than engaging in the pure mathematics investigations in the spirit of Polya and successors (e.g., which numbers are not sums of consecutive numbers), or the investigations that reform-oriented teachers offer to develop students' understandings of particular concepts (e.g., Chick's (2007) finding the dimensions of a rectangle of given perimeter with maximum area or Teacher B in Kendal et al. (2001) setting his class the problem of finding a general rule for the derivative of x^2, x^3, x^4 and then x^n by guessing rules from numerical values of the slopes of tangents). Mathematics is studied for its interest and its beauty and for its place in our cultural heritage, but its central role in the school curriculum is due to its usefulness. Teachers therefore need to understand deeply the way in which mathematics is applied. The presence of teachers coming into teaching as a second or subsequent career from a diversity of backgrounds is a strength here.

Mathematical modelling, using mathematics to answer questions about the real world, has a distinctly different flavour to investigation within the real world. It can be understood as consisting of four steps: formulating a mathematical problem from the real world problem, solving the mathematical problem (using all the techniques developed within mathematics itself), interpreting the mathematical solution in real world terms, and evaluating the solution to see if this solution is adequate for the task. The intention of mathematical modelling is similar to that of mathematical literacy as defined by the OECD (2003) for its PISA study of 15 year olds, although the possibilities of actually assessing modelling are severely curtailed by the written timed test format in PISA. Teachers need experience of mathematical modelling, in addition to pure mathematics investigations, because the process is distinctly different. Only in the simplest of word problems does a mathematical model capture all that is relevant to the real situation (e.g., 6 identical apples shared equally amongst 3 boys). The skill of the mathematical modeller is to identify what are likely to be the most critical variables, but the test for whether they are adequate choices can only come after a full modelling cycle when results are compared with reality. For example, to answer a question about how the times should be set for traffic lights to clear traffic at a busy intersection is it enough to assume that cars pass through the lights every 2 seconds in each lane (this is the time difference that is recommended to learner drivers), or should it be assumed that the first car takes longer and then others pass through at a constant rate, or is it necessary to go for a probabilistic model where cars pass through according to a selected probability distribution? Even the choice to include the rate at which cars pass through the lights as a variable in the model is part of the formulation stage, subject to later verification as to its usefulness. As with pure mathematics investigations, providing prospective teachers with experience of mathematical modelling is a high priority that it often not achieved. When it is achieved, a study by Nicol (2002) shows there may be further work to do to translate this into lively teaching. Prospective teachers were able to see how mathematics was being used in workplaces, but when they created lessons from the experience, the mathematics remained decontextualised. I noticed the same phenomena with prospective teachers from an engineering background. They were expert in applying mathematics in their previous work, but do not see how they could use these experiences to motivate students and illustrate applications.

KNOWING ABOUT MATHEMATICS

Beyond knowledge of mathematics and experience of doing mathematics, teachers need to know *about* mathematics. This is an area where the preparation of teachers is readily seen to require something different to preparation for other professions. Teachers who know about mathematics – its history in both the East and the West, its ways of working, its major events, and so on – can enliven their teaching and assist students to understand how mathematics works, where it comes from and its role in society. Some knowledge about mathematics comes incidentally as we learn mathematics (assisted by teaching), but some such as the history, epistemology or philosophy of mathematics can be studied separately from mathematics. The CBMS (2001) report recognises this need in both its recommended capstone course as well as in the attention it pays to 'habits-of-mind goals' (p. 141) and mathematical thinking.

There is long standing interest in courses on the history of mathematics. Since 1976 there has been, for example, an *International Study Group on the relations between the History and Pedagogy of Mathematics* (HREF4) affiliated to the International Commission for Mathematical Instruction. One of their aims is to assist mathematics teachers to gain insights on how the history of mathematics may be integrated into teaching and may help students to learn mathematics. Materials to support courses for prospective teachers are now becoming readily available on the Internet. For example, Mills (2007) describes an elective course intended for prospective teachers (although not exclusively), that is based on historical documents rather than a modern textbook. Mills' course aims to show how "mathematics is created by human beings and hence is connected with the culture, the times and the place where this creative activity takes place" (p. 195). Students study ancient Egypt (Rhind Papyrus), ancient Greece (Euclid) and medieval Europe (Fibonacci). In justifying his selection of elementary mathematics topics for the course, Mills (2007) notes that many more students can enjoy studying the history of elementary, rather than advanced mathematics. Whilst this is certainly the case, it is often not the case that the history of simple mathematics is itself simple. Matrices, for example, can be introduced in a straightforward way to junior secondary students as storage arrays for data or for coefficients of equations, but their important place in mathematics derives from advanced work by Cauchy, Lagrange and others (HREF5) on a variety of topics such as the use of differential equations to solve problems of celestial mechanics. It is not feasible to motivate the early study of matrices with this. A serious treatment of history can demand both difficult mathematical content and difficult historical material, both from the point of view of the prospective teacher and the instructor. As a consequence, the use of historical anecdotes to enrich the standard teaching of customary mathematical topics is a more widespread approach to increasing teachers' understanding of the history of mathematics than offering complete courses.

Whereas it is common to use history as a source of enrichment when teaching many topics, the philosophy of mathematics seems more difficult to encompass in teacher education. It seems reasonable that prospective teachers should be able to supply good answers to questions such as: what is a mathematical object?; what is the nature of mathematical truth?; is mathematics created or discovered?; and why does mathematics model the real world so well? However, there are no simple answers here; these are difficult questions at the interface of philosophy, logic and mathematics, which require serious study. In addition, they are questions which rarely trouble the working mathematicians who generally provide education in mathematics for prospective teachers. Davis and Hersh (1981) observed that most mathematicians act as though they are Platonists, acting on a naïve view that mathematical objects have an uncomplicated status, although when pressed they often retreat to a formalist view, where mathematics is viewed as a game played according to certain rules and where it is not required to specify any further meaning. In contrast to the concern with mathematical foundations that is attacked with the tools of logic and mathematics, many mathematics educators are keen to stress mathematics as a human endeavour and view it from a social perspective. For example, in their extensive article on mathematics for teacher education, Cooney and Wiegel (2003) promote the view that a fallibilist view of mathematics is the most productive to guide courses for prospective teachers – a view where truth in mathematics is seen as grounded not in pure reason, or on correspondence with data from the senses, but is a result of a social process. In their view, prevalent teachers' beliefs that mathematics is abstract, rigid, unchanging and not based in human experience have arisen from their mathematical training. They propose that these beliefs present a major obstacle to reform of mathematics in schools, and so should be countered by the fallibilist (social) view. My belief is that the view of mathematics as abstract (only), unchanging, rigid, and unrelated to human experience is a consequence of an inadequate mathematics education, not attending to the four components outlined in this chapter, rather than a consequence of a non-fallibilist philosophy. In a recommendation that I strongly endorse, Cooney and Wiegel also recommend that courses for prospective teachers should present mathematics as a pluralistic subject that includes elements of discovery and investigation alongside appropriate formalism, rather than being dominated by one view.

Beyond history and philosophy of mathematics, what else should teachers know about mathematics? For teachers of science, it is important that they 'keep up to date' with their subject, and there is a great deal of information in the press to help them and other concerned citizens, but this is harder for mathematics teachers since advances in mathematics are generally highly technical, and only slowly, if ever, become part of the school mathematics curriculum. Moreover, teachers tend to view mathematics as uncontested, often only as what their own educational jurisdiction sets down for them to teach (Wilson, Cooney, & Stinson, 2005). This view is too limited. At a minimum, teachers need some personal experience that new mathematics and new applications of mathematics continue to be invented and/or discovered. Mathematics 'general knowledge' does not have an easy place in formal mathematical training. The Black-Scholes equation is used for pricing options in financial markets by hedging against losing bets. It is now said to be the world's most used formula and so one might expect that most mathematics teachers would know about it. (Bulmer (2002) provides a suitable introduction for teachers.) However, since pricing options belongs to the mathematics of finance, the Black-Scholes formula is not a central part of a mathematics major today. Moreover it has become important only in recent years, after many teachers have graduated. As a consequence, it is probably the case that most of the world's mathematics teachers have not heard of the world's most used formula.

Infinity is a concept that fascinates people of all ages, including young students, and so one might expect that most mathematics teachers would have a good grasp of the infinite cardinals and how to do arithmetic with them. A teacher who understands why a mathematician says there is the same number of fractions as of all integers but more decimals than either, for example, can link into these widespread fascinations. Similarly, the fourth dimension is a fascinating idea and again one might expect that mathematics teachers could explain how the idea of a 2-dimensional net of a 3-dimensional cube can be generalised to the 3-dimensional net of a 4-dimensional cube. Mathematicians have also shown in recent years that it can be useful to calculate non-integer dimensions, for example the fractal dimension of a coast line. These, and many other ideas which are similarly prominent in the popular imagination, rarely have a firm place in a mainstream mathematics major study, because they are not central to the development of knowledge to participate in advanced mathematics. None of these illustrations above are of themselves essential knowledge for teaching (I expect that there will be individual readers disagreeing with my choice of each of these examples) but there is a cumulative effect of having teachers who can tap into the natural human interest in things mathematical and appreciate the ever increasing role of mathematics in society. This comes back to my point: mathematics teachers need to 'keep up to date' with mathematics and, over time, build up a wide general knowledge of mathematics. Consequently, there is a need for materials on new mathematical developments and on perennial favorites to be prepared for the teacher audience, and presented through teachers' journals and other media.

KNOWING HOW TO LEARN MATHEMATICS

Equally importantly, the need to keep up-to-date throughout a career points to the need for mathematics training at every level to develop skills in learning to learn mathematics. The CBMS report (2001) makes the same point: "Thus, college mathematics courses should be designed to prepare prospective teachers for the lifelong learning of mathematics, rather than to teach them all they will need to know in order to teach mathematics well" (p. 6). An initial preparation in any subject is not sufficient for an on-going career. Being an independent learner of mathematics, both to master new technical skills as required to deal with new topics in the curriculum, and to keep abreast of the concepts behind new developments, is as important for teachers as for any other professional. New demands from the workforce and national economies, new mathematical ideas and applications and new technologies for doing mathematics all contribute to making it a dynamic subject, with consequent needs for continual independent learning.

What do we know about courses that develop good skills for independent learning of mathematics? Seaman and Szydlik (2007) developed a concept of 'mathematical sophistication' to encompass a set of values and avenues for doing mathematics that is required to create fundamental understandings. They observed prospective primary teachers attempting to learn from an on-line resource and noted that many of them experienced difficulties that were due to characteristics such as not attempting to make sense of the relevant definitions provided, not focussing on giving meaning to the problem and attending precisely to language, and not using the explanations supplied. Although this was only a small study and it studied primary rather than secondary teachers, this study is relevant to this discussion because it points to the way in which independent learning of mathematics depends on an enculturation into mathematical practices and values. A detailed example of how understanding of the key role of mathematical definitions affects the mathematical work of teaching is given by Chick (2007). She reported episodes of teaching where teachers' knowledge of mathematics strongly influenced the outcome. In a classroom investigation, students who were finding rectangles with a certain property discarded a square as a solution, but the teacher skillfully drew their attention to how the square met the requirements (definition) of being a rectangle even though it had other properties as well. The point being made was that a definition provides minimal criteria, not a full

105

description. Mathematical practice has many other instances, large and small, in which teachers who are not enculturated into its language and practices may find an obstacle in extending their own knowledge. For example, even simple words such as 'some' and 'either' have mathematical meanings that contrast to their everyday meanings. It is true in mathematics that *some* women are called Kylie Minogue (even if there is only one person with this name, mathematicians can still say *some*) and it is true that a red square fulfils the criterion of being "*either* red *or* square" (being both is not excluded by a mathematical *either-or*).

The need for teachers to be able to learn mathematics independently is most critical for those teachers teaching 'out-of-field'. Unfortunately, these are the teachers who are likely to have the more difficulty with learning mathematics and also had less practice. With colleagues, I recently conducted professional development sessions for such teachers of junior secondary mathematics. In one instance, we wanted to focus on pedagogical content knowledge, to demonstrate the different degrees of difficulty of the three basic types of percentage problems. Given similar numbers, type 1 problems (given whole, given part and missing percentage) and type 2 problems (given whole, given percentage and missing part) are easier for students than type 3 problems (given percentage, given part and missing whole). In the professional development session, the demonstration was much more effective than we had intended. In every group, the type 3 problems could not be solved by a small but significant proportion of teachers currently teaching those grade levels that percentage is taught. It is likely that these teachers will avoid setting problems of this type for students, believing they are too difficult, and hence in effect setting expectations of students that are too low. Wilson and Berne (1999) comment on the dilemmas posed when voluntary professional development exposes teachers' lack of knowledge, and they also comment on the difficulties of research into teacher knowledge when it too can spotlight gaps in individual teachers' knowledge base. Even in professional development programmes with a strong focus on content knowledge, Wilson and Berne reported that opportunities to discuss mathematical content were repeatedly missed because instructors and fellow participants did not want to embarrass individuals. These sensitivities make it difficult for teachers to improve their content knowledge. Lachance and Confrey (2003) report similar observations, but note that teaching content in the context of new technology, new to all participants, eased the situation and fostered stronger helping relationships among teachers.

Another instance from the same professional development series highlights how teachers' 'big picture' of mathematics affects their flexibility in adapting teaching ideas. We introduced these 'out-of-field' teachers to the dual number line to solve percentage and ratio and proportion problems. The dual number line is marked on one side with the absolute amount and on the other with the percentage. It is used widely in Singapore but not in Australia where the professional development was held. By marking the data on a dual number line, a student can organise the information and hence see how to solve proportional reasoning problems, including problems related to speed, density, prices given cost per gram, and so on. From the view point of more advanced mathematics, all of these problems are problems of direct linear proportion, using the same mathematical techniques. After I commented quickly that the dual number line was also useful for these problems, I was surprised when teachers asked me how this could work. These teachers, learning mathematics independently and building only on their own school experience, have learned it topic by topic, without seeing the big picture of direct proportion and the multiplicative structure that links them all. After my short explanation of the similarity between the problems, it is likely that they over-generalised. They may have not seen that the dual number line needs serious modification to be used with other than direct proportion (e.g., conversion between Celsius and Fahrenheit).

GOOD POLICY IN AN ERA OF TEACHER SHORTAGE

The above sections focussed on the mathematics education that is desirable for mathematics teachers. In this section, I confront this discussion with reality. Le Métais (2002) notes that the trend of mathematics to decline in popularity in secondary schools across a number of western countries, has reduced the pool of specialist mathematics teachers. As a result, there are many non-specialists teaching mathematics, who may not have the expertise or confidence necessary to prepare and motivate students to pursue higher-level studies in mathematics. Stephens (2003) reiterates these concerns, and concludes that traditional pathways will not be able to provide sufficient mathematics teachers in the future, especially since the recent growth in occupations requiring a strong grounding in mathematics sciences exceeds supply.

The qualifications of mathematics teachers in Australia is reported in detail by Harris and Jensz (2006) in a study conducted on behalf of the Deans of Science of Australian universities, as a result of their concern about teacher supply and quality. Harris and Jensz report that 75% of teachers of senior (grade levels 11-12) mathematics had studied some mathematics to third year at university. This may not necessarily be sufficient for a major, as they may have taken mathematics as a small component alongside other major studies. Harris and Jensz express deep concern that about 8% of all secondary mathematics teachers (grade levels 7-12) studied no mathematics at university and 20% of all mathematics teachers studied no mathematics beyond first year (p. iv). The report also notes that many teachers, including a third of those teaching only junior secondary mathematics (grade levels 7-8) had studied no mathematics-specific education. Stephens (2003) cites data that over a quarter of high school students in the USA are taught by 'out-of-field' teachers.

It is also the case that the decline in the number of students studying mathematics, the increasing availability of well-paid careers for those qualified in the mathematical sciences, and a decline in the popularity of teaching as a career, leads to prospective teachers with a wide range of undergraduate qualifications (not a traditional mathematics major) entering consecutive courses of teacher education. For example, the University of Melbourne submission to the Australian Review of Teachers and Teacher Education (University of Melbourne, 2002) reported on the

107

discipline qualifications of entrants to the post-graduate diploma in education from 1998 to 2002. The submission noted that "demographics of current teacher education students do not conform to traditional expectations. They are older, better qualified and have substantial prior work experience" (p. 14). The report noted an increasing diversity of academic backgrounds, reflecting increasingly specialised undergraduate science training. Prospective mathematics and physics specialist teachers had an average age of 31 and about three quarters had previously worked in another profession, most commonly engineering. Only about a quarter of students had done their mathematics study within a Bachelor of Science degree, which indicates that they have mostly been trained in the applications of mathematics (e.g., engineering, applied science, information technology, commerce) rather than studying mathematics for its own sake. The decline in teachers with 'normal' qualifications is also indicated in a survey carried out in the Australian state of Victoria by the Mathematical Association of Victoria. The results of this survey indicated that a mathematics major in the undergraduate degree was held by 83% of teachers who had been teaching for more than 20 years but by only 61% of teachers who had been teaching less than 10 years (University of Melbourne, 2002). They have all met the requirements for amount of mathematics in the undergraduate degree as specified by state legislation (a sub-major), but the nature of this training is very different to what it might have been 20 years ago.

These trends in teacher supply raise important issues for answering the question of what mathematics teachers 'should' know. On the one hand, it is likely that most countries will have significant numbers of teachers who have studied little or no mathematics at university, and educational systems should plan to meet their needs for professional development in mathematics, as well as in other educational issues. These people will be an important part of the teacher workforce. On the other hand, a growing proportion of 'fully qualified' mathematics teachers will have studied mathematics in the service of another profession or discipline, rather than for its own sake. In answering the question of what mathematics teachers 'should' know, their needs must also be considered. Their expertise in another discipline is an advantage. The presence of many teachers who have used mathematical sciences in the workplace, in many different occupations, provides a considerable resource for enriching school students' experience of the applications of mathematics and for understanding the careers in which mathematical expertise is useful. Teacher education must empower these teachers to use these prior experiences in the classroom. On the other hand, having their expertise outside of mathematics means that there may be large gaps in their mathematical knowledge as exemplified in the article on prospective teachers' knowledge of proof by Stylianides et al. (2007) mentioned previously. It is extremely unlikely that prospective teachers who come to mathematics teaching from engineering or commerce will have experience of proof.

Reports such as that of the Deans of Science (Harris & Jensz, 2006) arise from concern about an inadequate supply of teachers well qualified in mathematics. They advocate that there should be stronger minimum standards of discipline study and of pedagogy for those teaching mathematics. This is one of the common policy responses to the widely recognised need to improve the quality of the teacher workforce. Boyd, Goldhaber, Lankford, and Wyckoff (2007) have compared the effects of this policy response (to tighten teacher certification requirements) with the opposite response of easing requirements and introducing alternative ways of being certified as a teacher, as implemented in the states of the USA. They conclude that tightening requirements is effective only if the tighter requirements focus on characteristics that lead to better outcomes for students and if they do not deter potential applicants who may become excellent teachers. In other circumstances, the opposite approach of easing requirements becomes the more attractive policy. Whilst calling for further research related to such policies, they note that teachers' content knowledge in mathematics is known to improve students' mathematics learning (hence can be seen as a characteristic that leads to better outcomes for students), but they also claim that there is some evidence that teacher certification requirements shrink the pool of people pursuing teaching careers. As a consequence, whilst it is appealing for teacher educators to identify substantial lists of the knowledge that teachers ought to have, it may be that better outcomes for students overall may arise from looser initial requirements and good opportunities for growth within the profession. Stephens (2003) makes the point that even with full teacher education, the powerful blend of content knowledge and pedagogical content knowledge that is envisioned by the Conference Board CBMS recommendations is unlikely to be able to be attained in initial teacher education, due to time constraints, lack of clarity of responsibility between discipline and education components, and lack of experience of the prospective teachers themselves with school student's mathematical thinking. As a consequence, the responsibility for deep understanding of content knowledge in a pedagogical context has to be taken up by education for practising teachers. These issues need careful consideration at the local level for the formation of good policy.

CONCLUSION

In the first part of this chapter, I outlined what a good education in mathematics for prospective teachers would be like. Working from an ideal of mathematics as a subject that is taught for both its interest and its applications, and from a basis of reasons rather than rules, a vision of what teachers should know and how they might know it emerges. The knowledge of teachers was classified into four: knowledge of the content of mathematics; experience of doing mathematics; knowledge about mathematics as a discipline; and knowing how to learn mathematics. In planning the content of mathematics courses for teachers in the past, it seems it was assumed that teachers had an adequate knowledge of school mathematics by having been successful students. However, led by research on the minute-by-minute mathematical requirements of teaching and by research which shows only weak links between university studies of mathematics and effectiveness as a teacher, there has been a movement (encapsulated in the CBMS report) to make school mathematics a central concern of university studies for teachers. The need to give prospective teachers an understanding of newly important mathematics (notably but certainly not restricted to statistics and computer science) has also put pressure on the traditional mathematics major, leading to a reassessment of the priorities for study. An important research question for the future will be to investigate whether courses along the lines envisaged by CBMS (2001) or initiatives as exemplified by Pierce et al. (2003) really do provide a major in mathematics that well-equips graduates for their chosen careers. In particular, it is important to investigate whether these initiatives do succeed in providing teachers with knowledge that really does enhance their teaching. Boyd et al. (2007) note that some knowledge of mathematics does improve student outcomes. Can we show that a theoretically excellent education for mathematics teaching actually makes a further measurable difference to student outcomes, and hence is worth requiring?

The later section examined the reality of teacher qualifications for mathematics and considers projections that in the future, shortages of well qualified mathematics teachers are likely to persist. Whereas the first section addressed an ideal with a teacher undertaking a mathematical major, the reality is that many teachers who are fully qualified to teach mathematics in the eyes of regulating bodies will in fact have been trained as users of mathematics in the service of other professions. More seriously, many will not be educated as mathematics teachers at all, but will do their best, as they understand it, from their own experience of being a high school student or undertaking a small component of university mathematics. This situation raises a substantial series of research questions related to how gaps in teacher knowledge can be overcome. There are some concerning reports in the literature (e.g., Wilson & Berne, 1999) that professional development that is intended to focus on content knowledge often avoids facing up to the challenge. In the literature there are many examples of teachers or prospective teachers not knowing the mathematics that will teach. How serious a problem is this in the long-term? What sort of knowledge is likely to be gathered during a teaching career, by teaching topics and engaging with students' thinking and what support does this require? To what extent do teachers (with differing backgrounds) learn mathematics by teaching it, and what support materials would encourage this? The CBMS report identifies that there is a special knowledge required for teaching, principally an overview of school mathematics as in the capstone course and the type of content that I have outlined above in the 'knowing about mathematics' section. How can this best be gained by teachers without the expected content background? I have also noted that many mathematics teachers now have substantial experience of using mathematics in a previous career. How can the educational system harness this?

In recent years, research has demonstrated how mathematical knowledge affects the minute-by-minute decisions that a teacher makes. Most of this research has been conducted with primary teachers, and most of the initiatives to address the identified deficiencies have also been aimed at primary teachers. Possibly this is because usually more of their education is within schools of education, and hence in the hands of those who conduct education research. Secondary teaching has been neglected on both these accounts. There is less research and the avenues for change are administratively more complex within institutions for secondary majors. Secondary mathematics is extremely important for individual life chances and for national prosperity yet it is often taught as rules without reasons, turning students away. Attending to the mathematics knowledge of the secondary teacher workforce, consisting, as it does, of people with mixed mathematical backgrounds, should be a high priority for researchers, teacher educators, mathematicians and educational systems.

REFERENCES

Aldrich, R. (1990). The evolution of teacher education. In N. J. Graves (Ed.), *Initial teacher education: Policies and progress* (pp. 12–24). London: Kagan Page.

Ball, D. L. (1990). The mathematical understandings that prospective teachers bring to teacher education. *The Elementary School Journal, 90*, 449–466.

Boyd, D., Goldhaber, D., Lankford, H., & Wyckoff, J. (2007). The effect of certification and preparation on teacher quality. *The Future of Children, 17*(1), 46–68.

Bulmer, M. (2002). The most used formula in the world. *Australian Senior Mathematics Journal, 16*(1), 14–19. [www.aamt.edu.au/content/download/744/19594/file/asmj-s.pdf]

Burkhardt, H., & Bell, A. (2007). Problem solving in the United Kingdom, *ZDM Mathematics Education, 39*(5–6), 395–403.

Chick, H. (2007). Teaching and learning by example. In J. Watson & K. Beswick (Eds.), *Proceedings of the 30th annual conference of the Mathematics Education Research Group of Australasia* (pp. 3–21). Hobart: MERGA.

Chinnappan, M., & Lawson, M. (2005). A framework for analysis of teachers' geometric content knowledge and geometric knowledge for teaching. *Journal of Mathematics Teacher Education, 8*, 197–221.

Conference Board of the Mathematical Sciences. (2001). *The mathematical education of teachers.* Washington, DC: American Mathematical Society and Mathematical Association of America.

Cooney, T., & Wiegel, H. (2003). Examining the mathematics in mathematics teacher education. In A. Bishop, M. Clements, C. Keitel, & F-K. Leung (Eds.), *Second international handbook of mathematics education* (pp. 795–828). Dordrecht, the Netherlands: Kluwer Academic Publishers.

Davis, P., & Hersh, R. (1982). *The mathematical experience.* Boston, MA: Houghton Mifflin Company.

Goulding, M., Hatch, G., & Rodd, M. (2003). Undergraduate mathematics experience: Its significance in secondary mathematics teacher preparation. *Journal of Mathematics Teacher Education, 6*, 361–393.

Graham, K., Li, Y., & Curran Buck, J. (2000). Characteristics of mathematics teacher preparation programs in the United States: An exploratory study. *The Mathematics Educator, 5*(1/2), 5–31.

Harris, K-L., & Jensz, F. (2006). *The preparation of mathematics teachers in Australia: Meeting the demand for suitably qualified mathematics teachers in secondary schools.* Report prepared for Australian Council of Deans of Science. Melbourne: Centre for the Study of Higher Education, The University of Melbourne.

Henry, M. (2000). Evolution and prospects of preservice secondary mathematics teacher education in France. *Journal of Mathematics Teacher Education, 3*. 271–279.

Hiebert, J. et al. (2003). *Teaching mathematics in seven countries: Results from the TIMSS 1999 video study.* Washington, DC: National Center for Education Statistics.

HREF1 Qualifications and Curriculum Authority. *International review of curriculum and assessment frameworks Internet archive.* (INCA) http://www.inca.org.uk Accessed Jan 6, 2008.

HREF2 German Education server http://dbs.bbf.dipf.de/zeigen_e.html?seite=480 Accessed Jan 6, 2008.

HREF3 Training and Development Agency for Schools. *Qualifying to teach. Professional standards for qualified teacher status and requirements for initial teacher training.* http://www.tda.gov.uk Accessed Jan 6, 2008.

HREF4 *International Study Group on the relations between the history and pedagogy of mathematics* http://www.clab.edc.uoc.gr/HPM/INDEX.HTM Accessed Jan 6, 2008.

HREF5 *Matrices and determinants.* School of Mathematics and Statistics, University of St Andrews, Scotland. http://www-groups.dcs.st-and.ac.uk/~history/HistTopics/Matrices_and_determinants.html. Accessed Jan 6, 2008.

Kendal, M., & Stacey, K. (2001). The impact of teacher privileging on learning differentiation with technology. *International Journal of Computers for Mathematics Learning, 6*, 143–165.

Kilpatrick, J., Swafford, J., & Findell, B. (2001). *Adding it up: Helping children learn mathematics.* Washington, DC: National Academy Press.

Lachance, A., & Confrey, J. (2003). Interconnecting content and community: A qualitative study of secondary mathematics teachers. *Journal of Mathematics Teacher Education, 6*, 107–137.

Le Métais, J. (2002). *International Developments in Upper Secondary Education: Context, provision and issues. INCA Thematic Study No. 8.* http://www.inca.org.uk/pdf/cav_final_report.pdf

Mason, J., Burton, L., & Stacey, K. (1982). *Thinking mathematically.* London: Pearson.

McNamara, O., Jaworski, B., Rowland, T., Hodgen, J., & Prestage, S. (2002). *Developing mathematics teachers and teaching.* http://www.maths-ed.org.uk/mathsteachdev/

Mills, T. M. (2007). A course on the history of mathematics. *The Australian Mathematics Society Gazette, 34*(4), 195–201.

Nicol, C. (2002). Where's the math? Prospective teachers visit the workplace. *Educational Studies in Mathematics, 50*, 289–309.

Organisation for Economic Co-operation and Development. (2003). *The PISA 2003 assessment framework: Mathematics, reading, science and problem solving knowledge and skills.* Paris: Author.

Pierce, R., Turville, C., & Giri, J. (2003). Undergraduate mathematics curricula – A new angle. *New Zealand Journal of Mathematics, 32* (Supp. Issue), 155–162.

Polya, G. (1962). *Mathematical discovery. On understanding, learning and teaching problem solving.* New York: John Wiley.

Robert, A., & Hache, C. (2000). Connecting research to French mathematics teacher education. *Journal of Mathematics Teacher Education, 3*, 281–290.

Ryve, A. (2007). What is actually discussed in problem-solving courses for prospective teachers? *Journal of Mathematics Teacher Education, 10*, 43–61.

Schoenfeld, A. (1985). *Mathematical problem solving.* Orlando, FL: Academic Press.

Seaman, C., & Szydlik, J. (2007). Mathematical sophistication among pre-service elementary teachers. *Journal of Mathematics Teacher Education, 10*, 167–182.

Shulman, L. S. (1986). Those who understand: Knowledge growth in teaching. *Educational Researcher, 15*(2), 4–14.

Stacey, K. (2005). The place of problem solving in contemporary mathematics curriculum documents. *Journal of Mathematical Behavior, 24*, 341–350.

Stacey, K., Stillman, G., & Pierce, R. (not dated). *RITEMATHS: Real World Problems and Information Technology Enhancing Mathematics.* http://extranet.edfac.unimelb.edu.au/DSME/RITEMATHS

Stephens, M. (2003). Regulating the entry of teachers of mathematics into the profession: Challenges, new models and glimpses into the future. In A. Bishop, M. Clements, C. Keitel, & F-K. Leung (Eds.), *Second international handbook of mathematics education* (pp. 767–793). Dordrecht, the Netherlands: Kluwer Academic Publishers.

Stylianides, G., Stylianides, A., & Philippou, G. (2007). Preservice teachers' knowledge of proof by mathematical induction. *Journal of Mathematics Teacher Education, 10*, 145–166.

University of Melbourne. (2002) *Review of teaching and teacher education. Australian government. Submission RTTE85.* http://www.dest.gov.au/schools/teachingreview/submissions/RTTE85.pdf

Van Dooren, W., Verschaffel, L., & Onghena, P. (2003). Pre-service teachers' preferred strategies for solving arithmetic and algebra word problems. *Journal of Mathematics Teacher Education, 6,* 27–52.

Wilson, P., Cooney, T., & Stinson, D. (2005). What constitutes good mathematics teaching and how it develops: Nine high school teachers' perspectives. *Journal of Mathematics Teacher Education, 8,* 83–111.

Wilson, S., & Berne, J. (1999). Teacher learning and the acquisition of professional knowledge: An examination of research on contemporary professional development. *Review of Research in Education, 24,* 173–209.

Kaye Stacey
Melbourne Graduate School of Education,
University of Melbourne
Australia

SECTION 2

MATHEMATICS FOR AND IN TEACHING

ANNA GRAEBER AND DINA TIROSH

5. PEDAGOGICAL CONTENT KNOWLEDGE

Useful Concept or Elusive Notion

Shulman's 1985 presidential address at AERA is frequently credited with launching increased attention to knowledge unique to teaching. In that address, Shulman coined the term Pedagogical Content Knowledge (PCK) and described it as "the particular form of content knowledge that embodies the aspect of content most germane to its teachability" (1986a, p. 9). Since then, the notion of PCK has been widely used in framing and describing research and practice in teacher education in many fields of education, including mathematics teacher education. In this chapter we first describe Shulman and others' attempts to define those aspects of teachers' knowledge that are unique to teachers and are related to their students' learning. We then consider the role of pedagogical content knowledge in mathematics teacher education. We end the chapter with reflections and future directions.

We begin by posing a task for readers and ask that they take some time to construct such a task before continuing.

> Write a multiple-choice item concerning decimal numbers that teachers will be able to answer but which will be a challenge to those in most other professions including mathematicians.

Hill, Schilling, and Ball (2004. p. 28) offer one example of such an item, as shown in Figure 1.

Mr. Fitzgerald has been helping his students learn how to compare decimals. He is trying to devise an assignment that shows him whether his students know how to correctly put a list of decimals in order of size. Which of the following sets of numbers will best suit this purpose?

a) .5   7   .01   11.4
b) .60   2.53   3.14   .45
c) .60   4.25   .565   2.5
d) Any of these would work well for this purpose. They all require the students to read and interpret decimals.

Figure 1. A task designed to tap an aspect of teacher knowledge.

P. Sullivan and T. Wood (eds.), Knowledge and Beliefs in Mathematics Teaching and Teaching Development, 117–132.

Teachers' knowledgeable about teaching decimals are most apt to know that students can order the decimals in two of the options, *a* and *b*, by ignoring the decimal points and ordering the resultant whole numbers (e.g., for option *a* they consider 5, 7, 1, 114 which they order correctly as 1, 5, 7,114 – a correct order for .01, .5, 7, 11.4). However such an approach to option *c* yields 2.5, .60, 4.25, .565, an incorrect ordering. Hill, Schilling, and Ball (2004) report that most non-teachers including mathematicians select option *d,* seeing no differences in the options offered. However teachers' familiarity with students' tendency to over generalise knowledge of whole numbers to decimal numbers example enables them to make the required distinction. This reliance on whole number ideas has been well documented (e.g., Grossman, A. S., 1983; Hiebert & Wearne, 1986; Sackur-Grisvard & Leonard, 1985) and has made its way into teacher education and teacher professional development materials (e.g., Barnett, Goldstein, & Jackson, 1994; Sconiers, Isaacs, Konold & McFadden, 1999; Van de Walle, 2007). The knowledge required to answer the item above is therefore somewhat unique to teachers. It requires more than knowledge of mathematics, namely knowledge of how students approach such tasks. This is one aspect of a construct that is frequently labelled pedagogical content knowledge, a term most closely identified with Shulman.

The driving question that led Shulman to formulate the term "pedagogical content knowledge" was – Are there specific types of knowledge needed for teaching? In this chapter we first describe Shulman and others' attempts to define those aspects of teachers' knowledge that are unique to teachers and are related to their students' learning. We also consider the role of pedagogical content knowledge in teacher education, and we end the chapter with reflections and future directions.

WHAT IS PEDAGOGICAL CONTENT KNOWLEDGE?

We begin by describing *pedagogical content knowledge* (PCK) as used by Shulman. We then outline how he and his colleagues' initial ideas were subsequently modified, critiqued, and expanded. Next we present some of the work of Ball and her colleagues that both expands on Shulman's notion of PCK and provides empirical support that such *knowledge for teaching* is indeed important for student learning. Finally we discuss the status of PCK in 2007.

Early Formulations of PCK

Shulman's 1985 presidential address at AERA is frequently credited with launching increased attention to knowledge unique to teaching. In that address (published in 1986), he proposed three categories of content knowledge: subject matter knowledge, pedagogical content knowledge and curricular knowledge. Shulman described PCK as "the particular form of content knowledge that embodies the aspect of content most germane to its teachability" (p. 9). In the 1985 address, Shulman considered PCK to include

> for the most regularly taught topics in one's subject area, the most useful forms of representation of those ideas, the most powerful analogies, illustrations, examples, explanations, and demonstrations ... an understanding of what makes the learning of specific topics easy or difficult; the conceptions and preconceptions that students ... bring with them ... knowledge of strategies most likely to be fruitful in reorganising the understanding of learners. (1986a, pp. 9–10)

Shulman also characterised PCK as "that special amalgam of content and pedagogy that is *uniquely* (emphasis added) the province of teachers, their own special form of professional understanding" (p. 8).

In Shulman and his colleagues later writings (e.g., Grossman, P., 1990; Marks, 1990; Wilson & Wineburg, 1988) the characterisation of PCK was expanded and elaborated, especially through the work of case studies of teachers working in different subject areas. P. Grossman (1990), who studied secondary English teachers, suggested four major components of PCK: knowledge of students' understanding, knowledge of curriculum, knowledge of instructional strategies, and purposes for teaching. Thus, P. Grossman expanded PCK to include aspects of Shulman's category of curricular knowledge. She also raised issues about the relationship of beliefs and values to PCK.

Adapting PCK to mathematics education, Marks (1990) interviewed fifth-grade teachers concerning their teaching of equivalence of fractions. He then suggested four components of PCK: students' understanding, subject matter for instructional purposes, media for instruction, and instructional processes. Marks elaborated on each of these, and upon close examination one finds that he has included aspects of Shulman's original category of curriculum knowledge in three of these components. For Marks, "subject matter for instructional purposes" included: "purposes of math instruction, justifications for learning a given topic, important ideas to teach a given topic, prerequisite ideas for a given topic, and typical 'school math' problems" (p. 5). Another contribution of Marks was his elaboration of the notion of students' understanding to include student learning processes, typical understandings, common errors, and those things that are hard or easy for students. Here, Marks also included knowledge of particular students' understanding. These modifications are consistent with Shulman's 1987 reflection that "the knowledge base for teaching is not fixed and final" but that much "remains to be discovered, invented, and refined" (p. 12).

Subsequent Extensions and Challenges

Indeed, both extensions and criticisms of Shulman's notion of PCK ensued. Shulman's claim that PCK "goes beyond subject matter per se" (1986a, p. 9) was the target of some criticism. Others interpreted Shulman's early work as reflecting only a direct instruction view of teaching or ignoring the role of teacher beliefs and values. Other researchers commented that the boundaries among PCK, content knowledge and pedagogical knowledge were blurred, or, that aspects of content knowledge or pedagogical knowledge should be included in PCK.

McEwan and Bull (1991) objected to the notion of pedagogical content knowledge, arguing against the division of subject matter knowledge into scholarly and pedagogic forms. These authors claim that "all subject matter knowledge is pedagogic" (p. 318). In fact, McEwan and Bull argued that "the distinction between content knowledge and pedagogical content knowledge introduces an unnecessary and untenable complication into the conceptual framework on which the research is based" (p. 318). Their objection is philosophically based, describing Shulman's work as harbouring an objectivist theory of knowledge. McNamara (1990) also questioned whether the distinction between pedagogical content knowledge could or should be made, but he acknowledged Shulman's contribution of helping to focus the profession on the "essential purpose of teaching which is the passing on of knowledge (however broadly or narrowly defined)" (McNamara, 1990, p. 157).

Other critics such as Meredith (1993, 1995) and Cochran, DeRuiter, and King (1993) argued that Shulman reflected "a teacher-directed didactical model of teaching" (Meredith, 1995, p. 176), a view of teaching that we note is consistent with an objectivist theory of knowledge. However, unlike McEwan and Bull who would dismiss the very notion of PCK, Meredith found the framework useful but called for a broadening of the framework to permit alternative forms of teaching. Cochran et al. (1993) also found Shulman's framework to focus so heavily on the "transformation of subject matter" (p. 266) that they were driven to modify the notion of PCK to that of Pedagogical Content Knowing (PCKg). For these authors the use of the form "knowing" signified an active process that is more consistent with a constructivist view of learning. They defined PCKg as "a teacher's integrated understanding of four components of pedagogy, subject matter content, student characteristics and the environmental context of learning" (p. 266).

Several researchers have proposed elaborations of aspects of PCK, especially attention to knowledge of students. In 1992, Fennema and Franke's chapter in the *Handbook of Mathematics Teaching and Learning* identified not only knowledge of content, but two other types of knowledge that are generally categorised within pedagogical content knowledge: knowledge of students; and knowledge of representations. Fennema and Franke's chapter raised teachers' knowledge of students to an important position. In considering teachers' knowledge of students, these authors presented evidence to show that knowledge of student's processes and thinking impacts teacher decision-making, allows teachers to attend to individual students, and influences educational outcomes. They also discussed teacher knowledge of mathematical representations in a manner that parallels Shulman's ideas about the importance of knowing useful representations, analogies and examples. In a similar way, Even and Tirosh (1995) emphasised the importance of studying the sources of knowledge that teachers use in responding to students' questions, ideas or hypotheses. One major source that teachers relied upon in order to formulate responses was knowledge about students. In an effort to unpack specific components of "knowledge of students", Even and Tirosh identified two, *knowing that* and *knowing why*. Knowing that refers to research-based and experienced-based knowledge about students' common conceptions and ways of thinking about the subject matter. Knowing why refers to general knowledge about possible sources of these conceptions, and also to the understanding of the sources of the specific students' reaction in a specific case.

A relatively recent framework derived from Shulman's work is offered by An, Kulm, and Wu (2004). These authors view PCK as including aspects of content, teaching, and curriculum; identifying teaching as the most important. An and colleagues characterise "profound pedagogical content knowledge" as broad and deep knowledge of teaching and curriculum. This concept parallels Ma's (1999) notion of "*profound understanding* (emphasis added) of fundamental mathematics" Ma characterised differences in understanding among teachers using the notion of "profound understanding of fundamental mathematics" as involving connectedness, multiple perspectives, basic ideas, and longitudinal coherence (p. 122). While generally more closely associated with content knowledge, Ma's descriptions also include knowledge that might be classified as pedagogical content knowledge or curriculum knowledge. For example, she argued that teachers with "deep, vast, and thorough understanding do not invent connections between and among mathematical ideas but reveal and represent them in terms of mathematics teaching and learning" (p. 122). Because such teachers understand which ideas are basic, they "revisit and reinforce these ideas" (p. 122). Thus Ma's concern was not simply with teachers' knowledge of mathematics but also with knowing when and how to use such knowledge in teaching. The aspects of content that An and colleagues include in their PCK, are consistent with the way Ma views knowledge of content in use in teaching.

An and colleagues acknowledged that knowledge of teaching includes preparing instruction and strategies for delivery of instruction. But, given their perspective of teaching for understanding, they identify "knowing students' thinking" as most critical. An and colleagues developed the following set of categories for knowing students' thinking: building on students' ideas, addressing students' misconceptions, engaging students in mathematics learning, and promoting students' thinking about mathematics (p. 155). These categories were defined by listing components of each. For example, the misconceptions category included "address students' misconceptions, use questions or tasks to correct misconceptions, use rule and procedure, draw picture or table, and connect to concrete model" (p. 155).

PCK AND MATHEMATICAL KNOWLEDGE FOR TEACHING

The notion of PCK dominated the literature for almost twenty years. In the last few years another construct built on Shulman's notion of PCK but specific to mathematics education has begun to gain much attention. The recent work of Ball

121

and Bass (2003) introduced the global term *mathematical knowledge for teaching*. This term was derived from their approach to uncovering the knowledge needed for teaching by looking at the work of teachers. Ball and Bass (2003) documented a year of teaching in a third-grade mathematics class in an attempt to tease out "core task domains of teachers work" (p. 6). As examples they cite "representing and making mathematical ideas available to students; attending to, interpreting, and handling students' oral and written productions; giving and evaluating mathematical explanations and justifications; and establishing and managing the discourse and collectivity of the class" (p. 6). The analyses of teacher work led to a framework of teacher knowledge that included two major aspects, subject matter knowledge and pedagogical content knowledge. Subject matter or content knowledge, comprises common content knowledge and specialised content knowledge. Common knowledge of content included what any well informed citizen would know. For example, what decimal is halfway between 1.1 and 1.11. An example of specialised content knowledge is shown below in Figure 2. Hill and colleagues (2007) describe such knowledge as "mathematical knowledge that is used in teaching, but not directly taught to students" (p. 132). Analysis of the student work and knowledge of whole number properties are needed to conclude that all three of the students have employed a method valid for any two whole numbers. The knowledge of mathematics is what is critical, but the item represents the type of mathematical task that is done by few adults other than teachers.

Imagine that you are working with your class on multiplying large numbers. Among your students' papers, you notice that some have displayed their work in the following ways:

Student A	*Student B*	*Student C*
35	35	35
x 25	x 25	x 25
125	175	25
75	700	150
875	875	100
		600
		875

Which of these students is using a method that could be used to multiply any two whole numbers? (Consortium for Policy Research in Education, 2004, p. 19)

Figure 2. An item that was designed to tap specialised content knowledge.

Pedagogical content knowledge comprises knowledge of content and students, knowledge of content and teaching, and knowledge of curriculum. The decimal-ordering item presented near the beginning of this paper is an item that was designed to measure knowledge of content and students. It taps into teachers' knowledge of how "students learn content," the characterisation Hill, Sleep, Lewis and Ball (2007) gave for knowledge of content and students (p. 133). In the case of Figure 1, this is the knowledge that students will likely apply whole number ideas to decimals. The item shown in Figure 3 is an example of an item designed to test knowledge of content and teaching. As the numbers given in the four choices are all correctly categorised as prime or composite, this item depends less on teachers knowing which numbers are prime and which are composite (content knowledge) but more on how to choose examples and representations (an aspect of the work of teaching) given knowledge of students' thinking. Hill and colleagues argued that success with the item in Figure 3 is dependent on teachers knowing that students have difficulty categorising 2 as a prime and are "likely to think that odd numbers cannot be composite" (p. 133). Hence choice d), with 2 listed as a prime and with its odd composite, 9, is the only set that challenges both of these faulty ideas.

> While planning an introductory lesson on primes and composites, Mr. Rubenstein is considering what numbers to use as initial examples. He is concerned because he knows that choosing poor examples can mislead a student about these important ideas. Of the choices below, which set of numbers would be best for introducing primes and composites? (Mark one answer.) (Hill et al., 2007, p. 133)

	Primes	Composites
a)	3, 5, 11	6, 30, 44
b)	2, 5 17	8, 14, 32
c)	3, 7, 11	4, 16, 25
d)	2, 7, 13	9, 24, 40
e)	All of these would work equally well to introduce prime and composite numbers.	

Figure 3. An item that was designed to tap knowledge of content and teaching.

Hill, Schilling, and Ball (2004) administered tests constructed around such categories and found that knowledge of content in a topical areas (e.g., number and operations or patterns, functions and algebra) differed from knowledge of students in that particular area.

This and other analyses (Ball & Rowan, 2004; Hill, Rowan, & Ball, 2005) support Shulman's claim that knowledge for teaching includes a specialised knowledge of content. This seems at least a start in addressing earlier concerns about whether the distinction between content knowledge and pedagogical content knowledge could or should be made.

PCK IN 2007

At the beginning of this section we raised the question: What is PCK? Here, we attempt to provide a response from the existing literature. Then we examine the extent to which the benefits Shulman anticipated from a framework of knowledge for teachers have accrued.

In reviewing the ways in which researchers have extended and modified Shulman's framework, we note that the direction of this evolution was to widen the definition. Researchers included within PCK aspects of Shulman's domains of subject matter content knowledge and curricular knowledge. The more recent frameworks (e.g., An, Kulm & Wu, 2004; Ball & Bass, 2003) identify aspects of content, teaching and curriculum within PCK. Within each of these domains, different researchers have explicated and stressed different concepts. Thus, Ma (1999) gives the field one way to think about content knowledge for teaching and Even and Tirosh (1995) another. Much interest has focused on characterising the "knowledge of students" sometimes included within the broader domain of teaching. The five components Marks (1990) offered (see above) overlap but differ from An et al.'s (2004) four components: students' prior knowledge; common misconceptions and strategies for amending; methods of engaging students; and methods of promoting students' thinking. These differences and the lack, at least to-date, of a widely agreed upon characterisation of PCK, suggest that while progress has been made, much remains to be done. The fact that many researchers do not offer a definition of PCK but rather attempt to characterise it with lists or examples is another indication that the concept is still somewhat ill defined.

In pursuing work on PCK, a number of questions, not all unrelated, have arisen. These include: 1) the role of beliefs and values in the development of a teacher's PCK, 2) whether different teaching/learning paradigms require different components of PCK, and 3) what are improved methods for assessing PCK.

A crucial trait of a valuable framework of teacher knowledge is the extent to which it identifies that knowledge needed for student learning and understanding. In fact, some limited progress has been made in identifying knowledge that is related to student achievement. Hill, Rowan, Ball (2005) found that teachers' mathematical content knowledge for teaching was positively related to first and third graders' achievement on a standardised achievement test. It is also the case that there is some research showing that individual components of PCK are positively related to student achievement. While such studies were not directed at establishing a foundation of an entire PCK framework, they may nevertheless testify to the importance of some individual components of PCK (e.g., knowledge about how students generally learn a topic as well as knowledge of specific students' thinking [Fennema, Carpenter, & Franke, Levi, Jacobs, & Empson, 1996]; and knowledge of and attention to misconceptions [Tsamir, 2005]).

Shulman began his quest for a framework for teacher knowledge at a time that he and others lamented the lack of attention given to the role of subject matter in research used to study teaching. He wished to bring to the fore questions such as

"Where do teacher explanations come from?, How do teachers decide what to teach and how to represent it?, etc." Such questions certainly have been addressed in research since 1985. Research by Lampert (2001) and by Sowder, Philipp, Armstrong, and Schappelle (1998) are but two examples of different genres of research on teaching that attend to the role of subject matter. Further, Shulman's categories have been used to frame research on teachers' knowledge of various topics. For example, Watson (2001) collected information about teachers' knowledge of statistics using Shulman's knowledge types to structure her questionnaire. Kieran (2007) noted that Shulman's PCK construct is the most widely used framework in studies of algebra teachers' knowledge (p. 739). Jones, Langrall and Mooney (2007) structure their review of teacher knowledge related to probability around Shulman's notions of content knowledge and pedagogical content knowledge by giving special attention to the knowledge of student understanding aspect of PCK (p. 932). Clearly Shulman's work has influenced research on teaching and teachers that does focus on subject matter, and it has also given researchers a way to organise the findings of such research.

A hope that Shulman had for a framework of teacher knowledge was the development of instruments that would test aspects of knowledge unique to teachers. He hoped for tests that could only be successfully completed by those specifically prepared to teach. If one believes that such knowledge is important to student learning and understanding, they could reasonably be used in a number of ways. For example, they could provide valuable information for policy makers, assist in the evaluation and modification of teacher education programmes, could conceivably be used in decisions about hiring, and provide information about individual teacher's strengths and needs. Given the paucity of empirical data on the various frameworks, it is clear that much research is needed in this area. The difficulty of obtaining such data, which involves testing of teachers and educated non-teachers, as well as teachers and their students, makes the task both practically and conceptually challenging. As noted above, Ball and colleagues have provided some data that positively relates aspects of teachers' PCK to student learning. Other projects attending to PCK, such as *Knowing for Algebra Teaching* (Ferrini-Mundy, Floden, McCory, Burrill, & Sandow, 2005*), Diagnostic Teacher Assessments in Mathematics and Science* (Bush, Ronau, Brown, & Myers), have constructed measures for the ultimate purpose of relating teacher knowledge to student achievement.

Shulman's overarching goal for a framework of teacher knowledge was that it be used to inform and legitimise the content of teacher education programmes (1986a, pp. 13–14) thereby establishing teaching as a profession with a well defined knowledge base, along with medicine and law. That is that the framework would both aid in the design of teacher education programmes and drive studies in order to establish a firm research base for teacher education. In the next section we consider the use of PCK components in mathematics teacher education.

PCK AND MATHEMATICS TEACHER EDUCATION

Designing a teacher education programme around elements of PCK would be an enormous task. First there are numerous aspects of PCK to consider. Then there are questions about when and how such knowledge is included and conveyed. In this section we first consider challenges involved in attempting to use components of the PCK framework as a basis of designing a mathematics teacher education programme. In this example we draw on knowledge of students' thinking. We then describe how one researcher addressed each of those challenges. In that case the attempt was to draw on the PCK component, knowledge of representations/explanations.

Design Challenge

Shulman proposed that teacher education should "draw upon the growing research on the pedagogical structure of students' conceptions and misconceptions, on those features that make particular topics easy or difficult to learn" (1986, p. 14). While this may sound like a rather straight-forward task, a closer examination reveals the many challenges that are involved in such an endeavour.

For example, suppose one were to decide to include knowledge of student conceptions in a mathematics teacher education programme. In the last decades many researchers have investigated students' mathematical ideas and conceptions in many topic areas, and there are numerous theories about the origin and impact of students' naïve conceptions on learning. Thus, among the first question one would face is, *what* (mis)conceptions[1] should one include? For example, a quick answer might be – choose the most salient conceptions. However, students' conceptions may differ according to the curricula they study, the classroom practices they experience, and other factors. The extent to which students' mathematical ways of thinking and difficulties are embedded in a particular approach to learning and teaching still needs to be studied. For instance, consider a curriculum in which percent is taught prior to decimal numbers. What types of (mis)conceptions might arise? Will they differ from those prompted by the more usual curriculum that places decimals before percents? Would this have any impact on the ordering-of-decimal difficulty highlighted in the task presented at the outset of this chapter? In addition to examples of (mis)conceptions in a specific domain, what, if any theories, concerning the origin or impact of (mis)conceptions should be included?

Suppose one has made the decision about what to teach, another question is – *how* is this knowledge addressed with teachers? Some options are: reading about conceptions, watching videos that capture students expressing (mis)conceptions, observing a class lesson, tutoring student. Which of these options, in what combination, and in what order should they be employed? Practical issues such as time and curriculum space will limit these options.

A third question that needs to be addressed is – *when* should this be addressed? Is a topic primarily for prospective or practising teachers' education? Which is optimal? Fennema et al. have suggested that there is some knowledge that can "only be acquired in the context of teaching mathematics" (1996, p. 432). There are conflicting perspectives as to when in the teacher's development is it best to incorporate attention to specific aspects of PCK?

Design Example

Kinach (2002), in describing a process she employed to transform prospective teachers instructional explanations from merely instrumental to relational (following Skemp, 1978), provided her answers to the *what, when,* and *how* questions posed above. Kinach selected as her aim, the *what,* the transformation of explanations from instrumental to relational. She observed that many prospective teachers know a great deal of mathematics but only instrumentally, and if we wish them to teach with relational understanding, their education must include opportunities for making such a transformation. For this particular article (2002), Kinach chose to illustrate the process using the topic, subtraction of integers. She selected this topic because she found that it is accessible but one in which prospective teachers' knowledge is generally limited to instrumental understanding. Kinach noted that she has used the same process (described below) with other computational as well as non-computational topics. We draw on Kinach's work not to hold up her resulting intervention as exemplary, although it may be so, but rather to illustrate one way in which a researcher used information about pedagogical content knowledge to design experiences in a teacher education programme.

For Kinach 'a methods course' answered the question of *when* to include this work. Her rationale was that in the teacher education curriculum the methods course is where "content and pedagogy are most likely to interact" (p. 65). Kinach noted that some teacher educators have argued that the methods course is not an appropriate site for changes in prospective teachers' views, because they are unable to reflect on such intangible educational goals (p. 68). However, Kinach argued that if a sufficiently powerful method is skilfully used; prospective teachers could make such a transformation.

The process, the *how*; which Kinach developed, employed, and evaluated a number of times; involved the following five-steps:

(1) Evoke an explanation of integer subtraction from each of the prospective teachers.
(2) Using the Perkins and Simmons' (1988) framework of four levels of understanding (concept level, problem solving level, epistemic level, inquiry level), have the class determine the level of understanding reflected in the initial explanations.
(3) Through discussion generate tension between the level of understanding reflected in the original explanation and that needed for effective teaching.
(4) Ask the prospective teachers to construct a second explanation for integer subtraction in another context known to present difficulties (e.g., number-line). Evaluate these explanations, using Perkins and Simmons' framework, in

class discussion and reshape explanations to match the problem solving and epistemic levels of the framework.

(5) Ask the prospective teachers to explain integer subtraction for a second context (e.g., algebra tiles). This second context is selected so that it will scaffold students' problems encountered in the number-line context.

Based on an evaluation of the levels of explanation reflected in steps 1, 4, and 5 above along with qualitative date gathered from video recordings of class discussions, student journal entries, and various homework assignments, Kinach concluded that this process was effective for helping the prospective teachers make the desired transformation to explanations that reflected relational understanding. This an example of an educator who drew on the PCK framework in designing experiences in teacher education. There is a need for empirical data for more ventures of this type.

REFLECTIONS AND FUTURE DIRECTIONS

We have traced, in this chapter, the evolution of PCK over the last twenty years. We began our discussion of PCK without noting that this notion has roots in earlier research and theory. Shulman (1987) cited Dewey, Scheffler, Green, Schwab, Fenstermacher, and others (p. 4) as researchers on whose work he drew. He also acknowledged that prominent others were working on similar questions (e.g., Leinhardt, Anderson & Smith) (Shulman, 1986a, pp. 8–9). This work continues by researchers within mathematics education (e.g., Wilson, Floden, & Ferrini-Mundy, 2001; An, Kulm, & Wu, 2004) and in other subject matter areas (e.g., Grossman, P., 2005).

The term, "pedagogical content knowledge" appears frequently in both scholarly papers and publications intended for less specialised audiences, a phenomenon that could be interpreted as an indication of the term's usefulness. It has helped frame the way researchers look at teachers' work and it has stimulated and guided considerable research on teacher knowledge. It has influenced mathematics teacher education and is beginning to influence teacher assessment (e.g., the recent work undertaken by Ball and colleagues in the United States and in the COACTIV project, the Cognitive Activation in the Classroom, undertaken in Germany by Baumert, Krauss, & Kunter, 2003)[2]. This term is now part of the mathematics educator's lexicon and has even found its way into the title of mathematics methods textbooks, (e.g., *Elementary mathematics: Pedagogical content knowledge;* Schwartz, 2008). However, we have shown that even within mathematics education those who have built upon Shulman's work in PCK have tended to use slightly different, broader definitions than did Shulman, and not all of these later definitions are equivalent to one another. This is one reason why the notion of PCK is still considered a bit elusive. Evidence that such knowledge is unique to teachers and more evidence that it is positively related to student achievement in mathematics will aid in the field's acceptance of PCK as a less elusive and a more useful construct.

We feel quite confident in conjecturing that in the coming years the mathematics education community will devote growing efforts to defining the specific types of knowledge needed for teaching mathematics and to provide evidence that these types of knowledge positively affect students' achievement. Our conjecture is based, among other factors, on the intense political pressure in many countries including Britain, Germany Israel, and the US, to raise "student achievement" in mathematics. The widespread acknowledgment of the critical role teachers have on student achievement leads to an increased interest in teacher knowledge and teacher "quality" that drives the search for ways of assessing teachers. Which teacher candidate should be hired? Which teachers are in "need" of professional development and on what should that professional development concentrate? Thus we believe that the current interest in defining the pedagogical, as well as subject matter, knowledge for teaching mathematics will remain. This effort appeals to researchers in mathematics education. For some it is a means of establishing the existence of important knowledge for teaching that is not simply more mathematics. As such it is also a part of the larger quest to establish a unique base of professional knowledge.

We would like to end this chapter by stating that we view the attempts to define the construct PCK within mathematics education as part of that larger quest to establish a unique base of professional knowledge, a hallmark of a true profession, for teachers of mathematics. Progress has been made, but much remains to be done. Further research and theory development are needed around profound questions concerning PCK, questions that are closely related to those originally posed by Shulman (1986b):

Are different components of PCK associated with different definitions of "quality teaching" in mathematics?

How specific must the teaching for PCK be? Are general instances illustrated with examples sufficient, or must specific element of PCK be identified and taught for each topic in mathematics education?

What is the standard for assessing the validity of proposed components of PCK for teaching mathematics?

What methods of assessing teachers' PCK are both valid and practical in large-scale studies?

Which components of PCK are best considered in the education of prospective teachers, and which are best learned in later professional development or, on the job?

GENERAL NOTES

1. We recognise that the use of the term "misconception" is particularly controversial in mathematics (as well as science) education. Some prefer naïve conceptions, child theories, or alternative conceptions.
2. See also Krauss, S., Kunter, M., Brunner, M., Baumert, J., Blum, W., Neubrand, M., Jordan, A., & Löwen, K. (2004). COACTIV: Professionswissen von Lehrkräften, kognitiv aktivierender Mathematikunterricht und die Entwicklung von mathematischer Kompetenz. In J. Dool & M. Prenzel (Eds.), Bildungsqualität von Schule: Lehrerprofessionalisierung,

Unterrichtsentwicklung und Schülerforderung als Strategien der Qualitätsverbesserung (pp. 31–53). Münster: Waxmann.

REFERENCES

An, S., Kulm, G., & Wu, Z. (2004). The pedagogical content knowledge of middle school teachers in China and the U.S. *Journal of Mathematics Teacher Education, 7*, 145–172.

Ball, D. L., & Bass, H. (2003). Toward practice-based theory of mathematical knowledge for teaching. In B. Davis & E. Simmt (Eds.), *Proceedings of the 2002 Annual Meeting of the Canadian Mathematics Education Study Group* (pp. 3–14). Edmonton, AB: CMESG/GCEDM.

Ball, D. L., & Rowan, B. (2004). Introduction: Measuring instruction. *Elementary School Journal, 105*(1), 3–10.

Barnett, C., Goldstein, D., & Jackson, B. (Eds.). (1994). *Fractions, decimals, ratios, & percents: Hard to teach and hard to learn?* Portsmouth, NH: Heinemann.

Baumert, J., Krauss, S., Kunter, M., & Brunner, M. (2003). COACTIV: Cognitive activation in the classroom: The orchestration of learning opportunities for the enhancement of insightful learning in mathematics. Retrieved January 13, 2008 from www.mpib-berlin,mpg.de/forschung/eub/projekete.coactiv.htm

Bush, W.S., Ronau, R., Brown, T. E., & Myers, M. H. (2006, April). Reliability and validity of diagnostic mathematics assessments for middle school teachers. Paper presented at the annual meeting of the American Educational Research Association, San Francisco, CA.

Cochran, K. E., DeRuiter, J. A., & King, R. A. (1993). Pedagogical content knowledge: An integrated model for teacher preparation, *Journal of Teacher Education, 44*, 263–272.

Consortium for Policy Research in Education. (2004). *Study of instructional improvement/Learning mathematics for teaching,* Ann Arbor: University of Michigan.

Even, R., & Tirosh, D. (1995). Subject-matter knowledge and knowledge about students as sources of teacher presentations of the subject matter. *Educational Studies in Mathematics, 29*, 1–20.

Fennema, E., Carpenter, T., Franke, M., Levi, L., Jacobs, V., & Empson, S. (1996). A longitudinal study of learning to use children's thinking in mathematics instruction. *Journal for Research in Mathematics Education, 27*(4), 403–434.

Fennema, E., & Franke, M. L. (1992). Teachers' knowledge and its impact. In D. A. Grouws (Ed.), *Handbook of research on mathematics teaching and learning* (pp. 147–164). New York, NY: Macmillan.

Ferrini-Mundy, J., Floden, R., McCrory, R., Burrill, G., & Sandow, D. (2005, April). Knowledge for teaching school algebra: Challenges in developing and analytic framework. Paper presented at the annual meeting of the American Educational Research Association, Montreal, Quebec.

Grossman, A. S. (1983). Decimal notation: An important research finding. *Arithmetic Teacher, 30,* (9) 32–33.

Grossman, P .L. (1990). *The making of a teacher: Teacher knowledge and teacher education.* New York, NY: Teachers College Press.

Grossman, P. L. (2005). Research on pedagogical approaches in teacher education. In M. Cochran-Smith & K. Zeichner (Eds.), *Studying teacher education: The report of the AERA panel on research and teacher education* (pp. 425–476). Mahwah, NJ: Lawrence Erlbaum Associates.

Hiebert, J., & Wearne, D. (1986). Procedures over concepts: The acquisition of decimal number knowledge. In J. Hiebert & P. LaFevre (Eds.), *Conceptual and procedural knowledge: The case of mathematics* (pp. 199–223). Hillsdale, NJ: Lawrence Erlbaum Associates.

Hill, H. C., Rowan, B., & Ball, D. L. (2005). Effects of teachers' mathematical knowledge for teaching on student achievement. *American Educational Research Journal, 42*, 371–406.

Hill, H. C., Schilling, S. G., & Ball, D. L. (2004). Developing measures of teachers' mathematics knowledge for teaching. *The Elementary School Journal, 105*(1), 11–30.

Hill, H. C., Sleep, L., Lewis, J.M., & Ball, D. L. (2007). Assessing teachers' mathematical knowledge: What knowledge matters and what evidence counts? In F. K. Lester, Jr. (Ed.), *Second handbook of research on mathematics teaching and learning* (pp. 111–155). Charlotte, NC: Information Age Publishing & National Council of Teachers of Mathematics.

Jones, G. A., Langrall, C. W., & Mooney, E. S. (2007). Research in probability: Responding to classroom realities. In F. K. Lester, Jr. (Ed.), *Second handbook of research on mathematics teaching and learning* (pp. 909–955). Charlotte, NC: Information Age Publishing & National Council of Teachers of Mathematics.

Kieran, C. (2007). Learning and teaching algebra at the middle school through college levels: Building meaning for symbols and their manipulation. In F. K. Lester, Jr. (Ed.), *Second handbook of research on mathematics teaching and learning* (pp. 707–762). Charlotte, NC: Information Age Publishing & National Council of Teachers of Mathematics.

Kinach, B. M. (2002). A cognitive strategy for developing pedagogical content knowledge in the secondary mathematics methods course: Toward a model of effective practice. *Teaching and Teacher Education, 18*, 51–71.

Lampert, M. (2001). *Teaching problems and the problems of teaching.* New Haven, CT: Yale University Press.

Ma, L. (1999). *Knowing and teaching elementary mathematics.* Mahwah, NJ: Lawrence Erlbaum Associates.

Marks, R. (1990). Pedagogical content knowledge: From a mathematical case to a modified conception. *Journal of Teacher Education, 41*, 3–11.

McEwan, H., & Bull, B. (1991). The pedagogic nature of subject matter knowledge. *American Educational Research Journal, 28*, 316–334.

McNamara, D. (1990), Research on teachers' thinking: Its contribution to educating student teachers to think critically. *Journal of Education for Teaching, 16*(2), 147–160.

Meredith, A. (1993). Knowledge for teaching mathematics: Some student teachers' views. *Journal of Education for Teaching, 19*(3), 325–336.

Meredith, A. (1995). Terry's learning: Some limitations of Shulman's pedagogical content knowledge. *Cambridge Journal of Education, 25*(2), 175–187. Retrieved February 2, 2006 from http://sas.epnet.com/citation.asp

Perkins, D. N., & Simmons, R. (1998). Patterns of misunderstanding: An integrative model for science, math, and programming. *Review of Educational Research, 58*(3), 303–326.

Sakur-Grisvard, C., & Leonard, F. (1985). Intermediate cognitive orientations in the process of learning a mathematical concept: The order of positive decimal numbers. *Cognition and Instruction, 2*(2), 157–174.

Schwartz, J. (2008). *Elementary mathematics: Pedagogical content knowledge.* Upper Saddle River, NJ: Allyn & Bacon/Pearson.

Sconiers, S. Isaacs, A., Konold, C., & McFadden, E. (1999). *Bridges to classroom mathematics.* Lexington, MA: COMAP.

Shulman, L. S. (1986a). Those who understand: Knowledge growth in teaching. *Educational Researcher, 15*(2), 4–14.

Shulman. L. S. (1986b). Paradigms and research programs in the study of teaching: A contemporary perspective. In M. C. Wittrock (Ed.), *Handbook for research on teaching* (pp. 3–33). New York: Macmillan.

Shulman, L. S. (1987). Knowledge and teaching: Foundations of the new reform. *Harvard Educational Review, 57*(1), 1–22.

Skemp, R. R. (1978). Relational understanding and instrumental understanding. *The Arithmetic Teacher, 26*(3), 9–15.

Sowder, J. T., Philipp, R. A. Armstrong, B. E., & Schappelle, B. P. (1998). *Middle-grade teachers' mathematical knowledge and its relationship to instruction.* Albany, NY: State University of New York Press.

131

Tsamir, P. (2005). Enhancing prospective teachers' knowledge of learners' intuitive conceptions: The case of *"same A--same B."* *Journal of Mathematics Teacher Education, 8,* 469–497.

Van de Walle, J. (2007). *Elementary and middle school mathematics: Teaching developmentally* (6th ed.). Upper Saddle River, NJ: Pearson.

Watson, J. M. (2001). Profiling teachers' competence and confidence to teach particular mathematics topics: The case of data and chance. *Journal of Mathematics Teacher Education, 4,* 305–337.

Wilson, S. M., & Wineburg, S. S. (1988). Peering at history though different lenses: The role of disciplinary perspectives in teaching history. *Teachers College Record, 89,* 525–539.

Wilson, S. M., Floden, R. F., & Ferrini-Mundy, J. (2001, March). Teacher preparation research: Current knowledge, recommendations, and priorities for the future. Center for the Study of Teaching Policy, University of Washington, Seattle, WA. (Available online at http://www.depts.washington.edu/ctpmail/ Reports.html#TeacherPrep.)

Anna O. Graeber
College of Education
University of Maryland, USA

Dina Tirosh
School of Education
Tel Aviv University, Israel

DOUG CLARKE

6. THE MATHEMATICS TEACHER AS CURRICULUM MAKER

Developing Knowledge for Enacting Curriculum

This chapter outlines a process by which a teacher begins with the intended curriculum as outlined in curriculum frameworks, guidelines or standards and enacts it. There is a discussion, placed within a narrative involving the teaching of fraction content, of how a teacher might identify the big ideas within a topic, sequence concepts within that topic, recognise and enhance connections between concepts, and match the curriculum to the developing understanding of students. The discussion also includes a consideration of the kinds of knowledge which a teacher might draw upon when being a curriculum maker, and some of the constraints which may prevent a teacher from fully enacting this role. The chapter concludes with a discussion of effective approaches to preparing prospective and practising teachers to be active curriculum makers, through appropriate professional development.

INTRODUCTION

Few people would disagree that the teacher is the key to worthwhile mathematical experiences for students in our schools. Although a whole range of circumstances need to be in place for teachers to carry out their work effectively, there is overwhelming evidence that two teachers working in similar circumstances with similar supports and constraints can provide quite different learning experiences for students (e.g., McDonough & Clarke, 2003).

In this chapter, I take the mathematics curriculum to be the teacher's experiences, intended or not, which occur within the mathematics classroom, and the processes on the part of the teacher leading up to the enactment of curriculum, including preparation and planning. This is a broader definition than that of some scholars. For example, Clements (2007) defined curriculum as "a specific set of instructional materials that order content used to support pre-K to grade 12 classrooms" (p. 36). Of course, my definition does not include all mathematical learning opportunities for teachers, but it clarifies my emphasis in this chapter, and allows me to focus on the teacher's role in the enactment of the mathematics curriculum.

A number of writers have distinguished between the *intended* curriculum, the *implemented* curriculum, and the *attained* curriculum (e.g., Robitaille et al., 1993).

P. Sullivan and T. Wood (eds.), Knowledge and Beliefs in Mathematics Teaching and Teaching Development, 133–151.

Gehrke, Knapp, and Sirotnik (1992) contributed the *planned, enacted* and *experienced* curriculum to this list, while Burkhardt, Fraser, and Ridgway (1990) referred to the *ideal, adopted, implemented, achieved*, and *tested* curriculum. Given my particular focus in this chapter on what the teacher knows and does my interest here is mainly in the *implemented* curriculum—the ways in which a teacher takes a syllabus or curriculum guidelines or standards and enacts them in the classroom. In the following sections, I provide a brief discussion of some of the influences and constraints on the work of teachers in relation to curriculum, before turning to the teacher's role in implementing curriculum.

INFLUENCES AND CONSTRAINTS ON MATHEMATICS TEACHERS

There are many factors which impact on mathematics teachers (primary or secondary) being able to teach in the way they would wish and achieving outcomes of the kind desired by educational institutions and systems. I discuss several of these factors below.

The Canonical Curriculum

In most countries, syllabus documents that define the content and approach to instruction are prepared centrally for school systems, and yet the mathematics curriculum in countries across the world do not generally reflect the diversity of cultures and contexts; in other words they are quite similar (Clarke, D. M., Clarke, B. A., & Sullivan, 1996). Howson and Wilson (1986) described the almost universal adoption of what they called the school mathematics "canonical curriculum". For example, they noted that in Japan and Mexico, where approximately 95% and 3% respectively complete secondary school, there is remarkable similarity in the year-by-year syllabuses. Of course, there are many factors leading to this situation. As Wilson (1992) noted, in discussing the situation in Africa:

> What did it matter that the chapters on stocks and shares, and rates and taxes were meaningless to an African pupil? Such relevance was simply not a criterion [...]. Any deviation would have been regarded by well-educated Africans as having their children fobbed off with a second-best or watered-down education. (p. 127)

It appears that the curriculum is so well established in many countries that societies do not wish to change it for fear of not operating a 'proper' education.

The Influence of State and National Assessment Schemes

Assessment at state and national levels appears to have a major influence in most countries on both content and teaching methods, particularly if the testing is 'high stakes'. As Wilson (2007) noted, the grade levels at which high-stakes testing occurred were more likely to experience more profound changes in curriculum and instruction than those grades which were not included in the evaluation. Phelps (2000) who examined data from 31 countries and provinces, concluded that there was an overall net increase internationally in all testing from 1974-1999, therefore the influence of such testing is likely to have increased over time. The influence of testing regimes on content and instructional practices is often channelled through the school system via the principal to the teacher in a top down approach; few teachers can claim to be unaffected by its influence.

Provision of Time and Resources

There are some basic requirements for teachers to be able to carry out their role. They need to be supplied with appropriate resources, including appropriate texts (student and teacher), relevant student materials (such as manipulative materials), relevant technology, and an appropriate physical environment. Just as importantly, teachers need time: to plan, alone and with colleagues, to assimilate new content and pedagogy into their teaching repertoire. They also need sufficient time on the school programme for students to engage with mathematics. In my own country for example, the issue of the 'crowded curriculum' is a common topic of conversation.

Large Scale Curriculum Development Projects

Around the world, there are a large number of curriculum development projects, increasingly linked to some kind of curriculum standards. In the United States for example, there were two large-scale, high-profile curriculum development efforts, the 'new math' and the recent curriculum reform of the 1990s. The "new math" emerged in the 1960s and had considerable impact on not only the U.S. but many countries around the world. Then again in the 1990s there was a strong move towards reforming mathematics education through changes presented in the *Curriculum and Evaluation Standards for School Mathematics* (National Council of Teachers of Mathematics, 1989), backed by substantial funding from the National Science Foundation (NSF) for developing, implementing and evaluating reform-based instructional materials to support the curriculum transformation (Hirsch, 2007). A major feature of these more recent curriculum projects was the strong commitment to funding to support teachers' professional development, in the belief that the absence of such financial support would lead to little real change in teaching and therefore little impact in the classroom (Bradley, 2007). However, many countries lack these extensive funds and/or political will to provide support in either instructional materials or professional development programmes.

The Ways in Which the Role of Teachers Are Perceived by Curriculum Developers

The form, size and style of curriculum documents developed for classroom teachers often provides insights into the ways in which the role of the teacher is perceived by the authors of such documents. Where teachers are seen as key players in curriculum implementation, such documents often take the form of general guidelines, upon which a teacher can place her/his stamp, as they work together with colleagues to adapt materials to the perceived needs of their students.

On the other hand, developers of highly prescriptive materials possibly think of teachers as incompetent or lacking experience, which are seen to be able to be used by *any* teacher. These materials are derived from an era in which curriculum developers attempted to provide 'teacher-proof' materials in order to bypass the influence of the teacher on student learning. This approach however does not allow for the impact of context and culture on the way in which materials might be implemented in classrooms. The distinctions between the types of curriculum discussed earlier (intended, enacted, experienced, etc.) is a recognition that the notion of teacher-proof materials is nonsense—not possible and, I would argue, not at all desirable.

In the remainder of this chapter, I focus on the teacher using the *intended* curriculum and the process by which she implements it, with a related discussion about teacher knowledge. In this scenario, I attempt to paint a picture of what could be described as an 'ideal' situation of a well-equipped and skilful teacher, who I will call Ms X, engaged in the implementation of relevant, meaningful and worthwhile learning experiences for her students. It is not claimed that this description is necessarily the norm; in fact it is clearly not. But the hope is that the reader will consider ways in which more teachers could be equipped and supported to prepare and teach in this way. I then discuss the knowledge which I argue necessarily underpins such implementation. Finally, I discuss principles of professional development which might enhance such knowledge.

A SCENARIO OF A TEACHER ENACTING THE CURRICULUM

I propose the following detailed scenario as an example of quality enactment of curriculum. The narrative is a fictitious account of a teacher's experience in teaching fractions, based on my own research, my reading, and the opportunity to observe some exemplary teachers in action. In order to make this discussion more concrete, I situate Ms X as about to teach the topic of comparing fractions (i.e., determining the relative size of two fractions) to a group of 7th grade students, around 13 years old, and describe the steps she might take in preparing for and teaching this topic.

1. Reflect on what has happened in previous related lessons.
When Ms X started to teach the topic of fractions to this 7th grade class, she knew that her students had a reasonable understanding of the part-whole notion of fractions. By this term, I refer to part-whole comparison, which Lamon (2006) states "designates a number of equal parts of a unit out of the total number of equal parts into which the unit is divided" (p. 125). Ms X determined from her reading, that part-whole ideas may have been overemphasised in many classrooms in relation to other constructs of fractions, such as measure, quotient, and operator (Kieren, 1976; Lamon, 2006). Ms X participated in a two-part professional development programme several months earlier when these ideas had been

discussed. Two lessons ago, the teacher engaged the students in a problem solving activity focused on partitioning strategies. This activity consisted of the following: 10 students come into the room one at a time, and choose to stand at one of three chairs, each having different amounts of chocolate (one block, two blocks, and three blocks, respectively), when all students are in the room, they are to share the chocolate at their chair with whoever else is standing at that chair (see Clarke, D. M., 2006, for more details of this activity). There is an assumption underpinning this activity, readily accepted on the part of students, that more chocolate is desirable.

One major purpose of this problem solving task was for students to become aware (if they were not already) that, for example, three blocks of chocolate shared between five people *automatically* means that each person would receive 3/5 of a block of chocolate, without the need to partition, or imagine partitioning the chocolate to determine each share. This activity emphasised the construct of fractions as *division* or *quotient*, that is, that a/b is the same as $a \div b$. After doing the activity, most students admitted that prior to this task they had no idea of this notion, even though many had learned in the previous year to convert fractions to decimals with a calculator or by hand, thereby enacting this principle.

At the end of the activity, in order to maximise the chances that the mathematical intent became clear to most students, Ms X formed a visual image which the students might retain to help them remember the notion. The teacher asked three students to hold a chair above their heads with the two chocolate blocks on it. She asked the class to observe the two blocks above the line of the chair (the line representing the vinculum), which was in turn above the three students, and pointed out "two blocks shared between three people is 2 (gesturing) over 3, so two-thirds".

In reflecting upon this lesson, Ms X felt a need to consolidate these ideas the following day. It was her general practice to attempt to build connections between a lesson and those which came before and after. A key finding of the effective teachers in the numeracy study in the UK (Askew, Brown, Rhodes, Johnson, & Wiliam, 1997) was that the most effective teachers could be described as "connectionist". Therefore, in the next lesson, Ms X attempted to build on this understanding of *fraction as division* (or quotient) by the provision of another problem, this time involving pizzas. The problem had been posed as follows: "Three boys share one pizza evenly, and seven girls share three pizzas of the same size evenly. Who gets more pizza, a boy or a girl?" Ms X had been interested to see how many students would build upon what they had learned in the previous lesson, thereby comparing 1/3 and 3/7. Only a small number did so. In fact, common solutions were of the following two kinds:

> For the girls' situation to be equivalent to the boys, six girls would have to share three pizzas. So, we effectively have one extra pizza and one extra girl, so clearly the girls must receive more on average.

> 'Scaling up' the boys' situation would mean nine boys and three pizzas, giving two more boys for the same number of pizzas as the girls. So the girls receive more.

Of course, these two solutions were innovative and more straightforward than comparing 1/3 and 3/7, but it was interesting that few saw the link with the previous lesson. In debriefing upon the different strategies, some students had come to compare 1/3 and 3/7 but had 'hit a brick wall', unsure as to which was larger, 1/3 or 3/7? This led quite appropriately for Ms X to a focus on strategies for comparing fractions in the following lesson.

2. Read through the written curriculum statements or guidelines (the intended curriculum).
As discussed previously, written curricula come in a variety of levels in terms of details and prescription. This is one aspect which varies considerably around the world. In some countries (e.g., Japan), a relatively thin book outlines all that should be 'covered' in one year, while in other countries (e.g., the United States), curriculum guides, particularly textbooks, are often very detailed, large and thick. The curriculum guidelines for this teacher were relatively brief, on the assumption that the teacher would work with colleagues, drawing upon her reading and insights which had emerged from professional development. In relation to this topic, the documentation indicated that students would require an understanding of equivalent fractions, and a process for finding the common denominator of two fractions, and converting both to this common denominator. The guidelines also indicated that such comparisons should be made successfully with both proper and improper fractions.

3. Consider what the 'big ideas' might be for the topic of fractions overall.
For any teacher, developing an understanding of what constitutes the 'big ideas' within a topic is an ongoing process, as curriculum statements, other readings, observations of students, conversations with colleagues, and teacher education and other professional development experiences come together. Sowder (2007) argued that effective mathematics teachers think about mathematics curricula "in terms of big ideas, such as proportional reasoning or the mathematics of change, around which to structure instruction" (p. 165). The kinds of big ideas which might be relevant here might include the following examples:

> Uses appropriate symbols to represent fractions, understanding the meaning attached to each part (e.g., denominator shows what 'denomination' is being counted, the numerator 'enumerates' how many of these parts).
>
> Understands that fractions (including whole numbers, mixed numbers and improper fractions) are entities that can be counted (e.g., 4/5 represents four things called 'fifths') and can recognise and use counting patterns and equivalences.
>
> Recognises a/b as a divided by b.
>
> Readily compares and orders fractions.
>
> Relates a given fraction to key benchmarks (e.g., 0, ½, 1).

4. Talk to colleagues about their experiences in teaching this topic.
Other 7th grade teachers indicated to Ms X that this is a difficult topic to teach, that they have had little success with it in the past, and that fractions generally is the least popular topic among students in the 7th grade curriculum. On a regular basis, the teacher used the IMPACT procedure (Clarke, D. J., 1989), which involves students responding every two weeks (for about ten minutes) to four or five questions of the kind, "What are you having most trouble with in mathematics at the moment?" "What is one new thing you can do in mathematics this week which you couldn't do last week?" and "How could we improve mathematics classes?" Ms X had noticed that even when students were not currently studying fractions, quite a few nevertheless nominated fractions as their greatest topic of concern. Her Grade 6 colleagues indicated that they taught the topic the previous year, but when assessed few students had a strong understanding, as revealed on a topic test after the completion of the topic. They indicated that their teaching approach had largely been *instrumental* (Skemp, 1976), involving converting fractions to common denominators, and that students seemed to do so all the time, even when the comparison should have been obvious. They indicated that they would be glad to hear of a better way of teaching this topic if Ms X finds one.

5. Consider articles which show research findings in this area with related teaching implications.
As part of a part-time study programme which Ms X was undertaking in her spare time, she had accumulated a number of 'research into practice' type articles. Articles which summarise research reinforced her perception that this is a difficult topic for teachers and students. They indicated that a major difficulty is that most students do not think of fractions as having a 'size', but are rather just one whole number over another whole number. One particular example was frequently cited in the literature. Students were asked to select "the nearest whole number to 7/8 + 12/13" from the four choices of 1, 2, 19 and 21. The majority of 13-year olds in the USA chose 19 or 21, almost certainly found by adding the numerators and denominators respectively (Carpenter, Kepner, Corbitt, Lindquist, & Reys, 1980). The research literature did however point to sense-making strategies which a number of students use, and which can be shared with others. They also recommended greater use of number lines, which help students to see things like the relationships between whole numbers, fractions and percentages. Number lines also support the idea of the density of rational numbers, namely that between any two distinct rational numbers, there is always an infinite number of rational numbers.

6. Gather some information from a sample of students on how they would choose to compare fractions.
During recess, Ms X chose carefully a selection of fraction pairs, and asked several volunteers (some of the more typically capable ones, and some who tend to approach problems in innovative ways) individually how they would compare them. The pairs were 3/7 and 5/8, 2/4 and 4/2, and 5/6 and 7/8. It is important to

note here the power of carefully chosen examples in eliciting and enhancing student thinking and bringing common misconceptions to the fore (Watson & Mason, 2005). As she worked with these students, she noticed that they found them very difficult, but several were using some number sense-based strategies and few were using common denominators. Some were using what research calls *residual* strategies (Clarke, Sukenik, Roche, & Mitchell, 2006), that is, deciding for each fraction how much would be needed to make the fraction up to 1 (the 'residual'). For 5/6, only 1/6 would be required, while for 7/8, 1/8 would be required—a smaller residual, so therefore 7/8ths is a larger fraction. There were also a couple of examples of *benchmarking*, where students compare each fraction to a well known benchmark, such as 0, 1/2 or 1. One student compared 3/7 and 5/8 by indicating that 3/7 is a bit less than 1/2, while 5/8 is clearly more than 1/2, which is most encouraging.

7. Use what has been learned from research and brief student interviews to structure a lesson.

Ms X decided that there was sufficient potential in the different strategies which some students had chosen to use when she spoke to them individually at recess, to make the next lesson a small group working session, with a focus on developing efficient strategies for comparing fractions. She started the lesson by reminding the class that when they left off yesterday, there was some confusion about how to compare 1/3 and 3/7. In 'friendship groups', students were given six pairs to work on, agreeing on which fraction was larger in each case, with a written reason on why. While methods involving common denominators were acceptable, groups were challenged to produce an additional method for each pair, which made sense to them. Ms X reminded the class that her emphasis all year was on mathematics making sense to them, and also helping us to make sense of the world. The class was accustomed to discussions about any proposed methods in terms of three things: Is the method mathematically valid? Is it efficient? Is it generalisable to many similar problems? (Campbell, Rowan, & Suarez, 1998). Once most groups had completed their set of six problems, she asked one person from each group to share one of their results, which they believe to have yielded a particularly impressive strategy, which could be generalised to many other pairs. Ms X listed each strategy on the board, and discussed it with the students, using the three criteria above.

8. Pose an assessment task for the first half of next lesson.

As an advance organiser (Ausubel, 1960), the teacher let the class know that in the next lesson they would be challenged to write five pieces of advice or hints for other students who are just learning how to compare fractions for the first time. For each piece of advice, they are to show what they mean with specific examples. This was to be their major assessment task for the week.

9. Encourage the students to share their knowledge with another group of students.
In this school, there was a regular expectation that a given class will share what
they have learned with another class, when some particularly helpful insights
emerge. The teacher therefore organises for one of the groups who have
particularly impressed her to share what they have found with another 7th grade
class who are just starting this topic, during a presentation to this class. She was
aware of Freudenthal's (1975) notion about students needing to create knowledge
for themselves (in the same way that particular procedures have developed over
hundreds of years)—what he termed reinvention as compared to the learning of
ready-made material. She emphasises that "the telling teacher is not the telling
teacher" and encouraged the group to create a way of scaffolding the students'
understanding and not rush to "tell," so that in time they will develop similar
understanding to that of her class.

In the following section, I will start to unpack the kinds of knowledge which
might lead to the hypothetical story I outlined above.

WHAT KIND OF KNOWLEDGE MIGHT A MATHEMATICS TEACHER HOLD TO UNDERPIN THIS ENACTMENT OF CURRICULUM?

In this section, I discuss the kinds of knowledge which might enable a teacher to
follow the path described in the narrative of Ms X.

Teachers' Knowledge

Various scholars have categorised the knowledge possessed by mathematics
teachers in a variety of ways. The best known is Shulman (1987) who identified the
components of teachers' knowledge (general and not specific to mathematics
teaching) as:

> content knowledge;
>
> general pedagogical knowledge, with special reference to those broad
> principles and strategies of classroom management and organisation that
> appear to transcend subject matter;
>
> curriculum knowledge, with particular grasp of the materials and
> programmes that serve as the 'tools of the trade' for teachers;
>
> pedagogical content knowledge, that special amalgam of content and
> pedagogy that is uniquely the province of teachers, their own special form
> of professional understanding;
>
> knowledge of learners and their characteristics;
>
> knowledge of educational contexts, ranging from the workings of the
> group or classroom, the governance or financing of school districts, to the
> character of communities and cultures; and
>
> knowledge of educational ends, purposes, and values, and their
> philosophical and historical grounds (p. 8).

Of course, it is not claimed that these are mutually exclusive, but I believe the distinctions are helpful. I focus on all of Shulman's categories now, relating them to the knowledge as evidenced by the decisions of the teacher in the above scenario.

Content knowledge. There is little doubt that effective teachers of mathematics need a clear understanding of the mathematics they wish to teach students, at least at the level at which they propose to teach. By understanding, I take the definition of understanding from Hiebert et al. (1997), namely that we understand something if we see how it is related or connected to other things we know. Clearly, the way teacher knowledge is organised and accessed as well as the nature of that knowledge is important. It must also be acknowledged that in many countries (including Australia) there has been a shift in focus from a transmission model of teaching to an emphasis on teaching for understanding (Fennema & Romberg, 1999) which changed the nature of student/teacher interaction. Moving to a more learner-centred approach from a teacher-centred stance places greater demands on teacher knowledge, as the lesson can take many possible directions, given the more responsive nature of the teaching process, and students' strategies and reasoning can provide additional challenges (Clarke, D. M., 1997).

Brophy (1991) argued in relation to content knowledge that

> where (teachers') knowledge is more explicit, better connected, and more integrated, they will tend to teach the subject more dynamically, represent it in more varied ways and encourage and respond fully to students' comments and questions. Where their knowledge is limited, they will tend to depend on the text for content, de-emphasise interactive discourse in favour of seatwork assignments, and in general, portray the subject as a collection of static, factual knowledge. (p. 352)

In the fraction narrative, Ms X needed a clear, connected knowledge of rational numbers, in order to deal with the ways in which students might choose to compare fractions. This is where the borders of content knowledge and pedagogical content knowledge become fuzzy (see Chapter 6, this volume). It is possibly helpful in determining the borders to consider what it is that teachers need to know in relation to this topic which is the special province of teachers, and unlikely to be possessed by an engineer, say. This will be discussed in more detail later.

Deborah Ball and her colleagues at the University of Michigan have explored further what they call "mathematical knowledge for teaching" (Hill, Rowan, & Ball, 2005). In their work they focus on subject matter knowledge, currently breaking it into *common content knowledge* (what people with reasonable mathematical knowledge know), the *specialised content knowledge of teachers*, and another category, which they call *horizon knowledge*, which can be thought of as knowledge of the mathematics which the student is likely to meet in coming years, and how this might connect to their current topics (D. Ball, personal communication, 2/10/07). The bulk of Ball and colleagues' current work is on describing the specialised content knowledge of teachers through the use of "records of practice".

General pedagogical knowledge. One example of this kind of knowledge in mathematics teaching might involve the capacity to form, manage and maximise the outputs of small group work and other organisational approaches in mathematics. Being clear on why groups might be formed in a certain way on a certain day is part of this. In the Early Numeracy Research Project (Clarke, D. M. et al., 2002), an extensive research, assessment and professional development project involving 35 'trial' schools and 353 teachers, data were collected at the end of the project from 220 teachers, on the ways in which trial school teachers organised their classes during the mathematics lesson.

When asked in the final weeks of the project to indicate the most common way in which they organised their students to work on tasks in the mathematics classroom during the main part of the lesson, there was an almost even split between: individual work, with discussion being allowed or encouraged (34%); children working in pairs (33%); and children working in larger groups (two or more) (34%). Slighty less than three-quarters of the teachers indicated that they used all three working group sizes at different times. Teachers were asked to identify the most common way in which groups were formed when children worked in pairs or other small groups. The distribution of the various forms of group assignment were heterogeneous (31.5%); homogeneous (28.5%); heterogeneous with one special group (26.0%); and student choice (14.0%).

Only 7.6% of teachers indicated that they used only one of these options. There was considerable variety in the ways in which groups were used and in how children were assigned to groups. Teachers indicated that the content and activities for the day were a major factor in these decisions. For example, one case study teacher paired "strong literacy children" with less strong literacy children for a mathematical activity with a high literacy demand.

Although these pedagogical decisions are important, Brown (1999) noted that quality teaching is more than this: "Quality teaching is more important than classroom organisation […] it's not whether it's whole class, small group or individual teaching, but rather what you teach and how you interact mathematically with children that seem to count" (p. 7).

In the fraction narrative, the teacher made at least two conscious decisions that were influenced by her pedagogical knowledge. First, she made several efforts to find out where her students were in terms of their understanding and use of strategies, by talking to individual students and to other teachers. She also made the decision to use small group work (friendship groups), thus encouraging students to pool their knowledge in working on the challenging fraction pairs. If she had chosen to use small groups based on ability, it is likely that some groups would have struggled, because they were merely "pooling their weaknesses".

Curriculum knowledge. This component of teacher knowledge also has clear links to pedagogical content knowledge. In knowing the materials and programmes that serve as the 'tools of the trade' for teachers as Shulman (1986) describes them, in the story above, this would include awareness of the curriculum guidelines, the kinds of manipulative material which are likely to be helpful in supporting learning, and the kinds of experiences which students are likely to have had in previous grades in relation to this topic, and where this topic might lead in subsequent years. We saw this, or the teacher's awareness for the need for this, in the fraction scenario, as Ms X referred to curriculum documents and to the experiences of other colleagues.

Pedagogical content knowledge. This is the area of knowledge which has received the most attention in the mathematics education research and professional development literature in the last five years (Chick et al., 2006; Hill, Rowan, & Ball, 2005). Shulman's contribution was to identify and elaborate the notion of pedagogical content knowledge which refers to how specific knowledge can be interpreted in teaching situations (Cooney, 1994).

Shulman (1986) summarised this knowledge as

> the most useful forms of representations of those ideas, the most powerful analogies, illustrations, examples, explanations, and demonstrations—in a word, the ways of representing and formulating the subject that make it comprehensible to others. ... Pedagogical content knowledge also includes an understanding of what makes the learning of specific topics easy or difficult: the conceptions and preconceptions that students of different ages and backgrounds bring with them to the learning of the most frequently taught topics and lessons ... if the preconceptions are misconceptions, which they so often are, teachers need knowledge of the strategies most likely to be fruitful in reorganising the understanding of learners. (p. 9)

To Shulman's list of the components of pedagogical content knowledge, Hill, Rowan, and Ball (2005) add knowing how to use pictures or diagrams to represent mathematical concepts and procedures, providing students with explanations for common rules and mathematical procedures, and analysing students' solutions and explanations.

In considering the fraction narrative, Ms X demonstrated her considerable pedagogical content knowledge. In Shulman's terms, she chose as an example the chocolate problem to encourage the students to explore, with obvious motivation, an important fraction construct. She collected information prior to the lesson (in class and out of it) on the kinds of difficulties which students face in studying this topic, and on some of the more important big ideas and strategies which might assist the students. Her thorough preparation increased the chances of helping students to reorganise their understanding where this was necessary.

Knowledge of learners and their characteristics. A teacher can be aware of curriculum documents and general patterns of student developing understanding in mathematics. In order however to meet the needs of individuals in classrooms, the teacher needs to know the students as individuals—their interests, their level of understanding, and their disposition for mathematics. There is a variety of ways of gaining this information and updating it on a regular basis, and many of these methods are in common use. Of particular personal interest is the potential of the one-to-one, task-based assessment interview in providing a detailed picture of individual learners' level of understanding and preferred problem solving strategies. As Bobis et. al. (2005) noted, an important feature of some of the largest research and professional development projects conducted in Australia and New Zealand in the past 10 years was the use of such interviews by classroom teachers. Although there was an assessment purpose behind the use of such interviews, the major emphasis was on assessment to inform teaching and thereby enhance learning

The teacher in the fraction scenario demonstrated a number of strategies to gain, and subsequently use, a detailed understanding of her students and their levels of understanding and preferred strategies. I would argue that one important component of teacher knowledge which is not always acknowledged in the literature is realistic expectations of students, for both individuals and the group as a whole. This component seems to overlap with pedagogical content knowledge, curriculum knowledge, and knowledge of learners and their characteristics. In the Early Numeracy Research Project (Clarke, D. M. et al., 2002), teachers were offered 22 statements about possible mathematical knowledge of their students (e.g., "knows that 78 is 7 tens and 8 ones"). Completing these items in both the entry and exit questionnaires (approximately three years apart) enabled quantification of whether their expectations of what students could do had changed over the course of the project (see also Volume 2, Chapter 10). One result of the regular use of the Early Numeracy Research Project task-based, one-on-one assessment interview by teachers in the project appeared to be changes in expectations, in two respects.

One change was in the "spread of expectations", where teachers seemed to be acknowledging the existence of considerable within-class variation. For example, in response to the questionnaires at the beginning and end of the project, all of the Grade 1 teachers at the end of the project (approximately 70 teachers) expected at least some of their children to "recall and use addition and subtraction facts to 20 (including 0)" compared to 29% at the beginning who thought that none of their children could do so. (Grade 1 children are typically six-year olds.)

There were also areas where the teachers had higher expectations of their children's understanding at the end of the project than at the beginning. For example, in relation to the item "knows that four hundred and two is written 402 and knows why neither 42 or 4002 is correct"), at the beginning of the project 61% of teachers of Preps (the first year of school) expected no child at the end of the first year of school (generally five-year olds) to have this knowledge. But, after three years of the project, the figure was only 30%, indicating considerably increased expectations over time. There were similar increased expectations among Grade 1 and 2 teachers.

A second factor which appeared crucial to teachers obtaining appropriate expectations for students was data provided by the research team about their own students' achievement of "growth points". The notion of growth points is discussed extensively in Volume 2 of this handbook series (see Barbara Clarke's chapter in that volume), but the idea was that the growing points were research-based 'big ideas' or strategies in students' developing mathematical understanding which had the following characteristics:

- reflect the findings of relevant research in mathematics education from around the world;
- emphasise important ideas in early mathematics understanding in a form and language readily understood and, in time, retained by teachers;
- reflect, where possible, the structure of mathematics;
- allow the description of the mathematical knowledge and understanding of individuals and groups;
- form the basis of planning and teaching;
- provide a basis for task construction for interviews, and the recording and coding process that would follow;
- allow the identification and description of improvement where it exists;
- enable a consideration of those students who may benefit from additional assistance; and
- have sufficiently high 'ceiling' to describe the knowledge and understanding of *all* children in the first three years of school.

By relating their own students' interview data to movement through these growth points, teachers were able to gain a sense of 'typical' performance and also variation across students, thereby enhancing the accuracy of their expectations. There is clear evidence in the literature that higher expectations have an impact on student outcomes. According to Brophy (1983), "higher expectations for student achievement are part of a pattern of differential attitudes, beliefs and behaviours that characterise teachers and schools who are successful in maximising their student learning gains" (p. 642).

Knowledge of educational contexts is the least relevant of the Shulman categories to the current discussion, and therefore will not be elaborated here. In the same way, *knowledge of educational ends, purposes, and values* is a more difficult area of knowledge to articulate, and it provides considerable overlap with beliefs, which are discussed in great detail in Forgasz and Leder's chapter in this volume. Thompson (1992), in her extensive review of the literature on beliefs and conceptions, took beliefs as a subset of conceptions, and on occasions, used them interchangeably. The picture painted earlier of Ms X gives a sense of a teacher who acts in harmony with the dynamic, problem solving view of mathematics (Thompson, 1992). Having said that, we need to remember that inconsistencies between stated beliefs and practices can occur for a variety of reasons, including the constraints mentioned early in this chapter. The statement to Cockburn by a teacher that she already knew how to teach twice as well as she was able to do (Desforges & Cockburn, 1987) is a sobering statement in relation to this inconsistency.

In the following section, I briefly report on several pieces of important research which link teacher knowledge of the kinds discussed above and other characteristics with student achievement.

ENHANCING TEACHER KNOWLEDGE OF CURRICULUM THROUGH PRINCIPLES OF PROFESSIONAL DEVELOPMENT

There are no easy ways for a teacher to build up the kinds of knowledge for teaching articulated in the previous sections, and which are illustrated in the fraction scenario. However, there is growing research evidence on the principles which might underpin effective professional development. By 'effective professional development', I am referring to those approaches which lead to substantial professional growth for teachers and also improvement in student learning.

Goals and Principles of Professional Development

Sowder (2007) proposed six somewhat overlapping goals for professional development in mathematics education that address both beliefs and knowledge: 1) developing a shared vision; 2) developing mathematical content knowledge, 3) developing an understanding of how students think about and learn mathematics; 4) developing pedagogical content knowledge; 5) developing an understanding of the role of equity in school mathematics; and 6) developing a sense of self as a teacher of mathematics (pp. 165–168).

Clarke, D. M. (1994) summarised research on the professional development of mathematics teachers and from this synthesis offered 10 principles which appeared to increase the effectiveness of professional development programmes. They were as follows:

1. Address issues of concern and interest, largely (but not exclusively) identified by the teachers themselves, and involve a degree of choice for participants.
2. Involve groups of teachers rather than individuals from a number of schools, and enlist the support of the school and district administration, students, parents and the broader school community.
3. Recognise and address the many impediments to teachers' growth at the individual, school and district level.
4. Using teachers as participants in classroom activities or students in real situations, model desired classroom approaches during sessions with practising teachers to project a clearer vision of the proposed changes.
5. Solicit teachers' conscious commitment to participate actively in the professional development sessions and to undertake required readings and classroom tasks, appropriately adapted for their own classroom.
6. Recognise that changes in teachers' beliefs about teaching and learning are derived largely from classroom practice; as a result, such changes will follow the opportunity to validate, through observing positive student learning, information supplied by professional development programmes.
7. Allow time and opportunities for planning, reflection, and feedback in order to report successes and failures to the group, to share 'the wisdom of practice', and to discuss problems and solutions regarding individual students and new teaching approaches.

8. Enable participating teachers to gain a substantial degree of ownership by their involvement in decision making and by being regarded as true partners in the change process.
9. Recognise that change is a gradual, difficult and often painful process, and afford opportunities for ongoing support from peers and critical friends.
10. Encourage participants to set further goals for their professional growth.

It is interesting to reflect on this list in relation to the narrative of Ms X, and to consider the extent to which, 14 years later, I might wish to revise this list. The experience of the Early Numeracy Research Project and the more recent work on rational number (Clarke, D. M., Sukenik, Roche, & Mitchell, 2006) have led me to see the powerful effect on teachers' professional learning of the two related strategies of 1) providing a framework of research-based growth points and, 2) a related, task-based, one-to-one student interview. These two components enable teachers to internalise both a sense of the 'big ideas' in a given content area and the reasonable expectations of what students know and can do, while increasing teachers' understanding of the incredible range of understanding within a given group of students.

In relation to the ten principles above, other writers outside the discipline of mathematics education have proposed similar principles (see, e.g., Elmore, 2002; Hawley & Valli, 1999), and there is no certainty that a programme with all of these principles in place would automatically achieve its aims, but it is clearly an important start.

Models of Professional Development

Sowder (2007) offered a helpful discussion of different approaches to professional development which have the potential to enhance "knowledge-in-practice" for teachers. The models included: a focus on student thinking (e.g., Cognitively Guided Instruction [CGI] Carpenter, Fennema, Franke, Levi, & Empson, 1999); a focus on curriculum (e.g., the various projects funded by the National Science Foundation in the 1990s in the USA); studying cases (e.g., Barnett, 1998); and formal course work. Of course, there are many more such models, one of the best known is that offered by Loucks-Horsley, Love, Stiles, Mundry, & Hewson (2003) which provides principles for the design of approaches to teacher professional development

DRAWING UPON APPROPRIATE KNOWLEDGE IN ENACTING THE CURRICULUM – AN IMPORTANT, COMPLEX BUT REWARDING TASK WHEN DONE WELL

In 1986, Shulman rejected the claim of George Bernard Shaw that "he who can does. He who cannot teaches," recognising that it gave no recognition to the highly specialised knowledge of good teachers. In this groundbreaking article, Shulman concluded with the statement, "those who can do. Those who understand, teach" (p. 14). In this chapter, I have attempted to describe the thoughtful artistry of a good teacher, to unpack the components of knowledge proposed by scholars, and have offered some thoughts on how such knowledge might be enhanced. I close with a quote from Andy Hargreaves, who like Shulman, acknowledged the key role played by the teacher in mathematics learning—the teacher as curriculum maker:

Teachers don't merely deliver the curriculum. They develop, define it and reinterpret it too. It is what teachers think, what teachers believe and what teachers do at the level of the classroom that ultimately shapes the kind of learning that young people get. (Hargreaves, 1994, p. ix)

REFERENCES

Askew, M., Brown, M., Rhodes, V., Johnson, D., & Wiliam, D. (1997). *Effective teachers of numeracy*. London: Kings College.

Ausubel, D. P. (1960). The use of advance organizers in the learning and retention of meaningful verbal material. *Journal of Educational Psychology, 51*, 267–272.

Ausubel, D. P. (1968). *Educational psychology: A cognitive view*. New York: Holt, Rinehart & Winston.

Barnett, C. (1998). Mathematics teaching cases as a catalyst for informed strategic inquiry. *Teaching and Teacher Education, 14*, 81–93.

Bobis, J., Clarke, B. A., Clarke, D. M., Thomas, G., Wright, R., Young-Loveridge, J., & Gould, P. (2005). Supporting teachers in the development of young children's mathematical thinking: Three large scale cases. *Mathematics Education Research Journal, 16*(3), 27–57.

Bradley, J. S. (2007). Foreword. In C. R. Hirsch (Ed.), *Perspectives on the design and development of school mathematics curricula* (pp. ix–xii). Reston, VA: National Council of Teachers of Mathematics.

Brophy, J. E. (1983). Research on the self-fulfilling prophecy and teacher expectations. *Journal of Educational Psychology, 75*(5), 631–661.

Brophy, J. E. (1991). Conclusion to advances in research on teaching, Vol 11: Teachers' knowledge of subject matter as it relates to teaching practice. In J. E. Brophy (Ed.), *Advances in research on teaching: Teachers' subject-matter knowledge and classroom instruction* (Vol. 2, pp. 347–362). Greenwich CT: JAI Press.

Brown, M. (1999). Is more whole class teaching the answer? *Mathematics Teaching, 169*, 5–7.

Burkhardt, H., Fraser, R., & Ridgway, J. (1990). The dynamics of curriculum change. In I. Wirszup & R. Streit (Eds.), *Developments in school mathematics around the world* (Vol. 2, pp. 3–30). Reston, VA: National Council of Teachers of Mathematics.

Campbell, P. F., Rowan, T. E., & Suarez, A. (1998). What criteria for student-invented algorithms? In L. J. Morrow & M. J. Kenney (Eds.), *The teaching and learning of algorithms in school mathematics* (pp. 49–55). Reston, VA: National Council of Teachers of Mathematics.

Carpenter, T. P., Fennema, E., Franke, M. L., Levi, L., & Empson, S. B. (1999). *Children's mathematics: Cognitively guided instruction*. Portsmouth, NH: Heinemann.

Carpenter, T. P., Kepner, H., Corbitt, M. K., Lindquist, M. M., & Reys, R. E. (1980). Results and implications of the second NAEP mathematics assessments: Elementary school. *Arithmetic Teacher, 2*(8), 10–13.

Chick, H., Baker, M., Pham, T., & Cheng, H. (2006). Aspects of teachers' pedagogical content knowledge for decimals. In J. Novotná, H. Moraová, M. Krátká, & N. Stehlíková (Eds.), *Mathematics in the centre* (Proceedings of the 30th Conference of the International Group of Psychology of Mathematics Education, Vol. 2, pp. 297–304). Prague: PME.

Clarke, B. A., Clarke, D. M., & Sullivan, P. (1996). The mathematics teacher and curriculum development. In A. J. Bishop (Ed.), *International handbook of mathematics education* (Vol. 2, pp. 1211–1238). Dordrecht, the Netherlands: Kluwer Academic Publishers.

Clarke, D. J. (1989). *Assessment alternatives in mathematics* (part of the Mathematics Curriculum and Teaching Program Professional Development Package). Carlton, Victoria, Australia: Curriculum Corporation.

Clarke, D. M. (1994). Ten key principles from research for the professional development of mathematics teachers. In D. B. Aichele & A. F. Croxford (Eds.), *Professional development for teachers of mathematics*. (pp. 37–48). Reston, VA: National Council of Teachers of Mathematics.

Clarke, D. M. (1997). The changing role of the mathematics teacher. *Journal for Research in Mathematics Education, 28*, 278–308.

Clarke, D. M. (2006). Fractions as division: The forgotten notion? *Australian Primary Mathematics Classroom, 11*(3), 4–10.

Clarke, D. M., Cheeseman, J., Gervasoni, A., Gronn, D., Horne, M., McDonough, A., Montgomery, P. & Roche, A., Sullivan, P., Clarke, B. A., & Rowley, G. (2002). *Early numeracy research project final report*. Melbourne, Australia: Mathematics Teaching and Learning Centre, Australian Catholic University.

Clarke, D. M., Sukenik, M., Roche, A., Mitchell, A. (2006). Asssessing student understanding of fractions using task-based interviews. In J. Novotná, H. Moraová, M. Krátká, & N. Stehlková (Eds.), *Proceedings of the 30th Conference of the International Group for the Psychology of Mathematics Education* (Vol. 2, pp. 337–344). Charles University in Prague, Czech Republic:

Clements, D. H. (2007). Curriculum research: Towards a framework for research-based curricula. *Journal for Research in Mathematics Education, 38*, 35–70.

Cooney, T. J. (1994). Research and teacher education: In search of common ground. *Journal for Research in Mathematics Education, 25*, 608–636.

Desforges, C., & Cockburn, A. (1987). *Understanding the mathematics teacher: A study of practice in first schools*. London: Falmer.

Elmore, R. F. (2002). *Bridging the gap between standards and achievement: The imperative for professional development in education*. Washington, DC: Albert Shanker Institute.

Fennema, E., & Romberg, T. A. (1999). *Mathematics classrooms that promote understanding*. Mahwah, NJ: Lawrence Erlbaum Associates.

Freudenthal, H. (1975). *Mathematics as an educational task*. Dordrecht, the Netherlands: Reidel.

Gehrke, N. K., Knapp, M. S., & Sirotnik, K. A. (1992). In search of school curriculum. *Review of Research in Education, 18*, 51–110.

Hargreaves, A. (1994). *Changing teachers, changing times: Teachers' work and culture in the postmodern age*. London: Cassell.

Hawley, W. D., & Valli, L. (1999). The essentials of effective professional development: A new consensus. In L. Darling-Hammond & G. Sykes (Eds.), *Teaching as the learning profession: Handbook of policy and practice* (pp. 127–150). San Francisco, CA: Jossey-Bass.

Hiebert, J., Carpenter, T. P., Fennema, E., Fuson, K. C., Wearne, D., Murray, H., Olivier, A., & Human, P. (1997). *Making sense: Teaching and learning mathematics with understanding*. Portsmouth, NH: Heinemann.

Hill, H. C., Rowan, B., & Ball, D. L. (2005). Effects of teachers' mathematical knowledge for teaching on student achievement. *American Educational Research Journal, 42*(2), 371–406.

Hirsch, C. R. (2007). Curriculum materials matter. In C. R. Hirsch (Ed.), *Perspectives on the design and development of school mathematics curricula* (pp. 1–8). Reston, VA: National Council of Teachers of Mathematics.

Howson, G., & Wilson, B. (1986). *School mathematics in the 1990s*. Cambridge: Cambridge University Press.

Kieren, T. (1976). On the mathematical, cognitive and instructional foundations of the rational numbers. In R. A. Lesh (Ed.), *Number and measurement: Papers from a research workshop* (pp. 101–144). Athens, GA: ERIC/SMEAC.

Lamon, S. J. (2006). *Teaching fractions and ratios for understanding: Essential content knowledge and instructional strategies for teachers* (2nd edition). Mahwah, NJ: Lawrence Erlbaum.

Loucks-Horsley, S., Love, N., Stiles, K. E., Mundry S., & Hewson, P. W. (2003). *Designing professional development for teachers of science and mathematics* (2nd edition). Thousand Oaks, CA: Corwin Press.

McDonough, A., & Clarke, D. (2003). Describing the practice of effective teachers of mathematics in the early years. In N. A. Pateman, B. J. Dougherty, & J. Zilliox (Eds.), *Proceedings of the 27th Conference of the International Group for the Psychology of Mathematics Education* (Vol. 3, pp. 261–268). Honolulu, HI: College of Education, University of Hawaii.

National Council for the Teachers of Mathematics (1989). *Curriculum and evaluation standards for school mathematics.* Reston, VA: Author.

Phelps, R. (2000). Trends in large-scale testing outside the United States. *Educational Measurement: Issues and Practice, 19*(1), 11–21.

Robitaille, D. F., Schmidt, W. H., Raizen, S., McKnight, C., Britton, E., & Nicol, C. (1993). *Curriculum frameworks for mathematics and science* (TIMSS Monograph No. 1). Vancouver: Pacific International Press.

Shulman, L. S. (1986). Those who understand: Knowledge growth in teaching. *Educational Researcher, 15*, 4–14.

Shulman, L. (1987). Knowledge and teaching: Foundations of the reform. *Harvard Educational Review, 57*(1), 1–22.

Skemp, R. R. (1976). Relational and instrumental understanding. *Mathematics Teaching, 77*, 20–26.

Sowder, J. T. (2007). The mathematics education and development of teachers. In F. K. Lester, Jr. (Ed.), *Second handbook on research on mathematics teaching and learning* (Vol. 1, pp. 157–224). Charlotte, NC: Information Age Publishing & National Council of Teachers of Mathematics.

Thompson, A. G. (1992). Teachers' beliefs and conceptions: A synthesis of the research. In D. A. Grouws (Ed.), *Handbook of research on mathematics teaching and learning* (pp. 127–146). New York: Macmillan.

Watson, A., & Mason, J. (2005). Mathematics as a constructive activity: Learners generating examples. Mahwah, NJ: Lawrence Erlbaum Associates.

Wilson, B. J. (1992). Mathematics education in Africa. In R. Morris & M. S. Arora (Eds.), *Studies in mathematics education* (pp. 125–147). Paris: UNESCO.

Wilson, L. D. (2007). High stakes testing in mathematics. In F. K. Lester, Jr. (Ed.), *Second handbook on research on mathematics teaching and learning* (Vol. 2, pp. 1099–1110). Charlotte, NC: Information Age Publishing & National Council of Teachers of Mathematics.

Doug Clarke
Faculty of Education
Australian Catholic University, Australia

ULLA RUNESSON

7. LEARNING TO DESIGN FOR LEARNING

The Potential of Learning Study to Enhance Teachers' and Students' Learning

The aim is to present an approach – learning study-for teacher cooperation in teaching and learning that has been shown to be a promising way to enhance teachers' learning about students' learning of a particular subject matter. A learning study is a hybrid of the Japanese lesson study model and design experiment. The teachers learn an inquiry approach to their teaching in which they systematically plan, enact and evaluate teaching and learning and are guided by some theoretical principles. A learning study centers on the object of learning and emphasises the learning problems the students have. In this paper I describe how a group of elementary teachers and their students learn about pre-algebra from a learning study. It is demonstrated that the teachers learned what was critical for students' learning the particular object of learning; how to write an algebraic expression for a given example and vice versa. These insights enabled the teachers to revise the lesson design in a way that enhanced students' learning. In that respect, the students' contribution, in terms of opening variation in the lesson, played a significant role. It is suggested that a parallel learning process of teachers and students' learning occurred and that the richness of 'meaning' of an algebraic expression was constituted and developed.

INTRODUCTION

How can teachers improve their knowledge about their students' learning obstacles? How can they learn about how their teaching affects students' learning and whether there was possibilities to learn that which was intended in the mathematics lesson? In this chapter I suggest an approach for teacher cooperation in teaching and learning that has been shown to be a promising way to enhance teachers' learning about students' learning of a particular subject matter. This approach – the *learning study* – centres on the object of learning, is grounded in a theoretical framework, and emphasises the learning problems of the students. It is a systematic planning process of reflection and revision, and entails follow-up and feedback. I describe the rationale behind the approach, the cyclic process the approach encompasses and provide an example from a learning study about the teaching of pre-algebra at elementary level.

P. Sullivan and T. Wood (eds.), *Knowledge and Beliefs in Mathematics Teaching and Teaching Development, 153–172.*

LEARNING STUDY – AN APPROACH FOR ENHANCING STUDENT LEARNING

In a learning study student learning is central. It has been reported that when teachers learn about students' understanding, their difficulties and strategies used, they can change their teaching in a way that facilitates students' learning (Carpenter, Fennema, Peterson, & Carey, 1988). In a learning study teachers try to learn from what takes place in the classroom. Hiebert, Morris, Berk, and Jansen (2007) have pointed out the potential of teachers learning from their teaching, and have proposed a framework for a teacher learning. However it should be noted, a learning study is more than reflective practice or cooperative effort among teachers. It is more than learning about students' strategies in mathematics. It is a systematic iterative process based on a theoretical framework for learning. It is not the lesson *per se* that is in focus, but rather the students' possibilities for learning during the lesson.

The Guiding Theoretical Framework

In a learning study the teachers try to develop their understanding of what it means to know something in mathematics, for instance, being able to do arithmetic calculations, operate with negative numbers, and so on. It involves asking questions about the object of learning. If you know what knowledge, understanding or skill you want the learners to develop and what that ability really implies, you are more likely to be able to help your students to learn. This includes taking the learners' perspective as well, by asking: What does it take to learn something from the point of view of the learners?

In a learning study a particular theoretical framework-variation theory (Bowden & Marton, 1998; Marton & Booth, 1997; Marton & Tsui, 2004) is used as a guiding principle. Nuthall (2004) is one of several (e.g., Floden, 2001; Levin & O'Donnell, 1999) who have pointed out the necessity for teachers to have a theory as an explanatory framework for understanding how their actions in the classroom affect students' learning.

> Teachers need an explanatory theory of the teaching-learning relationship that meets these requirements in order to plan, carry out, and evaluate their daily activities effectively and efficiently. (p. 277)

What kind of framework could help us to better understand the relation between what is taught and learned? It should not explain learning as an effect of teaching but should be powerful enough to help the teacher to know what to look for and interpret what they see when monitoring student learning. Nuthall (2004) advocates a theory which can help teachers to design learning.

The theoretical framework on which a learning study is based seems to be powerful and appropriate in that respect. Variation theory has been shown to have potential to explain how learning is afforded in the classroom and how this is reflected in students' learning (Marton & Morris, 2002). Variation theory is mainly a framework for learning, but has been used as an analytical tool when studying teaching and designing for learning (Lo, Chik, & Pang, 2006). A series of studies within this framework has addressed issues such as what matters for learning, what is possible to learn, what is learned in a specific learning situation, and how differences in learning outcomes can be understood in the light of the lesson. Since what is learned is the primary focus in a learning study, variation theory is particularly useful. From a variation theory perspective, learning always has an object: there is always something learned.

But why mind about the object of learning? Brentano (1838–1917), a prominent figure within phenomenology, stated that there is "no hearing without something heard, no believing without something believed, no striving without something striven" (Spiegelberg, 1982 p. 37). In the same way, you can say that there is no learning without something learned. When teachers and learners interact in the learning situation, they interact about something. Embedded in the activity and interaction in a classroom there is always an object that may be learned. So, apart from describing the teaching–learning process and the interaction between the teacher and the learners, it is also possible to suggest what may be learned about the specific topic taught (Runesson, 2005). Hence, classroom interaction affords an object of learning, in terms of a potential for learning. Therefore, it is significant to keep in mind what that is.

The object of learning is not equivalent to learning objectives. The object of learning refers to a certain capability that the students are expected to develop during a lesson, or during a limited sequence of lessons (Marton & Pang, 2006). Capabilities are not confined to theory or concepts only. They can also be associated with skills, values or attitudes. Every capability has two aspects, one general and one specific. The general aspect refers to the nature of the capability, for instance, 'understanding', 'calculating', 'explaining' or 'describing'. The specific aspect refers to what is acted upon, hence the subject matter; for instance, multiplication with two digits, linear equations or Pythagoras' theorem. To be able to afford vital learning possibilities for the learner, it is probably important for a teacher to focus on both aspects. Hence, teachers should be aware not only of what the students are trying to learn, but also of the way the students master that which is learned.

This does not mean that the interaction or the activity is not important itself. The character of the interaction, for instance, students' participation in a classroom discussion, can pave the way for or delimit learning (Emanuelsson & Sahlström, accepted). However, descriptions of activities, particular methods and so on are neutral to the topic taught and learned. Notions such as "student-centred" or "interactivity" do not say anything about what is possible to learn. Learning can be seen as two-fold, that is, it has a how-aspect and a what-aspect. These are two sides of the same coin and can hardly be separated. Next I provide some ideas of variation theory that are relevant for guiding and can help teachers to plan and evaluate their teaching in a more systematic and deliberate way.

Discernment, Variation and Critical Aspect – Central Elements of the Framework

From a variation theory perspective, learning is seen as a process of differentiation, rather than enrichment. This is in line with psychologists like Gibson and Gibson (1955) who pointed to the importance of differentiation when arguing that learning implies that "perception gets richer in differential responses" (p. 35). Thus, seeing learning as differentiation means seeing learning as a matter of being able to discern similarities and differences. From a variation theory perspective, to understand something in a certain way, it is necessary to discern certain necessary aspects simultaneously. For instance, there are probably several features that are necessary to discern to calculate the value of -5-(-3) of which the sign "-" is one. The "-" has different meanings in this expression. So, in line with Gibson and Gibson's line of reasoning, it is necessary to differentiate between "-" as a sign for the subtraction operation and "-" as a sign for the number. From a variation theory perspective the differentiation of the meaning is a *critical aspect* for learning. However, what is critical for learning to calculate -5- (-3) can probably not be prescribed on a general level, or be derived from mathematical theory alone. Knowledge about the object of learning always includes the learner; what s/he brings into the learning situation in terms of previous experiences and how s/he understands the object to be learned. The way something is perceived, understood or experienced is due to what extent the critical aspects are discerned by the learner. A student's failure or lack of understanding can be understood in the light of un-discerned aspects; for instance the learner does not differentiate the double meaning of the - sign in the operation above. So, the *discernment* of critical aspects is essential for learning.

Furthermore Gibson and Gibson argue that learning to differentiate objects is a matter of discovering and seeing differences between the objects and identifying their properties. Knowing what something is implies knowing what it is not. Seeing something (a situation, a concept, a principle and so on) in the light of its contrast brings out the characteristic properties of the object in question. Earlier educationalists have also emphasised the importance of contrast and variation. For instance, Maria Montessori stressed that the training of the senses is done by means of systematic variation in different sense modalities against a background that is invariant (Marton & Signert, 2005). A similar rationale was proposed by Dienes (1960) in his theory of mathematics learning. A concept must be taught by varying essential features of the concept, he argues. The same idea is found in Chinese mathematics education. The "bian shi" method is based on variation and invariance. When a pattern of variation and invariance is created, learners are given the opportunity to discern various aspects of, for instance, a concept.

The idea of *variation and invariance* is fundamental to variation theory. Discernment is a function of an experienced variation. That is, we attend to or discern certain aspects of a situation if they stand out. "Things tend to stand out when they change or vary against a stable background or when something stays unchanged against a changing background" (Lo et al., 2006, p. 19). For instance, if the same example (invariant) is solved by different methods (variant) it is likely that the learner will notice that the method could be different for the same example, thus the method will be discerned. However, if the case is the opposite (the same method is used to solve different examples) it is not opened up for possibilities to discern an alternative method. Or, in other words, the possibility to use different methods is not promoted.

Studying a learning situation from the point of view of what varies and what is "invariant" is an efficient way to describe the promoted space of learning. It is possible to study classrooms where the same topic is taught and the same teaching arrangements are used to identify differences in learning possibilities. To give an example, Runesson and Mok, (2005) studied how fractions were taught in two different classrooms. The aim was to describe and analyse how this topic was handled and what was possible to learn, that is the focus was on the enacted object of learning. In both classrooms the topic taught was comparison of fractions with different denominators. By using manipulatives, as well as applying the method of amplification, the students were able to learn, for instance, that $5/8>1/2$. However, in addition to this, in one of the classrooms, the students worked with the task, *"Is it possible for 5/8 to be smaller than 1/2? Discuss with classmates and explain the results in words and diagrams"*. This task was critical for what was possible to learn about the nature of fractions. After having established the fact that $5/8>1/2$, the learners were immediately confronted with the opposite idea, that it could be the reverse (if we imagine that we are talking about 1/2 of a big family pizza and 5/8 of a small pizza). Contrasting one situation where $5/8>1/2$ with another where $5/8<1/2$ created an opportunity to discern a critical aspect of fractions; that the size of the fractional part is relative; it is the related to the whole. It was then possible to simultaneously discern the part-part (i.e., 1/2 and 5/8) and the whole-whole relation (small and big pizza) at the same time. This did not happen in the other classroom. So, in one classroom the students were given the opportunity to gain a more complex or broad understanding (in terms of being able to discern more aspects) of the object of learning than was the case in the other.

It has been concluded that different patterns of variation, in different combinations and structures, create different learning opportunities. Do such subtle differences in how the object of learning is handled matter? Do they have an impact on students' learning outcomes? I do not claim that the handling of the content is the one and only factor that is significant for learning. Neither do I assert that there is a one-to-one correspondence between teaching and learning in terms of 'what is possible to learn is the thing learned'. A classroom situation is complex and, although one aspect may remain invariant in the lesson, the students themselves can open dimensions of variation on their own, or a dimension may be opened but still not discerned. What can be said is whether it is possible or not to discern certain critical feature. However, differences in the pattern of variation and invariance are reflected in student learning outcomes immediately after the lesson, but can also be noted in the long run. For instance, Holmqvist, Gustavsson, and Wernberg (2007) have demonstrated that the different nature of the enacted object of learning was observable even four weeks after the (single) lesson. It seems as if a particular pattern of variation and invariance generated new learning long after the initial learning situation itself.

LEARNING STUDY – AS A SYSTEMATIC AND ITERATIVE ENQUIRY INTO THE PROCESS OF TEACHING AND LEARNING

In the two classrooms described by Runesson and Mok (2005) one can assume that the two teachers handled the topic differently because of variation in their awareness of this particular aspect and its importance for a more advanced understanding of fractions differed. If teachers differ to the extent they are aware of critical aspects of the object of learning, would it not be possible to collectively investigate what the critical aspects are? Furthermore, if a pattern of variation and invariance is possible to identify in every lesson, would it not be possible to make teachers more aware of how they could use variation in a more thoughtful and systematic way to bring out significant features and thus promote possibilities for student learning? These questions were the point of departure for initiating a joint research project on a model of learning that first started in Hong Kong in 2000 and was taken up a couple of years later in Sweden. This initiative was named the learning study and was inspired by design experiment (e.g., Cobb, Confrey, diSessa, Lehrer, & Schauble., 2003) and the tradition of Japanese and Chinese teachers, who do in-depth and systematic analysis of their lessons (Ma, 1999; Stigler & Hiebert, 1999; Yoshida, 1999).

A learning study has points of similarity to a lesson study, particularly in the collective inquiry into how the intended goals are manifested in the 'research lesson'. A learning study is a cyclic process of planning and revision (see Figure 1).

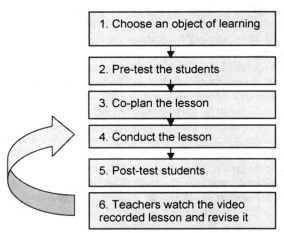

Figure 1. The learning study cycle.

The process starts with a group of teachers choosing and deciding about the object of learning – a capability or a value to be developed. (1) With the background of their previous teaching experiences and information from research findings, they design a pre-test (a written test or an interview) and give it to the students. (2) The teachers can study the results of the test to find out about the particular learning difficulties their students may have. This may lead to reconsideration or a delimitation of the object of learning. (3) They plan and one of the teachers in the group implements the research lesson. (4) The lesson is documented by video recording and after the lessons a post-test is given to the students. (5) The teachers meet again in a post-lesson session to analyse the recorded lesson and the results of the post-test. They reflect on students' performances and the enactments of the lesson. (6) If needed, they revise the lesson plan and another teacher implements this in her class (new students!). This continues in a number of cycles until all teachers in the group have conducted one lesson.

In the next section I illustrate the learning study process with an example from a learning study in a Swedish comprehensive school. My aim is to offer a deeper and more elaborated description of the learning study process, its stepwise and systematic character and the potential for teachers' learning in and from their practice.

LEARNING ABOUT TEACHING AND LEARNING ALGEBRAIC REPRESENTATIONS

Usually a learning study group consists of a group of three to five teachers teaching students of the same age. In the study reported here three teachers and their three mixed age-group classes (11-12 years old) were involved. The teachers' teaching experience varied; one of them had worked for more than 30 years as a teacher (T1), the other two had worked for 5 and 10 years, respectively. Since this learning study was included in a research project (Kullberg & Runesson, 2006) a researcher from the university worked together with the group as a tutor. This was the third learning study with this group of teachers. They were familiar with the principles of the guiding theoretical framework, both from their previous experience of learning study and from a one day expert seminar about variation theory and its application in the research of teaching and learning.

The analysis here draws on data from audio-recordings from the pre- and post sessions with the teachers, video recordings from the lesson and test-results from the pre- and post tests. The focus is on the teachers' reflections and comments on the recorded lesson, what they noticed and learned about how the content was handled, the students' reactions, and how this affected the planning and revision of the lesson as well as the manifested lesson.

First Planning Step: Choose an Object of Learning

The teachers met twice in sessions lasting 90 minutes to decide about the object of learning. Initially a particular topic, which the students found problematic to learn and the teachers thought was difficult to teach was identified. Since the duration of the research was restricted to one, or sometimes, two lessons they chose a specific capability as the object of learning. In this case the teachers had previously experienced that students often failed on particular test items in the Swedish National Assessment in Mathematics on converting algebraic expressions to sentences describing relationships, so they decided to do something about this. The students in question had not been taught about variables and letters as symbols in mathematics before, so it would be the first time they encountered this topic.

Much time of the pre-lesson sessions were devoted to constructing a pre-test. Inspiration came from literature, but mainly from their own experience. In learning study the pre-test serves two aims. It should 'scan' what the students know about the particular topic and related concepts, but also make it possible find out what the learning obstacles may be.

Second Planning Step: Pre-test the Students

In order to ascertain students' prior understanding it is advisable to combine the pre-test with a student interview; however, this was not the case in this study. In order to further define the object of learning and what specific capabilities to develop, the results on the pre-tests were analysed in a qualitative way, that is, it was not the total test-score that was of interest, but the different questions and how the students responded to these.

Third Planning Step: Co-planning of the Lesson

What was revealed from the test-results led to a shaping of the object of learning chosen; they wanted the students to be able to write algebraic expressions for a given example of an additive relation, that is, to find a general formula for an example with only one numerical value given (e.g., a chocolate bar costs 5 kronor more than a toffee) and vice versa. In the planning of the lesson, as well as in other steps of the study, the role of the researcher was merely supportive; for instance, she provided the group with literature or brought in ideas from her experience as a researcher. The researcher encouraged the teachers to come up with ideas of their own and try them. So, the way the lessons in this study were designed and enacted were principally based on the teachers' own ideas.

When planning the first lesson the teachers discussed possible explanations to students' failures on the pre-test. For example, they assumed that "X and Y are frightening" to the students, and "letters" would be less confusing if the notations were closer to the example, thus choosing a letter close to the variable would facilitate the understanding. For instance, Daddy's age would be represented by the letter D. They decided to start with saying. "Daddy is three years older than Mummy", after that writing "Daddy's age - Mummy's age = 3 years" and next, shorten this into "D-M=3". They planned for different patterns of variation; for instance, that the example (and thus the variable, for example, age, price, weight) must vary just as the positions of the symbols.

When planning the first lesson they also decided about the post-lesson test. A new assignment (compared to the pre-test) was chosen; the students were asked to find *different* expressions to *the same* example. At this point of the study, the teachers had met five times in total. Now the first lesson was ready to be conducted.

First Cycle: Conducting Lesson 1

The lesson shifted between plenary sessions (whole class) and student pairs with the focus on how the same example could be represented by different equations. The task was to find equations for the given example, or vice versa. In the discussion about the example (a chocolate bar costs 5 kronor more than a toffee), the following was written on the board:

$$C - T = 5$$
$$C - 5 = T$$
$$T + 5 = C$$
$$C = T + 5$$
$$T = C - 5$$
$$C - 5 = T$$
$$5 + T = C$$

The equations are all permutations of T +5=C, that is, the position of the symbols, and thus the operation, changes. The letters chosen to represent the variables are the initials for (the price of) a chocolate bar (C) and toffee (T). In all the examples taken in the lesson, no other letters but the above initials were used. The lesson was conducted in accordance with the plan. It was clearly demonstrated that the same example could be represented by different algebraic expression and that the variable is represented by a letter.

First Cycle: Post-session Meeting after Lesson 1

After being informed about the learning outcomes of the post-test, the teachers watched the video-recorded lesson and commented upon it. The teachers had conducted two learning study cycles before, so they were familiar with focusing on how the content was taught and the students' reactions, rather than on organisation and individual teacher behavior. This could be illustrated by the following example. Henry, one of the teachers (T2), commented on the learners' understanding when he said:

T2: The task was not 'write different formulas ...', still they do so. They turn the letters around. Hm ... interesting!

The teachers were satisfied with that the lesson was in accordance with what they had planned; that the same equation could be represented differently. However, when watching the recorded lesson 1, they noticed the way the teacher commented on the examples given to a specific equation by the students. She repeatedly said: "Does that [example] correspond with the formula?" and "Is it correct?" even though all the examples were correct. Teacher 1 (i.e., the teacher who had conducted the lesson) became aware of that and said:

T1: Here [in this situation] I could have given an example that was incorrect. Yes, I could have come up with that, one that was wrong!

Tutor: Yes, writing an incorrect one!

T1 Yes, I could. They should have had [an incorrect] one. That's why they failed on that [test-] item [in the post-test]. That's why they haven't got any further.

T2: Yes, when going through the first example you could have chosen…

T1 …I could had given the example 'I+7=9 [and asked] is that correct'?

Some minutes later Teacher 2 said:

T2: If you had taken an incorrect one there…!

T1: I think that is the point. You see they turn…they do that for this one [example] too, they [do] turn C+T=4 and T-4=C. This in is line with what I can see on the post-test.

T2: Wow. That's great!

They noticed that the expression C+T=4 is varied in the lesson and T1 also saw how that corresponds to the outcomes of the post-test, and what the students have learned. One of the tasks was to write *different expressions* for the example 'an apple and a cucumber cost 15 crowns'. This was in line with the intension of the lesson, with the pattern of variation and invariance that was planned and how the lesson was enacted. This is also what the students learned; those who solved the task correctly *all* used the initial letter of the variable but changed the positions (see Table 1).

When T1 observed herself teaching she discerned an alternative; that things could have been done differently and how she could have been able to increase the scope for learning. She commented on the question "Is it correct?" and probably realised that the question could be the key to the opening of another pattern of variation: "I could have given an example that was incorrect. Yes, I could have come up with that, one that was wrong!" thus, that it would have been possible to show an expression that did not represent the example. The idea of coming up with an incorrect expression was caught by the rest of the group. T2 said: "If you had taken an incorrect one there…!" This insight was new to them; that a variation of correct and incorrect expressions could be a potential for learning. Being familiar with variation theory, which states that that which is varied is likely to be discerned, they realised that in order to see what a correct expression was, one needed to know what was incorrect. So contrasting correct with incorrect expressions was added to the planning of lesson two.

The teachers also reflected upon whether the lesson opened up possibilities for understanding of the concepts of variable and constant. For instance, was it possible for the students to understand that the difference in age between two persons is the same independent of their age? They decided to bring up the idea of variable (i.e., something that varies) by substituting and varying values for the letters. In this way, they anticipated that the learners would learn that the relation between the variables is the same independent of the values taken.

Second Cycle: Conducting Lesson 2

To the original lesson plan some more dimensions of variation were added. So, besides varying the algebraic representation for the same example, it was planned to *contrast correct and incorrect expressions* and to substitute the letters with values (i.e., to keep the constant "in-variant" and varying the values of the variables). The lesson was similar to lesson 1 with respect to the shift between plenary and pair work and conducted in accordance with the planning. Just like in lesson 1 the tasks given were to find formulas for different examples, and vice versa (the example was "invariant" and the representation varied). For the example *"My cousin John is 10 years younger than me, Henry"*, permutations of J+10=H were suggested. Just as was planned, when this and similar examples were given, the teacher himself suggested an incorrect equation (e.g., H+10=J). In accordance with the planning, it was demonstrated that the letters could be substituted by numerical values. The teacher showed that no matter what values are used, all variations of J+10=H correspond to the example, (except for H+10=J). It could be noted that one of the students commented on this by saying: "it could correspond to another example". The teacher agreed, but without following up on this. Instead, he continued to explain that no matter how old Henry and John are the difference in age will be the same. So the students were clearly told that the different formulas correspond to the same example independent of the values of H and J. This aspect, the idea of a variable, was never brought out in lesson 1. Thus, in that respect the promoted space of learning was more complex than in lesson 1.

The remark from the student saying that H+10=J could correspond to another example is one example of a noticeable feature of lesson 2; that the students opened up for alternative interpretations and variation. Another example of this is when *"My cousin John is 10 years younger than me, Henry"* was written on the board and the teacher asked: "What do we use when we are doing maths?" Apart from replies like "numbers", "minus", "ruler and rubber", one student answered: "X" and "Y". This was probably not anticipated by the teacher and he did not comment on this at all. The teacher reacted in the same way some minutes later when he asked for a formula for the example and another student suggested:

S: You can write X minus ten equals Y!

T2 writes X-10=Y on the board.

T2: Explain. How did you work this out?

S: Mm, X that's you [your age] minus ten years and Y is John.

This suggestion from the student reveals a new aspect of the object of learning; that there are other possible ways of representing the variable than using the initials. However, the teacher does not pick this up at all. Instead he says:

T: Okay, So you changed our names to X and Y instead. Is it possible to change my name to something else besides X and Y? Elsie?

E: Er,..to letters.

T2: Yeah, what letters?

E: A or B, C.

T2: Yes, what else?

S?: (inaudible)

T2: Yes. Fiona?

F: If you knew the age you could take John's age plus yours equals ten.

The teacher agrees, but wants to wait a while with that. He wants them to come up with letters. He says:

T2: Right. If we knew how old they are. All right we'll get to that later on, I think. Can you use anything else? William has used X and Y and then Elsie and Mimmi said other things too. Could we use other letters? What letters? Roger?

Roger: A and B, maybe?

T2: Oh yes, we could use that. Albert?

Albert: H and J.

T2: Why?

Albert: Because your names are Henry and John.

T2: Aha! Yes we could actually use those, H and J, because they are symbols for Henry and John. Instead of writing the names out fully, you can write H and J instead.

This excerpt shows that the students suggest other letters than the initials. Although the teacher does not disapprove of using A and B or X and Y, my interpretation is that he gives prominence to the letters H and J. His comment: "Aha! Yes we could actually use that" is said in an encouraging way, and supports my interpretation. It is likely that he prefers the initials (H and J), which can be seen in the following also. One student suggested:

S: Circle plus 10 equals square.

T2: Ah. So instead of J and H you put in square and circle. Okay. We could have that, but let's stick to H and J so you all can follow me. We'll work with H and J, these abbreviations of John and Henry.

He accepts the suggestion "square and circle", but points out that H and J are the symbols he wants them to use and permutations of J+10=H are written on the board.

From this it appears that the students want to vary the symbols, whereas the teacher would like to see a variation of J+10=H. That is, he keeps the letters invariant but varies the algebraic expression. Probably he had a particular intention with that, since he later, after having substituted numbers for the letters in several expressions (J+10=H, H-10=J and so on), draws the students' attention to the formula H+10=J. This is supposed to be a counter-example, that is an incorrect expression for the example given, actually implying that "Henry is 10 years older than John", just as the teachers' group had planned.

Several similar examples were talked about in the lesson. Again the students suggested other letters than the initials. Although these were accepted by the teacher; the teacher himself constantly used the initials to represent the variables. Furthermore, for each and every example, he gave a counter-example, hence an incorrect formula, and asked if it correspond to the example; "Is it correct?" So, again we can see that the pattern of variation put forward by the teacher is different from the one put forward by the students. The teacher varies the algebraic J+10=H (correct as well as incorrect permutations) while keeping the letters invariant. The students varies the letters used (e.g., Y and X), *and* the algebraic expression (however, they never gave an incorrect expression). It was the students who suggested other letters than initials of the variable in the algebraic expressions-not the teacher. The teacher presented one pattern of variation and invariance, the students another. You could say that the students in the lesson opened a dimension of variation which was not planned by the teachers.

Second Cycle: Post-lesson Session 2

What features of the lesson caught the teachers' attention in the post-lesson session when watching the recorded lesson and what did they learn from lesson 2? When watching the recorded lesson the tutor noticed that one of the students suggested using X and Y:

Tutor: Nice comments from your students. It doesn't necessarily have to be H and J.

T2: That one should have been taken up!

When the tutor commented on this, teacher 2 (who conducted the lesson) immediately realised that the variation suggested by the students - using X and Y as letters for the variable - could have been useful and that he could have elicited that more. So, when observing the recorded lesson, the teachers became aware of the possibility of using other letters or other symbols as well. For instance, T1 expressed her awareness by asking:

T1: Did you write X and Y there?

T2: No, I didn't. I wanted to get to the abbreviations H and J. Therefore I didn't want to confuse them with X and Y. I didn't want to use that.

T2 confirms that he did not support the suggestion "X and Y"; he wanted to keep to the initials. He also explains why. When "circle and square" were suggested by one of the students in the lesson recording, T2 commented on this by saying: "I was guided by the manuscript". My interpretation is that since the group had much focus on contrasting correct and incorrect representations in the planning, in the lesson, the teacher was concentrated on that and not "tuned" to the opening of variation of symbols. So, it was not until the post-lesson session that T2 realised that the students' suggestion of using other symbols than the initials could create potential for learning. My interpretation is that, by carefully analysing the lesson and being exposed to a variation (the letters used could be others than the initials), he (and his colleagues who had planned the lesson together) became aware that by restricting the symbols to the initials of the variable, one significant aspect of the object of learning-how you choose symbols for the variables is arbitrary-was never brought out. This could be traced to the early planning sessions in the learning study. To, facilitate learning and not confuse the students with X and Y which they assumed were "frightening" and strange to the students, they decided to use letters as abbreviation.

That the teacher in the lesson was not tuned to the variation opened by the student may be an effect of the well planned lesson (cf., "I was guided by the manuscript" above). That is, T2 was focused on coming up with an algebraic expression that was incorrect, specifically a counter example (which was decided in the first post-lesson session), so that he was inhibited from giving his whole attention to what the students were coming up with. However, a new insight came from carefully watching the lesson recording. But above all, when they were exposed to a dimension of variation revealed by the students in the lesson, they experienced a critical aspect of the object of learning: that the symbols representing the variable are arbitrary, was never presented in the lesson. This pattern of variation created by the students afforded a learning space for the teachers in the post-lesson session.

This insight prompted them to revise the plan for the third lesson. They decided to deliberately introduce a variation of symbols. If the students did not come up with other letters and symbols than the initials, the teacher herself (T3) would take the initiative. Thus to the previous dimensions of variation proposed by the teachers yet another one was added. They also planned a change of assignments; to match each example with different (both correct and incorrect) expressions.

Third Cycle: Conducting Lesson 3

Initially two examples were chosen, *"My friend Anna is 5 years older than me, Joan"* and *"A chocolate bar costs five crowns more than a toffee"*. Besides varying the positions of the variables (and thus the operation), for instance, $T+5=C$, they also varied the symbols used. So the letters T and C (shorthand for toffee and chocolate) as variables in the expression were written on the board *simultaneously* with expressions with X and Y *and* other symbols (e.g., ⬚ and ⬚). Next, just as was planned, the assignment to match an example and different algebraic expressions was worked on in student pairs. The example given was the following: *"Martha has five more marbles than Colin"*. The expressions given were mixed; some of them corresponded to the example, others did not. After the pair work, when this example was discussed in the whole class, something happened that was probably not foreseen by the teacher. When the teacher asked if $M=C-8$ was a correct way to represent the example, most of the students said it was incorrect. Willie objected to this; the equation could represent the example provided that the number of marbles Martha had was represented by C, and Colin's marbles by M, he argued.

W: It could correspond if C were Martha and M were Colin.

T3: Listen to Willie.

Willie's suggestion was noticed by the teacher, who called for the students' attention. Several students disagreed. The students who had taken for granted that if a letter (other than X and Y) was chosen to represent the variable, it had to be the initial, probably found this idea provocative.

S1: No, it cannot, since Martha is M.

S2: Right. It cannot.

S3: That's not correct.

T3: But you could just as well write 'banana' here, or 'strawberries'. So $M=C-5$, is correct if $M=C$ and $C=M$.

Hence, besides opening the planned variation of the position of the symbols (and thus the operation) and the symbols (abbreviations/X and Y/⬚ and ⬚), it was demonstrated that it was possible to vary the symbols chosen by swapping them. My interpretation is that this pattern of variation and invariance brought out the arbitrariness of the symbols in an equation even more; it is possible to choose any symbol, provided it is defined.

In lesson 3 a more complex pattern of variation appeared compared to the

167

previous two lessons in the cycle, the potential space of learning was expanded by the opening of more dimensions of variation in lesson 3. This implied that more and critical aspects of the object of learning were revealed in lesson 3 just as lesson 2 was "richer" in that respect compared to lesson 1.

It could be suggested that during the learning study cycle the lesson plan and the enacted lesson developed in terms of critical aspects exposed to the learners. Taking their point of departure in the recorded lessons that is, the way they experienced how the object of learning was handled *and* the students' learning outcomes, the teachers successively became aware of aspects that they anticipated were critical and necessary for student learning and revised the plan accordingly. The awareness was sometimes a result of inputs from the students, who introduced a variation which was not planned by the teacher. For instance, in lesson 2 the students brought up a significant aspect by suggesting a variation of the representation of the variable. As was shown above, Teacher 2 did not pay much attention to that in the lesson. However, when watching the recorded lesson, this variation was experienced by the teachers and made them discern an aspect they had taken for granted. Due to this judgment, the teachers decided to revise the last lesson in the cycle, so this aspect would be elicited.

Teachers' Learning and Student Learning – A Parallel Process

The case described above suggests that it is possible for teachers to learn about the object of learning from their teaching and from the learners. My interpretation is that they successively developed their understanding about learning and teaching how to write algebraic expressions for examples with an additive structure, thus about the object of learning. Initially they learned that it is necessary to demonstrate different representations for the same example. When they planned the first lesson, they assumed that using other letters than the initials would be confusing; however, after lesson 2, when watching the recorded lesson, they realised what effect this assumption had on students learning possibilities, remarkably, by a variation suggested by the students. The new insight affected how the next lessons were planned and implemented. In the same way, they became aware that contrasting correct an incorrect representations would possibly bring out other learning affordances. From having planned and conducted a rather simple pattern of variation, in terms of bringing out few critical aspects in lesson 1, they became more and more aware of, and could discern, additional critical aspects as the cycle progressed. They also managed to implement the plans in a way that made it possible for the learners to discern these aspects. It is clear that the teachers went through a process in which their learning about their students' learning and what it takes to learn about algebraic expressions was developed.

If we take a look at students' learning outcomes of the post-test, we find a parallel process among the learners during the cycle (Kullberg & Runesson, 2006). One of the assignments on the post-test was to find *different* expressions for the example, *"An apple and a cucumber cost 15 kronor"*. The results are shown in Table 1.

Table 1. Percentage (number) of students who changed the positions of the symbols on the post-test

	The same letters, varying position	Varying letters, the same position	Incorrect or no answer
*Lesson 1 (N=23)	87% (20)	0% (0)	13%(3)
Lesson 2 (N=26)	73% (19)	19% (5)	8% (2)
Lesson 3 (N=27)	59% (16)	30% (8)	11% (3)

*NOTE: each lesson was conducted with a different class of students.

From Table 1 it can be seen that the majority in the three classes were able to write two different equations. Only 13%, 8% and 11 %, respectively, failed on this. However, the rate of students who changed the letters was greater after lesson 2 and 3 (19% and 30 %). Hence, it was more common that students, for instance, gave the answer A+C=15 and X+B=15. This was not found in any case after lesson 1. Besides, on the post-test after lesson 3 two students varied both the order and the chosen symbols (e.g., A+C=15 and 15-X=C). Our conclusion is that the post- test to some extent reflects the learning possibilities in the three lessons, where the last lesson afforded a more complex understanding of how to write an algebraic expression for a given example and how to choose symbols representing the variables. In my interpretation, the idea that the representations chosen are arbitrary was brought out in a more clear and distinct way in lesson 3. In this lesson it was pointed out that you could use any representation, but the symbol had to be defined as representing a specific variable. In this case, it is interesting that this condition was brought out by the students. How could that happen? It seems that the more complex pattern of variation presented invited the learners to explore other and more complex variations. Furthermore, this development of learning possibilities was parallel to a learning process among the teachers.

This parallel process is also interesting in that the awareness and the suggestions for variation from the teachers afforded an opening from the students just as if the variation opened up by the teachers invited the students to find other variations themselves. For instance, the more complex pattern of variation that was planned and constituted in lesson 3 seems to have invited the discovery of other critical aspects of the arbitrariness of the symbols on the initiative of one of the learners.

DISCUSSION AND REFLECTIONS

To summarise, in learning study the aim is to enhance student learning, not primarily to organise learning in general, nor implement a new curriculum or teaching arrangements. However, this could be the effect of the learning study, although it is not the point of departure. In a learning study the aim is to help the students to learn something specific. We ask: What are the necessary conditions for learning something and how can these be met in the learning situation? If students do not learn what we expected, we do not seek the answers to their failure in inadequacy of the student; neither do we seek them in the teaching arrangements or methods used. Instead we focus on the students' learning-what their difficulties are-and on how the content must be handled in the lesson in order to overcome the learning obstacles. We try to find out what it takes to know something; what kind of mathematical structure the specific capability has, what aspects of the object of learning are critical and, hence, are necessary to discern in order to learn. Once we think we know about these, we try to draw the students' awareness of them by planning the learning situation so it will open up variation in those particular dimensions.

In a learning study teachers get the opportunity to observe colleagues *teach the same thing.* This is one of the features of a learning study that makes it appropriate to mathematics teacher education. However, we have not been able to introduce learning study in a larger scale in prospective teachers training, but the approach seems to have several advantages in that respect. For instance, the prospective teachers could learn an inquiry approach to their teaching in which they systematically plan, enact and evaluate teaching and learning, guided by some theoretical principles. The theoretical framework does not tell us what the critical aspects are or what to do, but gives an analytical tool to understand learning obstacles from the point of view of the learner and how the object of learning must be enacted in order to overcome these. It could be assumed that learning study offers an opportunity to enhance the (prospective) teacher's subject knowledge as well as the pedagogical content knowledge. In learning study teachers receive immediate feed-back on their interactions with learners. It argued that the most effective place to improve teaching is to do something in the context of the classroom (Stigler & Hiebert, 1999). This is exactly what happens in learning study.

A key question is whether it is possible for teachers to work with learning study on regular basis. In learning study one can go deeply into a specific topic for a long period of time; sometimes for a whole semester. Teachers have competing demands, and operate under time constraints. However, our experience in working with teachers suggests that, by deeply investigating the particular, one can gain knowledge that is of general character also. So in that sense the benefit from a learning study might have effect on teachers' work in general. In learning study the teachers get insights into the nature of powerful instances of teaching and learning. Therefore, it may not be necessary to be engaged in learning studies all the time. One learning study a year or less might be sufficient.

There are other challenges with implementing the learning study approach in regular practice. In learning study one must be open for considering existing practice; thus the approach could be perceived as a threat. For example, a teacher might think, "my existing practice and that which I take-for-granted could be questioned, it may be necessary to combine my ideas with the ideas of my colleagues". Our experiences suggest that the collaborative nature of learning study creates a shared ownership of the lessons. A collective inquiry takes place which results in a collective responsibility for the planned lesson and, foremost, for students' learning (for more on collective teacher inquiry, see Chapters 14, 15, Volume 3).

REFERENCES

Bowden, J., & Marton, F. (1998). *University of learning*. London: Cogan.

Carpenter, T. P., Fennema, E., Peterson, P. L., & Carey, D. A. (1988). Teachers' pedagogical content knowledge of students' problem solving in elementary arithmetic. *Journal for Research in Mathematics Education, 19*, 385–401.

Cobb, P., Confrey, J., diSessa, A., Lehrer, R., & Schauble, L. (2003). Design experiments in educational research. *Educational Researcher, 32*(1), 9–13.

Dienes, Z. P. (1960). *Building up mathematics*. London: Hutchinson.

Emanuelsson, J., & Sahlström, F. (accepted). The price of participation – Teacher control versus student participation in classroom interaction. *Scandinavian Journal of Educational Research*.

Floden, R. E. (Ed.) (2001). *Research on the effects of teaching*. Washington, DC: American Educational Research Association.

Gibson, J. J., & Gibson, E. J. (1955). Perceptual learning: Differentiation or enrichment? *Psychological Review, 62*(1), 32–41.

Hiebert, J., Morris, A. K., Berk, D., & Jansen, A. (2007). Preparing teachers to learn from teaching. *Journal of Teacher Education, 58*(1), 47–61.

Holmqvist, M., Gustavsson, L., & Wernberg, A. (2007). Generative learning: Learning beyond the learning situation. *Educational Action Research, 15*(2), 181–208.

Kullberg, A., & Runesson, U. (2006). *Exploring teaching and learning of letters in algebra: A report from a learning study*. Paper presented at the 30th Conference of the International Group for the Psychology of Mathematics Education PME, Prague.

Levin, J. R., & O'Donnell, A. M. (1999). What to do about education research's credibility gaps? *Issues in Education, 5*, 177–229.

Lo, M. L., Chik, P. P. M., & Pang, M. F. (2006). Patterns of variation in teaching the colour of light to primary 3 students. *Instructional Science, 34*(1), 1–19.

Ma, L. (1999). *Knowing and teaching elementary mathematics: Teachers' understanding of fundamental mathematics in China and the United States*. Mahwah, NJ: Lawrence Erlbaum Associates.

Marton, F., & Booth, S. (1997). *Learning and awareness*. Mahwah NJ: Lawrence Erlbaum Associates.

Marton, F., & Morris, P. (Eds.) (2002). *What matters? Discovering critical differences in classroom learning*. Göteborg: Acta universitatis Gothoburgensis.

Marton, F., & Pang, M. F. (2006). On some necessary conditions of learning. *Journal of the Learning Sciences, 15*, 193–220.

Marton, F., & Signert, K. (2005, August). *Affordances for learning. Studying teaching in terms of the learning that the inherent pattern of variation and invariance makes possible: Maria Montessori's pedagogy as an example*. Paper presented at the 11th biennial Conference of the Association for Research on Learning and Instruction, Nicosia, Cyprus..

Marton, F., & Tsui, A. B. M. (Eds.) (2004). *Classroom discourse and the space of learning*. Mahwah: NJ: Lawrence Erlbaum Associates.

Nuthall, G. (2004). Relating classroom teaching to student learning: A critical analysis of why research has failed to bridge the theory-practice gap. *Harvard Educational Review, 74*(3), 273–306.

Runesson, U. (2005). Beyond discourse and interaction. Variation: A critical aspect for teaching and learning mathematics. *The Cambridge Journal of Education, 35*(1), 69–87.

Runesson, U., & Mok, I. A. C. (2005). The teaching of fractions: A comparative study of a Swedish and a Hong Kong classroom. *Nordisk Matematikdidaktik [Nordic Studies in Mathematics Education], 10*(2), 1–1.

Spiegelberg, H. (1982). *The phenomenological movement: A historical introduction* (3rd ed.). New York: Summit Books.

Stigler, J. W., & Hiebert, J. (1999). *The teaching gap: Best ideas from the world's teachers for improving education in the classroom*. New York: The Free Press.

Yoshida, M. (1999). *Lesson study: A case of a Japanese approach to improving instruction through a school based teacher development.* Unpublished Ph.D. Thesis, The University of Chicago, Chicago.

Ulla Runesson
University of Gothenburg
Sweden

HELEN J. FORGASZ AND GILAH C. LEDER

8. BELIEFS ABOUT MATHEMATICS AND MATHEMATICS TEACHING

In this chapter we trace the growing research interest in teachers' beliefs and describe the multiple ways the term belief is used. We also summarise and critique research on teachers' beliefs pertinent to the learning and teaching of mathematics. We focussed on articles published between 1997 and 2006 in influential and readily available journals. The work examined is clustered under various headings including: beliefs about pedagogy and learning, beliefs about the nature of mathematics and mathematics content areas, beliefs about technology, about gender and equity issues, and beliefs about aspects of mathematics achievement. Strengths and weaknesses of the research studies surveyed are discussed, methodological issues are highlighted, and some theoretical issues about teachers' beliefs are fore grounded. In the final section we indicate areas in which research consensus has been achieved and point to others still plagued by ambiguity and worthy of further, well planned, and focussed investigation.

INTRODUCTION

Studies on beliefs about mathematics and mathematics teaching and learning have been a relatively new addition to the mathematics education research agenda. "Indeed, in a comprehensive review of American and Canadian research in mathematics education reporting on research conducted primarily in the 1960s and 1970s, the word "belief" does not even appear in the index for this nearly 500-page volume" (Lester, 2002, p. 346). Nor does belief feature among the entries in the index of Wittrock's (1986) *Handbook of research on teaching*. However, more recent reviews of the mathematics research literature reveal a vastly different picture. For example, writing in a special journal issue on "affect and mathematics education" Leder and Grootenboer (2005) noted "Since 1995, MERGA [the Mathematics Education Research Group of Australasia] publications have invariably included a significant number [...] of articles and papers related to aspects of affect in mathematics teaching and learning. [...] Over the ten years (since 1995) beliefs have been a popular concern and the focus of between half to two-thirds of the papers within this subgroup in any given year" (p. 3).

Inspection of recent *Handbooks* concerned with mathematics and teacher education also confirms the burgeoning research interests on beliefs and mathematics teaching and learning. The *Second International Handbook of Mathematics Education* (Bishop, Clements, Keitel, Kilpatrick, & Leung, 2003) contains 30 entries under the index heading of belief; its predecessor The *International Handbook of Mathematics Education* (Bishop, Clements, Keitel,

P. Sullivan and T. Wood (eds.), Knowledge and Beliefs in Mathematics Teaching and Teaching Development, 173–192.

Kilpatrick, & Laborde, 1996), none. The *Handbook of International Research in Mathematics Education* (English, 2002) has 13 such entries; the *Handbook of Research on the Psychology of Mathematics Education* (Gutiérrez & Boero, 2006) features 38. Since some entries cover multiple references to beliefs on the same page, and others to multiple page sections in which beliefs and aspects of mathematics education are discussed, index entries provide, of course, only a crude measure of research interests in a particular area. This is illustrated clearly when belief index entries of the first (Grouws, 1992) and second edition of the *Handbook of Research on Mathematics Teaching and Learning* (Lester, 2007) are compared. The former has 19 index entries; the latter, surprisingly, just one although a full chapter is devoted to "Teachers' beliefs and affect".

More general handbooks such as the *Handbook of Educational Psychology* (Alexander & Winne, 2006) also deal in some depth with teacher beliefs. Topics discussed in a chapter devoted to "teacher knowledge and beliefs" include a veritable alphabet range of topics linked to teachers' beliefs. These, according to index entries, include the beliefs of teachers – from K to 12 – and:

> Adolescence and Assessment; Basic skills; Culture and Curriculum resources; Diversity and Democracy; Effort and Explicit knowledge; Family structure; Gender stereotypes; High stakes tests; Instructional decisions and Implicit knowledge; Journal data; Knowledge; Learning to teach; Mainstreaming and Mathematics knowledge; Nature of intelligence; Observational methodologies and Outcomes; Parental involvement and Problem behaviours; Quantitative and Qualitative methods; Race and Relating to students; Self efficacy and Student achievement; Tests and Teaching identity; Urban teacher; Values; "Whole" of teachers' mental lives; Young teachers.

These diverse entries evocatively convey the varied theoretical lenses through which affect and beliefs have been explored in the broader research literature: political science, history, anthropology, sociology, and psychology. A more restrictive set of theoretical avenues, it will be seen from this review chapter, has been taken in the exploration of teachers' beliefs.

Mason (2004) has creatively captured the many terms used as virtual synonyms for beliefs. His diverse list, which ranges from "A is for attitudes, affect, aptitude, and aims" through "E is for emotions, empathies, and expectations" and "J is for justifications and judgements" to "S is for sympathies and sensations" and "Z is for zeitgeist and zeal" (p. 347), highlights the importance of delineating the scope of this chapter.

As noted by Bar-Tal (1990), it is "especially social psychologists, who have devoted much effort into studying the acquisition and change of beliefs, their structure, their contents, and their effects mainly on individuals' affect and behaviour" (p. 12). Leder's (2007) inspection of papers presented at two recent major mathematics education research conferences, those of the International

Group for the Psychology of Mathematics Education [PME][1] and of the Mathematics Education Research Group of Australasia [MERGA][2] confirms Bar-Tal's observation.

Knowing that a range of definitions of beliefs have been adopted (see, for example, Leder & Forgasz, 2002a), we initially had difficulty deciding what to include in this review. To this end, Wilson and Cooney's (2002) observation with respect to teachers provided broad descriptors to assist in our literature searches, and permitted some degree of judicial choice in what to include and exclude:

> [T]here does not appear to be a consensus about what constitutes beliefs or whether they include or simply reflect behaviour. Generally speaking, neither does there seem to be agreement about the notions of teachers' conceptions or teachers' cognitions. However, regardless of whether one calls teacher thinking beliefs, knowledge, conceptions, cognitions, views, or orientations, with all the subtlety these terms imply or how they are assessed […,] the evidence is clear that teacher thinking influences what happens in classrooms, what teachers communicate to students, and what students ultimately learn. (p. 144)

Wilson and Cooney (2002) also identify a relationship between teachers' beliefs and students' learning. This suggests that researchers should not ignore teachers' beliefs as influencing learning outcomes. As noted above, researchers and curriculum developers use a range of terms interchangeably when discussing the affective domain. Three decades earlier than Wilson and Cooney (2002), Cockcroft (1982) had highlighted the effects of teachers' beliefs (attitudes) on students. In his influential publication, *Mathematics counts*, Cockcroft (1982) wrote:

> It is to be expected that most teachers will attach considerable importance to the development of good attitudes among the pupils whom they teach […] Attitudes are derived from teachers' attitudes […] and to an extent from parents' attitudes. […] Attitude to mathematics is correlated […] with the peer-group's attitude. (p. 61)

The *Programme for International Student Assessment* [PISA] "measures student performance in reading, mathematics and science literacy and also asks students about their motivations, beliefs about themselves and learning strategies" (OECD, nd). Again, as an acknowledgment of the interaction between affective factors and the learning of mathematics, those planning the PISA project explained:

> Mathematics related attitudes and emotions such as self-confidence, curiosity, feelings of interest and relevance, and the desire to do or

---

[1] The 31st annual PME conference held in Seoul, Korea, July 8–13, 2007. In recent years the goals of PME have been broadened beyond psychological to include "other aspects of teaching and learning mathematics and the implications thereof".
[2] The 30th annual MERGA conference held in Hobart, Tasmania, Australia, July 2–6, 2007.

understand things [...] are important contributors to it (i.e., mathematical literacy) [...] The importance of these attitudes and emotions as correlates of mathematical literacy is recognised. (OECD, 2004, p. 26)

The influential National Council of Teachers of Mathematics [NCTM] (2000) similarly argued:

> Students' understanding of mathematics, their ability to use it to solve problems, and their *confidence in*, and *disposition toward*, mathematics are all shaped by the teaching they encounter in school. (p. 16, emphasis added)

Thus, there is explicit recognition that concerns with teachers' beliefs goes beyond theoretical interests alone, and encompasses practical classroom-based issues.

Structure of This Chapter

In planning this chapter we took on board the advice seemingly given by Berliner and Calfee (1996) to the authors of their *Handbook* and reproduced by Winne and Alexander (2006).

> (Authors were charged) to prepare chapters that build on the history of a particular domain, lay out seminal issues and questions, and survey the major results and puzzlements, illuminating each with [...] descriptions of particular findings, and connecting the domain with important questions that warrant further investigation [...]. (p. xi)

Focussing on the years 1997 to 2006 the following databases were trawled for pertinent literature on the beliefs of mathematics teachers: *A+ Education, The Australian Education Index [AEI], ProQuest, ERIC*, and *Google Scholar*. Three high impact mathematics education journals were also examined: *Educational Studies in Mathematics*, the *Journal for Research in Mathematics Education*, and the *Journal of Mathematics Teacher Education*. The references found were analysed, and we concluded that the review could most conveniently be grouped under a number of headings: beliefs about pedagogy and learning, with separate discussions on teachers at different grade levels: primary, middle years, and secondary; beliefs about mathematics and mathematics content areas; beliefs about technology; gender, equity and beliefs; achievement and beliefs; and theoretical discussions and issues related to teachers' beliefs. It should be noted that in some research studies there was overlap in these dimensions. Thus, some studies are discussed in more than one section of the chapter with suitable links made between them.

THE LITERATURE ON TEACHERS' BELIEFS

Beliefs about Pedagogy and Learning

Teachers' beliefs about pedagogy are closely interwoven with their beliefs about the ways in which their students learn. In some articles this link can be inferred; in others it is made explicitly.

Primary teachers. In many of the articles in which primary teachers' pedagogical beliefs were explored findings were based on intensive scrutiny of a small number of case studies or investigations involving a small number of teachers. Semi structured interviews, classroom observations – in some research projects carried out by a participant observer; in others by a neutral recorder – lesson plans, and journals completed by the participating teachers and the researchers themselves were techniques frequently used for data gathering. In some studies, interviews were also held with parents and with colleagues of those involved in the study. Data obtained from surveys and questionnaires containing items with Likert-type response formats were reported in the relatively few large scale studies identified by our search of the literature. The duration of many of the studies, and in particular those aimed at changing teachers' pedagogical beliefs and any impact of this on instructional practices, spanned a substantial slice of the school year. Aspects of some longitudinal studies have also been reported. For example Steele (2001) and Wood and Sellers (1997) drew on data from longitudinal studies which respectively spanned four and two years.

The conceptualisation of mathematics and instructional practices as advocated by the mathematics reform movement featured prominently in a number of studies. The extent to which teachers' beliefs and practices reflected the aims of the movement and the curriculum content and instructional approaches promoted by it was identified in some studies (e.g., Archer, 2000). In others (e.g., Clarke, 1997; Senger, 1998; Steele, 2001), attempts were made to gauge whether the strategies advocated were actually adopted. Opportunities to reflect on their in-class practices seemed to enhance not only changes in teachers' beliefs but also to promote a stronger congruence between teachers' (changed) beliefs and their practices (e.g., Clarke, 1997; Raymond, 1997; Senger, 1998; Steele, 2001). Obstacles in the way of changing teachers' beliefs and their practices included preconceived ideas about students' (socioeconomic background related) needs (Sztajn, 2003), emphasis on practical constraints preventing the translation of beliefs into practice (Quinn & Wilson, 1997), teachers' limited mathematics background knowledge (Halai, 1998; Raymond, 1997; Steele, 2001), students' behaviours, and teachers' own school experiences. Indeed, prospective teachers' professional preparation courses, it was reported in several studies (e.g., Archer, 2000; Raymond, 1997), had less influence on teachers' beliefs and practices than teachers' own classroom experiences and their experiences as students of mathematics. Before turning to the next section, Sztajn's (2003) provocative caution on the link between teachers' beliefs and practices is worth noting. "Beliefs and practice", she argued, "are consistent – if in a study we find they are not, then I think we asked the wrong questions" (p. 74).

Prospective primary teachers. Prospective teachers are readily available to serve, within appropriate ethical guidelines, as subjects in research projects. It is therefore not surprising that this group, overwhelmingly comprised of females, was frequently targeted by those wishing to explore beliefs about mathematics and pedagogy. Some of the trends noted in the review of research on the mathematics related beliefs of primary teachers were also apparent when work involving prospective primary teachers was reviewed. Small sample studies again predominated, though this now typically comprised a relatively small group of students (e.g., the group taking a particular course) rather than just two or three individuals. Much emphasis was again given to the impact on participants' beliefs, and possibly their (intended) instructional practices, or exposure to reform-oriented and constructivist approaches during their professional training. Interviews, written materials, and group discussion were used for data collection in many of the studies surveyed (e.g., Ambrose, 2004; Langford & Huntley, 1999; Mewborn, 1999); in others heavy reliance was placed on survey responses. Some of the latter studies (e.g., Ambrose, 2004; Seaman, Szydlik, Szydlik, & Beam, 2005; Vacc & Bright, 1999; Wilkins & Brand, 2004) used previously constructed questionnaires; others – including Hart (2002) and Spielman and Lloyd (2004) relied on information obtained from surveys specifically constructed for the investigation described.

A strong theme that emerged from our survey of relevant articles was the positive effect on participants' beliefs of practicum and structured field work experiences, preferably coupled with times for reflection (e.g., Ambrose, 2004; Mewborn, 1999; Vacc & Bright, 1999). Ambrose's (2004) conclusion is representative of such findings.

> Providing prospective teachers with intense experiences that involve them intimately with children poses a promising avenue for belief change. Coupling these experiences with reflection allows the beliefs that arise from these experiences to be examined and refined. (p. 117)

The benefits of guided field work experiences are further reinforced by Langford and Huntley's (1999) study in which prospective teachers were given the opportunity to do a summer internship in a variety of settings: business, industry, scientific institutions, informal educational settings including museums and zoos, as well as in the more formal educational setting of a regular classroom. Coupled with the internship were extended collaborations with relevant professionals, for example, mathematicians, scientists or educators.

> It appears that the interns, on the heels of the challenge of their summer internship, had directed their thinking from what they *did* during the summer to what they *hoped to do* as teachers. They dared to take on challenging tasks; they envisioned themselves as risk-taking teachers who intended to question

and pursue understanding alongside their students [...]; they envisioned themselves as encouraging curiosity in their students [...]; they hoped to encourage their future students to take an active role in their own learning. (Langford & Huntley, 1999, p. 294, emphasis in the original)

Various "tools" to effect change were used in the research reports we identified. A strong emphasis on field experiences, including field work early in the course, has already been noted. Others found useful included using children's literature to identify ideological positions which in turn were reflected in instructional strategies (Cotti & Schiro, 2004) and, most commonly, course content carefully structured to capture child-centred, reform-movement advocated, and constructivist approaches (Anhalt, Ward, & Vinson, 2006; Quinn & Wilson, 1997; Scott, 2005; Spielman & Lloyd, 2004; Timmerman, 2004; Vacc & Bright, 1999). Authors typically concluded that appropriate course content could lead to changes in the beliefs of the prospective teachers. For example:

After one semester, teachers in the (innovative, reform oriented) curriculum materials section [...] placed significantly more importance on classroom group work and discussions, less on instructor lectures and explanations, and less on textbooks having practice problems, examples and explanations. They valued student exploration over practice. (Spielman & Lloyd, 2004, p. 32)

In contrast, for the group in which the courses relied heavily on a traditional textbook "there was little change in the teachers' beliefs, in which practice was valued over exploration" (Spielman & Lloyd, 2004, p. 32).

A cautious note about changes in beliefs captured during the study on which they were reporting, and not necessarily reflected in classroom practices, was injected by several researchers. Time constraints during prospective teacher education courses often prevented optimum practices from being implemented. "Considerable personal reflection on one's beliefs and behaviour would seem to be necessary for one to develop a coherent pedagogy... It is not clear whether pre-service teacher education programmes can structurally accommodate these needed 'reflection events'" (Vacc & Bright, 1999, p. 107). Ambrose (2004) concluded that new beliefs were often added to, rather than fully replacing, previously held beliefs. Scott (2005) indicated that when the prospective teachers in her study tried to reconcile conflicting theory and practice, they most frequently turned to practising teachers who did not necessarily share their beliefs about constructivist practices. Discrepancies between espoused beliefs and observed or intended practices were reported by Quinn and Wilson (1997) and Timmerman (2004). In many of the reports which contained positive accounts of functional changes in the prospective teachers' beliefs it was nevertheless concluded that the extent to which these changes would eventually be translated into practice in classrooms could only be a matter of speculation.

Middle school teachers and prospective teachers. Issues already identified in earlier sections were also found in work involving middle school teachers. Britt,

Irwin, and Ritchie (2001), for example, reported that the poor mathematical content knowledge of the middle school teachers involved in their two year professional development programme prevented them from making the changes in beliefs and practices towards reform-oriented teaching promoted by the programme. In contrast, experienced, mathematically knowledgeable secondary school teachers' beliefs and practices changed in the desired direction. Middle school teachers' lack of confidence to teach mathematics was also identified by Beswick, Watson, and Brown (2006) as they sought baseline information at the beginning of a three year study aimed at assisting teachers to improve student performance in mathematics. Given the decade long emphasis in many countries, including their own (Australia), on constructivist, student-centered teaching their finding that "in spite of progressive beliefs many teachers and their students work in quite traditional classrooms" (p. 75) suggests that the dichotomy between theory and practice, that is, the schism between espoused beliefs and actual practice, is remarkably persistent. Teachers, as already noted, are quite likely to have adopted reform oriented rhetoric without altering their instructional practices. Zevenbergen (2003) interviewed 20 middle school teachers on the implementation of a unit of work based on the New Basics framework (a reform-based curriculum introduced into Queensland, Australia). Three groups of teachers were identified: the conservatives, the pragmatists, and the contemporary. The three groups of teachers held different beliefs about mathematics pedagogy, curriculum, and assessment. Identifying beliefs in these areas, Zevenbergen (2003) maintained, might be a useful first step in affecting change.

The report of an action research collaboration between a middle school mathematics teacher and a mathematics teacher educator (Edwards & Hensien, 1999), aimed at making the former's instructional practices congruent with reform advocated instructional practices, confirmed just how difficult the road to change can be. "The interplay between teachers' beliefs and their instructional practices seems to be more dynamic, interactive, and cyclic than a simple linear cause-and-effect relationship", Edwards and Hensien (1999, p. 189) argued. Change in instructional practice consistent with changes in belief was gradually achieved through an intensive, long term (multiple years), collaborative partnership requiring levels of sustained commitment, time, mutual trust and understanding – features rarely available to busy practitioners with multiple demands on their time and services.

Secondary school teachers and prospective teachers. The data gathering methods described in the sections above were also used in many of the studies in which the beliefs of secondary school teachers about mathematics and pedagogy were examined. In studies in which surveys were used to gauge beliefs of larger groups of teachers, the dominance of females reported for studies involving prospective or practising primary teachers, changed to one of male dominance (e.g., Barkatsas & Malone, 2005). Secondary teachers, at least in those studies in which this information was sought, generally believed themselves to be competent mathematically (Britt, Irwin, & Ritchie, 2001; Doerr & Zanger, 2000) – a factor which influenced the extent to which they adopted or moved towards reform-oriented teaching. Whether it was access to, or professional development on innovative materials or problem-solving focussed text books that led to mathematics classroom practices consistent with the strategies advocated by the reform movement, seemed to depend heavily on the teachers' beliefs about their students' mathematical ability (Arbaugh, Lannin, Jones, & Park-Rogers, 2006; Quinn & Wilson, 1997), their beliefs about the nature of mathematics, and their broader social and cultural beliefs (Archer, 2000; Barkatsis & Malone, 2005). The importance of an individual's values in the formation of beliefs was also explored in some depth by Cooney, Shealy, and Arvold (1998) in their detailed study of a small group of prospective secondary mathematics teachers.

The limited "uptake" of mathematics reform movement sanctioned practices in the secondary mathematics classroom severely hampers, according to Frykholm (1999), their implementation by beginning teachers, including those fully familiar with, and accepting of, those principles. Frykholm's (1999) six cohorts of secondary mathematics student teachers, collectively spanning an investigative period of three years, contrasted the "large doses" of theory to which they were exposed during their training with the limited practical advice they received and experience they gained in how to implement the reform movement advocated strategies. In addition to the teacher dominated lessons they experienced during their own schooling, the bulk of the lessons they observed during their (semester long) teaching internship were again traditional, and teacher dominated. Thus although the prospective secondary mathematics teachers were "eager to gain knowledge of reform" and searched for "new models of instruction to emulate them [...] they recognised the ways in which their emerging beliefs often run counter to their teaching practices" (p. 102). Ensor (2001), too, described discrepancies between the participants' beliefs and practices as they began their career as secondary mathematics teachers. Her interpretation of this is reminiscent of the view expressed by Sztajn (2003) who hypothesised, as noted earlier, that when beliefs and practice are found to be inconsistent, then it is possible that the wrong questions may have been asked. Ensor (2001) similarly noted:

> The apparent discrepancy between Mary's words and her deeds [...] only emerged if the professional argot was taken to embody a fixed meaning for both teacher educators and student teachers. Once it was perceived to mean something different from Mary's perspective, she could be seen to be acting consistently with what she said. (p. 317)

In the studies reviewed so far, interest has centred on teachers' beliefs about pedagogy and learning. Their beliefs about mathematics and mathematics content areas are considered next.

Beliefs about Mathematics and Mathematics Content Areas

Since the number of studies of practising teachers' and prospective teachers' beliefs about mathematics and mathematics content areas was relatively small, the views of practising mathematics teachers and prospective mathematics teachers at all levels – primary, middle years, and secondary – are presented together.

Beliefs about the nature of mathematics Teachers' and prospective primary teachers' beliefs about the nature of mathematics have been the focus of several studies. Based on interview data from 17 primary and 10 secondary teachers, Archer (2000) reported marked differences in the views of primary and secondary teachers with respect to the nature of mathematics and its place in the curriculum. While primary teachers related mathematics to the everyday life experiences of students and recognised its inter-relationship with other dimensions of the primary curriculum, secondary teachers considered mathematics to be self-contained and not strongly linked to students' lives. The primary teachers' views were considered consistent with the holistic approach of primary education, and the secondary teachers' with the organisation of secondary schools. The primary teachers also identified differences in how mathematics had been taught to them and how they now taught. Seaman, Szydlik, Szydlik, and Beam (2005) administered the same instrument used by Collier (1972) to a cohort of prospective primary teachers in 1998 and found that compared to Collier's 1968 cohort, the beliefs of the 1998 cohort were more informal, that is, better aligned with constructivist principles. They argued that beliefs about mathematics and mathematics teaching are shaped by early educational experiences, a finding also reported by Lindgren (2000), and suggested that the differences between the two cohorts reflected changes over time in their learning experiences.

Beliefs and their relationship to other learning-related factors and outcomes have also been examined. Perry, Way, Southwell, White, and Pattison (2005) found a negative correlation between prospective primary teachers' achievement scores and their beliefs about the importance of computation and correct answers in mathematics. In a study exploring how nine primary teachers responded to observations of *reform-minded* teaching, Grant, Hiebert and Wearne (1998) found that reactions depended on the views of mathematics held by the observing teachers. Compared to teachers who believed in the learning of concepts and processes, those who considered mathematics to be a set of skills and algorithms to be taught did not implement what they had seen into their own practice as intended by the programme developers. McDonough and Clarke (2005) claimed that the Early Numeracy Research Project [ENRP], a professional development programme, had served as a catalyst to change primary teachers' beliefs about the nature of mathematics.

Gathering pre- and post-data from prospective primary teachers was a common means of identifying if changes in beliefs had taken place as a consequence of intervening experiences. In the Langford and Huntley (1999) study, discussed earlier, it was found that the summer internship experiences had challenged the students' conceptions of and beliefs about the nature and processes of mathematics and science. The researchers claimed that internships held promise for teacher reform in that those who had participated "intend to bring a holistic, conceptually oriented view of mathematics and science into their classrooms" (p. 296). Szydlik, Szydlik, and Benson (2003) and Timmerman (2004) gathered data on beliefs about the nature of mathematics and its teaching, at the beginning and end of particular pre-service courses. After the courses, Timmerman reported stronger disagreement with tradition-oriented beliefs, and Szydlik et al. (2003) found that students' beliefs were more supportive of autonomous behaviours.

Beswick (2005) and Barkatsas and Malone (2005) reported findings from large scale survey data on secondary teachers' beliefs about the nature of mathematics and the teaching and learning of mathematics; the former gathered data in Australia, the latter in Greece. Barkatsas and Malone (2005) indicated that "mathematics teachers' beliefs about mathematics could not be separated from their beliefs about teaching and learning mathematics" (p. 80) and data from one case study revealed that a very experienced teacher's espoused beliefs were less traditional than observed classroom practices would suggest. Beswick (2005) found that very few teachers held beliefs about the nature of mathematics that were solely consistent with Ernest's *problem solving view*; the extent to which classrooms could be characterised as constructivist was, however, related to how strongly teachers held this view. Based on data from one teacher who held a problem-solving view of mathematics and a constructivist view of mathematics learning, Beswick (2004) demonstrated that other beliefs about students and their abilities can affect teachers' practices in different contexts.

Beliefs about Mathematics Content Areas
There were surprisingly few studies which specifically focused on beliefs about mathematics content areas. However, teachers' and prospective teachers' beliefs about the mathematics curriculum in general, and the more specific content areas of problem-solving, modeling, proofs, and numeracy have been examined. Lloyd (2002) presented data from two case studies and discussed how experiences with innovative curriculum materials could change teachers' beliefs about mathematics and the content of the curriculum. Findings from one part of a survey administered to 42 middle years teachers (grades 5-8) by Beswick, Watson, & Brown (2006) indicated that the teachers were "convinced of the importance of being numerate" (p. 72), and that at least two-thirds of them believed that it was important to understand fractions, decimals, and percentage. Among other aims, Anderson, White and Sullivan (2005) used a mixed methods approach to examine primary teachers' beliefs about problem solving. Survey data indicated that many agreed that problem-solving was an important dimension of mathematics learning; open-ended and unfamiliar questions were considered by many to be more appropriate for high achieving students. Brown (2002) reported that International Baccalaureate examiners and assessors held a range of beliefs about the nature of mathematical modeling that were consistent with those reported by Kyleve and Williams (1996). Mingus and Grassl (1999) found that prospective primary and practising secondary teachers believed that proofs should be experienced fairly early in schooling. The secondary prospective teachers had more sophisticated

beliefs about the nature of proofs; beliefs about the role of proofs in mathematics learning were related to these beliefs.

Beliefs about Technology

In this section, beliefs about calculators, computers, and other forms of technology that can be used for the teaching and learning of mathematics are reported. Again, since the number of studies was quite small, findings for practising and prospective teachers at all levels are presented together.

While not directly focusing on beliefs about calculators in a study of one secondary teacher's implementation of graphing calculators into her teaching, Doerr and Zangor (2000) claimed that "the role, knowledge and beliefs of the teacher influenced the emergence of [...] rich usage of the graphing calculator" (p. 161). Based on questionnaire findings about their beliefs about graphics calculators – positive, neutral, and negative – Honey and Graham (2003) selected three prospective secondary teachers as participants in their study. Despite the differences in their beliefs, there were various reasons why each was generally reluctant to use the calculators during the teaching practicum. Forgasz and Griffith (2006) reported on teachers' beliefs about the effects of the imminent introduction of Computer Algebra Systems [CAS] calculators as compulsory tools into the final year of schooling mathematics courses in Victoria (Australia). It was found that the mathematics teachers were generally optimistic about the effects that CAS calculators would have on their teaching, on student learning, and on the curriculum. While there were a few dissenting voices, there was little difference in the views of male and female teachers.

Findings from a three-year study in which data were gathered on secondary teachers' and their students' views on whether computers assisted students' understanding of mathematics were described by Forgasz (2005) and Forgasz, Griffith, and Tan (2006). The students (30%) were less convinced than their teachers (60%) of the positive impact of computers on their learning. Another dimension of the study involved interviews with a small number of teachers and observations of their lessons in which students used computers. Forgasz (2006) summarised the differences in the teachers' beliefs about how boys and girls work differently with computers in the classroom:

> [...] boys' competence, confidence, and interest in computers generally, appear to advantage them over girls when computers are used in the mathematics classroom. It seems that teachers feel the need to focus boys' attention to the task at hand and encourage and support girls to engage with the technology. It would appear that without positive intervention with girls, it is more likely that boys will gain more from their interactions with computers in the mathematics classroom. (pp. 459–460)

Gender, Equity and Beliefs

Studies in which data were analysed by gender but in which gender was not the major focus of the research are not reported here. However, it should be noted that the findings from such studies reflect those of the work reviewed here. Practising teachers' and prospective teachers' gendered beliefs about boys and girls have been examined at both the primary and secondary levels. The patterns of beliefs found were generally consistent with those reported in earlier times (see, for example, Fennema & Leder, 1990). Based on quantitative data from 52 primary teachers in Germany, Tiedemann (2000, 2002), for example, found that the teachers held biased views that were more likely to disadvantage girls than boys. Tiedemann (2000) summarised the results as follows:

> Teachers rated mathematics as more difficult for average girls than for equally achieving boys. Teachers thought that average achieving girls were less logical than equally achieving boys. Girls were thought to profit less than boys from additional effort and to exert relatively more effort to achieve the level of actual performance in mathematics. With regard to girls, teachers attributed unexpected failure more to low ability and less to lack of effort than with boys. Nonetheless, teachers were aware of the girls' lower self-concept of mathematical ability. In summary an image emerges that, in the view of these teachers, girls, especially those of average or low achievement, must exert relatively more effort than boys to achieve a certain level of mathematical performance. (p. 204)

An instrument designed to tap beliefs about mathematics as a male domain devised by Leder and Forgasz (see Leder & Forgasz, 2002b) was administered to secondary prospective teachers in Australia and the U.S. (Forgasz, 2001a). The teachers were asked to respond to the items as they believed secondary school students would respond. The same instrument had previously been administered to large samples of secondary students in both countries and the results indicated that their beliefs about mathematics as a male domain were inconsistent with previous findings in the field (Forgasz, 2001b). The prospective teachers' views of the students' beliefs were more in-line with earlier research, that is, that mathematics was perceived to be a male domain. There was a remarkable similarity in the patterns of the results from Australia and the USA. Soro (2000) reported that Finnish lower secondary school teachers held different beliefs about boys and girls as mathematics learners. Boys were considered more likely than girls to succeed in mathematical tasks demanding high cognitive abilities, and some teachers had a tendency to stereotype mathematics as a male domain.

There appears to be a dearth of research in recent times on mathematics teachers' beliefs about other equity dimensions including race/ethnicity/culture and socio-economic backgrounds. Arguably, students with special needs can be considered under the equity umbrella. In this area the study by DeSimone and Parmar (2006) was somewhat unique. They surveyed a large group of middle school teachers to determine their beliefs about coping, in the regular classroom, with students with learning disabilities. It was found that many teachers considered their teacher education course preparation to have been insufficient to prepare them for the realities faced in the classroom with these students.

Achievement and Beliefs

Yun-peng, Chi-chung, and Ngai-ying (2006) argued that China is a country where there is great pressure to perform on public examinations, including the national mathematics Olympiad. While the Olympiad results had no effect on students' future opportunities, teachers' pay and promotion prospects were related to students' performance levels. In a case study of two schools, one urban and one rural, the authors claimed that the teachers' beliefs about what students needed to learn, the goals of learning, teaching approaches, and the perceived difficulty level of the textbook affected performance levels. The findings appear consistent with those of Arbaugh et al. (2006) and Quinn and Wilson (1977) with respect to the likelihood that lack of access to resources had contributed to differences in the teachers' beliefs about students' abilities, and that geographic location had served as a factor contributing to inequitable outcomes.

Using the TIMSS data from the U.S. and hierarchical regression modeling, the relationship between constructivist teachers' beliefs and practices and students' achievements were examined by Gales and Yan (2001). The relationship was also examined for behaviorist teachers. It was found that lower student achievement was related to the behaviorist teachers' belief that diversity in the classroom had a negative impact on achievement. A negative relationship was also found between the constructivist teachers' belief that mathematics is a practical, structured, and formal guide for addressing real world situations and student achievement. The latter finding may be indicative of the type of questions being asked in the TIMSS study, that is, the questions were inconsistent with this view of mathematics held by the constructivist teachers.

Theoretical Discussions and Issues Related to Teachers' Beliefs

In a reflective piece, Cooney (1999) wrote of prospective teachers' unsophisticated understanding of school mathematics, the need to match their mathematical experiences with what would be expected of the reflective and adaptive teacher, and theoretical considerations for the conceptualisation of teachers' belief structures. Gates (2006) described two teachers with strongly held, ideologically-based, opposing views on whether students should be in homogenous or heterogeneous achievement groupings for mathematics learning. He used these teachers as examples to illustrate why so many reforms in mathematics education may have failed. He argued that:

> What is required is not an approach based on hoping such difference can be resolved, but one based on recognising ideological diversity and social conflict, focusing on the way social structures influence meaning rather than

negotiation between individuals within different power structures and cultural communities. (p. 365)

Cooney's (1999) and Gates' (2006) views were implicit in many of the studies reviewed on teachers' beliefs about pedagogy and learning. Leatham (2006) challenged researchers to conceptualise teachers' beliefs as inherently sensible and to explore and explain apparent inconsistencies in beliefs and practices rather than simply pointing them out; similar ideas were expressed by Ensor (2001) and Sztajn (2003).

CONCLUSIONS AND RECOMMENDATIONS FOR FUTURE RESEARCH

In conducting this review of the literature for the period 1997–2006 on mathematics teachers' beliefs, we noted that extensive research had been undertaken in some areas but that there has been much less focus on others. For example, there was much more work on primary teachers' beliefs about pedagogy and learning with less attention being paid to the views of middle years and secondary level teachers. There was more research on teachers' beliefs about pedagogy and learning than on their views about mathematics and its content areas, mathematics achievement, or technology for mathematics learning. With the exception of a few studies in which teachers' gender-related beliefs were examined, there was a dearth of work on teachers' beliefs related to other equity dimensions or students with special needs.

We noted that the range of methodological approaches adopted in the studies discussed above was fairly limited. Larger scale quantitative data were generally gathered from surveys or questionnaires and, with few exceptions, the analyses were restricted to descriptive statistics. Small scale qualitative studies dominated the research on primary teachers' beliefs in particular. Although they were carefully conducted and analysed, the limited generalisability of the findings remains a challenge in the field.

It was found that in many studies there was no theoretical discussion of the construct "beliefs", let alone any definition offered prior to "beliefs" being measured or inferences about beliefs from interview data or observation of classroom practices being drawn. This observed methodological weakness lends further support to Mason's (2004) somewhat cynical discussion of the A-Z of synonyms used for the construct, and Wilson and Cooney's (2002) observation about what might constitute teachers' beliefs, cited earlier.

Based on the review of the literature presented, the following conclusions can be drawn:

− The beliefs about the teaching and learning of mathematics of teachers at all levels are affected by a range of factors and can be context and student dependent;
− Circumstances dictate whether teachers' beliefs about the nature of mathematics and their beliefs about the teaching and learning of mathematics are clearly related;

– There are many obstacles to overcome in attempting to change beliefs to be in line with contemporary understandings of good mathematics pedagogy;
– Appropriate practicum and field-related experiences can impact strongly on prospective teachers' beliefs about the nature of mathematics and its teaching and learning;
– Teachers' generally hold positive beliefs about the effects of technology on students' mathematics learning;
– Teachers' beliefs about boys and girls and mathematics learning remain gender-stereotyped.

The conclusions drawn from this review are generally consistent with those reported by Philipp (2007), with the exception of the more positive beliefs reported here of teachers' views about technology and mathematics learning. Da Ponte and Chapman (2006) were critical of continued efforts in researching teachers' beliefs without simultaneously exploring aspects of teachers' practices. There is some merit in this argument if the sole aim is to understand better why findings on espoused and enacted beliefs continue to reveal inconsistencies. However, as noted above, there is still a lack of knowledge on teachers' beliefs about a range of issues related to the teaching and learning of mathematics which can be explored without reference to practice even if there may be a direct bearing on practice. We advocate, however, that researchers carefully define what they mean by "beliefs" and that a breadth of methodological approaches is adopted in exploring them.

REFERENCES

Alexander, P. A., & Winne, P. H. (2006). *Handbook of educational psychology* (2nd ed.). Mahwah, NJ: Lawrence Erlbaum Associates.
Ambrose, R. (2004). Initiating change in prospective elementary school teachers' orientations to mathematics teaching by building on beliefs. *Journal of Mathematics Teacher Education, 7*, 91–119.
Anderson, J., White, P., & Sullivan, P. (2005). Using a schematic model to represent influences on, and relationships between, teachers' problem-solving beliefs and practices. *Mathematics Education Research Journal, 17*(2), 9–38.
Anhalt, C. O., Ward, R. A., Vinson, K. D. (2006). Teacher candidates' growth in designing mathematical tasks as exhibited in their lesson planning. *The Teacher Educator, 41*(3), 172–186.
Arbaugh, F., Lannin, J., Jones, D. L., & Park-Rogers, M. (2006). Examining instructional practices in Core-plus lessons: Implications for professional development. *Journal of Mathematics Teacher Education, 9*(6), 517–550.
Archer, J. (2000, December). *Teachers' beliefs about successful teaching and learning in English and mathematics.* Paper presented at the annual conference of the Australian Association for Research in Education, Sydney. Retrieved 20 October, 2007 from: http://www.aare.edu.au/00pap/arc00325.htm
Barkatsas, A. T., & Malone, J. (2005). A typology of mathematics teachers' beliefs about teaching and learning mathematics and instructional practices. *Mathematics Education Research Journal, 17*(2), 69–90.
Bar-Tal, D. (1990). *Group beliefs. A conception for analysing group structure, processes and behaviour.* New York: Springer-Verlag.
Berliner, D. C., & Calfee, R. C. (Eds.) (1996). *Handbook of educational psychology.* New York: Macmillan.
Beswick, K. (2004). The impact of teachers' perceptions of student characteristics on the enactment of their beliefs. In M. J. Hoines & A. B. Fuglestad (Eds.), *Proceedings of the 28th Annual Conference*

of the International Group for the Psychology of Mathematics Education (Vol. 2, pp. 111–118). Bergen: Bergen University College.

Beswick, K. (2005). The beliefs/practice connection in broadly defined contexts. *Mathematics Education Research Journal, 17*(2), 39–68.

Beswick, K., Watson, J., & Brown, N. (2006). Teachers' confidence and beliefs and their students' attitudes towards mathematics. In P. Grootenboer, R. Zevenbergen, & M. Chinappan (Eds.), *Identities cultures and learning spaces. Proceedings of the 29th Annual Conference of the Mathematics Education Research Group of Australasia*, (pp. 68–75). Adelaide: MERGA Inc.

Bishop, A. J., Clements, K., Keitel, C., Kilpatrick, J., & Laborde, C. (1996). *International handbook of mathematics education.* Dordrecht, the Netherlands: Kluwer Academic Publishers.

Bishop, A. J., Clements, M. A., Keitel, C., Kilpatrick, J., & Leung, F. K. S. (2003). *Second international handbook of mathematics education.* Dordrecht, the Netherlands: Kluwer Academic Publishers.

Britt, M. S., Irwin, K. C., & Ritchie, G. (2001). Professional conversations and professional growth. *Journal of Mathematics Teacher Education, 4,* 29–53.

Brown, R. (2002). Mathematical modelling in the international baccalaureate, teacher beliefs and technology usage. *Teaching Mathematics and its Applications, 21*(2), 67–74.

da Ponte, J. P., & Chapman, O. (2006). Mathematics teachers' knowledge and practices. In A. Gutiérrez & P. Boero (Eds.), *Handbook of research on the psychology of mathematics education* (pp. 461–494). Rotterdam, the Netherlands: Sense Publishers.

Clarke, D. M. (1997). The changing role of the mathematics teacher. *Journal for Research in Mathematics Education, 28,* 278–308.

Cockcroft, W. H. (1982). *Mathematics counts.* London: Her Majesty's Stationary Office.

Collier, C. P. (1972). Prospective elementary teachers' intensity and ambivalence of beliefs about mathematics and mathematics instruction. *Journal for Research in Mathematics Education, 3,* 155–163.

Cooney, T. (1999). Conceptualising teachers' ways of knowing. *Educational Studies in Mathematics, 38*(1–3), 163–187.

Cooney, T. J., Shealy, B. E., & Arvold, B. (1998). *Journal for Research in Mathematics Education, 29,* 306–333.

Cotti, R., & Schiro, M. (2004). Connecting teacher beliefs to the use of children's literature in the teaching of mathematics. *Journal of Mathematics Teacher Education, 7,* 329–356.

DeSimone, J. R., & Parmar, R. S. (2006). Middle school mathematics teachers' beliefs about inclusion of students with learning disabilities. *Learning Disabilities Research & Practice, 21*(2), 98–110.

Doerr, H. M., & Zangor, R. (2000). Creating meaning for and with the graphing calculator. *Educational Studies in Mathematics, 41*(2), 143–163.

Edwards, T. G., & Hensien, S. M. (1999). Changing instructional practice through action research. *Journal of Mathematics Teacher Education, 2,* 187–206.

English, L. D. (2002). *Handbook of international research in mathematics education.* Mahwah, NJ: Lawrence Erlbaum Associates.

Ensor, P. (2001). From preservice mathematics teacher education to beginning teaching: A study in recontextualising. *Journal for Research in Mathematics Education, 32,* 296–320.

Fennema, E., & Leder, G. C. (Eds.) (1990). *Mathematics and gender.* New York: Teachers College Press.

Forgasz, H. J. (2006). Teachers, equity, and computers for secondary mathematics learning. *Journal for Mathematics Teacher Education, 9,* 437–469.

Forgasz, H. (2005). Teachers' and pre-service teachers' gendered beliefs: Students and computers. *Australian Mathematics Teacher, 61*(2), 17–21.

Forgasz, H. J. (2001a). Australian and US preservice teachers' perceptions of the gender stereotyping of mathematics. In M. van den Heuvel-Panhuisen (Ed.), *Proceedings of the 25th Conference of the International Group for the Psychology of Mathematics Education* (Vol.2 (pp.2–433, 2–440). Utrecht University, The Netherlands: Psychology of Mathematics Education.

Forgasz, H. J. (2001b, April). *Mathematics: Still a male domain? Australian findings.* Paper presented at the annual meeting of American Education Research Association. Seattle, WA. [ERIC document: ED452071].

Forgasz, H., & Griffith, S. (2006). CAS calculators: Gender issues and teachers' expectations. *Australian Senior Mathematics Journal, 20*(2), 18–29.

Forgasz, H., Griffith S., & Tan H. (2006). *Gender, equity, teachers, students and technology use in secondary mathematics classro*oms. In C. Hoyles, J. Lagrange, L. H. Son, & N. Sinclair (Eds.), *Proceedings for the Seventeenth ICMI Study Conference: Technology Revisited,* Hanoi University of Technology,Hanoi [Paper No. c82 on CD-ROM].

Frykholm, J. A., (1999). The impact of reform: Challenges for mathematics teacher preparation. *Journal of Mathematics Teacher Education, 2,* 79–105.

Gales, M. J., & Yan, W. (2001, April). *Relationship between constructivist teacher beliefs and instructional practices to students' mathematical achievement: Evidence from TIMMS.* Paper presented at the annual conference of the American Educational Research Association Conference. Seattle, WA. Retrieved 5 January, 2007 from: http://www.eric.ed.gov/ERICDocs/data/ericdocs2sql/content_storage_01/0000019b/80/19/2b/8c.pdf

Gates, P. (2006). Going beyond belief systems: Exploring a model for the social influence on mathematics teacher beliefs. *Educational Studies in Mathematics, 63*(3), 347–369.

Grant, T. J., Hiebert, J. & Wearne, D. (1998). Observing and teaching reform-minded lessons: What do teachers see? *Journal of Mathematics Teacher Education, 1,* 217–236.

Grouws, D. A. (Ed.), (1992). *Handbook of research on mathematics teaching and learning.* New York: Macmillan.

Gutiérrez, A., & Boero, P. (Eds.) (2006). *Handbook of research on the psychology of mathematics education: Past, present and future.* Rotterdam, the Netherlands: Sense Publishers.

Halai, A. (1998). Mentor, mentee, and mathematics: A story of professional development. *Journal of Mathematics Teacher Education, 1,* 295–315.

Hart, L. (2002). Preservice teachers' beliefs and practice after participating in an integrated content/mathematics course. *School Science and Mathematics, 102*(1), 4–14.

Honey, S., & Graham, T. (2003). To use or not to use graphic calculators on teaching practice: A case study of three trainee-teachers' beliefs and attitudes. *The International Journal of Computer Algebra in Mathematics Education, 10*(2), 81–101.

Kyleve, J. I., & Williams, J. S. (1996). Measures of teachers' attitudes towards mathematical modelling. In L. Puig, & A. Gutiérrez (Eds.), *Proceedings of the 20th Conference of the International Group for the Psychology of Mathematics Education* (Vol. 3, pp. 209–216). Valencia, Spain: Universitat de València.

Langford, K., & Huntley, M. A. (1999). Internships as commencement: Mathematics and science research experiences as catalysts for preservice teacher professional development, *Journal of Mathematics Teacher Education, 2*(3), 277–299.

Leatham, K. R. (2006). Viewing mathematics teachers' beliefs as sensible systems. *Journal of Mathematics Teacher Education 9,* 91–102.

Leder, G. C. (2007). Beliefs: What lies behind the mirror? *The Montana Mathematics Enthusiast, Monograph 3,* 39–50.

Leder, G. C., & Forgasz, H. J. (2002a). Measuring mathematical beliefs and their impact on the learning of mathematics: A new approach. In G. C. Leder, E. Pehkonen, & G. Törner (Eds.). *Beliefs: A hidden variable in mathematics education?* (pp. 95–113). Dordrecht, the Netherlands: Kluwer Academic Publishers.

Leder, G. C., & Forgasz, H. J. (2002b). Two new instruments to probe attitudes about gender and mathematics. *ERIC, Resources in Education (RIE).* ERIC document number: ED463312.

Leder, G. C., & Grootenboer, P. (2005). Editorial. *Mathematics Education Research Journal, 17*(2), 1–8.

Lester, F. K. Jr. (2002). Implications of research on students' beliefs for classroom practice. In G. C. Leder, E. Pehkonen, & G. Törner (Eds.) *Beliefs: A hidden variable in mathematics education?* (pp. 345–353). Dordrecht, the Netherlands: Kluwer Academic Publishers.

Lindgren, S. (2000, June). *Teachers' beliefs about mathematics and the epistemology of their practical knowledge.* Paper presented at the Research on Mathematical Beliefs: Proceedings of the MAVI-9 European Workshop, University of Vienna, Austria.

Lloyd, G. (2002). Mathematics teachers' beliefs and experiences with innovative curriculum materials. In G. C. Leder, E. Pehkonen, & G. Törner (Eds.), *Beliefs: A hidden variable in mathematics education?* (pp. 149–159). Dordrecht, the Netherlands: Kluwer Academic Publishers.

McDonough, A., & Clarke, B. (2005). Professional development as a catalyst for changes in beliefs and practice: perspectives from the early numeracy research project. In P. Clarkson, A. Downton, D., Gronn, M. Horne, A. McDonough, R. Pierce, & A. Roche (Eds.), Building connections: Research, theory and practice. *Proceedings of the 28th annual conference of the Mathematics Education Research Group of Australasia* (pp. 521–528). Sydney: Mathematics Education Research Group of Australasia.

Mason, J. (2004). Are beliefs believable? *Mathematical Thinking and Learning*, 6(3), 343–351.

Mewborn, D. S. (1999). Preservice elementary mathematics teachers. *Journal for Research in Mathematics Education*, 30, 316–341.

Mingus, T. T. Y., & Grassl, R. M. (1999). Preservice teacher beliefs about proofs. *School Science and Mathematics*, 99(8), 438–444.

National Council of Teachers of Mathematics (2000). *Principles and standards for school mathematics.* Reston, VA: Author.

OECD. (2004). *The PISA 2003 Assessment Framework – Mathematics, reading, science and problem solving.* Paris: Author.

OECD. (nd). FAQ: OECD PISA. Retrieved 12 December, 2007 from: http://www.oecd.org/document/53/0,3343,en_32252351_32235731_38262901_1_1_1_1,00.html

Perry, B., Way, J., Southwell, B., White, A., & Pattison, J. (2005). Mathematical beliefs and achievement of pre-service primary teachers. In P. Clarkson, A. Downton, D. Gronn, M. Horne, A. McDonough, R. Pierce, & A. Roche (Eds.), *Building connections: Research, theory and practice* (pp. 625–632). Sydney: Mathematics Education Research Group of Australasia.

Philipp, R. (2007). Mathematics teachers' beliefs and affect. In F. K. Lester, Jr. (Ed.), *Second handbook of research on mathematics teaching and learning* (pp. 257–315). Charlotte, NC: Information Age Publishing & National Council of Teachers of Mathematics.

Quinn, R. J., & Wilson, M. M. (1997). Writing in the mathematics classroom: Teacher beliefs and practices. *The Clearing House, 71*(1), 14–20.

Raymond, A. M. (1997). Inconsistency between a beginning elementary school teacher's mathematical beliefs and teaching practice. *Journal for Research in Mathematics Education, 28*(5), 550–576.

Scott, A. L. (2005). Pre-service teachers' experiences and the influences on their intentions for teaching primary school mathematics. *Mathematics Education Research Journal, 17*(3), 62–90.

Seaman, C. E., Szydlik, J. E., Szydlik, S. D., & Beam, J. E. (2005). A comparison of preservice elementary teachers' beliefs about mathematics and mathematics teaching: 1968 and 1998. *School Science and Mathematics, 105*(4), 197–210.

Senger, E. S. (1998). Reflective reform in mathematics: The recursive nature of teacher change. *Educational Studies in Mathematics, 37*(3), 199–221.

Soro, R. (2000). *Teachers' beliefs about girls and boys and mathematics.* Research on mathematical beliefs: Proceedings of the MAVI-9 European Workshop, University of Vienna, Austria.

Spielman, L. J., & Lloyd, G. M. (2004). The impact of enacted mathematics curriculum models on prospective elementary teachers' course perceptions and beliefs. *School Science and Mathematics, 104* (1), 32–44.

Steele, D. F. (2001). The interfacing of preservice and inservice experiences of reform-based teaching: A longitudinal study. *Journal of Mathematics Teacher Education, 4*, 139–172.

Sztajn, P. (2003). Adapting reform ideas in different mathematics classrooms: Beliefs beyond mathematics. *Journal of Mathematics Teacher Education, 6*, 53–75.

Szydlik, J. E., Szydlik, S. D., & Benson, S. R. (2003). Exploring changes in pre-service elementary teachers' mathematical beliefs. *Journal of Mathematics Teacher Education, 6*, 253–279.

Tiedemann, J. (2000). Gender-related beliefs of teachers in elementary school mathematics. *Educational Studies in Mathematics, 41*(2), 191–207.

Tiedemann, J. (2002). Teachers' gender stereotypes as determinants of teachers' perceptions in elementary school mathematics. *Educational Studies in Mathematics, 50*(1), 49–62.

Timmerman, M. A. (2004). The influences of three interventions on prospective elementary teacher's beliefs about the knowledge base needed for teaching mathematics. *School Science and Mathematics, 104*(8), 369–382.

Vacc, N. N., & Bright, G. W. (1999). Elementary preservice teachers' changing beliefs and instructional use of children's mathematical thinking. *Journal for Research in Mathematics Education, 30*, 89–110.

Wilkins, J. L. M., & Brand, B. R. (2004). Change in preservice teachers' beliefs: An evaluation of a mathematics methods course. *School Science and Mathematics, 104*(5), 226–232.

Wilson, M., & Cooney, T. (2002). Mathematics teacher change and development. In G. C. Leder, E. Pehkonen, & G. Törner (Eds.), *Beliefs: A hidden variable in mathematics education?* (pp. 127–147). Dordrecht, The Netherlands: Kluwer Academic Publishers.

Winne, P. H., & Alexander, P. A. (2006). Foreword. In P. A. Alexander, & P. H. Winne, *Handbook of educational psychology*, Second Edition (pp. xi–xii) Mahwah, NJ: Lawrence Erlbaum Associates.

Wittrock, M. C. (1986). *Handbook of research on teaching*. New York: Macmillan.

Wood, T., & Sellers, P. (1997). Deepening the analysis: Longitudinal assessment of a problem-centered mathematics program. *Journal for Research in Mathematics Education, 28*, 163–186.

Yun-peng, M., Chi-chung, L., & Ngai-ying, W. (2006). Chinese primary school mathematics teachers working in a centralised curriculum system: A case study of two primary schools in north-east China. *Compare: A Journal of Comparative Education, 36*(2), 197–212.

Zevenbergen, R. (2003). Mathematics teachers' beliefs and practices: Reforming middle school mathematics in a context of new times. *Australian Journal of Middle Schooling, 3*(2), 6–14.

Helen J. Forgasz
Faculty of Education
Monash University, Australia

Gilah C. Leder
Faculty of Education
Monash University, Australia

SECTION 3

KNOWLEDGE OF EQUITY, DIVERSITY AND CULTURE IN TEACHING MATHEMATICS

JILL ADLER AND DANIELLE HUILLET

9. THE SOCIAL PRODUCTION OF MATHEMATICS FOR TEACHING

This chapter aims to show the impact of culture on the learning of mathematics and consequently that studies of mathematics for teaching require strong theoretical frameworks that foreground the relationship between culture and pedagogy. For this purpose, we describe two different research projects in Southern Africa, each focused on the notion of mathematics for teaching. The first study analyses teacher learning of the mathematical concept of limits of functions through participation in a research community in Mozambique, and is framed by Chevallard's anthropological theory of didactics. The second, the QUANTUM project, studies what and how mathematics is produced in and across selected mathematics and mathematics education courses in in-service mathematics teacher education programmes in South Africa, and is shaped by Berstein's theory of pedagogic discourse. We argue that separately and together these two studies demonstrate that mathematics for teaching can only be grasped through a language that positions it as structured by, and structuring of, the pedagogic discourse (in Bernstein's terms) or the institution (in Chevallard's terms) in which it 'lives'.

INTRODUCTION

Shulman (1986, 1987) posited the notions of *subject matter knowledge* (SMK), *pedagogical content knowledge* (PCK) and *curriculum knowledge* (CK), as critical categories in the professional knowledge base of teaching. In so doing, he foregrounded the centrality of disciplinary or subject knowledge, and its integration with knowledge of teaching and learning, for successful teaching. The past two decades have witnessed a range of studies related to SMK and an emphasis of research on PCK, many focused on mathematics (e.g., Ball, Bass & Hill, 2004; Ball, Thames & Phelps, 2007). As a consequence, a new discourse is emerging attempting to mark out *mathematics for teaching* as a distinctive or specialised form of mathematical knowledge produced and used in the practice of teaching. As noted in Adler and Davis (2006), this discourse is fledgling.

In this chapter we describe two different research projects in Southern Africa each focused on the notion of *mathematics for teaching*. We foreground the social epistemologies that informed and shaped these studies: Chevallard's anthropological theory of didactics (Chevallard, 1992, 1999) and Bernstein's theory of pedagogic discourse (Bernstein, 1996, 2000), and illuminate their critical

P. Sullivan and T. Wood (eds.), Knowledge and Beliefs in Mathematics Teaching and Teaching Development, 195–221.

role in each study. We argue that separately and together these two research projects demonstrate that *mathematics for teaching* can only be grasped through a language that positions it as structured by, and structuring of, the pedagogic discourse (in Bernstein's terms) or the institution (in Chevallard's terms) in which it 'lives'. From this perspective, mathematics is learned for some purpose, and within teacher education, this would be for mathematics teaching, and/or becoming a mathematics teacher. There are thus limits to the appropriateness of the use of general categories like PCK and SMK, as well as the distinctions between them.

MOZAMBICAN TEACHERS RESEARCHING THE LIMIT CONCEPT

We begin with a study of teacher learning through participation in a research community in Mozambique, motivated by the desire to impact on teachers' knowledge of advanced mathematical concepts. The study drew inspiration for its questions from Chevallard's notions of personal and institutional relations to concepts, and from his elaborated anthropological theory of didactics for framing and interrogating the notion of *mathematics for teaching* in this study. It shows how the institutional relation to the mathematical concept of limits of functions, as well as each teacher's position within the new institution influenced the development of a new personal relation to this concept. However, the weight of strong institutions such as Mozambican secondary school and Pedagogical University hindered the development of a more elaborated relation to the mathematical concept of limit that allows the challenging of these two strong institutions' relation to this concept. This opens up questions about both SMK and PCK and their inter-relation, particularly in teacher education practice.

Starting Point of the Study

In Mozambican didactic institutions, the teaching of limits of functions typically has two components: a formal component, the ε-δ definition, derived from within mathematics that students are sometimes asked to memorise; and a procedural component, the calculation of limits using algebraic transformations. Mozambican teachers study the limit concept in these didactic institutions, secondary schools and university. As a consequence, their mathematical knowledge of limits is reduced to these two aspects (Huillet & Mutemba, 2000). Their teaching mirrors the way they have been taught as students, and thus, the secondary schools' routine for teaching limits. This study started from reflection on the conditions for changing these institutional routines. Considering that teachers are the main actors in the didactical relation in the classroom, teaching limits in a more elaborated way would only be possible if teachers develop their mathematical knowledge of this concept. This led to the following questions:

- How could limits of functions be taught in Mozambican secondary schools so that students not only learn to calculate limits but also give meaning to this concept?

- What kind of knowledge does a teacher need to teach limits in schools in that way?
- How could Mozambican secondary school teachers acquire this knowledge?

These questions have been addressed in this study through the lens of the Chevallard's anthropological theory of didactics.

Chevallard's Anthropological Theory of Didactics

The anthropological theory of didactics (ATD) locates mathematical activity, as well as the activity of studying mathematics, within the set of human activities and social institutions (Chevallard, 1992). It considers that "everything is an object" and that an object exists if at least one person or institution relates to this object. To each institution is associated a set of "institutional objects" for which an institutional relation, with stable elements, is established.

An individual establishes a personal relation to some object of knowledge if s/he has been in contact with one or several institutions where this object of knowledge is found. S/he is a "good" subject of an institution relative to some object of knowledge if his/her personal relation to this object is judged to be consistent with the institutional relation. For example, in this study, the relation that Mozambican mathematics teachers established with the limit concept was shaped by the relationship to this concept in the institutions in which they learned it. For most teachers, this contact occurred in Mozambican institutions (secondary school as students, university as students, and as secondary school teachers). The institutional relation to an object of knowledge can be analysed through the social practices involving this object inside the institution. Chevallard (1999) elaborates a model to describe and analyse these institutional practices, using the notion of praxeological organisation or, in the case of mathematics, mathematical organisation. The first assumption of this model is that any human activity can be subsumed as a system of tasks (Chevallard, 1999; Bosch and Chevallard, 1999). Mathematics, as a human activity, can therefore be analysed as the study of given kinds of problematic tasks.

The second assumption of this theory is that, inside a given institution, there is generally one technique or a few techniques recognised by the institution to solve each kind of task. Each kind of task and the associated technique form the *practical block* (or know-how) of a *mathematical organisation* (MO). For example, in Mozambican secondary schools, students are taught to calculate limits using algebraic transformations. A specific algebraic transformation is associated to each kind of limit, constituting the practical block of a specific MO. Other kinds of tasks could be: to read limits from a graph, to sketch the graph of a function using its limits, to demonstrate the limit of a function using the definition, etc. These kinds of tasks are hardly used in Mozambican secondary schools, but can be found in other institutions, for example in secondary schools or universities in other countries. Students are then expected to solve each of these tasks using a specific technique. The institutional relation to an object is shaped by the set of tasks to be performed, using specific techniques, by the subjects holding a specific position inside the institution. In an institution, a specific kind of task T is usually solved using only one technique τ. Most of the tasks become part of a routine, the task/technique practical blocks [T, τ] appearing to be *natural* inside this institution.

The third assumption of the theory of mathematical organisations is that there is an ecological constraint to the existence of a technique inside an institution: it must appear to be understandable and justified (Bosch & Chevallard, 1999). This is done by the technology θ, which is a rational discourse to describe and justify the technique. This constraint can be interpreted at two levels. At the students' level, it means that students should be able to understand the technique. At the mathematics level, we must ensure that the technique is "mathematically correct" with reference to scholarly knowledge.[1] These ecological constraints can sometimes lead to a contradiction, given that the ability of students to understand will be constrained by their development and previous knowledge. It can be difficult for a technique to be both understandable and justified at the same time.

The technology θ itself is justified by a theory Θ, which is a higher level of justification, explanation and production of techniques. Technology and theory constitute the *knowledge block* [θ,Θ] of a MO. According to Chevallard (1999), the technology-theory block is usually identified with *knowledge* [un savoir], while the task-technique block is considered as *know-how* [un savoir-faire].

The two components of a MO are summarised in the diagram below.

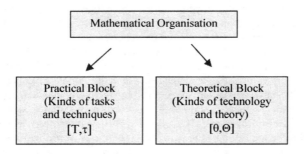

Figure 1. Mathematical organisation.

A MO around a particular kind of task in a certain institution is specific. For example, calculating the limit of a rational function when x goes to infinity by factorisation and cancellation is a specific MO. The corresponding technology would be, for example, the theorems about limits, and the corresponding theory the demonstration of these theorems using the ε-δ definition. The integration of several specific MOs around a specific technology gives rise to a local MO. For example, calculating several kinds of limits using algebraic transformation constitutes a local

---

[1] We mark out mathematical knowledge intentionally in order to signal that what counts as scholarly mathematical knowledge is not unproblematic.

MO. In the same way, the integration of several local MOs around the same theory gives rise to a regional or global mathematical organisation.

In order to teach a mathematical organisation, a teacher must build a *didactical organisation*[2] (Chevallard, 2002). To analyse how a didactical organisation enables the set up of a mathematical organisation, we can first look at the way the different moments of the study of this MO are settled in the classroom. Chevallard (2002) presents a model of six moments of study. They are the following: *first encounter* with the MO, *exploration of the task* and *emergence of the technique*, construction of the *technological-theoretical bloc*, *institutionalisation*, work with the MO (particularly *the technique*), and *evaluation*[3]. The order of these moments is not a fixed one. Depending on the kind of didactical organisation, some of these moments can appear in a different order, but all will probably occur. For example the study of mathematical organisations at university level is often divided in theoretical classes and tutorials. The theoretical block is presented to students in lectures, as already produced and organised knowledge, and tasks are solved using some techniques (practical block) during tutorials. In that way there is a disconnection between the theoretical component of the organisation and its applications. This is what happens in Mozambique with limits of functions. At the university level, the ε-δ definition and the theorems about limits and their demonstrations using this definition are usually taught in theoretical classes, while tutorials are dedicated to calculating limits using algebraic transformations (Huillet, 2007a). In that case, the reasons why the theory exists gets lost. And so we see the institution as structuring of, and being structured by, the particular mathematics in focus.

The Use of Anthropological Theory of Didactics in this Study

The anthropological theory of didactics (ATD) has been used in this study to analyse the teachers' personal relation to this concept and its evolution through their work within a new institution, using different aspects of mathematics for teaching limits.

In the first place, ATD has been used as a tool for analysing the institutional relation of Mozambican didactic institutions to the limit concept, in particular the secondary school institution and the Pedagogical University where most mathematics teachers are trained. For each of these institutions, the practical block and the knowledge block of the mathematical organisation related to limits of functions have been analysed through the examination of the syllabus, the national examinations (secondary school), worksheets used in secondary schools (there is no textbook for this level in Mozambique), textbooks used at the Pedagogical University and the exercise book of a student. This analysis highlighted a

---

[2] We note here that didactical organisations are specific to certain topics or contents in mathematics.
[3] There is an interesting similarity between these moments of study and the interpretation of Hegelian moments of judgement in pedagogic discourse as described by Davis (2001), and referred in Adler and Pillay (2007).

dichotomy between two regional mathematical organisations: the algebra of limits based on the ε-δ definition, and the existence of limits, based on algebraic transformations to evaluate limits. This dichotomy, which also exists in other secondary schools in other countries (Barbé, Bosch, Espinoza, & Gascón, 2005) and is explained by the nature of the limit concept, seems to be exacerbated in the Mozambican case. This can explain the limited personal relation to limits of Mozambican teachers (Huillet, 2005a).

Secondly, anthropological theory of didactics was used to design the research methodology. Considering the institutional relation previously described and how it strongly shaped teachers' personal relations to this concept, this personal relation could only evolve if teachers were in contact with this concept through a new institution where this concept lived in a more elaborated way.[4] Other institutional or personal constraints could influence the usual way of teaching limits in schools. The argument was that their personal relation did not allow them to challenge the institutional routines. The evolution of their knowledge was a necessary, although not sufficient, condition for any change of the way of teaching limits in Mozambican secondary schools. Consequently a new institution was set up, where four final-year student-teachers from the Pedagogical University researched some aspects of the limit concept and shared their findings in periodic seminars. The researcher was both supervisor of the teachers' individual research and facilitator of the seminars.

In the third place, ADT was used to analyse a mathematics teacher's task(s) when planning a didactical organisation, using Chevallard's model of the moments of study (Chevallard, 2002). This allowed the development of a general framework for describing the knowledge needed by a teacher to perform these tasks. It includes scholarly mathematical knowledge of the MO, knowledge about the social justification for teaching this MO, how to organise students' first encounter with this MO, knowledge about the practical block (tasks and techniques) using different representations, knowledge on how to construct the theoretical block according to learners' age and previous knowledge, and knowledge about students' conceptions and difficulties when studying this MO. This description of *mathematics for teaching*[5] was used to define research topics for the teachers involved in the research group. In line with the overall approach in this study, within these aspects of *mathematics for teaching* limits, the boundary between SMK and PCK as developed by Shulman is blurred. Rather, and this is elaborated further below, each aspect has two components, a mathematical and a pedagogical component. Some aspects are more mathematical, some others more pedagogical, but they are necessarily merged in the human activity of mathematics teaching.

---

[4] Obviously, it cannot be claimed that a change in teachers' personal relation would automatically result in a change of their way of teaching limits at school.

[5] The expression *mathematics for teaching* to design the knowledge needed by a mathematics teacher is the same as defined by Ball et al. (2004) and Adler and Davis (2006).

The Evolution of Teachers' Knowledge through the New Institution

The new institution set up for this study was a research group, where four teachers, honours students at the Pedagogical University, researched different specific aspects of the limit concept and shared their findings in periodical seminars. The researcher was their supervisor and the facilitator of the seminars. The evolution of these teachers' knowledge through the new institution was analysed in detail for five aspects, or sub-aspects, of mathematics for teaching limits in schools: how to organise students' first encounter with limits of functions, the social justification for teaching limits in secondary schools, the essential features of the limit concept (part of the scholarly mathematical knowledge), the graphical register (part of the practical block) and the ε-δ definition (also part of the scholarly mathematical knowledge). For each of these aspects, categories were defined both for teachers' mathematical knowledge (ranked in several degrees from "knowing less" to "knowing more") and for teachers' ideas about teaching, related to this aspect (ranked again in several degrees from "being close to the secondary school institutional relation to limits" to "challenging this institutional relation"). An example of each of these can be found in Appendix 1, where the co-presence of both mathematical and teaching knowledge is evident. These further illuminate that learning of mathematics through the range of tasks in this research institution was for the purposes of teaching mathematics.

In this chapter we will not detail the methodology used to collect and analyse data in the study. We only present some results that help understand the role of the new institution in the development of a new personal relation to limits and discuss the weight of this institution in comparison with strong Mozambican didactic institutions as are the Secondary School and the Pedagogical University. We focus on two teachers, selected because they represent two extreme situations in relation to their teaching experience and to their position within the group: Abel,[6] an experienced teacher who had taught limits in school for years; and David, the youngest teacher in the group, with very little teaching experience. The evolution of these two teachers' personal relation to limits during the research process, for the five aspects selected for the study, is presented in Table 1 below.

This table shows that while both teachers' personal relation to limits evolved, this was uneven, particularly for the two last aspects of the limit concept: the use of the graphical register and the ε-δ definition. In this chapter we focus on these two aspects.

---

[6] These are pseudonyms.

Table 1. Evolution of Abel's and David's personal relation to the limit concept according to five aspects of mathematics for teaching limits

	Categories	Abel	David
First Encounter	FE-MK1 to FE-MK2	FE-MK1→FE-MK2	FE-MK1 → FE-MK2
	FE-T1 to FE-T6	FE-T2 → FE-T4	FE-T1 → FE-T5
Social Justification	SJ-MK1 to SJ-MK4	SJ-MK2 → SJ-MK4	SJ-MK1 → SJ-MK4
	SJ-T1 to SJ-T3	SJ-T1 → SJ-T1	SJ-T1 → SJ-T3
Essential Features	EF-MK1 to EF-MK4	EF-MK1→ EF-MK4	EF-MK2→ EF-MK4
	EF-T1 to EF-T2	EF-T1→ EF-T2	EF-T1→EF-T2
Graphical Register	GRRR to GRR6	GRR1 → GRR3	GRR2 → GRR5
	GRRS to GRS6	GRS2 → GRS2	GRS3 → GRS6
	GR-T1 to GR-T3	GR-T1 → GR-T2	GR-T1 → GR-T3
ε-δ Definition	D-MK1 to D-MK4	D-MK1 → D-MK3	D-MK1 → D-MK2
	D-T1 to D-T4	D-T1 → D-T3	D-T4 → D-T2

FE-MK   *Mathematical knowledge about the first encounter with the limit concept.*
FE-T   *Ideas about teaching related to the first encounter with the limit concept.*
SJ-MK   *Mathematical knowledge about the social justification.*
SJ-T   *Ideas about teaching related to the social justification.*
EF-MK   *Mathematical knowledge about essential features.*
EF-T   *Ideas about teaching related to essential features.*
GRRR   *Knowledge about how to read limits from graphs.*
GRRS   *Knowledge about how to represent a limit on a graph.*
GR-T   *Ideas about teaching related to the graphical register.*
D-MK   *Mathematical knowledge about the definition.*
D-T   *Ideas about teaching related to the definition.*

In the wider study, Huillet (2007b) shows the limited evolution of all four teachers' knowledge about the graphical register, and explained this in relation to the general difficulty that the teachers had in working with graphs. The teachers in this study did not display deep understanding of basic mathematical knowledge such as the concept of function, and the use and interpretation of graphs in general. Nevertheless, the evolution of Abel's and David's knowledge about the use of the graphical register for studying limits was very different from each other, with David's knowledge about this aspect evolving more than Abel's (as well as the other teachers in the study). We suggest two explanations for this uneven outcome. Firstly, this aspect was directly linked to David's research topic (Applications of the limit concept in mathematics and in other sciences). Secondly, and this explanation is more speculative, David used the interviews as a means for learning.

By positioning himself more as a student than as a teacher, David was able to take advantage of each opportunity for learning, by asking questions and attempting to solve more tasks. In contrast, Abel did not try to solve many graphical tasks. He assumed more of a teacher's position and thus one who should already know. As a consequence, he did not engage in the interviews in ways that could have enabled his knowledge about the use of graphs for teaching limits to evolve.

The ε-δ definition belongs to the scholarly mathematical knowledge and, like the graphical register, requires a deep understanding of basic mathematical concepts. Furthermore, it is intrinsically difficult (Huillet, 2005b) and it is part of the syllabus of Mozambican secondary schools. At the beginning of the research process, none of the teachers could explain this definition, and their understanding of it evolved slightly during the study. Again, Abel's and David's ideas about teaching this definition in secondary schools evolved differently, curiously in opposite directions. At the beginning of the research process, Abel, the experienced teacher who had taught this definition in schools, argued that it was right that it be taught in school. By the end of the study, he had reached the conclusion that it was not appropriate to teach this definition at secondary school level: students were not able to understand it in that form. In contrast, David was initially inclined not to teach the definition. At the end, however, he was willing to teach it while acknowledging students' difficulties in understanding this definition.

Let's analyse the evolution of how these two teachers positioned[7] themselves within the new institution, that is, within the research group and so with the possibilities for their relations to the limit to evolve. At the beginning of our work together, Abel positioned himself as an experienced teacher. During the seminars, he volunteered to explain some aspects of limits to his colleagues, particularly the ε-δ definition, trying to show that he had mastered this topic. During the first interview, he constantly referred to what was done in schools when teaching this concept, showing that he knew the syllabus and the way limits are usually taught in secondary schools. However, he faced difficulties during his explanations to his colleagues and felt 'ashamed' about it, as he told the researcher during the second interview. He then faced difficulties during his research study - an experiment in a secondary school. He experienced these difficulties as his failure as a teacher, and not as the result of the research, or as a researcher. He also became aware that he had been teaching limits in school, in particular the ε-δ definition and L'Hôpital's Rule, in ways that were problematic for his students. This reflection on his practice, although very hard for him, offers an explanation as to why, at the end of the research process, Abel said that the ε-δ definition should not be part of the secondary school syllabus.

In contrast, David's initial position within the research group was of learner-teacher, a university student teaching as he completed his studies. During the first interview, he analysed the way limits are usually taught in Mozambican secondary

---

[7] What we mean by 'positioned' here is the way in which this particular teacher related to both the researcher and others in the group.

schools as a student who did not understand the ε-δ definition. He did not participate much in the discussion during the first seminars, giving way to his more experienced colleagues. However, he was able to argue with them in the last seminars. The end of the research process coincided with the conclusion of his teacher training course, and it seems that at that point, he then positioned himself more as a teacher than as a student. He was thus anticipating the institution where he was going to teach limits i.e., the secondary school institution. He knew that secondary school students were not able to understand this definition, but at the same time that it is part of the Mozambican Grade 12 syllabus. He remembered studying it in that grade. It is arguable, that as a prospective teacher, the weight of the institution he was moving to became more influential in his thinking.

The analysis of the evolution of these two teachers' personal relation to limits of functions related to two critical aspects of this concept shows that these teachers experienced the weight of the two institutions in different ways, particularly where relations to the limit concept was in conflict.

Institutional Strengths and Weaknesses

Chevallard's anthropological theory of didactics points out the importance of institutional relations to an object of knowledge and how an individual's personal relation to this object is shaped by the institutions' relations where this individual met this object. The study of the personal relation of four Mozambican student-teachers, who had mainly[8] been in contact with the limit concept through Mozambican institutions, showed how their personal relation to limits at the start of the study was consistent with the Mozambican Secondary School's and the Pedagogical University's institutional relations to this concept. It also showed that this personal relation evolved during their contact with this object of knowledge through another institution, the research group, holding a different institutional relation. However, this study also pointed out some limitations in the evolution of this knowledge.

These results lead to the following questions:
- Why, at the end of the work within the research group, were the teachers' personal relations to limits of function not fully consistent with the relation of the new institution?
- How could the new institution be modified so as to enable teachers to learn more about limits, according to the expected (and more elaborated) personal relation?

Elements of answers to these questions have been given in the previous section. One of them is the lack of basic understanding of some mathematical concepts that hindered the evolution of teachers' knowledge, especially the mathematical components of this knowledge. It seems that, in these cases, more direct engagement with these aspects of the limit, supported by explanations and

---

[8] One of the teachers also studied in a university in East Germany.

systematic solution of tasks was necessary for teachers to overcome their difficulties. This is what happened with David. During the third interview he tried to solve many graphical tasks, asking questions and drawing on the researcher's explanations to solve them. He thus engaged with the limit concept in various and new ways.

The mathematical component in the new institution was apparently not strong enough. In the first case, the researcher did not anticipate the extent of the weakness of the teachers' knowledge of basic mathematical concepts. For example, she knew that the teachers were not used to using graphs in the study of limits, but she did not imagine that they would have so many difficulties working with graphs in general. For example, they sometimes confused x-values and y-values (or the two axes), or a limit with the maximum of the function (Huillet, 2007b). Secondly, the researcher was reluctant to play the role of a teacher within the group, because she wanted to observe how the teachers' personal relation to limits evolved through research. She felt that teaching them would influence the results of her research.

With regard to the more pedagogical component of the teachers' personal relations to limit, we already saw that, during the research process, all teachers changed their ideas about teaching the ε-δ definition in secondary schools. While the experienced teacher said that he would not like to teach the definition any more, the other three teachers argued that this definition should be taught in schools. This evolution was explained by the weight of the secondary school institutional relation to limits: they were now positioned as teachers and not as students, as at the beginning of the research process. This suggests another weakness of the research group as an institution. Relative to well established institutions such as the Mozambican Secondary School and the Pedagogical University, institutions with a strong tradition of teaching and well established routines, the research group appears as a very weak institution. That this institution enabled the teachers to become aware of strong gaps in the teaching of limits in secondary schools and at university does not necessarily imply that they will be able to stand up against strongly institutionalised routines. Organising students' first encounter with limits in a different way, introducing different kinds of tasks, for example graphical tasks or tasks to link limits with other mathematical or other sciences concepts, do not mean going against the secondary school syllabus, but adding something to it. Not to teach the ε-δ definition, even knowing that the students will not understand it, is a bigger step to take because this definition is part of the syllabus. It can be seen as an act of rebellion against the institution. Elsewhere, Huillet (2007a) has argued that these research outcomes emerging as they are from the Mozambican context and through a study that placed mathematics at its centre open up important questions about the literature in mathematics education on teachers-as-researchers. In the "teachers as researchers" movement, teachers usually studied some pedagogical aspect of their teaching, taking the mathematical content for granted; this did not allow them to challenge the content of their teaching. This can also be seen as the result of the dichotomy between mathematics and pedagogy in teacher education. This dichotomy is reproduced in Shulman's distinction between SMK and PCK, as if SMK were some kind of 'universal mathematical knowledge' and PCK mathematical knowledge specific for teaching. However, his description of SMK's substantive and syntactic structures contradicts this separation.

> The substantive structures are the variety of ways in which the basic concepts and principles of the discipline are organised to incorporate its facts. The syntactic structure of a discipline is the set of ways in which truth or falsehood, validity or invalidity, are established. (Shulman, 1986, p.9)

The syntactic structure of the discipline is important for teachers to engage in mathematics in a way that enables the construction of new didactical organisations. This study shows that the teachers involved in the research group did not grasp the syntactic structures of the limit concept during their training, but were only able to lead with substantive structure. From our perspective, this is not sufficient to teach limits in a way that challenges institutional routines, so making it comprehensible to students. We can then ask the question: does the syntactic structure of mathematics belong to SMK or PCK? We argue that this distinction is not appropriate and that, in teacher education, mathematics should live in a way that enables reflection at the same time on the mathematical and pedagogical aspects of the content to be taught. Where, when and how, then, in teacher education (particularly in professional development) practice, are teachers to have opportunities for further engagement with both syntactic and substantive aspects of the limit function. Could a research institution be strengthened so as to offer teachers further possibilities for elaborating their knowledge of limits of functions, and if so, how? The institution of mathematics teacher education itself – its objects and tasks, in Chevallard's terms – are in focus in the QUANTUM research project. In the next section we describe aspects of QUANTUM, foregrounding the theoretical resources drawn on to enable us to 'see' this "inner logic of pedagogic discourse and its practices" (Bernstein, 1996, p. 18), and specifically how it comes to shape mathematics for teaching in teacher education practice.

THE QUANTUM RESEARCH PROJECT IN SOUTH AFRICA

QUANTUM is the name given to a research and development project on quality mathematical education for teachers in South Africa. The development arm of QUANTUM focused on qualifications for teachers underqualified in mathematics (hence the name) and completed its tasks in 2003; QUANTUM continues as a collaborative research project. Between 2003 and 2006, the QUANTUM project has studied selected mathematics and mathematics education courses offered in higher education institutions as part of formalised (i.e., accredited) mathematics teacher education programmes for practising teachers in South Africa. Our analysis of these courses led to deeper insights into and understanding of what and how *mathematics for teaching* comes to 'live' in such programmes. We drew on, and elaborated, a set of theoretical resources from Bernstein in our study. These are our focus in this section of the chapter.

Starting Point of the Study

An underlying assumption in QUANTUM is that mathematics teacher education is distinguished by its dual, yet thoroughly interwoven, objects: *teaching* (i.e., learning to *teach* mathematics) and *mathematics* (i.e., learning *mathematics for teaching*). It is these dual objects that lead to what is often described as the subject-method tension. Others describe this as one of the dilemmas in teacher education (Adler, 2002; Graven, 2005). The inter-relation of mathematics and teaching is writ large in *in-service* teacher education (INSET) programmes (elsewhere referred to as professional development for practising teachers) where new and/or different ways of knowing and doing school mathematics, new curricula, combine with new and/or different contexts for teaching. Such are the conditions of continuing professional development for practising teachers in South Africa. The past ten years saw a mushrooming of formalised programmes for practising teachers across higher education institutions in South Africa, in particular, Advanced Certificates in Education (ACE) programmes.[9] The ACE qualification explicitly addresses the inequities produced in apartheid teacher education, where black teachers only had access to a three-year diploma qualification. As a result, most ACE programmes are geared to black teachers, at both the primary and secondary levels. Many of these are focused on the content of mathematics and constituted by a combination of mathematics and mathematics education courses. Debate continues as to whether and how these programmes should integrate or separate out opportunities for teachers to (re)learn *mathematics* and to (re)learn how to *teach*.

A consequent assumption in QUANTUM is that however the combinations are accomplished, both mathematics and teaching as activities and/or discourses are always simultaneously present in all components of such programmes. Moreover, their interaction within pedagogic practice will have effects. This latter assumption is derived from a social epistemological approach to knowledge (re)production in pedagogic practice, and motivated by the work of Basil Bernstein, specifically how he deals with the conversion or translation of knowledges into pedagogic communication. And it is this orientation that leads us to reframe the broad problematic discussed as the following research question: What is constituted as *mathematics for teaching* in formalised practising mathematics teacher education practice in South Africa, and how is it so constituted?[10]

---

[9] The ACE (formerly called a Further Diploma in Education – FDE) is a diploma that enables teachers to upgrade their three-year teaching diploma to a four-year diploma. The goal is to provide teachers with a qualification regarded as equivalent with a four-year undergraduate degree.

[10] In Chevellard's terms, the question would be: what is the institutional relation to mathematics that is set up and how does it function?

Bernstein's Theory of the Pedagogic Device and Related Orientations to Knowledges

In the introduction to this chapter, we noted that Chevallard and Bernstein share a social orientation to knowledge. Both hold that rigour in educational (or didactics) research is a function of coherence between an overarching theoretical orientation, research questions and methodology. For Chevallard, a didactic organisation needs to be built to teach a mathematical organisation. The reciprocal effects of this are inevitable. Bernstein too sees knowledges in school, or any pedagogic context, as structured by pedagogic communication. His theory of the pedagogic device describes a set of principles and rules that regulate this structuring. It is these that we have brought to bear on our investigation into *mathematics for teaching* in teacher education practice.

For Bernstein, the principles of the transformation of knowledge in pedagogic practice are described in terms of the 'pedagogic device' (Bernstein, 2000). The pedagogic device is an assemblage of rules or procedures via which knowledges are converted into pedagogic communication.[11] It is this communication (within the pedagogic site) that acts on meaning potential. That is, pedagogic discourse itself shapes possibilities for making meaning, in this case of *mathematics for teaching*. The pedagogic device is the intrinsic grammar (in a metaphoric sense) of pedagogic discourse, and works through three sets of hierarchical rules.

Distributive rules regulate power relations between social groups, distributing different forms of knowledge and constituting *different orientations to meaning* (Bernstein refers to pedagogic identities). In simpler terms, the regulation of power relations in pedagogic practice effects who learns what. Whereas for Chevallard, orientations to meaning lie in 'institutional and personal relations' to a concept, the distributive rule brings social structuring *effects* to the fore, a function of Bernstein's concern with educational inequality and its social (re)production.

Recontextualisation rules regulate the formation of specific pedagogic discourse. In any pedagogic practice *knowledges are delocated, relocated and refocused*, so becoming something other. In the context of QUANTUM, the recontextualising rule at work regulates how mathematics and teaching, as a discipline and a field respectively, are co-constituted in particular teacher education practices. Here there is further resonance with didactic transposition, and with Chevallard's notion of institutionalisation, particularly the effects of strong and weak institutions on changing practices. The recontextualising rule is possibly the most well known and used element of Bernstein's work, and elaborated through the concepts of classification and framing. Classification refers to "the relations between categories" (2000, p. 6),[12] and how strong or weak are the boundaries between categories (e.g., discourses or subject areas in the secondary school) in a pedagogic practice. Framing refers to social relations in pedagogic

---

[11] In Chevallard's terms, this transformation occurs in the setting up of the didactical organisation.

[12] For Bernstein, boundary maintenance is through power and changing or weakening the insulation between categories will reveal power relations – and so be contested (p.7).

practice, and who in the pedagogic relation controls what (2000). For our purposes in this chapter, the issue is whether and how mathematics and teaching as two domains are insulated from each other or integrated and then through what principles. The way knowledges are classified and framed, in any educational practice, the varying strength or weakness of the insulations, will constitute a range of pedagogic modalities[13] and shape what comes to be transmitted.[14] In particular, they will impact on what comes to be *mathematics for teaching*.

Acquisition, in Bernstein's terms, is elaborated by what he refers to as 'recognition' and 'realisation'. In any pedagogic setting, learners need to recognise what it is they are to be learning, and further, they need to be able to demonstrate this by producing (realising) what is required – what he refers to as a 'legitimate text'.[15] Recognition and realisation link with the third set of rules operating within the pedagogic device. *Evaluative rules* constitute specific practices – *regulating what counts as valid knowledge.* For Bernstein, any pedagogic practice "transmits criteria" (indeed this is its major purpose). Evaluation condenses the meaning of the whole device (2000), so acting (hence the hierarchy of the rules) on recontextualisation (the shape of the discourse) that in turn acts on distribution (who gets what). What comes to be constituted as *mathematics for teaching* (i.e., as opportunities for learning *mathematics for teaching*) will be reflected through evaluation and how criteria come to work.

Despite the significance of evaluation in this theory, and in contrast to recontextualising rules, Bernstein's evaluative rules are not elaborated. Much of the pedagogical research on teacher education that has worked with Bernstein's framework focused on his rules for the transformation of knowledge into pedagogic communication, and particularly the distributive and recontextualising rules of the pedagogic device (e.g., Ensor, 2001, 2004; Morais, 2002). These studies foreground an analysis of classification and framing in a particular pedagogic modality, and related recognition and realisation rules that come to play. Ensor's study of mathematics prospective teacher education and its recontextualisation in the first year of teaching has advanced our understanding of the what, how and why of recontextualisation across sites of practice (university and school). The study argues that the 'gap' between what is taught in a programme for prospective teachers, and the practice adopted by teachers in their first year of teaching is not simply a function of teacher beliefs on the one hand, or

---

[13] Bernstein describes two contrasting educational codes – ideal types – formed by strong and weak classification. A collection code has strong classification and strong framing; in contrast, an integrated code has weak classification and framing. In the latter boundaries between contents and between social relations are both weak.

[14] As Graven (2002) explains, "in educational terms, Bernstein's use of the terms 'transmitter' and 'acquirer' may seem pejorative. However, he uses them throughout various pedagogic models and they are merely sociological labels for descriptive purposes. They should therefore not be interpreted to imply transmission pedagogies" (Ch. 2, p.28).

[15] In Chevallard's terms, when learners are able to produce the legitimate text, they show that their personal relation fits the institutional relation (that they are "good subjects" of the institution).

constraints in schools on the other. The gap is explained through the principle of recontextualisation. The privileged pedagogy enacted in the teacher education programme was unevenly accessed by the teachers in her study. Ensor, drawing on Bernstein, shows how this distribution was a function of what and how criteria for the privileged practice were marked out, and so what teachers were or were not able to recognise as valued mathematical practice, and then realise this in their school classrooms. Morais' work focused on primary science, and tackles the phenomenon of primary teachers not being subject specialists. She argues that because of their weaker science knowledge base, the pedagogic modality in their teacher education should combine strong classification with weakened framing. In this way primary science teachers can be offered an enabling set of social relations within which to engage further learning of science. Science content needs to be clearly bounded and visible (i.e., strongly classified), and structured by sequencing and pacing to suit primary teacher interests and needs (weakly framed).

However, as Davis has argued (Davis, 2005) a focus on classification and framing, while productive, backgrounds the special features of the content to be acquired. Even in Morais' study, the *specificity* of the science to be learned by primary teachers remains in the background. The concern with mathematical production in teacher education has thus led the QUANTUM project to focus instead on evaluation, and on the criteria for the production of legitimate (mathematical) texts. This required elaboration of the evaluative rule. Before we describe the methodology we have developed and used in QUANTUM to foreground the content to be acquired, one additional aspect of Bernstein's work requires discussion.

Mathematics and Teaching as Differing Domains of Knowledge.

Bernstein (2000) provides conceptual tools to distinguish different forms of knowledge and so to interrogate mathematics and teaching. In the first instance, he distinguished vertical and horizontal discourses, the criteria for which are forms of knowledge, and the most significant of which is whether knowledge is organised hierarchically or segmentally (2000). But, as he argues, this broad distinction does little to assist with understanding discourses in education, and ensuing issues of pedagogy. Education (and so too mathematics education) invokes a wide range of vertical discourses. He thus developed further distinctions, insisting that while these were accompanied by additional conceptual apparatus, they were important analytically.

For Bernstein, within vertical discourses we can distinguish between hierarchical and horizontal knowledge structures; and within the latter, between strong and weak grammars. Different domains of knowledge are differently structured and have different grammars. The natural sciences have hierarchical knowledge structures and strong grammars. They have "explicit conceptual syntax" and so recognition of what is and is not physics, for example, is apparent. Development is seen as "the development of theory which is more general and more integrating than previous theory" (2000, p. 162). The social sciences (hence education), in contrast, have horizontal knowledge structures, where development proceeds through the introduction of "new languages" that "accumulate" rather than integrate. Within the social sciences, some have relatively strong grammars i.e., their conceptual syntax enables "relatively precise empirical descriptions" (e.g., linguistics, economics); while others have weak grammars (e.g., sociology, education). Bernstein describes mathematics as a horizontal knowledge structure as it "consists of a set of discrete languages for particular problems", with a strong grammar.[16] While mathematics largely does not have empirical referents, there is little dispute as to what is and is not mathematics from the point of view of the kinds of terms used, and the ways they are connected and presented. Education, in contrast, is horizontally structured but with a weak grammar. Empirical descriptions of educational phenomena vary widely, a function of the multiple languages used to describe these, many of which lack precision.

What then might be the effects of weakening of knowledge boundaries between two domains of knowledge when one has a weak and the other a strong grammar? There has been a great deal of contestation over curriculum policy in South Africa and elsewhere that has advocated weakening the boundary between mathematics and everyday knowledge. The motivation for this move lies in the view that horizontal discourses of 'realistic' or 'relevant' settings for mathematics provide access to and meaning for abstract mathematical ideas. The critique of this arises within a Bernstein framework, and posits that 'realistic' or 'relevant' settings can work instead to background mathematical principles, and so result in denying access, particularly to those already disadvantaged by dominant discourses.[17] In a similar vein, Taylor, Muller and Vinjevold (2003), for example, draw on Bernstein to argue that integration in teacher education through the weakening of boundaries around content knowledge can result in methods of teaching dominating pedagogic discourse in teacher education at the expense of content development of teachers. Here too, effects will then be skewed against the already disadvantaged. They see a danger for teachers in greatest need for access to further content knowledge being subjected to an education dominated instead by examples of supposed good practice. In QUANTUM we share this concern. However, our assumptions are different. In our analysis, forms of integration are inevitable in contemporary educational practice. The issue is how these are and can be accomplished without damage to agents. Hence the need to understand varying practices and thus our focus in QUANTUM: what is at work in mathematics teacher education in South

---

[16] We are not convinced of the distinction drawn here between mathematics as horizontal and physics as vertical. Physics too has discrete languages. The inter-related distinctions here are, in our view, questionable, but full discussion beyond the scope of this chapter. The significant distinction, which in our view is productive and illuminating, is between week and strong grammars. Physics and mathematics both have strong grammars.

[17] It is beyond the scope of this chapter to detail this debate. It is well known in the field of mathematics education. Interested readers might find the work of Cooper and Dunne (1998) interesting, as well as the debate between Jo Boaler (2002) and Sarah Lubienski (2000) in the Journal for Research in Mathematics Education.

Africa when there is more or less integration of mathematics and teaching/education in these programmes?

Putting the Evaluative Rule to Work in the Study

One major difficulty that arises in an integrated educational code (or when here is a weakening of classification in a curriculum), is what is to be assessed and the form of assessment.[18] Criteria must be worked out. Whether or not this is explicitly done, criteria will emerge and be transmitted. In QUANTUM's terms, implicit criteria can be rendered visible because any act of evaluation has to appeal to some or other authorising ground in order to justify the selection of criteria. In Adler and Davis (2006) and Davis, Adler and Parker (2007), we describe in more detail how we have worked from the proposition that the authorising grounds at work in teacher education pedagogic practice illuminate what comes to be privileged (in terms of knowledges and their integration).[19] Given the complexity of teaching and more so teacher education, we started from the assumption, and related concern, that what comes to be taken as the grounds for evaluation is likely to vary substantially within and across sites of pedagogic practice in teacher education. Our methodology and language of description have allowed us to examine the diverse ways in which mathematics and teaching come to be co-produced in mathematics teacher education practice.

The QUANTUM research project began in 2003 with a survey of 11 higher education institutions offering formalised (i.e., accredited) mathematics teacher education programmes in South Africa. We collected information on courses taught including formal assessments. Phase 1 of the overall study focused on formal assessment carried out across courses in our data archive. We focused on actual assessment tasks, examining what and how mathematics and teaching competence were expected to be demonstrated in these tasks. We developed an analytic tool, using the notion of "unpacking" (Ball, Bass, & Hill, 2004), but redescribing it in line with our methodology. For Ball et al., "unpacking" captures the specificity of mathematical know-how required in the practice of teaching. We were particularly interested in whether assessment tasks demanded some form of 'unpacking' of mathematics.

A full account of this phase of QUANTUM's work is provided in Adler and Davis (2006). We started from the assumption that there are (in the main) two specialised knowledges to be (re)produced in mathematics teacher education: mathematics and mathematics teaching. That these knowledges are specialised implies there is some degree of internal coherence and consistency. However, in line with the discussion on knowledge structures and grammars above, the ways in which coherence and consistency are established in mathematics and mathematics

---

[18] See Moore (2000) for an interesting discussion of the challenges of disciplinary integration in a university foundation course in South Africa, and how these manifested in assessment practices.
[19] See Davis and Johnson (2007) for further development of 'grounds' at work in school mathematics classrooms.

teaching differ. In mathematics a strong internal "grammar" allows for a degree of relatively unambiguous evaluation of that which is offered as mathematical knowledge; in mathematics teaching the ambiguity is greatly increased because the field is populated by academic, professional, bureaucratic, political and even popular discourses. However, we asserted that despite those differences, where the knowledge to be reproduced is relatively coherent and consistent, justifications can be structured in a manner that conforms to the formal features of syllogistic reasoning. Whether or not explicit coherent reasoning (be it mathematical reasoning or reasoning about teaching mathematics) was required by tasks thus provided the analytic resource we needed to identify "unpacking" consistently across different tasks.

Our examination of each task involved identifying the primary and secondary objects (mathematics and/or teaching) of the task, and then whether an understanding of the logical chains (explicit coherent reasoning) relevant to the knowledge to be reproduced was explicitly demanded. As these tasks arise in mathematics teacher education, we expected that their objects may well be both teaching and mathematics and that they could vary in their demands for unpacking. Our analysis of tasks across formal evaluations in our data set was very interesting. Simply, we found that the kind of mathematical work required in teaching was infrequently assessed, with assessment tasks in mathematics focused predominantly on the reproduction of some mathematical content or skill. There was evidence, though limited and infrequent, of assessment of 'unpacking' of mathematical ideas – what specific mathematics teachers need to know and know how to use in practice to make mathematics learnable in school. There was thus a disjuncture between what is valued at the level of intention, and what comes to count as legitimate and valued knowledge in mathematics teacher education. Of course, this analysis did not provide any insight into the pedagogical practice of which these assessments were but a part.

In phase 2 of our study, we focused on in-depth study of selected courses. This, in turn, required an elaboration of the language we had developed so far, the details of which are in Davis, Adler and Parker (2007). Pedagogic practice functions over time, unlike static assessment tasks. The unit of analysis thus required rethinking. As already noted, we accepted as axiomatic that pedagogic practice entails continuous evaluation, the purpose of which is to transmit criteria for the production of legitimate texts. Further, any evaluative act, implicitly or explicitly, has to appeal to some or other authorising ground in order to justify the selection of criteria. Our unit of analysis became what we call an *evaluative event*, that is, a teaching-learning sequence that can be recognised as focused on the 'pedagogising' of particular mathematics and/or teaching content. In other words, an evaluative event is an evaluative sequence aimed at the constitution of a particular mathematics/teaching object.

Each course, all its contact sessions and related materials, were analysed, and chunked into evaluative events. Following on from Phase 1, after identifying starting and endpoints of each event or sub-event, we first coded whether the object of attention was mathematical and/or teaching, and then whether elements of the object(s) were the focus of study (and therefore coded as M and/or T) or were assumed background knowledge (and then coded either m or t). We worked with the idea that in pedagogic practice, in order for some content to be learned it has to be represented as an object available for semiotic mediation in pedagogic interactions between teacher and learner. The semiotic mediation that follows involves moments of pedagogic reflection that in turn involve (following Davis, 2001) pedagogic judgement. All judgement, however, hence all evaluation, necessarily appeals to some or other locus of legitimation to ground itself, even if only implicitly. Legitimating appeals can be thought of as qualifying reflection in attempts to fix meaning. We therefore examined *what* was appealed to and *how* appeals were made over time and in each course, in order to deliver up insights into the constitution of MfT in mathematics teacher education.

Given the complexity of teaching, and more so of teacher education, as previously intimated, we expected that what came to be taken as the grounds for evaluation was likely to vary substantially within and across the courses we were studying. Indeed, through interaction with the data, we eventually described the grounds appealed to across the three courses in terms of six ideal-typical categories: (1) mathematics, (2) mathematics education, (3) the everyday, (4) experience of teaching, (5) the official school curriculum, and (6) the authority of the adept. In each course we found differences in what was appealed to and how, differences that point to very different opportunities for teachers to (re)learn *mathematics for teaching*.

In one course (focused on teaching and learning algebra) mathematics was integrated with methods for teaching mathematics. In this course, the grounding of objects reflected on during class sessions was predominantly in what we called empirical mathematics (particular examples). In a course that focused on teaching and learning mathematical reasoning, the emphasis was in the domain of mathematics education, and so specific mathematics backgrounded. As could then be expected, a substantial grounding of objects reflected on during class sessions in this course was in mathematics education, particularly texts reporting research related to teaching and learning mathematics. Interestingly, when mathematical objects were in focus, and this occurred through the class, grounding for these was both empirical (with examples) and principled (discussion was expected to conform to demands of mathematical discourse).

There are many reasons to explain why these two courses differed as such. Our interest, however, was that very different forms of *mathematics for teaching* were constituted in these courses, offering very different opportunities for learning. Mathematics teachers, whatever level, in our view, need to grasp mathematics in principled ways if they are themselves to enable mathematical learning in their classrooms. In-service mathematics teacher education should offer opportunities for engaging with mathematics as a principled activity. Of course, this is not to say that these two courses each capture the *mathematics for teaching* in the overall programmes of which they were each but a part. In Davis et al. (2007) our discussion of these courses is elaborated through a further analysis of how in each, the way teaching is modelled appears to link with what and how mathematics and teaching are integrated, and then too with how *mathematics for teaching* is constituted. We argue there that modelling the practice is a necessary feature of all teacher education.[20] There needs to be some demonstration/experience (real or virtual) of the valued practice; that is, of some image of what mathematics teaching performances should look like. In the Algebra course, the model was located in the performance of the lecturer whose concern (stated repeatedly through the course) was that the teachers themselves experience particular ways of learning mathematics. This experiential base was believed to be necessary if they were to enable others to learn in the same way. The mathematical examples and activities in the course thus mirrored those the teachers were to use in their Grades 7–9 algebra class. In the Reasoning course the model of teaching was externalised from both the lecturer and the teacher-students themselves, and located in images and records of the practice of teaching: particularly in videotapes of local teachers teaching mathematical reasoning, and related transcripts and copies of learner work. The externalising was supported by what we have called discursive resources (texts explaining, arguing, describing practice in systematic ways).

Our findings in both phases of the study need to be understood as a result of a particular lens, a lens that we believe has enabled a systematic description of what is going on 'inside' teacher education practice at two inter-related levels. The first level is 'what' comes to be the content of *mathematics for teaching*, i.e., the mathematical content and practices offered in these courses. We are calling this MfT. It is not an idealised or advocated set of contents or practices, but rather a description of 'what' is recognised through our gaze. Some aspects of MfT here can be seen as closer to SMK, and others to PCK in Shulman's terms. However, each of these categories is limiting in describing 'what' mathematics is offered in these courses. At the second level, is the 'how'. This content is structured by a particular pedagogic discourse; and a key component in the 'how' that has emerged in the study, is the projection and modelling of the activity of teaching itself. In Bernstein's terms we have seen, through an examination of evaluation at work and of how images of teaching are projected, that different MfT is offered to teachers in these programmes. The research we have done thus suggests in addition, that developing descriptions of what does or should constitute maths for teaching outside of a conception of how teaching is modelled is only half the story.[21]

MATHEMATICS FOR TEACHING: A SOCIAL PRODUCTION

We stated in the introduction to this chapter that studies and developments related to *mathematics for teaching* have their roots in Shulman's seminal work in the

---

[20] This further supports our assumption that forms of integration are internal to pedagogic practice in teacher education.

[21] We note here that a similar point is made in Margolinas, Coulange and Bessot (2005) pointing further to resonance between the orientation to knowledge for teaching in QUANTUM and didactical theory as developed and used in studies in France.

1980s that placed disciplinary knowledge at the heart of the professional knowledge base of teaching. We also noted that while there has been considerable research, the discourse of *mathematics for teaching* is fledgling. Neither of the two studies drew directly on the categories of professional knowledge as posited by Shulman, despite being driven by the same concern: to develop or deepen mathematical knowledge as it is (or needs to be) used in teaching, and a starting point that the way mathematics is used in teaching has a specificity. From our perspective, all mathematical activity (and hence all mathematics wherever it is learned) is directed towards some purpose, and within teacher education, this would be for mathematics teaching, and/or becoming a mathematics teacher. While the notion of PCK in particular is compelling in teaching and teacher education – it emphasises that pedagogic reasoning in mathematics teaching is content-filled – it does not live outside of the institutions where it functions – and these are inherently social. There are limits to the appropriateness of general categories like PCK and SMK, as well as to the distinctions between them.

Shulman's work spurred several studies (and continues to do so) attempting to build on his notions, particularly PCK, but as Ball, Thames and Phelps (2007) point out, these notions remain poorly defined. In this paper Ball et al. pull together the accumulation of their work over the past decade that has included (a) describing *mathematics for teaching* from close observation of a detailed archive of a year of mathematics teaching in a third-grade class taught by Ball in the United States and (b) developing measures of content knowledge for teaching. This research has led them to strengthen and elaborate Shulman's initial work by providing clear definitions and exemplars of distinctive categories within and across SMK and PCK. A particular move they make is to define two new categories within SMK – or content knowledge for teaching: what they call common content knowledge and specialised content knowledge. They argue that this distinction is necessary to capture the specificity of teachers' mathematical work – and that recognition of this specificity lies at the heart of effective mathematics teaching. In simple terms, teachers need to know aspects of mathematics that is not required by 'others' (i.e., in common use). But what is common use? From a social epistemological perspective, all mathematical activity is towards some purpose, and occurs within some or other (social) institution. The notion of 'common' content knowledge is thus problematic, and so too then, the marking out of specialised content knowledge.

We nevertheless share with Ball and her colleagues a concern with *mathematics for teaching*. In the two studies we have presented here, we have shown how two different social epistemologies have been productive for studying *mathematics for teaching*. The Mozambique study described and explained teachers' evolving personal relations to the limit through their participation and engagement with this concept in a new institution. We showed that this evolution was uneven, across teachers, and then also in relation to different aspects of *mathematics for teaching*. We elaborated in particular, the relatively poor evolution of the teachers' grasp of graphical representations and the ε-δ definition. We argued that these outcomes were a function of the strength of the research institution relative to the dominant

216

institutions of the secondary school and Pedagogical University. An important element of this argument was an interpretation of aspects of *mathematics for teaching* through an ATD lens that reflected the limits of the distinction posited by Shulman between SMK and PCK. The evolution of each of the teachers' personal relation to the limit concept was described in terms of both subject knowledge and knowledge of teaching. Emerging from this study is the observation that professional development programmes for practising teachers in a context like Mozambique need to provide opportunities for substantive engagement with the content of mathematics, opportunities that were not available in the research institution set up, despite placing mathematics at the centre. So where and how then, is this engagement with mathematics to function in mathematics teacher education?

In the South African study of courses within formalised in-service mathematics teacher education programmes – where engagement with mathematics was a goal - we described the mathematics that came to be constituted (came to 'live') in and across different courses. By examining evaluation at work in the courses we were able to 'see' what and how mathematics and teaching are co-constituted through pedagogic discourse. We showed that different models of teaching combine with varying selections from mathematics, mathematics education and teaching practice to produce different kinds of opportunities for teachers in these courses to learn mathematics (for teaching).

Separately and together these two studies demonstrate that *mathematics for teaching*, and its learning in any institutional setting can only be grasped through a language that positions *mathematics for teaching* as structured by, and structuring of, the pedagogic discourse (in Bernstein's terms) or the institution (in Chevallard's terms) in which it 'lives'. Both provide strong conceptual tools with which to interrogate how mathematics is recontextualised in pedagogic settings. Separately and together they contribute to the growing body of knowledge related to the *what* of mathematics teacher education, and particularly to subject knowledge for teaching.

APPENDIX 1

Categories of teacher's mathematical knowledge about the graphical register (reading and sketching)

GRR1	The teacher is not able to read any limit from the graphs.
GRR2	The teacher is able to read some limits along a vertical or a horizontal asymptote (when the graph does not cross the asymptote).
GRR3	The teacher is able to read limits along a vertical or a horizontal asymptote (when the graph does not cross the asymptote), and infinite limits at infinity ($x \to \infty$, $y \to \infty$).
GRR4	The teacher is able to read limits along a vertical or a horizontal asymptote (even when the graph crosses the asymptote), and infinite limits at infinity ($x \to \infty$, $y \to \infty$).
GRR5	The teacher is able to read most limits but faces small difficulties.
GRR6	The teacher is able to read all kinds of limits.
GRS1	The teacher is not able to sketch any graph using limits or asymptotes.
GRS2	The teacher is not able to indicate any limit on axes. He is able to sketch a standard graph having two asymptotes, one vertical and one horizontal.
GRS3	The teacher indicates limits along a vertical or a horizontal asymptote as a whole branch. He does not acknowledge that drawing several branches may produce a graph that is not a function.
GRS4	The teacher indicates limits along a vertical or a horizontal asymptote as a whole branch. He acknowledges that the produced graph does not represent a function.
GRS5	The teacher indicates limits along a vertical or a horizontal asymptote as a local behaviour.
GRS6	The teacher is able to indicate any kind of limit on axes.

Categories of teacher's ideas about the use of graphs to teach limits

GR-T1	The teacher would not use graphs when teaching limits.
GR-T2	The teacher acknowledges the importance of the graphical register in teaching limits.
GR-T3	The teacher acknowledges the importance of the graphical register and explains how he would use it or articulate it with other registers.

ACKNOWLEDGEMENTS

This chapter forms part of the QUANTUM research project on *mathematics for teaching*, directed by Jill Adler, at the University of the Witwatersrand. This material is based upon work supported by the National Research Foundation (NRF) under Grant number FA2006031800003. Any opinion, findings and conclusions or recommendations expressed in this material are those of the author(s) and do not necessarily reflect the views of the NRF. Dr Huillet's study in Mozambique was supported by QUANTUM and the Marang Centre at the University of the Witwatersrand.

REFERENCES

Adler, J. (2002). Global and local challenges of teacher development. In J. Adler & Y. Reed (Eds.), *Challenges of teacher development – An investigation of take-up in South Africa* (pp. 1–16). Pretoria: Van Schaik Publishers.

Adler, J., & Davis, Z. (2006). Opening another black box: Researching mathematics for teaching in mathematics teacher education. *Journal for Research in Mathematics Education, 36*(4), 270–296.

Adler, J., & Pillay, V. (2007). An investigation into mathematics for teaching: Insights from a case. *African Journal of Research in Mathematics, Science and Technology Education, 11*(2), 87–108.

Ball, D., Thames, M., & Phelps, G. (2007). Content knowledge for teaching: What makes it special? Retrieved November 20, 2007, from http://www-personal.umich.edu/~dball/papers/ BallThamesPhelps_ ContentKnowledgeforTeaching.pdf

Ball, D., Bass, H., & Hill, H. (2004). Knowing and using mathematical knowledge in teaching: Learning what matters. In A. Buffler & R. Laugksch (Eds.), Proceedings from SAARMSTE 2004: *The 12ʰ Annual Conference of the Southern African Association for Research in Mathematics Sciences and Technology Education* (pp. 51–65). Cape Town: SAARMSTE.

Barbé, J., Bosch, M., Espinoza, L., & Gascón, J. (2005). Didactic restrictions on the teacher's practice: The case of limits of functions in Spanish high schools. *Educational Studies in Mathematics, 59,* 235–268.

Bernstein, B. (2000). *Pedagogy, symbolic control and identity: Theory, research, critique* (Revised edition). Lanham, MD: Rowman & Littlefield Publishers, Inc.

Bernstein, B. (1996). *Pedagogy, symbolic control and identity: Theory, research, critique.* London: Taylor & Francis.

Boaler, J. (2002). Learning from teaching: Exploring the relationship between reform curriculum and equity. *Journal for Research in Mathematics Education, 331,* 239–258.

Bosch, M., & Chevallard, Y. (1999). Sensibilité de l'activité mathématique aux ostensifs. *Recherches en Didactique des Mathématiques, 19*(1), 77–123.

Chevallard, Y. (2002). Organiser l'étude. 1. Structures & fonctions. In J-L. Dorier, M. Artaud, R. Berthelot, & R. Floris (Eds.), *Actes de la 11ᵉ École d'Été de Didactique des Mathématiques,* Version électronique du cédérom d'accompagnement. Grenoble: La Pensée Sauvage.

Chevallard, Y. (1999). L'analyse des pratiques enseignantes en théories anthropologiques du didactique. *Recherches en Didactique des Mathématiques, 19*(2), 221–265.

Chevallard, Y. (1992). Fundamental concepts in didactics: Perspectives provided by an anthropological approach. In R. Douady & A. Mercier (Eds.), *Recherches en didactique des mathématiques : Selected papers* (pp. 131–167). Grenoble: La Pensée Sauvage.

Cooper, B., & Dunne, M. (2000). *Assessing children's mathematical knowledge: Social class, sex and problem-solving.* Buckingham, UK: Open University Press.

Davis, Z. (2005). *Pleasure and pedagogic discourse in school mathematics: a case study of a problem-centred pedagogic modality.* Unpublished Ph.D. Dissertation. Cape Town: University of Cape Town.

Davis, Z. (2001). Measure for measure: Evaluative judgment in school mathematics pedagogic texts. *Pythagoras, 56,* 2–11.

Davis, Z., Adler, J., & Parker, D. (2007) Identification with images of the teacher and teaching in formalized in-service mathematics teacher education and the constitution of mathematics for teaching. *Journal of Education, 42,* 1–28.

Davis, Z., & Johnson, Y. (2007). *What functions as ground for mathematics in schooling? Further remarks on the constitution of school mathematics, with special reference to the teaching and learning of mathematics in five secondary schools.* Paper presented at the 13th Annual National Congress of the Association for Mathematics Education of South Africa (AMESA), Mpumalanga. http://www.amesa.org.za/AMESA2007/abstractslong.htm

Ensor, P. (2004). Modalities of teacher education discourse and the education of effective practitioners. *Pedagogy, Culture and Society, 12*(2), 217–232.

Ensor, P. (2001). From pre-service mathematics teacher education to beginning teaching: A study in recontextualising. *Journal for Research in Mathematics Education, 32,* 296–320.

Graven, M. (2005). *Mathematics teacher learning, communities of practice and the centrality of confidence.* Unpublished Ph.D. Dissertation. Johannesburg: University of the Witwatersrand.

Graven, M. (2002). Dilemmas in the design of in-service education and training for mathematics teachers. In R. Vithal, J. Adler, & C. Keitel (Eds.), *Researching mathematics education in South Africa* (pp. 206–246). Cape Town: HSRC Press.

Huillet, D. (2005a). Mozambican teachers' professional knowledge about limits of functions. In H. Chick & J. Vincent (Eds.), *Proceedings of the 29th Conference of the International Group for the Psychology of Mathematics Education* (Vol. 3, pp. 169–176). Melbourne: Psychology of Mathematics Education.

Huillet, D. (2005b). The evolution of secondary school Mozambican teachers' knowledge about the ε-δ definition of limits of functions. In C. Kasanda, L. Muhammed. S. Akpo, & E. Ngololo (Eds.), Proceedings from SAARMSTE 2005: *The 13th Annual Conference of the Southern African Association for Research in Mathematics Sciences and Technology Education* (pp. 271–278). Windoek, Namibia: SAARMSTE.

Huillet, D. (2007a). *Evolution, through participation in a research group, of Mozambican secondary school teachers' personal relation to limits of functions.* Unpublished Ph.D. Dissertation. Johannesburg: University of the Witwatersrand.

Huillet, D. (2007b). The evolution of secondary school Mozambican teachers' knowledge of the use of graphs for studying limits. In I. Mutimucuiu & M. Cherinda (Eds.), Proceedings from SAARMSTE 2007: *The 15th Annual Conference of the Southern African Association for Research in Mathematics Sciences and Technology Education* (pp. 193–198). Maputo: SAARMSTE.

Huillet, D., & Mutemba, B. (2000). The relation of Mozambican secondary school teachers to a mathematical concept: The case of limits of functions. In S. Mahlomaholo (Ed.), Proceedings from SAARMSTE 2000: *The 8th Annual Conference of the Southern African Association for Research in Mathematics Sciences and Technology Education* (pp. 309–316). Port Elizabeth, South Africa: SAARMSTE.

Lubienski, S. (2000). Problem solving as a means towards mathematics for all: An exploratory look through the class lens. *Journal for Research in Mathematics Education, 31,* 225–248.

Margolinas, C., Coulange, L, & Bessot, A. (2005). What can the teacher learn in the classroom? *Educational Studies in Mathematics, 59,* 205–234.

Moore, R. (2000). The (re)organisation of knowledge and assessment for a learning society: The constraints on interdisciplinarity. *Studies in Continuing Education 22*(2), 183–199.

Morais, A (2002). Basil Bersntein at the micro level of the classroom. *British Journal of Sociology of Education, 23*(4), 559–569.

Shulman, L. (1987). Knowledge and teaching: Foundations of the new reform. *Harvard Educational Review 57*(1), 1–22.

Shulman, L. (1986). Those who understand: Knowledge growth in teaching. *Educational Researcher 15*, 4–14.

Taylor, N., Muller, J., & Vinjevold, P. (2003). *Getting schools working*. Cape Town: Pearson Education South Africa.

Jill Adler
Marang Centre for Mathematics and Science Education
School of Education
University of the Witwatersrand
Johannesburg
South Africa
and
Department of Education and Professional Studies
King's College
London
United Kingdom

Danielle Huillet
Mathematics Department
Faculty of Sciences
Eduardo Mondlane University
Maputo
Mozambique

PAOLO BOERO AND ELDA GUALA

10. DEVELOPMENT OF MATHEMATICAL KNOWLEDGE AND BELIEFS OF TEACHERS

The Role of Cultural Analysis of the Content to Be Taught

We claim that the cultural analysis of the content to be taught (CAC) is one of the most important components of teacher education, if we want to develop teachers' mathematical knowledge and at the same time call into question their beliefs about mathematics and mathematics teaching. In this chapter we discuss the importance of CAC and its place in mathematics teacher education. We also provide some criteria for choosing content, tasks, and methodology to develop CAC. Some examples of CAC activities are presented that concern probability and statistics as well as conjecturing and proving.

INTRODUCTION

The first part of the title underlines the fact that teachers, when entering an education programme, already have some mathematical knowledge "to be developed". Implicitly, it suggests the need to clarify in what direction development must be oriented in order both to intervene on teachers' beliefs about mathematics in general and about specific mathematical subjects, and to provide them with useful knowledge for planning and analysing teaching.

Consistent with our 30 years' experience with mathematics teacher education in different situations and current literature and trends in the field, in this chapter we stress the importance of the cultural analysis of the content to be taught (CAC) as one of the crucial components of mathematics teacher education. CAC adds to professional knowledge, usually considered in the literature as "subject matter knowledge", "pedagogical content knowledge," and "general pedagogical knowledge" (see Shulman, 1986), by including the understanding of how mathematics can be arranged in different ways according to different needs and historical or social circumstances, and how it enters human culture in interaction with other cultural domains (economics, physical sciences, philosophy, etc.). As such, CAC can lead teachers to radically question their beliefs concerning mathematics in general and specific subject matter in particular.

The relevance of CAC in teachers' preparation is related to presenting mathematics as an evolving discipline, with different levels of rigour both at a specific moment in history (according to the cultural environment and specific needs), and across history, and as a domain of culture as a set of interrelated

P. Sullivan and T. Wood (eds.), Knowledge and Beliefs in Mathematics Teaching and Teaching Development, 223–244.

cultural tools and social practices, which can be inherited over generations (see Hatano & Wertsch, 2001).[1]

CAC is not intended to be taught through regular lectures about mathematics by a university professor but it can be used to open new windows for teachers as "decision makers" (see Sullivan & Mousley, 2001; Malara & Zan, 2002), provided that suitable mathematical subjects are selected and teachers are personally involved in suitable mathematical activities and related educational reflections.

Consequently, in this chapter we present: the place of CAC in mathematics teacher education; a short discussion of methodological issues (related to the difficulty of providing evidence for our assumptions through ordinary comparative methods); some criteria for choosing mathematical subjects, tasks, and educational methodology for teacher education, in order to make CAC involving and profitable for teachers; and some examples of how CAC concerning two delicate subject areas (probability and statistics; and conjecturing and proving) can enter teacher education and affect teachers' beliefs about these subject areas, as well as mathematics in general.

THE PLACE OF CAC IN MATHEMATICS TEACHER EDUCATION

Taking the relevance of "subject matter knowledge" and "general pedagogical knowledge" for granted (see Boero, Dapueto, & Parenti, 1996), current mathematics education literature on teacher education stresses the importance of "pedagogical content knowledge" (PCK) as defined by Shulman (1986) as one possible direction for integration and development of teachers' professional knowledge. Following Shulman, for

> the most regularly taught topics, [...] the teacher should become acquainted with the most useful forms of representation of those ideas, the most powerful analogies, illustrations, examples, explanations, and demonstrations- in a word, the ways of representing the subject that make it comprehensible to others [...] what makes the learning of specific topics easy

---

[1] In the last three decades, the nature of mathematics as a culture (or part of a culture) has been investigated by several scholars with reference to different definitions of "culture". In particular, Wilder (1986, p. 186) writes that "A culture is the collection of customs, rituals, beliefs, tools, mores, etc. which we may call cultural elements, possessed by a group of people", and applies this general definition to mathematics.

We prefer to make reference to the definition of culture proposed by Hatano and Wertsch (2001), because it better accounts for the systemic character of mathematics (including mathematical activities), its "inheritance over generations", and the relevance of symbolic and social tools.

"'Culture' means the special medium of human life consisting of a set of interrelated artefacts (Cole, 1996), shared to some extent among members of the community and often inherited over generations. These artefacts include physical tools, common sense knowledge and beliefs, social organisations, and conventional patterns of behaviour associated with the physical, symbolic, and social tools" (Hatano & Wertsch, 2001, p. 80).

or difficult: the conceptions and preconceptions that students of different ages and backgrounds bring with them to learning. (1986, p. 9)

Some studies in the educational sciences (see Hiebert, Gallimore, & Stigler, 2002) and in the field of mathematics education (Mason, 1998) have discussed or further elaborated PCK, distinguishing between its different components and their effects on teachers' beliefs (see Torner, 2002, also Chapter 6, this volume). Focusing on PCK can help call into question students' and teachers' beliefs about mathematics, specific subject matter, and how to present it. However, this scarcely contributes to CAC, the cultural analysis of the content to be taught (its possible different axiomatic organisation, its relevance in mathematics, its links with other subjects, and so forth.). As we have seen, according to the original definition of Shulman, PCK concerns knowledge of the content that is directly related to teaching (ways of illustrating, exemplifying, explaining it), and students' content-related "conceptions and pre-conceptions". Connections between PCK and some aspects of CAC may be established only when dealing with different ways of representing a given topic or the relationships between students' conceptions and the social and historical roots of mathematical knowledge. However, neither mathematics as a culture (its possible organisations and evolution across history), nor the dynamic relationships between mathematics and other cultures (two key aspects of CAC) are taken into consideration in the construct pedagogical content knowledge. The following two examples are aimed at clarifying the above issues. More detailed examples will be presented in the second part of this chapter.

The first example (relevant for primary school mathematics teacher education) concerns cardinal (Cantor) and ordinal (Peano) axiomatic organisations of the content "natural numbers", and their relationships with the roots of the concept of natural number in its uses in everyday life situations and in different past and present cultures.

The second example (relevant in particular for high school mathematics teacher education) concerns rigour in mathematical proof: historical-epistemological evolution (from Euclid to Hilbert); relationships with rigour in ordinary arguing in different domains (law, natural sciences, philosophy); acceptable, semantic based rigour (mathematicians' ordinary proofs) versus formal rigour (proof as formal derivation, according to the logicians' models).

In both cases the considered pieces of CAC knowledge escape the borders of PCK as defined by Schulman, and do not enter ordinary taught content knowledge (see later).

In our opinion, CAC is relevant for different purposes: on one hand, to allow the teacher to consider the content not as a given object to be presented in an efficient way, but as a multifaceted cultural entity that can live different lives in the realm of mathematics, according to the context (mathematicians' community in different historical periods, school, professional contexts, etc.); on the other hand, to gain some distance from the content to be taught and evaluate its importance in the mathematics and scientific culture (thus becoming aware of the wider consequences of poor learning). CAC can also contribute to interpretations of students' learning difficulties and preconceptions; in particular, it can reveal the nature of some difficulties as related to didactical obstacles inherent in the ways of presenting a given content in school, or to epistemological obstacles inherent in its very nature (for a distinction between didactical obstacles and epistemological obstacles, see Brousseau, 1997).

Let us move now to possible relationships between CAC and the acquisition of content knowledge. When Shulman (1986, p. 9) defines "subject matter knowledge" as "the amount and organisation of the knowledge per se in the mind of the teacher", he claims that "to think properly about content knowledge requires [one] to go beyond knowledge of the facts or concepts of a domain. It requires understanding the structures of the subject matter." However, in Shulman's definition, "structures of the subject matter" are considered as given; the need to discuss them in relation to different social, cultural, and historical contexts in which the mathematics was and is used (a crucial component of CAC) is not taken into account. In another research perspective, the theoretical construct of Didactical Transposition (Chevallard, 1985) implies a need to analyse differences and relationships between mathematicians' mathematics and school mathematics and to consider different contexts for use of mathematics (with their constraints on the nature of mathematical activities) as possible occasions for "re-contextualisation" of mathematical knowledge. When mathematics teacher education is considered within this perspective, the role of CAC in the development of teachers' professional knowledge is not evident (Chevallard, 2000); instead the focus of investigations are on the mathematical, institutional, and didactic constraints that "determine the teacher's practice and ultimately the mathematical organisation actually taught" (Barbé, Bosch, Espinoza, & Gascon, 2005, p. 235).

Properly speaking, at least some parts of CAC (those related to different axiomatic organisation of mathematical content, and to mathematical modeling) should be developed in the teaching of mathematics for all those who have to deal with mathematics in a critical way (not only mathematics teachers, but also physicists, economists, statisticians, etc.). This is not the case in most universities all over the world!

Considering how teachers acquire content knowledge, we observe that CAC is not usually included in the ordinary mathematical curricula that provide prospective teachers with "subject matter knowledge." In particular, in Italy (like in many other countries) most prospective high school mathematics teachers are taught "subject matter knowledge" in university courses that are not specific for prospective teachers and are intended to provide students only with a strong technical background in mathematics. Even in papers concerning what content knowledge should be acquired by practising teachers and how, when possible, to organise specific mathematics courses for them, we find limited evidence of CAC. Attention is mainly given to the choice of tasks (cf., Zaslavsky, Chapman, and Leikin, 2003) and educational methodology, usually based on a problem-centred approach, in order that teachers learn mathematics and at the same time experience learning of mathematics in an educational environment suitable for transposition to their professional activities. Connections with CAC are implicitly evoked in a few sources. In particular, Schifter (1993) describes a mathematics course for teachers in which the intended major goal was to enable participants to experience genuine mathematical activities and reconsider and broaden their understanding of what mathematics is. Even in that situation, the real focus was more on teachers' reflection on their mathematical practices than on the increase (and/or change) in their knowledge about what mathematics is with respect to different historical, social, and cultural contexts. The conclusion is that attention to CAC as a component of teachers' preparation is lacking both in theoretical perspectives and in practical teacher education.

We add that it is not easy to find instructors or space in the curriculum for CAC in teacher education. Teacher educators coming from the educational sciences usually have poor competencies in CAC. Mathematics educators with a scientific background in teaching of mathematics and a technical background in mathematics (this is the case of most mathematics educators in Italy) usually concentrate on PCK and eventually on subject matter technical knowledge (when they realise that teachers do not know enough of the specific subjects they will teach). On the mathematicians' side, most of them (in Italy like in many other countries) think that teacher education should extend (in terms of quantity and/or technical depth) teachers' mathematical knowledge in those fields that are strictly related to what they teach, in order to make them more sure and comfortable with the content to be taught. Other mathematicians (a minority) insist that teachers' mathematical knowledge be updated (especially in the case of practising teacher education for the high school level), so that they learn new ways of thinking about traditional mathematical content and new directions of development for the mathematical sciences. This position theoretically provides a place and space for CAC. However, it usually results in lectures that go far beyond the content to be taught. Their focus is on presenting research perspectives in mathematics. In both cases, the underlying assumption is that "better" (i.e., deeper, broader, or updated) knowledge of mathematics translates into better teaching of mathematics. Both positions do not tackle the problem of teachers' beliefs concerning mathematics and related distortions; also, neither provides teachers with relevant knowledge and tools for the "didactical transposition" of mathematical knowledge.

The previous analysis shows how it is difficult to locate CAC in existing theoretical perspectives and practical situations of mathematics teacher education; we aim to show that CAC can be a reasonable, feasible, and useful component in this endeavor. In general, we acknowledge the importance of PCK and we do not deny the necessity of integrating teachers' content knowledge (especially when teachers' previous preparation has not covered important content areas to be taught), but we would like to stress the importance of developing teachers' mathematical knowledge while at the same time integrating their content knowledge and calling into question their ways of thinking about mathematics. In order to attain this aim, we think that relevant tools can be derived from epistemology of mathematics and history of mathematics, in order to frame and substantiate the CAC component of teacher preparation. Psychology of learning and mathematics education can provide further tools in order to benefit from the

227

CAC component and relate its contributions to educational choices (as we will illustrate in the examples presented below).

As a final remark related to feasibility, we point out again that CAC is sterile if it enters mathematics teacher education only as the subject of lectures. Standard lectures are received by teachers as cultural contributions that in the best case contribute to what they say when they speak with their colleagues or with the mathematics teacher educator, not to what they do in the classroom (here the distinction between "knowing about" and "knowing to act", proposed by Mason & Spence, 1999, is appropriate). We think that mathematical content for teacher education, tasks related to that content (concerning the crucial role of tasks in teacher education, as in Zaslavsky, Chapman, and Leikin, 2003), and methodology of teacher education should be three interrelated components for mathematics teacher education on CAC. Together, these can contribute to the image of mathematics (and the image of mathematics teaching as well) conveyed to teachers.

REMARKS ABOUT OUR RESEARCH METHODOLOGY

Our contribution is based on more than 30 years of work with teachers at different school levels (from primary school to high school) in different situations:
- prospective teacher preparation at the university (where many "students" are already practising teachers who need a university degree in order to get tenure at a school, or to move from one school level to another);
- practising teacher education (sometimes promoted by the university, more frequently organised by schools, districts, or the ministry of education);
- cooperative efforts with teachers that are engaged in educational research and didactic innovations promoted by university researchers; in this case, they act as "teacher-researchers" who share responsibilities with university researchers (see Arzarello & Bartolini Bussi, 1998; Malara & Zan, 2002).

CAC is one of the common components of our mathematics teacher education interventions in all the abovementioned situations. We must say that its importance grew progressively in our courses during the past three decades; indeed, we observed how it can work (in well arranged teacher education activities) as the component of teacher development most suitable to challenge some of teachers' deep beliefs about mathematics and to raise doubts about the cultural foundation of many traditional educational choices and their effect on students.

We cannot provide any results of comparative studies substantiating our above claim, although we have a lot of materials at our disposal (teachers' written texts and recorded oral interventions collected during teacher professional development activities, and follow-up of teacher education in terms of tasks for their students and analyses of their students' behaviors). The reasons for this serious limitation of our discourse are inherent: first, in the changes in the school system (programmes, commitment of teachers, and their ideological orientations) and in our expertise in managing teacher education over the last 30 years; second, in the impossibility of isolating the component "CAC" from the other components of teacher education, and measuring (or at least evaluating in an objective way) its short- and long-term specific effect on teachers' professional performances. However, we think that there are some elements that can support our claim about the effects of CAC in teacher education: the analysis of CAC tasks and teachers' behaviors shows how teachers' beliefs are intentionally called into question as they answer the open-ended questions posed by the instructor; also, the qualitative analysis of the evolution of teachers' answers and their planning of didactical situations shows their increase in awareness about both the crucial cultural nodes of their educational choices and on what aspects of students' behaviour to focus.

For this reason, our presentation of examples of tasks and related teachers' behaviours shows how tasks encouraged teachers to take the CAC component into account and resulted in changes in their cultural and educational perspectives (including an awareness of the importance of CAC), emerging both in their planning of didactical situations and in their texts at the end of the education programme. Concerning these teachers' written products, we have used two kinds of final evaluation tasks: in some cases, cultural analyses of the content are explicitly required for specific subjects; more frequently, tasks do not concern CAC in explicit terms but give the teachers an opportunity to demonstrate competencies in CAC either in presenting difficulties, doubts and questions related to a specific subject, or in planning didactical situations for it. These tasks can also reveal the effects of CAC education on the teachers' beliefs.

THE CHOICE OF MATHEMATICAL CONTENT FOR CAC

We think that not all mathematical content is suitable for developing teachers' awareness of the nature of mathematical knowledge and calling into question their beliefs. We also think that exemplary CAC activities on well-chosen topics can have an effect on other topics, if teacher education challenges teachers to reflect on those experiences and their cultural meaning beyond the specific content dealt with in the CAC perspective.

In Italy, well-established content areas (e.g., in the case of high school: Euclidean geometry, analytic geometry, or rational numbers) are well-known by teachers (or, at least, they think they know them rather well). Reflective activities about those content areas can provide teachers with new ideas, but it is difficult to engage teachers in restructuring their knowledge with educational intentions. They know main definitions and theorems, they can solve ordinary problems, and current textbooks offer a variety of well-established guidelines of how to teach the subject matter. Tasks could be chosen in order to raise questions about deep aspects of teachers' knowledge, but those tasks would be removed from ordinary teaching practices, and teachers' difficulties would appear to them as artificially generated (with no impact on their professional duties). Historical and epistemological contributions by the instructor could enrich teachers' knowledge and cultural framing of the content to be taught (and possibly provide them with information to be conveyed to their students), but this would not put the core of their content knowledge and related images into question. For instance, the transition from Euclid's geometry to Hilbert's axiomatic perspective can be presented to teachers in more or less detail (as we have experienced several times). The effect is that teachers stick to some anecdotal information and eventually present it to their high school students in order to illustrate the spatial referent-free validity of Hilbert's statements, but it remains detached from the students' actual geometrical activity in the classroom. Incidentally, we observe that even descriptions of students' learning processes and psychological interpretations of their difficulties in well-established content areas are insufficient to call into question ordinary teaching practices.

In teacher education, we would like to challenge teachers' knowledge in order to help them to learn more about mathematics and mathematical activities (from the mathematical, epistemological, historical, psychological, and didactical point of view). At the same time, we would like to call into question some general views of teachers about mathematics (for instance, the idea that mathematical rigour is an absolute across history, or that rigour only depends on the use of mathematical formalisms, or that the crucial aim to attain in school is students' knowledge of mathematical objects and structures: definitions, statements with their proofs, algorithms, etc.). Having these aims in mind and taking previous considerations into account, we think that it is better for CAC activities to exploit "important" content areas where teachers' previous knowledge is lacking or rudimentary and "important" mathematical activities where teachers' performances are usually poor ("important" depending on both present evolution of curricula and relevance in mathematics). Based on current literature and our direct knowledge of the Italian situation, we have selected (amongst the possible content areas and mathematical activities that can be chosen according to the previous criteria--as important mathematical subjects to develop CAC and put teachers' beliefs into question in an exemplary way): a) the domain of probability and statistics; and, b) the activities of conjecturing and proving (particularly in the domain of elementary arithmetic).

With reasonable adaptation to fit teachers' different professional needs and mathematical background inherent in their previous curricula, we think that these subjects can work well for teacher education for all school levels (from primary school to the last grades of high school). In our teacher education activities, there are other subjects that are suitable for productive CAC interventions; in particular, mathematical modeling for high school teacher education and decimal numbers for primary school teacher education. The advantage of presenting examples in the areas a) and b) consists in the fact that we can see how CAC on the same subject can be adapted to teachers of different grade levels.

Probability and Statistics

In Italy, probability and statistics is still a marginal subject in high school and in university mathematical preparation of teachers. When probability is taught in depth (as happens sometimes at university, for teachers who are required to obtain a Mathematics degree), it is ordinarily taught at a formal, sophisticated level (substantially, as a "chapter" of measure theory, endowed with specific terminology and results). When probability is taught in secondary school, it is taught as a set of rules to solve standard exercises. In both cases, the modeling aspect of probability is neglected (or reduced to rote exercises), and no room is left for a discussion about the cultural importance of probabilistic thinking. During the last two decades in Italy, pressure on schools has been exerted (by national "programmes" and prescriptions for "curricula") in order to develop teaching of probability and statistics as an important area of mathematical thought related to several applications and cultural aims (including scientific education of new generations). Thus, we are in the optimal situation of having at our disposal an "important" subject with no established teaching tradition, potentially rich from a cultural point of view, and possible to develop at different levels of symbolic treatment, with interesting problems accessible at each level. CAC activities in the field are potentially rich in connection with other cultural fields (e.g., natural sciences, social sciences.), and with teachers' and students' frequent specific misconceptions. The activities can also open a window on genuine mathematical modeling as one of the crucial aspects of mathematical culture.

Conjecturing and Proving

Conjecturing and proving in mathematics is recognised today as a major source of educational challenges all over the world, because it is one of the characterising features of mathematical culture. It is also a source of difficulty for students in high school and university mathematics courses (particularly as concerns the capacity of checking the validity of a statement, finding counter-examples, producing elements for a general justification, evaluating justifications). It depends on linguistic and logic skills that must be developed very early (beginning in kindergarten, according to the U.S. National Council of Teachers of Mathematics (NCTM, 2000) standards).

Usually, secondary school mathematics teachers have learned (as high school and/or university students) to understand and repeat proofs for standard theorems in different areas (Euclidean geometry at the high school level; calculus, linear algebra, and so forth, at the university level). Primary school teachers have a poor preparation in proving (most of them have encountered only some Euclidean geometry theorems at the secondary school level). Almost no teacher has expertise in producing conjectures, finding counter-examples, and producing justifications for unknown statements. Thus, the area of genuine conjecturing and proving is a virgin field for almost all teachers! As we will see, the impact on teachers of CAC education in this area might be: first, to let them experience these aspects of mathematical activities; second, to induce them to distinguish between the development of productive processes, on one side, and the elaboration of their products (according to cultural constraints), on the other, as different sides of mathematical competency.

TASKS FOR CAC

Detailed criteria for choosing tasks for CAC depend on the chosen content area of intervention in mathematics teacher education: for instance, tasks concerning algorithmic performances have more scope in arithmetic than in geometry. However, we can point out some general ideas about how to choose and shape tasks.

First of all, tasks must be clearly related to crucial educational issues in the chosen area. According to our experience, other tasks are not attractive for most teachers and not suitable for challenging their ways of thinking. This criterion does not mean that tasks must be the same at a given school level; teachers willingly engage in other tasks provided that they see the connection with their professional work. For instance, to analyse a given problem situation (once the problem has been solved) in terms of prerequisites is an acceptable task, even if the level of the problem is not accessible for primary or high school students. And a "difficult" (out of the reach of students) problem can be acceptable if it serves to clarify how the difficulties met at an adult level need a long-lasting educational intervention to be managed in a successful way.

Tasks suitable to an approach using CAC can be:
— solutions of mathematical problems (problems that need new tools for teachers can be proposed as well.);
— analysis of students' or colleagues' solutions, according to criteria of correctness, clarity, and efficiency;
— analysis of tasks (in suitable cases, comparison can be proposed between a-priori analysis of tasks and a-posteriori analysis, according to produced solutions and difficulties met by solvers);
— reconstruction of the conceptual hierarchy of a given subject (with the aim of producing its "conceptual map"); and
— production of tasks for students, related to the main issues of a given task proposed at the adult level (with the aim to develop prerequisites, or to meet students' crucial difficulties, or to justify the introduction of further tools for students).

This list of tasks does not include tasks that directly call into question teachers' beliefs (about the subject matter, or about mathematics in general), nor tasks that directly offer CAC elements (for instance, comparing different axiomatic treatments of the same subject). We stress the importance of teachers discovering the need to reconsider their own beliefs and to know more about the subject, starting from what the teachers easily recognise as a mathematical task or an educational task. It is the nature of tasks (related to the opportunities offered by the chosen subject) that create the interest for CAC perspectives and discussion of teachers' beliefs. The difficulties met by teachers on apparently "easy" questions, their different answers, their different evaluations of colleagues' and students' solutions and mistakes, and their different educational proposals can work as occasions in that direction. Here, the choice of suitable mathematical subjects (as discussed in the previous subsection) plays a crucial role – according to our experience it is more difficult to provoke such surprises and puzzling diversity in the case of well established school mathematics areas.

INCORPORATING CAC INTO MATHEMATICS TEACHER EDUCATION

In mathematics teacher education, CAC activities on a given subject can be planned according to a plurality of individual and collective tasks, and instructors' interventions, conveniently organised in teaching routines. A complete, ideal routine can include individual problem-solving, followed by collective comparison and discussion of individual solutions (chosen by the instructor as representative of the whole set of solutions – possibly including mistakes), then individual analysis of the task in terms of prerequisites and difficulties, followed by collective discussion guided by the instructor, and systematic "injection" of CAC elements. In some cases, individual creation of tasks suitable for students, and related collective discussion of proposed tasks, can bring the sequence of activities to a satisfactory conclusion for teachers.

As we see in the examples below, in some cases (especially in short education interventions, or when teachers are already accustomed to the previously described style of work) the same individual task can include some of the listed steps and guided discussion can be organised at the end, as a premise for the "injection" of CAC elements by the instructor.

The "transfer" problem is one of the most delicate for mathematics teacher education on CAC. The very nature of CAC does not allow acquired knowledge (concerning historical, epistemological and socio-cultural aspects of the content) to be directly transferred to other domains. For instance, knowledge concerning the origin of calculus of probability in the XVII century and its multiple roots in the study of gambling, in rational philosophies, in demographic studies (see Hacking, 1975) is a relevant CAC knowledge for teachers at all school levels. Indeed it suggests how deeply probabilistic thinking is related to different cultural domains. This knowledge cannot be transferred to other domains of mathematics.

Also, the knowledge of different axiomatic treatments of a mathematical content and their historical evolution is "local" knowledge related to that specific content. Transferability can (and should) concern the teachers' attitude towards the content, *"How did this notion, or method, or activity develop over history? How did its organisation and symbolic representation change?", "What was, and is now its relevance in mathematics? And in the applications of mathematics?", "What are the analogies with other domains of mathematics?"* are crucial questions related to CAC that the teacher should learn to pose and (at least in some cases) to answer with the help of appropriate sources and or experts. The role of the instructor should be to demonstrate the general character of those questions when he/she deals with them in CAC education on a given content or activity, and to assist teachers to formulate them in suitable ways on further content or activity (see examples at the end of the next sections, where some teachers come to ask questions in the spirit of CAC that can open possibilities of effective transfer).

In general, the didactical organisation of mathematics teacher education activities on CAC should be as coherent as possible with the model of classroom teaching suggested in the other education activities (particularly those concerning PCK and general pedagogical knowledge). This parallelism cannot be maintained in a systematic way, especially in the case of primary school teacher education. In that case, teachers can be invited to discuss why the choice of the instructor at a given moment was contradictory with the proposed principles for classroom work, and the related consequences.

We observe that the instructor's role in CAC education activities is not only that of a facilitator of the development of teachers' knowledge and a stimulator for their beliefs to be put into question. CAC involves specific knowledge that teachers do not have and cannot reconstruct on the basis of their culture. The problem for the instructor is to motivate (in the teachers' eyes) the need for further knowledge to better interpret difficulties, situate problems, and frame subject knowledge according to different needs. From the perspective of teachers' professional preparation, this example of a "mediating role" in action can be useful for their educational choices.

MATHEMATICAL WORK AND ITS CULTURAL IMPACT: THE CASE OF PROBABILITY AND STATISTICS

CAC in probability and statistics offers several opportunities to develop teachers' knowledge and call into question teachers' beliefs related to the specific field as well as to mathematics in general. We present some snapshots from our teacher education experience for primary school, lower secondary school and high school teachers. They concern some of the tasks that we consider crucial for our work with teachers in the field (independent from the number of hours at our disposal)

First, let us consider the "classical" definition of probability as the ratio between the number of favourable outcomes and the number of all possible outcomes, provided that they are equally likely. Many teachers at all school levels are not aware of the crucial importance of the condition *"provided that they are equally likely"* and (if they are acquainted with it) of its possible epistemological limitation (the definition seems to depend on the notion of *"equally likely"*, thus on the application of the defined notion). Depending on the school level, we use different tasks to provoke discussions on these issues. For instance, in primary school teacher education a suitable task is, *"Let us throw two dice and consider the sum of the upper digits. Is it preferable to bet on odd or on even?"* Many teachers (including more than one third of those who learned probability in high school) answer *"even, because the even outcomes are 2, 4, 6, 8, 10, 12, while the odd outcomes are 3, 5, 7, 9, and 11: only five odd outcomes, against six even outcomes"*. The discussion of the produced solutions, conveniently guided by the instructor, usually brings teachers to the correct solution and to the discovery (or re-discovery) of the condition that outcomes must be "equally likely"; incidentally, we observe that the same task is suitable for approaching one of the crucial nodes of probability in primary school (see Consogno, Gazzolo, & Boero, 2006). The ensuing discussion can be oriented to reveal the meaning and the status of the condition *"equally likely outcomes"* in the classical definition of probability, and to approach the issue of rigour in mathematics. This aspect became relevant at different levels for different reasons: on one hand, teachers consider as rigorous many definitions and proofs that are not rigorous at all; on the other hand, they pretend to require an "absolute" rigour from their students (according to their standard models of rigour), without taking into account the fact that rigour must be related to the needs inherent in the situation to be dealt with.

For teachers of every school level, we consider it important that they can experience different kinds of knowledge organisation in the field of probability. In this field, it is easy to find problems that can be solved in substantially different ways, according to the theoretical tools available to the solver. For primary school teachers, we have chosen the task:

"A box contains 8 counters with numbers 1, 2, 3, 4, 5, 6, 7, 8. They are drawn out without replacement. The first four drawn out numbers were 1, 2, 4, and 8. What is the probability that the next three drawn out numbers are odd?"

An inelegant but safe solution consists in considering all possibilities: 3,5,7; 3,7,5; 5,3,7; 5,7,3; 7,3,5; 7,5,3; 6,3,5; 6,3,7; ...; then evaluating the ratio between the 6 favourable outcomes and the 24 possible outcomes. Another strategy can be based on the notion of conditional probability and the theorem of compound probability: the probability of getting an odd number is 3/4 for the fifth counter drawn out, 2/3 for the sixth one, (provided that the previous number was odd), 1/2 for the seventh one (provided that the previous two numbers were odd); thus the probability of getting three odd numbers is $3/4.2/3.1/2 = 1/4$. One could arrive at the same result by considering the fact that 1/4 is the probability of getting the counter that carries the number 6 as the last counter drawn out.

We have observed how many teachers with an extensive background in probability do not choose the second way of reasoning (even if the instructor invites the teachers to find "other solutions"). The reasons for this are sometimes inherent in a poor operational mastery of the necessary notions (Mason & Spence, 1999) would say that those teachers know about them, but they do not know to act with them). Teachers typically comment, *"I have studied them six years ago, but I am not confident with them."* Sometimes, reasons depend on a deeper doubt: *"by counting all possible outcomes and those that are "favourable," I am sure to control the situation; when applying theorems, I feel uncomfortable, because theorems and rules are like black boxes for me, and I do not know their exact boundaries of validity, or whether formal manipulations can introduce mistakes".* These remarks are suitable (under the teachers' guidance) to open important windows on the ways of functioning of mathematics: how theorems represent an economy of thought; and how theory works as a mathematical model (according to Norman: see Dapueto & Parenti, 1999) for those situations to which theory is applied.

The last, easiest way of solving the problem is chosen by few teachers. During the comparison of solutions produced by teachers, is interesting to discuss the reasons for it: *"I have thought about it, but it seemed to me too easy"*; *"I was surprised when Norma presented her solution: she was able to understand that the complementary event was easier to manage"*. Again, teachers' comments can put important educational and cultural facts into evidence. The first comment above calls for the relevance of the didactical contract (Brousseau, 1997) and the nature of problem solving in school, which is strongly influenced by it. The second comment opens another window on some aspects of productive mathematical activities (particularly the need to achieve some distance from the problem situation and consider it from different points of view).

In high school mathematics teacher education, occasion for reflection on the same issues comes with the proof of Bernoulli's theorem. Combinatorics offers useful tools for proving it (but the proof needs a lot of steps). Reasoning based on random variables allows one to get the solution quickly. Again, we find that some teachers think that reasoning based on random variables is too far from the nature of the problem and does not allow them to perform the step-by-step monitoring of reasoning necessary to prevent possible mistakes. *"Reasoning is in another place, it is as if it does not concern the problem. And how to be sure that reasoning with random variables fits the problem in a sure way?"*

In our experience in teacher education, links between probability and statistics are a delicate subject. We think that it is necessary to deal with this subject because it can open windows on important cultural issues (e.g., why people are convinced that chance tends to equilibrate too frequently on outcomes of unlikely events? When can we derive sure conclusions from outcomes of random events?) and on the modeling potential inherent in probability theory. Also, the cultural value of mathematics as a component of scientific rationality can be demonstrated.

For teachers of all school levels, we enter the subject through the "black bottle experiment". It can be organised as follows: the teachers are divided into groups of two or three. Each group has one closed bottle that contains the same unknown quantities of blue and red marbles (e.g., 6 red marbles and 4 blue marbles in each bottle). The colour is the only difference between marbles. It is not possible to see the contents of the bottle; when the bottle is inverted, it is only possible to see one marble. Each group must produce a sequence of 300 or 400 outcomes (requiring less than 15 minutes), then they must draw a diagram of the cumulative frequencies (after 20, 40, 60, etc. outcomes). Finally, they answer some questions:

− what are the features of the diagram?
− is it possible to guess the number of red marbles?
− what about the difference between the number of red marbles and the number of blue marbles?
− what information can we derive from the collected data?

The comparison of the diagrams and the answers to the previous questions, together with the construction of the diagram that represents the cumulative frequencies of the outcomes collected by all the groups, allow teachers to realise that: *"we cannot get any information about the number of red marbles in the* bottle, we can only guess the ratio between the number of red marbles and the total number of marbles"; "the number of trials can influence the 'stabilisation' of the frequency diagram near to a value that suggests the ratio between the number of red marbles and the total number of marbles"; "the difference between the number of red outcomes and the number of blue outcomes tends to increase, in spite of the fact that the ratio between red outcomes and blue outcomes tends to become stable".

The following step consists in individually answering to the following question: "In some diagrams produced by groups we see that, in spite of an initial prevalence of red or black outcomes, the tendency (when the number of trials increases) is to approach the same value. How can we explain this fact?"

Here, we can observe how some teachers reflect common misconceptions: "Chance balances out the initial prevalence of red or blue marbles," "After too many red marbles, chance makes more blue marbles come out, so equilibrium is reached". Other teachers explicitly refuse such explanations, but they are not able to explain what happens. Only a few teachers write that "The increasing number of trials has the initial prevalence of red marbles absorbed in the ratio". The comparison of different answers allows teachers to move towards a shared answer to the initial questions and reflect on the reasons why people think that "chance tends to balance irregular outcomes".

The final step usually consists of a collective discussion of the question: "How many trials should we perform, in order to be sure that the proportion of the red and blue marbles in the bottle is that suggested by the frequency diagram?"

In primary school teacher education, the aim of this question is to encourage discussion of the notion of "sure answer". With 10-12 groups (each group producing one series of 300 or 400 trials) it is easy to find at least one diagram (derived from one series of trials) that suggests a hypothesis "rather different" from the other ones. There is not time to experience several series of 3000 or 4000 trials, but teachers can rely on their instructor's words and imagine that even a cumulative diagram derived from 3000 or 4000 trials could suggest a "relatively bad" hypothesis. Teachers can come to understand that the notion of "sure answer" cannot be absolute, but instead it depends on the "acceptable discrepancy" (inherent in the use of expressions like "rather different"), on the number of trials, and on the "acceptable risk" for the validity of the hypothesis.

In secondary school teacher education, the aim is to motivate the introduction of theoretical tools (in our opinion, at least Bernoulli's theorem and Tchebichev's inequality must be presented) that allow one to measure the degree of uncertainty of a hypothesis derived from the analysis of frequencies.

In both cases, the discussion should be guided to consider the importance of the posed question in different domains (physical sciences, medical sciences, polls, etc.).

Traces of the impact of the CAC activities in the case of probability and statistics can be found in the planning of didactical situations concerning the introduction of such subject matter in school, in the analysis of students' products, and in the answer to open ended questions concerning *"discoveries, doubts, open problem."* Criteria to evaluate such traces are:

- precision in the language to deal with topics in the field;
- focus on relevant cultural issues; and especially (for answers to open ended questions)
- quality of doubts and open problems that are posed.

For instance, we consider important (in the CAC perspective and keeping teachers' current beliefs in mind) that a secondary teacher writes: *"I have understood that (differently from other domains of mathematics) in the field of probability and statistics the answers to many problems must be formulated in terms of 'it is more likely that', instead of 'it is true that'. But it seems to me that also in probability and statistics theory provides true statements: the statement 'the probability that… is less than…' seems to me true like a normal statement in other fields. I would like to know more about this issue".* Statements like this one are not rare in our corpus of teachers' texts. On one hand, they show how teachers formulate questions in the CAC perspective; on the other hand, they can be exploited by the instructor to fuel further discussions aimed at transferring the CAC way of looking at mathematics to other mathematical domains.

MATHEMATICAL PRODUCTS AND PRODUCTION PROCESSES: THE CASE OF CONJECTURING AND PROVING

Let us consider the following individual task:
"Evaluate whether the following texts, produced by Grade IX students that are just beginning to prove in Mathematics, are satisfactory to 'Provide a general justification. i.e., a mathematical proof, for the statement: the sum of two consecutive odd numbers is divisible by four.' Give reasons for your evaluation."

(note that d is the initial letter of *dispari, odd* in Italian, and p is the initial letter of *pari, even* in Italian)

The following are three proofs that can be used as the basis of discussion.

Proof I. $d+d+2=2d+2=2+2d=4d$; $4d$ is clearly a number divisible by 4.

Proof II. By making some trials, like for instance 3+5, 15+17, 31+33, I realise that I always get sums made by the first odd number and by the same odd number increased by two, thus I get the double of an odd number plus two. This result is divisible by four because the sum of two equal odd numbers would be (alone) an even number divisible only by two, but if I add two I get the consecutive even number, which is divisible by four because even numbers follow each other with the rule that if one is divisible only by two, the following one is divisible by four (like: 2, 4; 6, 8; 22, 24; etc) because the multiples of four are four units far from each other.

Proof III. $d=p+1$, the following odd number is $d+2=p+3$; I must make the addition $d+d+2$ that makes $p+p+4$ because $d+d+2=p+1+p+3=p+p+4$.

This task is systematically used as an introductory task in an 8 to 10 hour introduction of CAC elements in teacher education, which takes place in a 30-hour course of mathematics education mostly taken by practising primary school teachers. It has also been used with lower secondary school teachers and high school teachers (within a 15 to 21 hour course on conjecturing and proving).

It is interesting to analyse how teachers react to this task and notice the differences between primary school teachers and high school teachers. Most primary and high school teachers write that Proof II is *"a less mathematical proof than Proof I and Proof III"*, and more than one half of high school teachers add that Proof II *"is not a true mathematical proof because it uses examples."*

The discussion after the individual task reveals that most teachers in both cases did not engage in understanding the text of Proof II; the presence of "algebraic proofs" I and III reveals the teachers' conception of the ideal mathematical proof as a formal algebraic derivation (even if high school proving in Euclidean geometry was a long lasting experience of verbal proving for all of them!). Seeing some examples in Proof II (without considering their real function within the text) induces the majority of high school teachers to think that *"the student has not understood that the validity of mathematical proof cannot rely on examples"*. Few teachers (three out of a sample of 18, in a education course last year), after reconsidering Proof II under solicitation of the instructor, realise that *"in this case examples have only a heuristic or illustration function; they are not good in the text of a standard mathematical proof, but this text works substantially well as a general justification!"*.

In contrast, most primary school teachers do not consider examples as mistakes or inappropriate in a mathematical proof; when the instructor suggests they read the text again, they simply conclude that *"it works,"* although *"it is less mathematical than the other ones."*

Coming now to Proof I and Proof III: most teachers (even primary school teachers) recognise the mistake within Proof I. High school teachers explain that *"the student does not know the rules of algebraic transformations."* Under the request of the instructor, they say that *"There is nothing to save in that proof."* Primary school teachers are more indulgent; some of them say that (provided that the algebraic transformation would have been managed in a correct way) *"4d would have brought the correct conclusion of divisibility by 4"*.

Proof III usually receives different evaluations by high school teachers and by primary school teachers, and within both groups of teachers. The fact that the algebraic transformations work well causes about one half of high school teachers, and about three quarters of primary school teachers, to be satisfied with Proof III. Very few primary school teachers identify the lack of a crucial step (proving divisibility of $p+p+4$ by 4). In contrast, one third of high school teachers speak of *"incomplete proof"* (other teachers write that the student *"had the intuition that it worked, but did not feel the need to make the last steps"*). Invited by the instructor

239

to consider again Proof II, most teachers of both school levels do not realise that the author of Proof II was able (in the substance) to move verbally from odd+odd+2 to the full justification of its divisibility by 4.

According to this synthetic description of teachers' behaviour in an individual task and related collective discussion, it is clear how the task provides a rich source of occasions (for the instructor) to call into question many stereotyped conceptions teachers have about proving and, more generally, about mathematics and their role as mathematics teachers. In particular, the dominant idea of the necessity of mathematical formalism in proving, the lack of distinction between a valid justification and its conventional style of presentation, and more attention paid to the correctness of the product than to the quality of the process.

Starting from the aforementioned task and depending on the time available and the school level, CAC education can be developed in different directions with different aims. For primary school teachers, one of the main final aims can be to discover the importance of specific logic-linguistic skills inherent in exhaustive, logical arguing; as well as reflecting on the fact that many statements in mathematics can be validated without a specialised symbolic apparatus. The same aims can be intermediate steps for education high school teachers, but in this case further goals can be considered:

- to make clear why Proof III is not satisfactory from a mathematical point of view;
- to make clear why Proof I, in spite of the student's mistake, contains some valid elements (if we consider the underlying process);
- to identify and discuss the various functions of algebraic language in mathematics and in mathematical proving.

In our experience, a second, common task for high and primary school teachers (in the domain of conjecturing and proving) is: *"To produce a conjecture about the GCD of all the products of three consecutive integer numbers, and prove it"*. Usually, some words must be added, in order that teachers understand what they must do (by itself, this fact offers an occasion for reflecting on characteristics of mathematical language).

The analysis of the task in terms of CAC shows relevant potential in different directions, suitable for different developments according to the teachers' school level. Many high school teachers in the conjecturing phase, and most of them in the proving phase, try to solve the problem using algebraic language, which results in an impasse. Most primary school teachers prefer to explore the situation with numerical examples. They produce suitable conjectures, but when they try to prove them, many are not able to move from verification of examples to a general justification. High school teachers' conceptions about the privileged role of algebraic language in every non-geometrical activity come again to the foreground (in spite of the discussions following the previous task). Other conceptions that must be called into question (in the perspective of high school teaching) are revealed by the analysis of teachers' behaviours and the collective discussion on the second task: a limited use of examples (justified by saying that *"whenever possible, when we deal with theorems we must avoid the use of examples"*, with a clear extension to conjecturing of warnings concerning proving); when examples are used, the difficulty of exploring them in order to find the common "structure," in particular the difficulty in moving from the fact that 6 appears to be the GCD to the discovery of the reasons why it happens in all cases (teachers say that *"examples only help to see, in some cases, if the statement is reasonably true"*; the possibility of discovering structural regularities by exploring examples is ignored).

After the first two tasks and related discussion guided by the instructor (4-5 hours of work), the injection of elements of history and epistemology of mathematics by the instructor is usually a turning point in the teachers' ways of conceiving some aspects of conjecturing and proving: in particular, the analysis of Euclid's proofs of some arithmetic theorems legitimates the use of verbal language as a genuine tool for mathematical proving at all school levels; the comparison between different styles of presentation of proofs (Euclid, Lobacevsky, Hilbert) illustrates the historical non-linear evolution of the style of proofs; (for high school teachers) the discussion of some claims by Thurston (1994) raises the question of what is relevant in mathematics and in the communication of mathematical knowledge.

For high school teacher education, one of the most useful tasks is the following (used also with prospective teachers): *"Generalise the proposition*: 'The sum of two consecutive odd numbers is divisible by four', *and prove the generalised proposition"* (see Boero, Douek, & Ferrari, 2002, for details about difficulties and strategies). Teachers' difficulties in understanding what *"Generalise"* could mean in such a situation, the plurality of possible generalisations, the difficulties in proving some of the conjectures (depending on the difficulties of translating them into suitable algebraic expressions) are all sources of reflection on important CAC aspects of mathematical activities and on teachers' related beliefs. In particular, the following question is frequently raised by teachers when they discover that many generalisations have been produced within their group: *"What are the criteria to decide whether this is a meaningful generalisation? And who decides this in mathematics?"*

At the end of the activities, evidence in teachers' written texts and oral interventions reveals that their beliefs on conjecturing and proving, and related educational choices, have been at least partially re-oriented: under open-ended tasks (*"Write down your discoveries, persisting difficulties, doubts, open questions"*), teachers' texts show how the activities have put into question some previous firm convictions (*"Now, I feel much more free to write in Italian my thoughts and solutions in mathematics; my teachers had always discouraged me from doing it, with the motivation that I had to learn the language of mathematics, and I was reproducing the same with my students"*) and have contributed to opening new windows for further learning (*"It seems to me that well chosen numerical examples can work as generic examples in geometry, from the point of view of discovering structural facts: am I right?"*) in the perspective of transfer.

On tasks concerning evaluation of samples of students' proofs (or justifications, at the primary school level), teachers not only take into account the distinction between correctness of the product and quality of the process (this might merely depend on the need of satisfying the instructor's requests), but also spontaneously move to personal considerations about the relationships between students' performances and their educational context: *"Ivan's proof has some gaps, but they concern implications that the student probably thinks to be obvious; it would be necessary to know better the level of rigour that is requested by his teacher".*

CONCLUSION

CAC, the cultural analysis of mathematical content, has been presented in this chapter as one of the most important components of teacher education, in spite of the fact that little room is devoted to it in teacher education and in current literature on teacher education. Through snapshots derived from our experiences in teacher education, we tried to show how CAC activities can be organised using suitable subject matters, tasks, and educational methods. We tried also to provide evidence for the impact of CAC activities on teachers' beliefs related to the specific field, and concerning mathematics in general.

There is an unsolved problem that we would like to pose in this concluding section – that is the preparation of mathematics teacher educators to work from a CAC perspective. As remarked in the second section of this chapter, today mathematics teacher educators are mostly interested in developing teachers' competencies related to PCK, and also their preparation is oriented in the same direction (e.g., Zaslavsky & Leikin, 2004). Mathematicians who engage in teacher education do not seem interested in the CAC perspective, and their scientific career as mathematicians does not depend on CAC competencies. The CAC perspective needs competencies coming from epistemology of mathematics, history of mathematics, and philosophy of mathematics. However, experts in these fields do not intervene in teacher education, or, if they do, their involvement is not designed to call into question teachers' beliefs and the cultural orientation of their teaching – only standard lectures in those fields are offered to teachers.

REFERENCES

Arzarello, F., & Bartolini Bussi, M. (1998). Italian trends in mathematics education: A national case study from an international perspective. In A. Sierpinska & J. Kilpatrick (Eds.), *Mathematics education as a research domain: A search for identity* (pp. 243–262). Dordrecht, the Netherlands: Kluwer Academic Publishers.

Barbé, J., Bosch, M., Espinoza, L., & Gascon, J. (2005). Didactic restriction on the teacher's practice: The case of limits of function in Spanish high schools. *Educational Studies in Mathematics, 59,* 235–268.

Boero, P., Dapueto, C., & Parenti, L. (1996). Didactics of mathematics and the professional knowledge of teachers. In A. J. Bishop, M. A. Clements, C. Keitel, J. Kilpatrick, & C. Laborde (Eds.),

International handbook of mathematics education (Vol. 2, pp. 1097–1122). Dordrecht, the Netherlands: Kluwer Academic Publishers.

Boero, P., Douek, N., & Ferrari, P. L. (2002). Developing mastery of natural language: Approaches to theoretical aspects of mathematics. In L. English (Ed.), *Handbook of international research in mathematics education* (pp. 241–268). Mahwah, NJ: Lawrence Erlbaum Associates.

Brousseau, G. (1997). *Theory of didactical situations in mathematics.* Dordrecht, the Netherlands: Kluwer Academic Publishers.

Chevallard, Y. (1985). *La transposition didactique: Du savoir savant au savoir enseigné.* Grenoble: La Pensée Sauvage.

Chevallard, Y. (2000). La recherché en didactique et la formation des professeurs: Problématique, concepts, problèmes. In M. Bailleul (Ed.), *Actes de la X-ème Ecolse d'Eté de didactique des mathématiques* (pp. 98–112). Caen, France: IUFM.

Consogno, V., Gazzolo, T., & Boero, P. (2006). Developing probability thinking in primary school: A case study on the constructive role of natural language in classroom discussions. In J. Novotná, H. Moraová, M. Krátká, & N. Stehlková (Eds.), *Proceedings of the 30th Conference of the International Group for the Psychology of Mathematics Education* (Vol. 2, pp. 353–360). Charles University in Prague, Czech Republic.

Dapueto, C., & Parenti, L. (1999). Contributions and obstacles of contexts in the developments of mathematics knowledge. *Educational Studies in Mathematics, 39,* 1–21.

Hacking, I. (1975). *The emergence of probability.* Cambridge, UK: Cambridge University Press.

Hatano, G., & Wertsch, J. V. (2001). Sociocultural approaches to cognitive development: The constitution of culture in mind. *Human Development, 44,* 77–83.

Hiebert, J., Gallimore, R., & Stigler, J. (2002). A knowledge base for the teaching profession: What would it look like and how can we get one? *Educational Researcher, 31,* 3–15.

Malara, N., & Zan, R. (2002). The problematic relationship between theory and practice. In L. English (Ed.), *Handbook of international research in mathematics education* (pp. 553–580). Mahwah, NJ: Lawrence Erlbaum Associates.

Mason, J. (1998). Enabling teachers to be real teachers: Necessary levels of awareness and structure of attention. *Journal of Mathematics Teacher Education, 1,* 243–267.

Mason, J., & Spence, M. (1999). Beyond mere knowledge of mathematics. The importance of knowing-to act in the moment. *Educational Studies in Mathematics, 38,* 135–161.

Schifter, D. (1993). Mathematics process as mathematics content: A course for teachers. *Journal of Mathematical Behavior, 12,* 271–283.

Shulman, L. S. (1986). Those who understand: Knowledge growth in teaching. *Educational Researcher, 15,* 4–14.

Sullivan, P., & Mousley, J. (2001). Thinking teaching: Seeing mathematics teachers as active decision makers. In F.-L.-Lin & T. J. Cooney (Eds.), *Making sense of mathematics teacher education* (pp. 33–52). Dordrecht, the Netherlands: Kluwer Academic Publishers.

Torner, G. (2002). Mathematical beliefs – A search for a common ground: Some theoretical considerations on structuring beliefs, some research questions, and some phenomenological observations. In G. Leder, E. Pehkonen, & G. Torner (Eds.), *Beliefs: A hidden variable in mathematics education?* (pp. 73–94). Dordrecht, the Netherlands: Kluwer Academic Publishers.

Thurston, W. P. (1994). On proof and progress in mathematics. *Bulletin of the American Mathematical Society, 30,* 161–177.

Wilder, R. L. (1986). The cultural basis of mathematics. In T. Tymoczko (Ed.), *New directions in the philosophy of mathematics* (pp. 185–199). Boston, MA.: Birkhauser.

Zaslavsky, O., Chapman, O., & Leikin, R. (2003). Professional development in mathematics education: Trends and tasks. In A. J. Bishop, M. A. Clements, C. Keitel, J. Kilpatrick, & F. K. S. Leung (Eds.), *Second international handbook of mathematics education* (Vol. 2, pp. 877–915). Dordrecht, the Netherlands: Kluwer Academic Publishers.

Zaslavsky, O., & Leikin, R. (2004). Professional development of mathematics teacher educators: Growth through practice. *Journal of Mathematics Teacher Education, 7*, 5–32.

Paolo Boero
DIMA
Genoa University
Italy

Elda Guala
DIMA
Genoa University
Italy

SECTION 4

ASSESSMENT OF, AND RESEARCH ON, TEACHER KNOWLEDGE

ANNE D. COCKBURN

11. ASSESSMENT OF MATHEMATICAL KNOWLEDGE OF PROSPECTIVE TEACHERS

In this chapter I use four case studies – two from primary and two from secondary – to illustrate the key issues surrounding the assessment of prospective mathematics teachers' knowledge. The examples are taken from cross-cultural settings and demonstrate the universal complexities involved in planning and assessing future teachers efficiently and effectively. Criteria for successful teaching – as defined by Ball, Bass and Hill (2004) – and students' views on the assessment procedures in two of the cases provide an added dimension to the discussion.

INTRODUCTION

A hundred years ago teaching was seen as a highly transmissive activity: children were perceived as empty vessels to be filled with knowledge. During this same time, no formal qualifications for teaching were required. It was not until the middle of the last century that teachers were required to gain a formal qualification in teacher education before they could practise in government schools in the U.K. Prior to that, for example, a degree in mathematics was sufficient to teach the subject in secondary schools. Since then there have dramatic changes in the view of teaching and the view of students. The widespread acceptance of a more constructivist approach views teaching and learning as active and interactive processes. There is now an almost universal requirement that individuals need to successfully complete some recognised form of teacher education before they can practise regardless of the age they wish to teach. Teaching mathematics is no longer seen as passing on a series of formulae and procedures which need to be drummed into – often very reluctant – learners. Indeed, more than 20 years ago Shulman (1986) articulated the necessary content knowledge required for teaching in terms of three categories, which he describes as:

- *Subject matter content knowledge* which goes beyond the basic facts to encompass teachers', [...] understanding of the subject matter and the ability to, [...] be able to explain why a particular proposition is deemed warranted, why it is worth knowing, and how it relates to other propositions, both within the discipline and without, both in theory and practice (p. 9).
- *Pedagogical content knowledge* which, as the phrase implies, extends to subject knowledge for teaching or, '[...] the ways of representing and

P. Sullivan and T. Wood (eds.), Knowledge and Beliefs in Mathematics Teaching and Teaching Development, 247–272.

formulating the subject knowledge that make it comprehensible to others' (ibid, p 9).

- *Curricular knowledge* which is a knowledge of the full range of topics which might be taught within a subject area together with an understanding as to if, when and how they might best be presented.

More recently, Hill, Rowan, and Ball (2005) stressed that, "Effectiveness in teaching resides not simply in the knowledge a teacher has accrued but how this knowledge is used in classrooms" (pp. 375–376). Elsewhere Ball, Bass, and Hill (2004) discuss extensive research they have done with teachers to expand on Shulman's work and present some important insights for teacher education. Firstly, they demonstrate that, unlike the untrained mathematicians in the past who had been taught, "...to *compress* information into abstract and highly usable forms" (Ball et al., 2004, p. 10), teachers are required to "unpack" (Ball et al., 2004, p. 10) ideas and thus be able to both explain how mathematical concepts evolve but also be able to unravel a pupil's thinking processes when they have misunderstood some aspect of their work.

Secondly, they stress that, "Teaching involves making connections across mathematical domains, helping students build links and coherence in their knowledge" (Ball et al., 2004, p 11). Thus, for example, a teacher might present a 3 × 5 rectangle as shown in Figure 1 below and then rotate it through 90° to demonstrate that multiplication is commutative, that is 3 × 5 = 5 × 3.

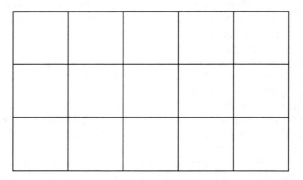

Figure 1. A 3 x 5 rectangle which might be used to demonstrate that multiplication is commutative.

Thirdly, they argue that teachers need to be aware of future mathematics their pupils will encounter to reduce the likelihood of misconceptions developing with regard to, for example, subtraction where, in the past, it was common to teach in the early grades that you always subtract the smaller number from the larger.

Finally, they conclude that, "Knowing mathematics for teaching often entails making sense of methods and solutions different from one's own, and so learning to size up other methods, determine their adequacy, and compare them, is an essential mathematical skill for teaching [...]" (Ball et al., 2004, p. 15). These views – although not generally articulated in such detail – are apparent in some of the key practitioner documents available around the world. For example the six principles for school mathematics issued by the National Council of Teachers of Mathematics (2000) in the United States include statements such as,

- *Curriculum.* A curriculum is more than a collection of activities: it must be coherent, focused on important mathematics, and well articulated across the grades.
- *Teaching.* Effective mathematics teaching requires understanding what students know and need to learn and then challenging and supporting them to learn it well.
- *Learning.* Students must learn mathematics with understanding, actively building new knowledge from experience and prior knowledge.

While in England teachers are advised that,

> In good mathematics teaching the skills and knowledge that children are expected to learn are clearly defined and the teacher has mapped out how to lead the children to the mathematics. Children know that they can discuss, seek help and use resources as and when they need to. They like to be challenged and enjoy the opportunities to practise and apply their learning. [...] Children who need more support than others are identified quickly and receive early intervention to help them maintain their progress…The teacher or practitioner recognises that mathematics is a combination of concepts, facts, properties, rules, patterns and processes. Leading children's learning must take account of this and requires a broad repertoire of teaching and organisational approaches. [...] Good mathematics teaching requires a good knowledge of the subject, an understanding of the progression in the curriculum being taught and a recognition that some teaching approaches are better suited to promote particular learning and outcomes. (Department For Education and Skills, 2006, pp. 65–66)

Reviewing the above it would appear that, over the past 100 years there has been a marked shift in several significant quarters as to how mathematics teaching and learning is perceived. Education is now seen as a much more dynamic process which requires high levels of knowledge and understanding with successful teachers being highly skilled in a range of pedagogical techniques. Although there might be fairly widespread agreement about that, however, when it comes to assessing teachers' practice, "[…] there is little agreement on what, whom, and how to measure, and for what purpose" (Hill, Sleep, Lewis, & Ball, 2007, p. 149).

While this observation might create an interesting challenge, it becomes a major issue when the spotlight is turned away from practising teachers and focused on prospective teachers. As a profession we need to be convinced that they have reached the necessary requirements to become efficient and effective practitioners. No longer are mathematics examinations sufficient. What is required are far more sophisticated and wide ranging techniques which capture, as far as possible, the subtleties and complexities involved in mathematics education for primary and secondary pupils.

Thus this chapter considers how prospective mathematics teachers are assessed when undertaking their teacher education. It uses four case studies as catalysts for discussion. These are presented as in-depth examinations of experienced educators' thoughts and actions when planning and implementing assessment of prospective mathematics teachers. The choice of examples allows for comparisons and similarities to be made across countries (three were selected) and across age phases (e.g., a primary and secondary programme within the same institution are considered). Semi-structured interviews (Robson, 1993) were conducted to elicit data on common issues across programmes and yet ensure that the integrity and individuality of each course description was explored. A qualitative descriptive approach was adopted (Sandelowski, 2000). Key issues to emerge were the range of strategies adopted, the high levels of tutor involvement required for comprehensive assessments of prospective teachers' performance and the extent to which outside agencies are involved in the process.

CASE 1: ASSESSMENT OF ELEMENTARY TEACHERS IN A MIDDLE EASTERN CONTEXT

The first case is a 3-year first degree course for prospective primary teachers undertaken at a teachers' training college in a middle-eastern context. To qualify for one of the 20 places in this undergraduate course applicants must pass examinations set by both their schools and the college in - among other subjects - mathematics. Once accepted they study units in mathematics, psychology, pedagogy and the language of instruction while also gaining practical teaching experience in local schools. On qualification the majority of these teachers will teach 6-12 year-olds.

In each year of their three years of study, students do four mathematics courses which combine to result in eight hours of mathematics per week for 30 weeks per year. Typically each course comprises subject knowledge and how to teach mathematics in a ratio of 3:1. All the courses and their assessments are designed by the person/people who teach them. No external bodies are involved although every year the mathematics tutors from all the colleges in the country meet for a day to share their programmes as a way of stimulating new ideas rather than anything more formal such as moderation.

When preparing her mathematics teaching, the course tutor said that, not only does she change her courses each year, but she also reviews how she assesses the students' work as part of the course planning process. For every course unit she teaches she employs two assessment strategies:

1) examinations to assess key points. These tests last 90 minutes and are used to assess subject knowledge and its application. For an example of a typical problem see Figure 2.

A child solved the following exercises as follows:

$$10 + 4 \times 2 = 28$$
$$10 \times 4 + 2 = 42$$
$$10 - 4 - 2 = 4$$
$$10 - 4 : 2 = 3$$

a. Correct his work.
b. Explain his mistakes.
c. Give some more examples which help you to diagnose his knowledge. Write the expected answers in each case.
d. What are the prerequisite skills required for the above?
e. Suggest how you might teach this child.

Figure 2. Example of an examination question for prospective primary teachers.

2) exercises, which are set three or four times a semester, and require students to reflect on an issue in depth. For example students might be asked to read a research paper on the different forms of subtraction. They then discuss it as a group, formulate some questions on the topic which they use as a basis for an interview with children in school. They analyse the data collected and present a report of their findings to their seminar group. Another activity might be for each student to select a non-routine task which they have enjoyed completing in a seminar and try it with a class of primary pupils. They observe the children at work, analyse their actions with the expectation of recounting their observations and providing an in-depth account of their conclusions to their colleagues.

In addition, every week the students are on teaching practice they are observed and assessed by a pedagogical supervisor from the college. This individual may not be a subject specialist but, particularly in cases of concern, they may then discuss a student's progress with colleagues in the mathematics department at the college.

Towards the end of their third year the prospective teachers undertake a project for which they select a series of sessions on a specific topic – such as addition – to teach in school. They are required to plan these in the light of their knowledge and experience together with reference to the research literature. The prospective teachers then teach the unit in school with some of their lessons being observed in the manner described above. Following the series of lessons, the prospective teachers are required to do an oral presentation at college explaining what they prepared and why and how they adapted their planning in the light of their classroom experiences. These presentations are observed and commented on by several college tutors although it is only the course mathematics tutor who formally assesses them and assigns a mark. As an aside, the respondent said that she would like the students to do more such reading but added that this could be a problem as there are few appropriate native language texts and some students have difficulty in reading English.

If, at any time during the process of their teacher education, the tutor notices that a student's performance is weak, she explains, "I do my best to give all the help the students need. I spend a lot of time on this". As a result, she added that students seldom fail any aspects of the course. On the rare occasions that they do not perform to a sufficiently high standard, students are required to re-take the year they have completed unsatisfactorily.

The tutor of the above programme does not assess all aspects of her mathematics courses and, indeed, she argues that it might be counter productive to do so. She does, however, adopt a rather unusual – and seemingly effective – strategy which she believes develops her students' confidence and understanding without the burden of assessment anxieties. Specifically, she sets a problem at the start of some of her sessions for students to complete in their own time. At the next meeting she asks for volunteers to discuss their solution. This practice is repeated throughout the year, and at no time are students put under pressure to explain their work unless they wish to do so. As a result of this strategy, over the years she discovered that students become self-motivated and those who had difficulty solving problems, set early in the year, research the topics in detail and, in so doing, gain confidence and a willingness to experiment in the classroom.

First Commentary

Clearly the design of the above course involved detailed thinking about the teaching, learning and assessment processes. Of paramount importance to the tutor seemed to be the need for her prospective teachers to know considerably more than mathematical facts. Their knowledge was assessed using regular examinations but the application of this knowledge was also monitored in a variety of ways to ensure that the prospective teachers had an in-depth appreciation of the facts and knew how to incorporate them into the educational process. This was done through the frequent exercises set each semester and the observation of practical teaching in a school environment.

Reflecting on the above, it would appear that both Shulman's (1986) and Ball et al's. (2004) criteria for successful teaching are assessed and, in several cases – such as pedagogical content knowledge and knowing mathematics for teaching – on more than one occasion. Indeed, there are ample opportunities where students could *potentially* demonstrate Ball et al's criteria as summarised in Table 1. This notwithstanding, one of the tutor's approaches to advancing the students' own mathematical knowledge, understanding and confidence was not formally assessed but appears to be a highly effective teaching and learning technique.

Table 1. Potential opportunities for prospective teachers to demonstrate Ball et al.'s criteria for successful teaching in Case 1

Assessment to demonstrate students' ability to….	Case 1	
'Unpack' information	*1.*	*examination*
	2.	*exercises*
	3.	*teaching practice*
	4.	*project*
Make connections	*1.*	*examination*
	2.	*exercises*
	3.	*teaching practice*
	4.	*project*
Anticipate pupils' future mathematical needs	*2.*	*exercises*
	3.	*teaching practice*
	4.	*project*
Evaluate and incorporate other methods/solutions	*1.*	*examination*
	2.	*exercises*
	3.	*teaching practice*
	4.	*project*

CASE 2: ASSESSMENT OF ELEMENTARY TEACHERS IN THE U.K. CONTEXT

The majority of prospective teachers in the first case – apart from those opting to teach 5- and 6-year-olds – will only teach mathematics once qualified. In contrast, those in the second case study are likely to teach the full range of primary curriculum subjects when they complete their initial teacher education course. When comparing and contrasting the two case studies therefore one should take cognisance of the fact that both groups of prospective teachers are being prepared to teach approximately the same age range of children and, although there may be some cultural variations, the range of mathematical topics they will teach elementary pupils will be broadly the same.

Every year approximately 170 graduates embark on a 39-week course which prepares them to teach all subjects across the nursery and elementary sector. They will, however, have opted for particular age ranges making them most highly equipped to teach 3-7 year-olds or 5-11 year-olds. To qualify for this over-subscribed course all of the prospective teachers have gained a good honors degree (in any subject), have had experience working with children and have undergone a rigorous interview including a short presentation. The only entry requirement which specifically refers to mathematics is a pass at C grade or above (available grades are A*, A - G) in GCSE mathematics – a public examination typically taken by 16 year-olds but which can be taken at any age.

During the course of their initial teacher education all prospective teachers study the full range of curriculum subjects taught in primary schools. Their mathematics course comprises eight lectures on key mathematical topics – such as number, calculation, children's errors, curriculum structure – and twelve hours of workshops which focus on the practical aspects of mathematics teaching in areas such as shape and space, measurement, data handling. In addition, those studying to teach 3-7 year-olds have 20 hours input on mathematical development in the early years. Prospective teachers who fail their audit (see below) also attend up to five hours of mathematics clinics. Others, with a particular interest in the subject, may opt for a 10-hour project in planning and conducting mathematics in out-of-school contexts. The prospective teachers spend approximately half of their course working at the university and the other half in two schools where they develop their expertise in practical teaching. In order to be eligible for qualified teacher status at the end of their year's course all prospective teachers are required to:

1) pass a mathematics audit prepared and marked by the course tutors but which, periodically, may be scrutinised by external examiners and government inspectors from the Office for Standards in Education (Ofsted). This audit is taken under examination conditions and may take up to two hours to complete. Every year questions, such as using informal methods to calculate a percentage, are designed to test mathematical knowledge while others are included to assess understanding and application. Typically the latter might be of the type, "Which of the following is true/false and give reasons why". An example of such a question is given in Figure 3. Prospective teachers who fail the first attempt at the audit attend the clinics described above

> A cuboid-shaped container has sides of lengths 0.5m, 0.8m and 0.25m. It would need to be used 40 times to fill a tank with 4 cubic metres of water.
>
> This is true/false, because…*[delete as appropriate, and explain/show why]*

Figure 3. A typical question in a mathematics audit in Case 2.

and then undertake a re-examination. Prospective teachers have a further chance if they fail again, but a second failure results in their not qualifying for a teaching certificate.

2) work in groups of three students plan and deliver a 20-minute workshop for colleagues on a specific mathematical topic such as fractions. They present the material – including practical tasks and a display – explaining how the concept can be developed across the primary years of schooling. The work is then written up in 500 words by each member of the group. This, together with the

presentation, is assessed. If students fail they are given one opportunity to re-do the work.

3) successfully complete their teaching practices in two placement schools. To do so, for the mathematics component, prospective teachers need to demonstrate sufficient competence in the preparation, planning, teaching, assessment and evaluation of their practice. For all prospective teachers this assessment is done by their class teacher working in collaboration with a university tutor who may, or may not, be a mathematics specialist. Evidence used in making these judgments is collected from the teaching practice files which all prospective teachers are expected to prepare and maintain. These include records of the key written documents the prospective teachers use as part of their practice such as schemes of work, lesson plans, pupil assessment details and reflections on sessions taught. In addition prospective teachers are observed teaching on several occasions by both their class teacher and their tutor. At least one of these observations must be of a mathematics session. Should a student fail to meet the specified criteria (see below) they are usually given the opportunity to undertake a further teaching practice in the following academic year.

Every year a sample of prospective teachers (i.e., about 10%) are also observed by an external examiner from another school or higher education institution by way of a moderation exercise. Additionally, when an institution is inspected by Ofsted – typically every 3-4 years – government inspectors observe a range of prospective teachers across the ability range working in schools. The inspectors' role is not to assess the prospective teachers per se but rather to judge the way in which the higher education institution monitors and works with individuals.

4) the final form of assessment the prospective teachers are required to undergo is a centrally prepared online (QTS) test required by the government Department for Education and Skills. In essence it is a basic skills test in numeracy and it may be taken as many times as necessary. Individuals are not, however, allowed to work as fully qualified teachers until they have passed this exam. The tests include typical questions you might ask pupils – such as '46 x 8 equals?' and 'A science teacher has £100 left in his budget. How many books at £ 6.95 each can he buy?' This notwithstanding, the focus is not so much on the teaching of mathematics, but rather on the numeracy of the prospective teacher and especially their competence to interpret professional data – for example, graphs and tables of examination results.

The above four criteria are designed to determine whether the prospective teachers have fulfilled the professional standards for qualified teacher status as defined by the Training and Development Agency and set out in the Appendix. As discussed, prospective teachers are generally given the opportunity to re-take any aspect of the course they have failed. A second failure – with the exception of the QTS test which can be taken as often as necessary – means, however, that they are unable to graduate as a qualified primary teacher.

Second Commentary

The aim of this chapter is not to compare and contrast the input in mathematics education the different groups of prospective teachers receive on their various courses but, in passing, it is interesting to note that the difference in contact time focusing specifically on mathematics is markedly different in Cases 1 and 2, although, ultimately, the prospective teachers will teach much the same mathematics curriculum in their respective countries.

Another notable difference between the courses is the number of prospective teachers enrolled in each. Teaching arrangements are not central to this chapter although the idea of holding certain classes only for the weaker mathematicians – and thus reducing class size and increasing individualised attention – is noteworthy. For the purposes of this discussion, class size is relevant in so far as it impacts on assessment strategies. For example in both Cases 1 and 2, audits (termed 'examinations' in Case 1) are taken of the prospective teachers' subject knowledge. Given that there are only two mathematics specialist tutors in Case 2, however, it would be impossible for them to assess three or four detailed exercises per semester for each of 170 individuals. The tutor in Case 2 emphasised that the audits included questions to, 'assess understanding and application', but, to an outsider, it seems unlikely that this could be as thorough as the regular tasks concentrating on specific issues in depth as described in Case 1.

In part, the practical teaching of mathematics was assessed in similar ways in the two cases with prospective teachers being observed working in the classroom by someone who may or may not be a mathematics specialist. Again, however, the larger cohort in Case 2, seems to restrict the possibility for a more in-depth approach to student assessment. Certainly the prospective teachers are observed teaching mathematics and their paperwork (e.g., long- and short-term planning, pupil assessment records, and self evaluation records) are thoroughly scrutinised but, unlike their counterparts in Case 1, there is only a limited requirement for them to provide detailed work on a topic such as in the form of a workshop rather than a formal presentation. The sheer number of prospective teachers – 170 versus 20 – would make this an impossible task for the subject specialists in Case 2. Table 2 provides a summary of opportunities where the prospective teachers in Case 2 might *potentially* demonstrate their ability to meet Ball et al's (2004) criteria for successful teaching. As might be predicted there is less scope for them than in Case 1.

Table 2. Potential opportunities for prospective teachers to demonstrate Ball et al's criteria for successful teaching in Case 2

Assessment to demonstrate students' ability to....	Case 2	
'Unpack' information	*1.*	*audit*
	2.	*group work*
	3.	*teaching practice*
Make connections	*2.*	*group work*
	3.	*teaching practice*
Anticipate pupils' future mathematical needs	*1.*	*audit*
	3.	*teaching practice*
Evaluate & incorporate other methods/solutions	*3.*	*teaching practice*

Another marked difference between the two cases for discussion at this point is the fact that the tutor in Case 1 appears to have full control over how her prospective teachers' work in mathematics is assessed. She involves her non-specialist colleagues on occasion and once a year she discusses her strategies with professionals at other institutions but the responsibility for the assessment of prospective teachers' work in mathematics clearly resides with her. In contrast, in Case 2 all of the prospective teachers have to take, and pass, a centrally set online test. Failure to pass it prevents prospective teachers from taking up a teaching post as a fully qualified practitioner. In addition, all of the assessment techniques used in Case 2 are open to scrutiny by two external parties. The first are external examiners who may or may not be mathematics specialists but who, in their capacity as expert practitioners in primary education, may voice an opinion as to the rigor and suitability of the assessment arrangements employed. They cannot insist that anything is altered but their opinions are usually highly regarded and therefore, on the rare occasions they make suggestions, their advice is generally heeded. The other group who periodically (i.e., every three or four years or so) take an interest in the course assessment are government inspectors from the Office for Standards in Education (Ofsted). Their views on the strategies used, together with their thoughts on the entire elementary education programme, determine how the course is rated nationally: since these gradings began over 10 years ago, Case 2 has consistently been ranked as one of the top three primary teacher education courses in the country. This has had a significant impact on the number of student places allotted to the course (this is determined centrally) and the caliber of the applications made to the institution. Poor gradings can result in the ultimate closure of a course.

To summarise the above in the light of Shulman (1986) and Ball et al.'s (2004) criteria, students in both cases seem to be assessed across all of the aspects listed although, as discussed below, there is a question over the extent that students' mathematical knowledge is thoroughly measured in Case 2. Finally, consider whether it is better to produce 20 fully prepared and thoroughly assessed elementary teachers whose primary task is to teach mathematics each year or to produce 170 generalist teachers whose performance – although perhaps not so intensely assessed – is deemed to be of a recognised national standard? Despite the lack of a simple answer, the question raises some important issues and as the reader, your initial reaction to it might also be worthy of examination.

CASE 3: ASSESSMENT OF PROSPECTIVE HIGH SCHOOL TEACHERS IN A EUROPEAN CONTEXT

Case 3 comprises a 5-year university programme course which is available for those wishing to teach mathematics in secondary (high) schools. Every year there are 40 places on the course: generally about 15 are taken by those wishing to do mathematics with the remaining 25 going to individuals opting to teach mathematics and physics. Most of the prospective teachers on the course have spent three of the five years studying courses in mathematics although some will have undertaken broader programmes of study combining mathematics with, for example, components in physics, statistics or engineering. Prior to entry onto the final two years of the course prospective teachers are required by law to undertake firstly, a multiple choice written test to assess their knowledge of mathematical topics at university; secondly an oral test to assess how this knowledge might influence the mathematical topics taught in high schools.

Over the 2-year teacher education period the prospective teachers take 12 examinations and receive 1,200 hours teaching comprising:
* 300 hours of educational studies (undertaken with secondary prospective teachers studying other subjects),
* 300 hours on the didactics, history and epistemology of mathematics,
* 300 hours of laboratory work on the didactics of mathematics, and
* 300 hours on school placements.

With the exception of the school placements, the assessment is decided at an institutional rather than a national level. As will be described below, school experience is assessed using a state examination set at regional level.

All of the 270 prospective teachers undertaking secondary school teacher education courses, regardless of subject specification, take four written examinations as part of their educational studies course which focus on topics such as psychology and sociology. Prospective teachers take two courses in didactics and two in the history and epistemology of mathematics. At the end of each they take a written examination. Typically prospective teachers might be given a mathematical problem from a school textbook to solve and then be required to discuss the didactical (epistemological) issues surrounding it. The better prospective teachers not only solve the problems successfully but they also refer to appropriate literature on the subject and analyse the suitability of the text for teaching secondary school pupils. Each essay is marked by four university tutors. Should there be any disagreement in the grading, or should a student be borderline, an oral examination is arranged to further explore what the student has written and to ask them more general questions about their knowledge and understanding of the teaching of secondary school mathematics.

The prospective teachers also attend two laboratory courses each semester and, working in self chosen groups of two or three individuals, decide on an area, for example, the teaching of parabolas in secondary school, to work on. Their task is to consider how the topic might best be treated from (a) a mathematical and (b) a didactical point of view. There is no word limit set but, through successive dialogues with their colleagues and with their tutor, each group has to produce a portfolio of their work by the end of the academic year. Each student is then interviewed by a panel of four (i.e., two school teachers and two university tutors) to determine their individual contribution to their group's work, their mathematical knowledge and understanding of the topic selected and their thinking on how the topic might best be taught. Each of these orals is specifically tailored to the student under consideration. Course attendance is deemed sufficient to gain the necessary credits to pass two second-year laboratory courses on the didactics of mathematics, however, formative assessment plays a key element in the teaching of these units.

The final aspect of the mathematics prospective teachers' programme is their school placements. These are arranged by specially trained school teachers who are employed by the university as supervisors and who spend approximately half of their time working in school and the other half at the university. There are three components to a student's school experience. Firstly, they spend time observing how a school operates at a general level noting what is required of the school and how the organisation is managed. Secondly, they spend time observing at least two teachers. Finally, having planned mathematics sessions in conjunction with a teacher (to ensure that the pupils' programme is not interrupted) the prospective teachers then practise and refine their teaching skills. This third component of the school placement is assessed by both a practising school teacher and the student's supervisor in that they are asked to comment on the student's strengths and weaknesses. In addition, prospective teachers compile a report on the three aspects of their practical teaching experience. These are usually of the order of 100 -120 pages but they have been known to be as long as 300 pages. The intention is that the report demonstrates a student's understanding of children's mathematical, social and emotional needs. Following their school experience prospective teachers undertake a 3-hour written test set by the State. In essence they select three topics at random from a bowl and from these topics they have to choose one, such as the introduction of derivatives, polynomials or matrices and determinants. In the assigned 3-hour period they then prepare what might best be termed medium term plans for the topic including the intended school type, the age group to be taught, the pre-requisite skills required for successful learning, assessment strategies and teaching techniques. On the following day each student then orally presents the same work in front of a panel of four teaching practice supervisors and four university tutors. On this occasion, however, the work is supplemented with a discussion of the resources which might be used and any reflections the prospective teachers might have on their presentation. This is followed by questions from the panel regarding the choices the student made when planning their scheme of work and their general thoughts on their teaching practice experience as documented in the report described above.

None of the assessment strategies employed include the involvement of external examiners. Nor is there any assessment of the prospective teachers' mathematical beliefs but, as in Cases 1 and 2, these may have been apparent in their practical teaching and written work. Prospective teachers who fail their first year assessments are required to repeat the year if they wish to continue their studies.

Third Commentary

Although it is not the focus of this chapter, it is clear that the above is a thorough course. Moreover, not only are a range of assessment strategies used, but there is a high commitment of specialist tutors' time for marking and moderation. The prospective teachers' level of mathematical knowledge is assessed prior to the course and then, less explicitly, throughout their teacher education programme when, for example, their ability to plan, teach and reflect on their practical teaching is monitored. It is interesting to note that the prospective teachers' understanding of students' mathematical, social and emotional needs is also considered to be sufficiently important to be assessed (see below). Thus, it would appear that prospective teachers are assessed in a very comprehensive manner which, as shown in Table 3, includes the criteria specified by Ball et al. (2004).

Table 3. Potential opportunities for prospective teachers to demonstrate Ball et al's criteria for successful teaching in Case 3

Assessment to demonstrate students' ability to....	Case 3	
'Unpack' information	1.	*examination*
	2.	*lab task*
	3.	*teaching practice+ report*
Make connections	1.	*examination*
	2.	*lab task*
	3.	*teaching practice+ report*
Anticipate pupils' future mathematical needs	2.	*lab task*
	3.	*teaching practice+ report*
Evaluate and incorporate other methods/solutions	3.	*teaching practice+ report*

CASE 4: ASSESSMENT OF PROSPECTIVE SECONDARY SCHOOL TEACHERS IN A UK CONTEXT

Case 4 focuses on a secondary school teacher education course at the same university in England as the second case. To obtain a place on the 1-year postgraduate 36-week (PGCE) course, the majority of applicants are required to have a first degree at least 50% of which is mathematics. This is a requirement of the national body, the Teacher Development Agency. At the discretion of the course tutor, however, individuals without such a strong mathematical background but who are otherwise deemed to be appropriate candidates for the course – for example because of extensive school experience – may be required to take a full time 6-month mathematics enhancement course or a 2-week subject booster course depending on their mathematical competence. In addition applicants are only accepted into the course if they have, or are about to gain prior to beginning the course, experience of working in school. Every year approximately 20 mathematics prospective teachers enroll on the programme which caters for 200 potential high school teachers in total.

The course comprises 24-weeks practical teaching in two different schools and 12 weeks university based work of which 120 hours is devoted to preparing prospective teachers to teach mathematics to pupils in the 11-18 age range and 108 hours to general professional development. Subject knowledge per se is not taught although, as described below, it is assessed.

The course tutor designs some aspects of the prospective teachers' assessment but others are determined by the broader university secondary school programme team and yet others were required by external agencies (see below). Being new to teacher education the tutor said of the assessments she designed, "I've kind of collected what other people do at other institutions". More specifically,

1) During the course of their PGCE year all the prospective teachers complete and mark an audit of their subject knowledge. The audit comprises past examination papers for pupils aged 14-, 16- and 18-years-old and the intention is that the exercise helps student teachers identify gaps in their mathematical knowledge which they will endeavour to fill during the course of their training. The tutor takes no part in the process and says, "I don't know that they don't cheat".

2) Also informally the tutor set, "[…] my own mini assignments to build up to the formal PGCE assignment and to build up the prospective teachers' written skills". So, for example, a student might be asked to prepare a written presentation on an article they have read on mathematics education which they then present to their peers. This is followed by a discussion and informal assessment by the tutor and other prospective teachers. Another task might be to teach their peers something that they considered that they taught well in school and ask for feedback.

3) More formally, irrespective of the subject they are preparing to teach all of the prospective teachers on high school programmes at this university are required to write a curriculum assignment. They are all given the same topic and their work is assessed using common criteria. This assessment strategy has been widely discussed and developed by the course tutors over the past 10 years and has met the formal approval of professional partners (i.e., practitioners in schools), external examiners from other higher education establishments and government Ofsted inspectors (see below). The assignment (which should be approximately 5200 words in length) requires prospective teachers to describe

261

the selection of a scheme of work with the rationale for doing so, how they taught and assessed it, how they would modify it in the future giving particular attention to any two lessons in the scheme and what they learnt from the exercise. A common marking sheet is used by all secondary curriculum tutors and focuses on the professional and academic choices the prospective teachers made and their justifications for doing so (see Figure 4 for marking criteria – the possible ratings for each statement are "good", "satisfactory", "borderline", and "unsatisfactory"). Each assignment is marked by the appropriate curriculum tutor, a moderation meeting takes place and then a sample are selected for marking by another member of the course team – who might, for example, be a scientist or a geographer – to ensure equity across the secondary programme. Should a student fail this assignment they are given one opportunity to do it again. Should they fail again they fail the written component of their PGCE course although, in some instances – depending on the extent of the fail – they may be given the opportunity to re-submit the work the following academic year.

PGCE Criteria for Curriculum Assignment

1   Description and analysis of Scheme of Work A drawing on your personal
     experience
2   Literature on pupils' learning and progression from one key stage to the next
     drawing on research literature and national assessment related report evidence.
3   Rationale for the revised scheme of work describing how it improves on Scheme A
     and matches teaching methods to the learning objectives.
4   Assessment in the revised scheme of work explaining how formative and
     summative assessment tasks allow you to assess pupils' learning.
5   Detailed comment on two lessons in the scheme.
6   Comment on your professional development making explicit how the new scheme
     improves upon the first, and how the process will inform your future practice.

General criteria for coursework assignments

7   Reference to a wide range of relevant literature
     integrated into your assignment
8   Quality of the communication of your ideas
     (including fluency, structure, coherence, awareness of reader)
9   Accuracy (spelling, punctuation, grammar)

     Referencing: Is the referencing system used clear and consistent?

MA Criteria for Curriculum Assignment

1   Has the writer related personal experience and professional practice to broader
     principles and to relevant literature?
2   Does the writer provide evidence of having developed exposition and argument that
     goes beyond description and unsubstantiated opinion?
3   Does the work show that personal insight has been gained through reflection and
     analysis?

Figure 4: Common marking criteria used in Case 4.

4) Additionally, in common with all the other high school student teachers (i.e., covering other subject specialisations), the mathematics prospective teachers undertake two other formal written assignments. The first is a learning assignment of 4000-6000 words which has to be completed in their first term. In essence it requires prospective teachers to reflect on pedagogical processes by comparing and contrasting sessions in their own and other subjects. The other task they are required to complete is of similar length and focuses on a whole-school issue of their choice albeit in consultation with a teacher in one of their schools. This has to be completed in their second term and might consider issues such as bullying, health education or home/school relationships.

5) During their PGCE year prospective teachers undertake practical teaching in two schools. Following six-day visits they spend 34 days in 'school A' in their first term and then four separate days, followed by 70 days in 'school B' which they begin half way through their second term. In both cases the intention is that they are given, '[...] a broad range of practical experience' and 'complementary advice, guidance and support of placement school staff and university staff' (Secondary Team, 2006, p. 42). Although the mathematics tutor will visit every student during a practice, each school takes the lead responsibility for their student's formative and summative assessment. In essence this involves assessing prospective teachers': professional values and practice; their mathematical knowledge and understanding; their ability to plan and set appropriate targets for pupil learning; the quality of their monitoring and assessment; and their teaching and management skills. These requirements were set out by the Training and Development Agency (2007) and these standards must be met by all prospective teachers prior to qualification (see Appendix). Should there be any question as to whether a student is meeting the necessary criteria, a representative of the school is asked to inform the university with the result that the mathematics tutor will observe the student teach a range of classes and discuss the student's progress with the mathematics specialists in the school. A joint decision is then made on the student's readiness to enter the teaching profession. Should an individual be deemed unready to qualify, assuming they are making sufficient progress, they will fail the course but be given the opportunity to undertake an additional placement the following academic year. Each year a cross section of prospective teachers are visited by an External Examiner from either a secondary school or another university. This is not to determine whether a student should pass or fail the course but rather it is a form of moderation exercise to ensure that, as far as possible, individuals deemed to be of a certain standard in one institution would be of similar quality in another. In addition, Ofsted inspectors, as discussed in Case 2, observe a sample of prospective teachers every 3-4 years as a means of monitoring the quality of provision provided by an institution.

6) Finally, as part of the Department of Education and Skills requirements, all the prospective teachers complete successfully the same centrally produced online numeracy test as described above for the primary prospective teachers in the same UK institution. This can be done at any time during their PGCE year and

may be taken as many times as necessary until the student has passed. Until they do so, however, they cannot be awarded Qualified Teacher Status.

Fourth Commentary

An unusual feature of the above programme is that the student teachers are responsible for auditing their own subject knowledge and taking remedial action as appropriate. Anyone who has tried to teach something they know but do not fully understand will appreciate that it can be both unwise and highly embarrassing to attempt to teach anybody anything unless you are well versed in the subject matter. Having said that, although they are enrolled on a professional course, the prospective teachers in this case might not have reached the realisation that acquiring a sound subject knowledge is in their best interest. They might also be anxious to pass their course and appear to do well casting doubt on the reliability of such an assessment strategy.

The range of mini-assignments appears to be a good way to encourage prospective teachers to read and think about teaching from a range of perspectives and this idea was further developed in the task requiring them to compare and contrast the pedagogical processes involved in two different subject areas.

Comparing assessment strategies on the two high school teacher education courses it is clear that in both cases, prospective teachers embark on their programme of study with sound mathematical knowledge and, with the exception of the mathematics audit undertaken by Case 4 prospective teachers, much of the assessment is based on the application of this knowledge within an educational context.

As with Case 3 the prospective teachers had to plan a series of sessions, teach them and then evaluate their performance. In theory, prospective teachers in Case 4 might have more autonomy when planning as those in Case 3 are required to plan with their teachers for the sake of curriculum continuity. That being said, the topics available to them are likely to be limited as most secondary schools in England follow a nationally prescribed curriculum and many pupils are in the process of preparing to sit national examinations.

Prospective secondary school teachers in both cases are observed teaching by subject specialists and practising teachers although, only in Case 4 do the latter take the lead responsibility for the prospective teachers' final assessment of practical teaching. This will be discussed further below.

Two final significant differences between the assessments of the two secondary school education courses surround the planning and preparation of schemes of work. As discussed above, in both cases prospective teachers plan and prepare work which they then teach and, presumably, in both cases they are given ample warning, resources and preparation time in which to do this. Additionally, however, prospective teachers in Case 3 are also expected to select one of three topics picked at random and, within a 3-hour period, produce hypothetical teaching plans as a result. In other words, unlike Case 4 prospective teachers, they are expected to demonstrate the facility to prepare one of a range of topics at short notice. Further, unlike their UK colleagues discussed above, they are then expected to present, discuss and justify their work in detail to a panel of experts. Although this must take a considerable amount of time, it is almost certainly thorough and appears to be a good measure of prospective teachers' potential to prepare and reflect on their planning.

Thus, to conclude, in both cases students appeared to be assessed across the range of criteria set out by Shulman (1986) and Ball et al. (2004) but in Case 3 it was in a more thorough and interactive manner (see below). Additionally, in Case 4 there was greater possibility that students could manipulate their assessment tasks – for example by selecting the topics they were most knowledgeable about or, even, cheating – so that they would be seen in the best possible light. With this proviso, Table 4 provides a summary of the *potential* opportunities for the prospective teachers in Case 4 to demonstrate Ball et al's. criteria for successful teaching.

Table 4. Potential opportunities for prospective teachers to demonstrate Ball et al's criteria for successful teaching in Case 4

Assessment to demonstrate students' ability to....	Case 4	
'Unpack' information	*1.*	*audit*
	2.	*mini assignment*
	3.	*curriculum assignment*
	4.	*teaching practice*
Make connections	*3.*	*curriculum assignment*
	4.	*teaching practice*
Anticipate pupils' future mathematical needs	*1.*	*audit*
	2.	*mini assignment*
	3.	*curriculum assignment*
	4.	*teaching practice*
Evaluate & incorporate other methods/solutions	*4.*	*teaching practice*

SOME REFLECTIONS FROM PROSPECTIVE TEACHERS

Although it was not part of the original plan the opportunity arose to ask prospective teachers in Cases 2 and 4 to complete a short questionnaire outlining their thoughts on the assessment procedures they were undertaking as part of their courses. It was not intended to be a comprehensive survey. Nor, indeed, can the data necessarily be taken to be representative. Some of the information provided, however, was thought-provoking and therefore worthy of inclusion in such a discussion paper.

In Case 2 80% of the prospective teachers and 72% of Case 4 prospective teachers considered the levels of assessment on their courses to be 'about right'.

6% and 16% respectively judged that they were over-assessed and, as one pointed out, all assessment is potentially stressful. This may, indeed, be the case for some or all of the cases described above but, as will be discussed later, it may be necessary to adopt a variety of approaches to ensure as broad and as fair an assessment programme as possible for all. What might be missing, however, is sufficient explanation to the prospective teachers as to why such detailed assessment is necessary. In part this should be part of the educational process but also, equally importantly, it seems appropriate that professional educators should share their thinking and expertise with future professional educators. Thus, for example, as implied in the discussion of Ball et al.'s work (2004) at the beginning of the chapter, future teachers of the very youngest school children need to have a thorough knowledge and understanding of the mathematics well beyond their chosen age range in order to reduce the likelihood of mathematical misconceptions arising as they teach. An example of this is graphically described in Iannone and Cockburn (2006) when, in response to a child, a grade 2 teacher finds it necessary to call upon her knowledge of negative numbers to explain subtraction.

In Case 2, 14% of the prospective teachers and only one of the Case 4 prospective teachers deemed that they were insufficiently assessed. As a future teacher of 3-5 year-olds revealed, "We are tested on mathematical ability but not on our understanding and ability to apply it to children except during an observation – which can of course be arranged to be in an area of strength!" Many of the respondents found that lesson observations were extremely helpful explaining,

"It provided a rich tapestry of feedback and useful relevant advice." (Jack)

"Being observed by mentor/curriculum tutor [...] (is most effective) [...] because the feedback can be very useful and encouraging." (Helen)

Some found written assignments valuable,

"Essays have been good for reflection but can be hard for some mathematicians to get the most out of." (Paul)

"They (essays) enabled me to analyse my teaching and develop new strategies to improve." (Susie)

However others questioned the worth of such exercises noting,

"[...] Many very able trainees struggled to express their views on paper." (Jack)

"Just because you can write an essay, it doesn't mean you can teach. Likewise if you struggle with essays, it doesn't mean you can't teach." (Rona)

DISCUSSION

The main aim of teacher education is not preparing the students to a sufficiently high standard so that they do well in their assessments; nor should it be. It would, however, be both irresponsible and naïve not to assess their performances to ensure that, as far as possible, they are well equipped to enter the profession as effective teachers of mathematics. At the beginning of the last century, this was perceived to be a straight-forward process: students' mathematical knowledge was tested and, if deemed to be of a sufficiently high standard, they were considered fit to pass this knowledge on to the next generation.

At the outset of this chapter the attributes associated with successful teachers by Shulman (1986) and Ball et al. (2004) were described. These are markedly different from those of over 100 years ago. Now successful teaching is considered to be a dynamic, interactive activity which requires considerable knowledge and understanding of children and adolescents, mathematics, and the process of education. Were the students in the above case studies assessed in terms of these more complex criteria? Moreover, could they be? Reviewing the information provided it appears that, on paper, all the courses measured the students' knowledge, understanding and professional expertise in such terms to a greater or lesser extent. Was this, however, the case in reality?

The art of the assessment involves measuring the students' attainments as comprehensively and as accurately as possible while making efficient use of the available resources and, most crucially, not adversely affecting the education process itself. It is possible, for example, for a course to be so rigorously assessed that it takes an inordinate amount of time, worry and attention – on the part of both students and their tutors – and proves to be highly expensive. None of the courses described above appeared to fall into that category although, as mentioned above, the assessment of the students in Case 3 in particular was highly demanding of tutors' time and expertise.

In 1979 Doyle memorably concluded that prospective teachers 'exchange performance for grades'. Whether the various tests and examinations given in these cases resulted in an exchange of performance for grades they had the desired effect on some, "The audit forced me to really develop my own maths skills and undertake personal study" (Rob) and "The maths audit gave me confidence. I found I knew more than I thought and could explain how I found the answers" (Beth). That being said, someone remarked, that they revised [studied] for the audit, "[…] and forgot key concepts soon after". Earlier in the chapter, on discussing the prospective teachers' self-monitoring an audit of their subject knowledge in Case 4, it was noted that they were future professionals and that one would hope that they would take responsibility for filling the gaps in their learning rather than attempting to cheat the system by pretending that they performed well. Some of the prospective teachers gave the impression that passing the course was more important than securing knowledge commenting, for example, that test situations were the most effective form of assessment as you "can't cheat" (Paul) and any assessment involving others were ineffective as, "you only need to do a little work" (Sam). Another student clearly missed the intended value of an assignment when she complained,

> For the last assignment (curriculum) we were told we needed to have 20-30 references however other subjects were told only one would be enough (Rona).

Another aspect of 'exchanging performance for grades' is that it has the potential for skewing attention. If, for example, an aspect of the course is not assessed will prospective teachers fully engage? Data from Case 1 – where the prospective teachers were invited (rather than expected) to discuss a problem they had been set – suggested that, certainly for some of them, focusing on assessment was not what drove them to succeed. Indeed, if they saw the value of the work and did not feel pressured, the absence of formal assessment enhanced their performance in the course. Further insight into this issue comes from an ongoing international study of mathematical misconceptions in the primary school funded by the British Academy[1]. The project involves practitioners discussing children's difficulties in mathematics across the 5-11 age range. A by-product of the work is that it has become clear that several of the teachers – all of whom are qualified to teach across the primary age range – were fairly selective in what they attended to when they were student teachers,

> Today has been useful from my point of view as a teacher. Now I'm going down to a younger year group, I have a better understanding of what I need to be really careful about. (Suzanne)

> You focus on your own group and forget what they are going on to […] (Ivan)

Although these data are anecdotal, they support the case for explicitly teaching and assessing student teachers on their knowledge and understanding as to how a mathematical concept develops across several years. This idea is further supported by findings from the same project which indicate that misconceptions may begin early in a child's schooling and yet not become fully manifest until several years later, as Ivan suddenly appreciated,

> I have done, "if you add two things it gets bigger and if you subtract gets smaller" […] you don't tend to think what you do has bearing on what others do further up the school. (Ivan)

Such data also demonstrate the value of continuing professional development (CPD) for teachers with particular reference to more advanced mathematical concepts which were perhaps not fully covered and assessed in some of the above courses. For teachers CPD serves as an opportunity to reflect on issues which were not necessarily apparent to them in their inexperienced days as a prospective teacher. For others CPD is a chance to fill in some of the gaps they chose to ignore during their teacher preparation course. More specifically, it would be naïve not to acknowledge that there are invariably be some prospective teachers in every cohort who focus their learning and preparation predominantly on their perception of the most probable topics for assessment. It may be worth it for tutors – particularly in Cases 1, 2 and 4 – to adopt a less predictable approach. For example, if their prospective teachers were asked to discuss a topic selected from a wide range of possibilities at random (as in Case 3), prospective teachers might broaden the scope of their attention during their teacher education programme.

Finally it is important to consider the extent to which outside agencies were involved in the various assessment processes. To some – such as government agencies in the U.K. – they are seen as key for accountability purposes. They could, however, also be perceived as being both intrusive and a waste of time. In Case 1 there was no external involvement; in Case 3 it was only in the sense of setting – rather than marking – some of the assessment but in Cases 2 and 4 there was considerable scope for contributions from other interested parties. In both of these cases it was clear that having external examiners visit from other institutions was generally supportive and useful. The best examiners took on the role of critical friends and provided an objective commentary on the nature of the assessment tasks, procedures and outcomes. Some, being closely engaged in similar teacher education programmes in their own institutions, were also able to give suggestions on other possible assessment strategies and to compare the quality of prospective teachers with their own. Other external examiners were head teachers in primary and secondary schools and, as such, usually had an excellent understanding of the environment awaiting the prospective teachers on qualification. They therefore were able to comment on the trainees' readiness to enter the profession and confirm our judgments on such matters. Some of these benefits might be available less formally in Cases 1 and 3 for the tutor in the former met annually with national colleagues working in similar roles and, in both cases, there was considerable involvement and collaboration with practising mathematics teachers in schools.

The other form of external intervention experienced in Cases 2 and 4 was not a significant part of the assessment process in the other institutions considered other than in setting part of the final assessment in Case 3. Every three or four years initial teacher education programmes in Cases 2 and 4 undergo an Ofsted inspection. The details of these inspections varies from time to time but, in essence, they involve a team of government appointees scrutinising vast amounts of course paperwork prior to coming to an institution for several days. These visits generally include meetings with the programme team, detailed interviews with individual tutors, examination of the prospective teachers' work and observations of a sample of prospective teachers (selected by the inspectors) teaching in school. There is no doubt that they create a tremendous amount of extra work and stress for all concerned. All the inspections in Cases 2 and 4 to date have had very successful outcomes. If, however, an inspection result is deemed less than satisfactory a programme is put under intense scrutiny and closely monitored every year. The number of prospective teachers assigned to the institution is reduced and, if there are not marked – and rapid – signs of improvement the course may well be closed. The process feels draconian but it is intended to maintain high standards. Obviously future teachers should experience the best possible education but it would appear that market forces – rather than government inspectors – play that role in Cases 1 and 3 to equally good effect.

CONCLUDING REMARKS

The four cases presented in this chapter exemplify some of the carefully planned assessment strategies adopted by teacher education programmes in different settings at the beginning of 21st century. Gone are the days when chalk-talk and a knowledge of mathematics sufficed for teaching in primary and secondary classrooms. Nowadays teaching is perceived as being more interactive, complex and intellectually challenging. It is not for the mediocre, the passive or those simply concerned with passing a few tests and securing a job. Recruiting and retaining mathematics teachers is a major concern (Cockburn & Haydn, 2004), however, not at any price. It is of paramount importance, therefore, that those involved in teacher education ensure that only those who understand and demonstrate the potential to be successful mathematics teachers succeed in entering the profession.

APPENDIX

Requirements for Newly Qualified Teachers as set out by the Training and Development Agency (2007)

The standards specifically pertaining to mathematics in case studies two and four are that prospective teachers must demonstrate that they have:

Q10 Have a knowledge and understanding of a range of teaching, learning and behaviour management strategies and know how to use and adapt them, including how to personalise learning and provide opportunities for all learners to achieve their potential.

Q11 Know the assessment requirements and arrangements for the subjects/curriculum areas they are trained to teach, including those relating to public examinations and qualifications.

Q12 Know a range of approaches to assessment, including the importance of formative assessment.

Q14 Have a secure knowledge and understanding of their subjects/curriculum areas and related pedagogy to enable them to teach effectively across the age and ability range for which they are trained.

Q15 Know and understand the relevant statutory and non-statutory curricula and frameworks, including those provided through the National Strategies, for their subjects/curriculum areas, and other relevant initiatives applicable to the age and ability range for which they are trained.

Q16 Have passed the professional skills tests in numeracy, literacy and information and communications technology (ICT).

Q17 Know how to use skills in literacy, numeracy and ICT to support their teaching and wider professional activities.

ACKNOWLEDGEMENT

The author gratefully acknowledges the financial support of the British Academy for the research study Mathematical Misconceptions in the Primary Years (Grant number: LRG – 42447).

REFERENCES

Ball, D. L., Bass, H., & Hill, H. C. (2004, April). *Knowing and using mathematical knowledge in teaching: Learning what matters.* Invited paper presented at the Southern African Association for Research in Mathematics, Science and Technology, Cape Town, South Africa.

Cockburn, A. D., & Haydn, T. (2004). *Recruiting and retaining teachers.* London: Routledge Falmer.

Department for Education and Skills (2006). *Primary framework for literacy and mathematics.* London: Author.

Doyle, W. (1979). Making managerial decisions in classrooms. In D. L. Duke (Ed.), *Classroom management* (pp. 42–74). Chicago, IL: University of Chicago Press.

Hill, H. C., Rowan, B., & Ball, D. L. (2005). Effects of teachers' mathematical knowledge for teaching on student achievement. *American Educational Research Journal, 42*(2), 371–406.

Hill, H.C., Sleep, L., Lewis, J.M., & Ball, D.L. (2007). Assessing teachers' mathematical knowledge. In F. K. Lester, Jr. (Ed.), *Second handbook of research on mathematics teaching and learning* (pp. 111–155). Charlotte, NC: Information Age Publishers & National Council of Teachers of Mathematics.

Iannone P., & Cockburn A. D. (2006): Fostering conceptual mathematical thinking in the early years: A case study. In J. Novotná, H. Moraová, M. Krátká, & N. Stehliková (Eds.), *Proceedings 30th Conference of the International Group for the Psychology of Mathematics Education* (Vol 3, pp. 329–336). Charles University in Prague, Czech Republic.

National Council of Teachers of Mathematics (2000) *Principles and standards for school mathematics.* http://standards.nctm.org/document/chapter2/index.htm (accessed 16/11/07)

Robson, C. (1993). *Real world research.* Oxford: Blackwell Publishers.

Sandelowski, M. (2000). Whatever happened to qualitative description? *Research in Nursing and Health, 23,* 334–340.

Shulman, L. S. (1986). Those who understand: Knowledge growth in teaching. *Educational Researcher, 15*, 4–14.
Training and Development Agency (2007). *Professional standards for teachers.* London: Training and Development Agency for Schools.

Anne Cockburn
School of Education and Lifelong Learning
University of East Anglia
U.K.

TIM ROWLAND

12. RESEARCHING TEACHERS' MATHEMATICS DISCIPLINARY KNOWLEDGE

At the substantive heart of this chapter is a framework for mathematics lesson observation. The framework was developed in research in the UK between 2002 and 2004, and modified in important ways in 2007. The research which led to the development of the framework drew on videotapes of mathematics lessons prepared and conducted by prospective elementary teachers towards the end of their initial training. A grounded theory approach to data analysis led to the emergence of a framework – the 'Knowledge Quartet' – with four broad dimensions, through which the mathematics-related knowledge of these teachers could be observed in practice. This methodological paper describes in detail the process by which the Knowledge Quartet evolved, the chronology of that process, and some of the associated theoretical influences and pragmatic constraints. The chapter concludes with remarks on the ways that the research is being applied to teacher education, in the analysis and improvement of mathematics teaching, and also in its evaluation.

INTRODUCTION

In his 1985 presidential address to the American Educational Research Association, Lee Shulman proposed a taxonomy with seven categories that formed a knowledge-base for teaching. Three of these elements are 'discipline knowledge', being specific to the subject matter being taught. They are: subject matter knowledge, pedagogical content knowledge and curricular knowledge. Shulman (1986) notes that the ways of conceptualising subject matter knowledge (SMK) will be different for different subject matter (discipline) areas, but in his generic account he includes Schwab's (1978) notions of substantive knowledge (the key facts, concepts, principles and explanatory frameworks in a discipline) and syntactic knowledge (the nature of enquiry in the field, and how new knowledge is introduced and accepted in that community). For Shulman, pedagogical content knowledge (PCK) consists of "the ways of representing the subject which make it comprehensible to others [...] [it] also includes an understanding of what makes the learning of specific topics easy or difficult [...]" (Shulman, 1986, p. 9). The notion of PCK as a distinct domain has been disputed (e.g., McNamara, 1991), but Shulman's intention seemed essentially to be to reify the hitherto 'missing link' between knowing something for oneself and being able to enable others to know it.

P. Sullivan and T. Wood (eds.), Knowledge and Beliefs in Mathematics Teaching and Teaching Development, 273–298.

This chapter is set in the context of UK research on beginning teachers' mathematics disciplinary knowledge. It charts research undertaken since 1998 by teams in London and Cambridge. This account is mainly methodological, and references are given to reports elsewhere of substantive findings. The majority of this chapter concerns a research project which investigated how mathematics teachers' disciplinary knowledge is made visible in teaching itself.

UK RESEARCH ON MATHEMATICS TEACHER KNOWLEDGE

Recent government initiatives have been taken in a number of countries to enhance the mathematics knowledge (typically vaguely conceptualised in the rhetoric) of prospective and serving elementary teachers. The rather direct approach to a perceived 'problem' in England was captured by an edict in the first set of government 'standards' for Initial Teacher Training (ITT) issued in 1997:

> All providers of ITT must audit trainees' knowledge and understanding of the mathematics contained in the National Curriculum programmes of study for mathematics at KS1 and KS2,[1] and that specified in paragraph 13 of this document. Where gaps in trainees' subject knowledge are identified, providers of ITT must make arrangements to ensure that trainees gain that knowledge during the course [...]. (Department for Education and Employment, 1997, p. 27)

The process of audit and remediation of subject knowledge within primary ITT became a high profile issue following the introduction of these and subsequent government requirements (Department for Education and Employment, 1998). Within the teacher education community, few could be found to support the imposition of the 'audit and remediation' culture. Yet the introduction of this regime provoked a body of research in the UK on prospective elementary teachers' mathematics subject-matter knowledge (e.g., Goulding, Rowland, & Barber, 2002; Goulding & Suggate, 2001; Jones & Mooney, 2002; Morris, 2001; Rowland, Martyn, Barber, & Heal, 2000; Sanders & Morris, 2000). The proceedings of a symposium held in 2003 usefully drew together some of the threads of this research (BSRLM, 2003). In every case, the participants were prospective (so-called 'trainee') elementary school teachers, on three- or four-year undergraduate or one-year graduate teacher preparation courses. The methodology at the heart of these studies involved a questionnaire – a test – taken at some time before or during the course. The subject matter being assessed was typically determined by that specified by the Department for Education and Employment (1998), mainly related directly to the elementary school curriculum, but also including some topics in the school curriculum up to about Year 9 (pupil age 14). The logic of the situation pointed to auditing the trainees' mathematics knowledge at the beginning

---

[1] In England and Wales, Key Stage 1 (KS1) is the first phase of compulsory primary education, between the ages of 5 and 7. Similarly, KS2 covers ages 7 to 11.

of their course, to establish where the 'gaps' were at the outset, and this was the case in most of the studies.

An exception was that of Rowland, Martyn, Barber, and Heal (2000), in which the audit was administered four months into a one-year course, after the prospective teachers had encountered the mathematics content within the teaching methods course, "giving them maximum opportunity and professional motivation to recall those topics they had forgotten (for lack of use) since they did mathematics at school" (p. 4). The research of this London-based team included an investigation of the relation between the prospective teachers' SMK, as assessed by a 16-item written audit instrument, and their teaching competence. The audit was administered by the research team; the assessment of teaching, on a four-point scale based on criteria in regular use, was made jointly by their university-based tutor and a practising teacher-mentor in the participant's placement school. A chi-square test showed a significant association between audit score and an assessment of teaching competence. This finding turned out to be robust when we replicated it with a different cohort of prospective teachers (Rowland et al., 2001). Participants obtaining high (or even middle) scores on the audit were more likely to be assessed as strong numeracy teachers than those with low scores; whereas those with low audit scores were more likely than other participants to be assessed as weak numeracy teachers.

INTO THE MATHEMATICS CLASSROOM

Although this was interesting in itself, and attracted some media attention, we wanted to find out more about what was 'going on'. By now, several UK-based researchers had formed a consortium named *SKIMA* ('subject knowledge in mathematics') and a five-person Cambridge-based *SKIMA* subgroup took forward this new line of enquiry.

The reasoning behind this move was, if superior SMK really does make a difference when teaching elementary mathematics, it ought somehow to be observable in the *practice* of the knowledgeable teacher. Conversely, the teacher with more limited SMK might be expected to misinform their pupils, or somehow to miss opportunities to teach mathematics 'well'. In a nutshell, we (the Cambridge team) wanted to identify, and to understand better, the ways in which elementary teachers' mathematics content[2] knowledge, or the lack of it, is evident in their teaching. Certain parallels can be drawn with recent studies of Deborah Ball and her colleagues that studies of the "work" of teaching with the goal of providing a "practice-based theory of knowledge for teaching" (Ball & Bass, 2003). The same description could be applied to our own study, but while parallels can be drawn between some of the outcomes, the two theories are very different. In particular, the theory that emerges from Ball et al. unravels and clarifies the formerly somewhat elusive and theoretically-undeveloped notions of SMK and PCK.

---

[2] By 'content' knowledge, we include any kind of disciplinary (in this case mathematics-related) knowledge. In particular, 'content' knowledge encompasses both SMK and PCK.

Shulman's SMK is separated into 'common content knowledge' and 'specialised content knowledge', while his PCK is divided into 'knowledge of content and students' and 'knowledge of content and teaching' (Ball, Thames, & Phelps, submitted). In our theory, the distinction between different kinds of mathematical knowledge is of lesser significance than the classification of the situations in which mathematical knowledge for teaching surfaces in the classroom. In this sense, the two theories may each have useful perspectives to offer to the other.

As a research group, we tended to think and talk about research goals more than research questions, but a key research question would be: in what ways is (novice elementary) teachers' mathematical knowledge made visible in their teaching? The parentheses capture the sense that while our interest in this question clearly focused on mathematics teaching, it extended beyond 'novice elementary' to all phases of teachers' careers and pupils' ages. The phrase "made visible" in the putative research question is intended to contain a strong element of "observable". From the outset, we envisaged this research as a classroom observation study. We were genuinely curious to know what knowledgeable teachers do in the classroom that might enhance their pupils' experience of learning mathematics, and what others did not, or could not, do. Our interest in whether teacher knowledge *can* be observed may well have been influenced by our previous and ongoing roles as tutors in initial teacher education. By 2002, the official guidance to teacher education 'providers' (mostly university education departments) on the assessment of trainee teachers' mathematics knowledge had shifted from some form of 'testing' (cf., Department for Education and Employment, 1997) towards seeking evidence for this knowledge *in the act of teaching itself*, in particular within the prospective teachers' *practicum* placements.

> Evidence of secure subject knowledge and understanding is most likely to be found in trainee teachers' teaching, particularly in how they present complex ideas, communicate subject knowledge, correct pupils' errors and in how confidently they answer their subject-based questions. (Teacher Training Agency, 2002, p. 19)

This is one of those statements about education that must seem self-evident, to its author[3] at least, but whose warrants are not at all clear to others. It seemed possible, however, that our intended classroom observation might go some way to finding out whether the claim, about evidence for teachers' subject knowledge being "found" in their teaching, was sustainable.

From Questionnaire to Observation

We were somewhat apprehensive as we set about planning for this project. Earlier *SKIMA* studies of trainee teachers' mathematical knowledge, located within the

---

[3] A culture of anonymity entered into English government documents of this kind more than a decade ago, so we are not privy to the identity of the person(s) who made this assertion or any other in the Guidance.

earlier 'audit' culture, had been more straightforward. A 90-minute written assessment consisting of 16 test items in mathematics had been administered to a whole PGCE cohort at the same time, in each of the *SKIMA*-participant universities. The scripts were collected, marked and the response to each question coded on a 5-point scale from 0 (not attempted, no progress towards a solution) to 4 (full solution with convincing and rigorous explanations). Each code corresponded to explicit descriptions of different responses developed from trials. The key boundary was between 2 and 3: a score of 3 or 4 indicated that the prospective teacher was 'secure' in this area of knowledge, in the sense that they appeared to know the topic adequately for their professional purposes. Scores of 0, 1 and 2 did not offer this assurance, and guided study and peer tutoring was advised in such cases. This was followed by various quantitative and qualitative analyses of the written responses. This seemed a good deal more tangible than our proposal to look for evidence of teacher knowledge in their work in classrooms. We had, at best, a vague idea of what we might be looking for, and the content of the classroom scenarios we would be observing would be beyond our control.

Participants and Ethical Desiderata

In the UK, the majority of trainees follow a one-year, full-time course leading to a Postgraduate Certificate in Education (PGCE) in a university education department (or school, institute or faculty), about half the year being spent working in a school under the guidance of a school-based mentor. All primary trainees prepare to be generalist teachers of the whole primary curriculum. Later in their careers, most take on responsibility for leadership in one curriculum area (such as mathematics) in their school, but, almost without exception, they remain generalists, teaching the whole curriculum to one class.

Most of the data collection for this study took place in 2002, in the context of a one-year PGCE course in which each of the 149 trainees followed a route focusing either on the 'lower primary (LP)' years (ages 3-8) or the 'upper primary (UP)' (7-11). In the first instance, we obtained mathematics content knowledge data for the whole cohort of prospective teachers, using the 16-item audit discussed above. This was administered four months into the course, for the reasons stated earlier. The next phase, the heart of our study, entailed observations of lessons taught by some of the 149 participants. Since we were interested in the relationship between mathematics content knowledge and classroom teaching, it seemed to us that the participants observed ought to represent a range of subject knowledge competence, as measured by the audit. For the purpose of this research, the total scores for each paper (maximum 64) were used to identify groups with 'high', 'medium' and 'low' scores. In practice, these vague notions were operationalised by defining a high score to be in the range 64-60, medium 59-48, and low 47 and below. Of course, these are crude measures, not least because these totals are aggregates of ordinal measures. These boundaries were further determined by the professional judgement by experienced course tutors about these prospective teachers' need for significant remedial support, modest support (or self-remediation), or none. The proportions of trainees in these three categories were not pre-ordained. In the event, the boundaries turned out to be close to the 20th and 70th percentiles in this cohort. In order to compare and contrast the teaching of trainees with different levels of audited content knowledge, we decided to observe equal numbers of participants from each of the three categories. Finally, because the curriculum would appear to make different demands on content knowledge in the lower primary and upper primary years, we also wanted these two phases to be equally represented. Our resources made it possible to devote the equivalent of one person full-time for two weeks to the observation; each classroom visit would take about half a day to observe and videotape one lesson. These factors and constraints eventually influenced the decision to identify 12 trainees for observation, and to observe each of them teaching a whole mathematics lesson on two separate occasions. The 12 trainees represented the intersection of each subject knowledge category with each of the two LP/UP age-phase groups, with two participants in each cell of the 3x2 grid of possibilities. This seemed a sensible compromise between the alternatives of observing 6 trainees (too few trainees) 4 times each, and observing 24 trainees just once (too few observations per person). Once the SMK/phase restrictions and geographical location of their school-based placements was taken into consideration, we had very little room to manoeuvre in selecting the 12 participants, of which three were male, reflecting reasonably well (if it were relevant) the 1 in 6 proportion in this PGCE cohort as a whole. These 12 were invited to participate in the video study phase of our project, and all agreed.

It was made clear to them, in writing, that in observing them, our role would be that of researcher, not university tutor (although four of the research team also fulfilled that role in other circumstances). They were therefore assured that our observations would play no part in the university's summative assessment of their teaching competence, or any other aspect of their certification. We sought and gained their permission to use data from the videotapes of their lessons in research papers, and to use short extracts from some of the tapes for research presentations, within future teacher education programmes, and at future 'partnership' meetings with cooperating schoolteachers ('mentors'). Later, it was also necessary to obtain similar permissions from mentors and headteachers in these prospective teachers' placement schools, and from the parents or carers of the children in their classes. In a few cases this parental permission was withheld, and practical arrangements (such as ensuring that certain children were off-camera, or supervised in an annexe to the class) were made to respect this choice without abandoning the observation altogether.

Procedure

Data collection. The two lesson observations took place in the 5th and 7th weeks of an 8-week final teaching placement. By this late stage of their training, the participants had completed the mathematics methods course at the university, and had taught in two schools for about 15 weeks in total. The school mid-term break occurred between the two observed lessons. Trainee-participants were asked to provide a copy of their planning for the observed lesson. The focus and content of the lesson were chosen by the trainee teacher. The observer operated a tripod-mounted video camera from the back of the class, while the trainee-teacher being observed wore a clip-on radio microphone linked to the camera audio input. The camera tracked the trainee-teacher, but would occasionally capture some artefact in the classroom (such as a set of exercises displayed on a wall) which had some immediate relevance to the mathematics teaching being observed. When and if necessary, the observer made handwritten field notes about anything that interested her, or which might be particularly relevant to the focus of our enquiry: specifically, how the teacher's mathematics content knowledge is evidenced in the classroom. These included notes of any relevant aspects of the lesson that might not have been captured on the video recording, such as off-camera pupil comments or interactions. Pupils' spoken contributions were audible on the video-recording if they were picked up by the radio microphone: for the most part, this included pupils' remarks during the whole-class teaching portions of the lesson and during seatwork portions when the trainee-teacher was working closely with an individual pupil or a group. Our assessment of the obtrusiveness of the observer and the technology can be anecdotal at best, but in the video recordings it is rare to see any evidence of the pupils taking any interest in their 'visitor'. The demeanour of the trainee-teachers themselves appears much as it might be when we visit to observe them as tutors. None of this is to deny that our presence might have caused some perturbation in the 'usual' classroom processes. At the conclusion of the lesson, the observer took care not to give any feedback or evaluative comments on the lesson to the teacher-trainee, in order to emphasise that they were not there in their role as teacher educator.

Data preparation. As soon as possible after the lesson (usually the same day) the observer/researcher wrote what we call a *Descriptive Synopsis* of the lesson. This was a brief (around 500 words) account of what happened in the lesson, so that a reader might immediately be able to contextualise subsequent discussion of any events within it. These descriptive synopses were typically written from memory and with the use of the field notes, with occasional reference to the videotape if necessary.

Mason (2002) suggests that there are three ways in which data may be 'read': literally, interpretively and reflexively. She describes the first of these as documenting a 'literal' version of "what is there", but points to the difficulties for interpretive researchers in attempts to do this, since "what is there" is necessarily interpreted by the observer. Mason suggests that in most qualitative research a construction of what data means, or what can be inferred from it, will be made. This involves the reading of data interpretively. In a reflexive reading of data, the researcher considers the way in which their own experiences and concerns might influence their interpretation (Winter, 1989).

The Cambridge research team subscribed to the view that every human account of events is an interpretation of the messenger/teller's experience, and every 'reading' of such an account is the reader's interpretation of the message, which itself is an artefact, a set of signs. Therefore no 'objective' account of a lesson can be written, and none can be read. However, we guarded against 'smuggling' interpretive and inferential passages into these descriptive synopses. With this in mind, in addition to what the observer believed to be their best efforts at straightforward description, different text styles were used to identify in the synopses (a) anything that the observer/researcher thought might turn out to be significant, or critical, moments or episodes with respect to the trainee-teacher's mathematics content knowledge, for consideration later by the research team (b) any evaluative comment within the descriptive synopsis; this was to allow occasional (in fact, quite rare) comments of the kind that one might write, as a tutor, on a lesson observation report (acclaim or criticism), yet which went beyond description. This was in part to alert others to the fact that the observer had imposed their own evaluation onto the description, but also in recognition that such remarks might be found to have some analytical value later. The descriptive account offered by the observer could be challenged by a member of the team for its 'objectivity', and if the challenge were conceded, one of these two formats would be applied to the hitherto 'normal' text in the account.

A pilot lesson was videotaped and analysed in this way, as a kind of rehearsal of our intended means of 'capturing' the lesson. We also discussed aspects of the content of the lesson that caught our immediate interest with respect to our intended focus on teacher knowledge. In retrospect, that was an extraordinarily rich lesson. The teacher, Trudy, was an undergraduate primary teacher education student, and therefore not a participant in the main study. Trudy's university subject specialism was music. She had not studied mathematics since the age of 16, however, in our audit she scored a perfect 4 on every item. Any temptation we might have felt to include her lesson in the data was subsequently lifted because the videotape of Trudy's lesson was mislaid, and has never been found. However, this raises interesting questions about 'exciting' data from pilot studies, and what researchers could do and should not do with it.

We note in passing, and with some regret, that we did not look to the trainee-teachers themselves as potential sources of interpretive data on the lesson that they taught. Our reasons were pragmatic; we appreciated the willingness of our participants to have their lessons observed and recorded, and we decided not to impose on their goodwill, or that of the personnel in their placement schools, any further.[4]

---

[4] In a later, separate phase of the project, *after* the Knowledge Quartet had been developed as a conceptual tool, we interviewed the trainee-teacher at the end of the school day, when one team member met with him or her to view the videotape and to discuss some of the episodes. In the first part of this stimulated recall interview (Calderhead, 1981), the trainee was invited to 'think aloud' about any aspect of the mathematical content of the lesson. Then the interviewer drew the teacher's attention to key issues that had been identified by the team earlier in the day, and invited the trainee to comment and offer their own perspective on the relevant episodes (Thwaites et al., 2005).

Coding

After all the video tapes of the lessons were collected, the hard work of analysing these 24 lessons began. We took a grounded approach to the data for the purpose of generating theory (Glaser & Strauss, 1987). At the outset, we did not know what kind of 'theory' might emerge from our close scrutiny of the lesson videotapes. It might have been an explanatory theory of the kind "Because this teacher knew x, he or she did (or did not do) y in the lesson". Alternately, it might have been a 'lens' type of theory – a new way of seeing classroom events from the perspective of teacher knowledge. In the event, the theory that materialised was more of the second kind.

In our grounded theory approach to the videotapes of the lessons, we watched the tapes of all the lessons, usually in two and threes, sometimes as a whole team. We articulated and compared our interpretations of episodes from each of the 24 videotaped lessons. We identified specific actions in the classroom that seemed to provide significant information about the trainee's mathematics content knowledge or their mathematical pedagogical knowledge. We reflected later that most of these actions related to various choices made by the trainee, in their planning or more spontaneously. In this way, we homed in on particular moments or episodes in the tapes. Each such moment or episode was assigned a preliminary code (or more than one if appropriate). We developed these codes as we went along (examples will be given later), and most of them recurred as we saw what looked like the same kind of phenomenon in different episodes within the same, or another, lesson. It soon became apparent that the majority of the salient moments and episodes, and the corresponding codes, related to issues of mathematics pedagogy[5] rather than knowledge of mathematics per se. Perhaps this is not surprising, since the subject-matter was elementary mathematics, and half of the lessons were with children aged 4-7. For example, the issue in introducing subtraction to young children is not whether an educated adult teacher can himself, or herself, subtract one small integer from another, but whether they know the fundamental subtraction structures or models, appropriate contexts for these structures and ways of representing them, and a range of relevant student mental strategies.[6] Nevertheless, pupils' spontaneous remarks and questions did, on occasion, tax the trainees' overt knowledge and understanding of mathematics, in unexpected ways (see Jason below).

At first the identification of such moments, and accounts of their significance for our research, was in the form of proposals, or conjectures, for consideration by the team. They could be challenged or supported, and retained or rejected by consensus. The grounds for such a challenge included *relevance* and *significance*.

---

[5] What our colleagues in other parts of Europe would more likely call 'didactics'.

[6] We probably depart from Ball et al., (submitted) here, in that they seem to regard these aspects of mathematics content knowledge as aspects of specialised content (i.e., subject matter, for them) knowledge. This is unimportant, for the present purpose at least: we could re-frame our observation by saying that what Ball et al. call common content knowledge was rarely an issue, either for concern or celebration, in the 24 lessons we analysed.

Relevance is subjective to a degree, but the coding was expected to be relevant to the focus of our research: the role of teachers' mathematics-related knowledge in mathematics teaching. For this reason, 'child demonstration' (CD), which was at one time one of 18 agreed codes in use, was challenged and discarded, leaving 17 codes. Whilst on several occasions the teachers *did* invite a child to demonstrate something to the class, it was agreed that this could happen irrespective of the teacher's SMK or PCK. The notion of significance is also subjective: while we did not attempt to define what made an event sufficiently 'significant' to merit being coded, decisions by individuals or subgroups in the team were often challenged on the grounds of significance. For example, one of our codes was called 'overt subject knowledge' (OSK). It related to moments when the teacher displayed some aspect of their SMK. One such example was when Nathalie compared the probabilities of two particular outcomes when two dice are thrown, by identifying and listing the sample space and isolating the events. The label itself (OSK) could have been improved, but it stuck. On one occasion, another trainee had been teaching how to add 10 by adjusting the tens digit in the numeral (e.g. $47 \rightarrow 57$). One of the team had provisionally coded OSK the prospective teacher's fluency with the strategy. This was successfully challenged, on the grounds that there was nothing special or unusual about that. It is the kind of knowledge that the 'average citizen' would be expected to have, whereas OSK was intended to mark knowledge that somehow went beyond the ordinary and everyday. This same significance criterion applied equally to codes that related to PCK more than SMK. In fact, there would be circumstances where the "how to add 10" might be coded, but with a code more related to PCK.

It was important for us to keep in mind that our research focus was mathematics content knowledge, and not other more general kinds of pedagogical awareness or expertise. For example, ensuring that all children are positioned to be able to see, say, a demonstration of counting by one of their peers is undeniably important, but not within the scope of our current enquiry. There were also times when we had to remind ourselves that we were not in the role of 'partnership tutors' (school placement supervisors). In fact, our analyses took place after the outcome of the trainees' teaching placement had been decided. This was helpful to ourselves and to the participants, because our task was to look for issues relating to their mathematics knowledge for teaching, and not to make summative judgements about or high-stakes assessments of their competence as mathematics teachers.

An initial 'long list' of codes was rationalised and reduced by negotiation and agreement in the research team. Typically this came about through identifying and unifying duplicate codes, and by eliminating the codes associated with events that were agreed to be weak in significance.

Responding to Children's Ideas

By way of illustration of this coding process, we give here brief accounts of two episodes that we labelled with the code RESPONDING TO CHILDREN'S IDEAS (RCI). It will be seen that the contribution of a child, in each case, was unexpected.

Within the research team, this code name was understood to be potentially ironic, since the observed response of the teacher to a child's insight or suggestion was often to put it to one side rather than to deviate from the planned lesson 'script', even when the child offered further insight on the topic at hand.

Illustrative episode 1. Jason was teaching elementary fraction concepts to a Year 3 (pupil age 7-8) class. The pupils each had a small oblong whiteboard and a dry-wipe pen. Jason asked them to "split" their individual whiteboards into two. Most of the children predictably drew a line through the centre of the oblong, parallel to one of the sides, but one boy, Elliott, drew a diagonal line. Jason praised him for his originality, and then asked the class to split their boards "into four". Again, most children drew two lines parallel to the sides, but Elliott drew the two diagonals. Jason's response was to bring Elliott's solution to the attention of the class, but to leave them to decide whether it is correct. He asks:

Jason:	What has Elliott done that is different to what Rebecca has done?
Sophie:	Because he's done the lines diagonally.
Jason:	Which one of these two has been split equally? [...] Sam, has Elliott split his board into quarters?
Sam:	Um ... yes ... no ...
Jason:	Your challenge for this lesson is to think about what Elliott's done, and think if Elliott has split this into equal quarters. There you go Elliott.

At that point, Jason returned the whiteboard to Elliott, and the question of whether it had been partitioned into quarters was not mentioned again. What makes this interesting mathematically is the fact that (i) the four parts of Elliott's board are not congruent, but (ii) they have equal areas (iii) this is not at all obvious. Furthermore, (iv) an elementary demonstration of (ii) is arguably even less obvious. This seemed to us a situation that posed very direct demands on Jason's SMK and arguably PCK too. It is not possible to infer whether Jason's "challenge" is motivated by a strategic decision to give the children some thinking time, or because he needs some himself.

Illustrative episode 2. Naomi was introducing the subtraction 'comparison' structure (e.g., Carpenter & Moser, 1983) to a Year 1 class (pupil age 5-6). She set up various comparison (or "difference": see Rowland, 2006) problems, in the context of frogs in two ponds. Magnetic 'frogs' are lined up on a board, in two neat rows. In the first problem, Naomi says that her pond has four frogs, and her neighbour's pond has two. The class agreed that she had two more frogs than her neighbour.[7] Then Hugh offered the following thought:

Hugh:	You could both have three, if you give one to your neighbour.

---

[7] We reflected that this particular example, with equal subtrahend and difference, is pedagogically problematic (see e.g. Rowland, Thwaites, & Huckstep, 2003).

Like Jason, Naomi acknowledged the child's idea, but in this case she dismissed any further consideration of the alternative avenues that it could lead down.

> Naomi: I could, that's a very good point, Hugh. I'm not going to do that today though. I'm just going to talk about the difference. Madeleine, if you had a pond, how many frogs would you like in it?

One can readily sympathise with Naomi's response to Hugh's insight, which seems to deviate too far from the agenda that she had set for the lesson. Naomi acknowledges Hugh's observation, but refuses to be diverted from her course. With the benefit of hindsight, one can see that she had the option, if she were brave (or confident, or reckless) enough to choose it, to take Hugh's remark as the starting point of rather a nice enquiry. This would almost certainly have prompted investigation of the difference between two numbers, as intended, as well as halving, the concept of arithmetic mean, and the distinction between even and odd numbers.

The *identification* of opportunities to respond to children's ideas (RCI), whether taken or sidestepped in the videotaped lessons, was not intended to suggest – and certainly not at the data analysis stage being described here – what the teacher (prospective teacher in this case) should or should not have done. The immediate context here is research, and the enlightenment of the research team. In a different context, that of mathematics teacher development, as I shall explain later, identification of such an opportunity by an observer raises the possibility for the teacher to reflect on it, to add to their knowledge for teaching, and to inform future action. I am *not* suggesting that every potential diversion should be pursued. Before deviating from their plan, the teacher must make a more-or-less instantaneous cost-benefit assessment of the outcome of doing so, whether they feel sufficiently confident to depart from their 'script', and whether the time available is sufficient to see the new venture through to a meaningful conclusion.

Reflexive Interpretation

We viewed and considered episodes like these without knowing in advance what we might 'find' in them, or what to expect. We had no theories in advance – at a level other than Grand Theory such as constructivist epistemology and grounded theory methodology – to shape the way that we looked at them. We were looking for ways in which these teachers' mathematical content knowledge 'played out' in their work in the classroom and, to the best of our knowledge, no existing framework existed to "organise the complexity"[8] of what we saw in the 24 lessons with that particular focus on teacher knowledge. We did not come to our analysis of the tapes *tabula rasa* however. Our *reflexive* interpretation (Winter, 1989) of the data was made explicit in subsequent 'analytical accounts' of the lessons (see

---

[8] This phrase, in connection with the Knowledge Quartet, is due to Michael Neubrand (personal communiqué, May 2005).

below), in which we made reference to connections of various kinds that came to mind when we viewed the lessons. These might be, for example, to something we had witnessed in the past, something someone had said in a discussion, or in a lecture, or something we had read. An instance of a connection of the latter kind that we made with the episodes of Jason and Naomi (above) is the following.

On more than one occasion, Bishop (e.g., 2001, p. 244) has recounted an anecdote about a class of 9- and 10-year-olds who were asked to give a fraction between ½ and ¾. One girl answered 2/3. When the teacher asked how she knows that it lies between the two given fractions she replied "Because 2 is between the 1 and the 3, and on the bottom the 3 lies between the 2 and the 4". Bishop uses the anecdote to illustrate how a teacher's response is determined by the values that they espouse. Through the lens of our research question, we also note two things about the situation. First, the girl's answer is probably not one that the teacher had expected, even less one that s/he had hoped for. For me, it hints at the notion of the Farey Mean of two fractions, (sometimes called their 'mediant'), but this topic is not standard material for the school curriculum, in England at least. More to the point, it would be perfectly possible to have gained a first degree, or even a doctorate, in mathematics without having encountered it. Even to begin to entertain the girl's proposal would necessitate substantial deviation for the teachers' planned lesson script. The teacher could ignore or effectively dismiss the girl's proposal (saying, for example, "You couldn't be sure that way"). To take it seriously would probably involve probing her answer or instituting some investigation of the generality of her reasoning. It follows that responding to children's ideas (RCI) of this kind potentially entails recourse to mathematics content knowledge resources, either substantive or syntactic, or both (Schwab, 1978).

This story (Bishops') is re-told here not because it comes from our data, but because it is an example of the kind of 'baggage' - our existing ways of thinking about the world in general and mathematics classrooms in particular - that shaped the 'reflexive' interpretation of our data.

A Staging Post

The inductive process described above generated an initial set of 18 codes which were reduced to 17 soon after. Next, each of us focused in detail on about five videotapes, and elaborated the Descriptive Synopsis into an *Analytical Account* of each lesson. In these accounts, significant moments and episodes were identified and coded, using the agreed set of codes and code-names, with appropriate justification and analysis concerning the role of the trainee's content knowledge in the identified passages, with links to relevant literature. Other members of the research team then re-visited and re-considered three or four of these codes in every analytical account. This intensive activity took place in the summer months, from June to August. In September, we presented some findings at a conference (Huckstep et al., 2002). Our presentation focused on three of the 18 codes: namely *choice of examples, making connections* and *responding to children's ideas*. We illustrated our talk with clips from the videotapes. The presentation was well-received, and we envisaged making another five similar presentations before we had exhausted the codes. In the event, our thinking took a different turn, one we had not planned from the outset – though, arguably, we should have.

THE EMERGENCE OF THE KNOWLEDGE QUARTET

Perhaps as a consequence of feedback received at the conference presentation, around that time we began to realise the practical potential of what we had 'found' in our research study for our work, and for that of our colleagues, in teacher education. In the UK, a large part (typically a half to two-thirds) of the graduate initial training (PGCE) year is spent teaching in schools under the guidance of a school-based mentor. The proportion of time differs in other countries, but *practicum* placement is more-or-less universal. Placement lesson observation is normally followed by a review meeting between a school-based teacher-mentor and the prospective teacher. On occasion, a university-based tutor will participate in the observation and the review. Research shows that such meetings typically focus heavily on organisational features of the lesson, with little attention to mathematical aspects of mathematics lessons (Brown, McNamara, Jones, & Hanley, 1999; Strong & Baron, 2004). Our 'pure' research clearly offered a basis for us to develop an empirically-based conceptual framework for lesson reviews with a clearer focus on the mathematics content of the lesson and the role of the trainee teacher's mathematics SMK and PCK. Such a framework would need to capture a number of important ideas and factors about content knowledge within a small number of conceptual categories, with a set of easily-remembered labels for those categories.

The identification of the 17 categories could be a stepping stone in the development of a framework for observing and reviewing mathematics teaching with prospective teachers, and potentially not only these novices. We (the Cambridge team) did not want a 17-point tick-list, like an annual car safety check, but a readily-understood scheme which would serve to frame an in-depth discussion between teacher and observer. Our codes were useful to the extent that we had a set of concepts and an associated vocabulary sufficient to identify and describe various ways in which mathematics content knowledge plays out in elementary mathematics teaching. In the autumn of 2003 we began to think about how we could group the codes into a smaller set of 'big ideas' for mathematics teaching.

Eventually, we made a large paper label for each of the codes, spread these labels out on the floor, and began to separate them into sets. Each suggestion for putting two or more codes in the same subset had to be backed up with a reason of some sort. For example, someone put *choice of examples* and *choice of representation* together, saying that these were both ways that teachers use to make an abstract idea accessible when they are teaching it. In fact, this person said, these two codes are characteristic examples of the ways that teachers 'transform' their subject knowledge, as Shulman (1987) put it, in order to help others to learn it. Another grouping included the three codes *decisions about sequencing;*

anticipation of complexity, and *recognition of conceptual appropriateness.* The last two of these capture instances of planning, or of in-the-moment decision-making, that appeared to be informed by the teacher's awareness of the level of challenge and conceptual complexity entailed in the mathematical subject matter in hand. This is a well-documented topic in the research and professional literature, and much can be learned from experience too. Indeed, as remarked earlier, the original conception of PCK "includes an understanding of what makes the learning of specific topics easy or difficult ..." (Shulman, 1986, p. 9). These kinds of teacher knowledge contribute to decisions about the sequencing of instruction and student activity and the sequencing of exercises – considerations encompassed in the first of the three codes in this grouping. The crucial awareness and consensus, for us, was that these three codes contribute to students' sense of coherence within a lesson, and from lesson to lesson: that the shifts of focus and activity were by design, and not by chance. As we discussed and tried to capture this unifying quality with respect to these three codes, the words, 'coherence', 'cohesion' and 'connection' came to mind.

By an extended process of argument, debate and negotiation, we eventually agreed on grouping the 17 codes into four superordinate categories which, together, we later called the *Knowledge Quartet.* Each of the four categories is a unit, or *dimension* of the Knowledge Quartet. We have named the four dimensions: *Foundation; Transformation; Connection; Contingency.* These four units represent more comprehensive, higher-order concepts, in keeping with standard practice in grounded theory research (Strauss & Corbin, 1998, pp. 113–114), which involves first categorising the data ('open' coding), then connecting categories ('axial' coding') before finally proposing a core category (selective coding). "First analyse, then synthesise, and finally prioritise" (Dey, 1999, p. 98). This is certainly a way of describing what we had done in grouping the 17 codes into four categories, and conceiving the whole (the Quartet) as a tool for focused mathematics lesson observation.

Not only the constituents, but also the names of these four Knowledge Quartet categories were in flux for more than a year. Indeed, notes of a research team meeting late in 2002 record *five* superordinate categories, with tentative names like Knowing (a precursor of Foundation) and Showing (a blend of elements of Transformation and Connection). A separate category had been created to group just two codes: adherence to textbooks (AT); concentration on procedures (CP). The thinking had been that these, in some way, marked instrumental attitudes and beliefs about the nature of mathematics and mathematics teaching. Eventually these fundamental affective considerations were subsumed by the Foundation dimension. Three months later, the components of the categories had more or less stabilised but their names were still not settled, being: theoretical background and beliefs; transformation, presentation and explanation; coherence; contingent action (Huckstep et al., 2003). 'Coherence' was originally chosen in preference to 'Connection', a term which had gained popularity in the UK in connection with the *Effective Teachers of Numeracy* study (Askew et al., 1997). Our conceptualisation of the corresponding unit of the Knowledge Quartet was specific in its inclusion of codes related to the sequencing of instruction, and we wanted to distinguish our notion from the 'connectionist' beliefs orientation which headlines the *Effective Teachers* study. In the end, we decided that it would be sensible to 'go with the flow', and explain our nuanced use of 'connection' as and when necessary.

We had reduced the names of all the dimensions to single words by the end of 2003 (Rowland, Huckstep, & Thwaites, 2003). A further refinement of the codes was judged to be necessary in 2004 as we prepared the manuscript for a journal article (Rowland et al., 2005). As we listed the elements of each dimension, we could not avoid the feeling that a code that we had labelled 'making connections' (MC) now seemed rather limp as a component (admittedly one of four) of the dimension that we were calling Connection. Looking back at our data, we saw that the code 'making connections' had been used – in keeping with Askew et al. (1997) – to refer to the participant teachers' efforts (or missed opportunities) to make connections between *concepts*, or to show how two *procedures* might be related. Consequently, the rather tautologous MC was subdivided into two codes: making connections between concepts (MCC) and making connections between procedures (MCP). I should emphasise that there were instances of both of these new codes in our original data: it was not a case merely of imagining ways to make 'making connections' more focused. Indeed, a clear instance of MCP can be seen in the case of Laura (Rowland et al., 2004). It could be argued that a code 'making connections between procedures and concepts' ought to be necessary, since it relates to the important notion of procept (Gray & Tall, 1994). However, there were no instances of these particular novice teachers making such a connection, or missing an opportunity to make one, in our data. In principle, the code could be added later – as we shall propose later in this chapter.

In this way, our description and understanding of the Knowledge Quartet more-or-less stabilised a year after it was conceived. Since then, our experience of using the Knowledge Quartet has shown that it covers the various ways that the teacher's subject-specific knowledge comes into play in the classroom. It has also been shown to be a useful tool for thinking about mathematics teaching, and a framework for professional discussions of lesson planning and lesson review. Many moments or episodes within a lesson can be understood in terms of two or more of the four units; for example, a contingent response to a pupil's suggestion might helpfully connect with ideas considered earlier. Furthermore, the application of subject knowledge in the classroom *always* rests on foundational knowledge.

Conceptualisation

Since this chapter is envisaged, principally, as methodological, this is not the place to spell out the substantive conceptualisation of the four dimensions of the Knowledge Quartet at length. Such an account can be found in Rowland et al. (2005). However, a brief characterisation of each unit of the Knowledge Quartet is as follows. The first category, *foundation*, consists of trainees' knowledge, beliefs and understanding acquired 'in the academy', in preparation (intentionally or otherwise) for their role in the classroom. The key components of this theoretical background are: knowledge and understanding of mathematics per se and knowledge of significant tracts of the literature on the teaching and learning of mathematics, together with beliefs concerning the nature of mathematical knowledge, the purposes of mathematics education, and the conditions under which pupils will best learn mathematics.

The second category, *transformation*, concerns knowledge-in-action as demonstrated both in planning to teach and in the act of teaching itself. As Shulman indicates, the presentation of ideas to learners entails their re-presentation (our hyphen) in the form of analogies, illustrations, examples, explanations and demonstrations (Shulman, 1986, p. 9). Of particular importance is the trainees' choice and use of examples presented to pupils to assist their concept formation, language acquisition and to demonstrate procedures (Rowland, Thwaites, & Huckstep, 2003).

The third category, *connection*, binds together certain choices and decisions that are made for the more or less discrete parts of mathematical content. In her discussion of "profound understanding of fundamental mathematics", Ma (1999, p. 121) cites Duckworth's observation that intellectual 'depth' and 'breadth' "is a matter of making connections". Our conception of this coherence also includes the sequencing of material for instruction, and an awareness of the relative cognitive demands of different topics and tasks.

Our fourth and final category, *contingency*, is witnessed in classroom events that are almost impossible to plan for. In commonplace language it is the ability to 'think on one's feet'. As indicated earlier, in the comments on episodes with Jason, and Naomi, it includes the readiness to respond to children's ideas and a consequent preparedness, when appropriate, to deviate from an agenda set out when the lesson was prepared. The Knowledge Quartet framework is summarised in Table 1.

THEORETICAL SAMPLING: THE CASE OF MÁIRE

Since its initial development, the Knowledge Quartet has been put to the test as an instrument for mathematics lesson observation and analysis. This testing has taken a number of forms, including its application in varying degrees in three doctoral studies, including one longitudinal study of the knowledge, beliefs and practices of early career elementary teachers (Turner, 2007). Although our experience to date indicates that the Knowledge Quartet is comprehensive in its scope, we take the view that the details of its component codes, and the conceptualisation of each of its dimensions, are perpetually open to revision. This fallibilist position (Lakatos, 1976) seems to us to be as appropriate for a theory of knowledge-in-mathematics-teaching as it is for mathematics itself. In grounded theory methodology, it is also inherent in the notion of 'theoretical sampling' (Glaser & Strauss, 1967), whereby the application of the theory exposes some shortcoming, and thereby lays it open to refinement, modification and possible improvement.

Table 1. The Knowledge Quartet (adapted from Rowland et al., 2005)

	The Knowledge Quartet
Foundation	Propositional knowledge and beliefs concerning: *the meanings and descriptions of relevant mathematical concepts, and of relationships between them; *the multiple factors which research has shown to be significant in the teaching and learning of mathematics; *the ontological status of mathematics and the purposes of teaching it. *Contributory codes: awareness of purpose; identifying errors; overt subject knowledge; theoretical underpinning of pedagogy; use of terminology; use of textbook; reliance on procedures.*
Transformation	Knowledge-in-action as revealed in deliberation and choice in planning and teaching. The teacher's own meanings and descriptions are transformed and presented in ways designed to enable students to learn it. These ways include the use of representations, analogies, illustrations, explanations and demonstrations. The choice of examples made by the teacher is especially visible: *for the optimal acquisition of mathematical concepts and procedures; *for confronting and resolving common misconceptions; *for the justification (by generic example) or refutation (by counter-example) of mathematical conjectures. *Contributory codes: choice of representation; teacher demonstration; choice of examples.*
Connection	Knowledge-in-action as revealed in deliberation and choice in planning and teaching. Within a single lesson, or across a series of lessons, the teacher *unifies* the subject matter and draws out *coherence* with respect to: *connections between different meanings and descriptions of particular concepts *or* between alternative ways of representing concepts and carrying out procedures; *the relative complexity and cognitive demands of mathematical concepts and procedures, by attention to sequencing of the content. *Contributory codes: making connections between procedures; making connections between concepts; anticipation of complexity; decisions about sequencing; recognition of conceptual appropriateness.*
Contingency	Knowledge-in-*inter*action as revealed by the ability of the teacher to 'think on her feet' and respond appropriately to the contributions made by her students during a teaching episode. On occasion this can be seen in the teacher's willingness to deviate from her own agenda when to develop a student's unanticipated contribution might be of special benefit to that pupil, *or* might suggest a particularly fruitful avenue of enquiry. *Contributory codes: responding to children's ideas; use of opportunities; deviation from agenda; teacher realisation.*

An illuminating instance of this incremental process is the case of Máire, one of the prospective teacher participants in the study by Dolores Corcoran, located in Ireland. Máire was observed teaching a lesson on whole-number division. The lesson was analysed at length, through the lens of the Knowledge Quartet, in Corcoran (2007) and also in Rowland (2007). The class was a mix of 3rd and 4th Class girls (age 9-10 years). Máire had written separate worksheets on division for each age group, both set in a fantasy Harry Potter[9] scenario. The first problem for each of the two groups was as follows:

3rd Class: Ron has 18 Galleons[10] and a pack of cards costs 3 Galleons. How many packs can he buy?

4th Class: Fred and George want to buy magic worms to put in everyone's bed. They had 44 Galleons, and each worm costs four Galleons. How many worms could they buy? [This question continues: if there are 30 beds, how many more worms would be needed?]

One of the ways in which pupils make sense of mathematical operations, procedures or concepts is by appreciating the range of different situations to which they apply. The various problems and scenarios relevant to a particular operation can be grouped into a small number of categories, each with the same fundamental structure. In the case of division, there are at least two key problem structures (e.g. Vergnaud, 1983), variously called partition (or sharing) and quotition (or measurement, or grouping). In the partition version of 20 divided by 4, for example, we share 20 things among 4 people, and each receives the same quota of 5 things; in the quotitive scenario, we distribute a pre-set quota of 4 things to 5 people.

In each of the two Harry Potter problems under discussion, the problem structure is *quotition*. They both begin with a certain supply of Galleons, and a fixed quota (3 Galleons, 4 Galleons), whereas the 'answer unit' is packs for one problem, worms for the other. However, in exploring how to resolve the problem, Máire drew on the language and concepts of *partition*. In the case of the 3rd class problem, for example,

Máire had provided butter beans as manipulatives for the 3rd class, to represent the Galleons. One pupil, Rosin, read out the 'packs of cards' problem, while Megan volunteered to count out 18 butter beans. As Megan counted out the 18 butter beans, Máire offered a few words of explanation about the "wizard money", then she asked:

Máire: How many groups does she [Megan] need to break it into and can you tell me why? Hannah, what do you think?

Hannah: Into three groups.

---

[9] The Harry Potter novels by J. K. Rowling are well-known in Ireland, and in most parts of the world for that matter.

[10] Galleons are the fictional currency in use at Hogwarts, which is Harry Potter's school.

291

> Máire: Into three groups. Well done, and why? You can read the question again if you want.

As observed above, the problem structure here is quotition. However, Máire's query here to the *number of groups* and not to their size, points inappropriately to a partition structure, and this is picked up by Hannah. This is hardly surprising since, as Brown (1981, cited in Dickson et al., 1984) found, primary school children have a propensity to opt for partition in preference to quotition when asked to supply a problem for a 'bare' division sentence. Indeed, Ball (1990) found the same to be true of prospective teachers. Máire congratulates the child ("Well done") on her inappropriate suggestion. However, for some reason, Máire is then inspired to ask Hannah to explain ("and why?"). The interaction then takes a different direction.

> Hannah: Because there's three packs of cards.
> Máire: It's not that there's three packs of cards. But what is it about the cards?
> Hannah: It costs three galleons.

It is interesting to note that the child's first justification ("there's three packs of cards") would be entirely appropriate for the partitive division model that she proposed earlier i.e., 18 Galleons, 3 packs of cards, therefore 6 Galleons for each pack. But, for reasons that we can only speculate, Máire is pulled up short at this point. She knows that there are *not* three packs of cards. Máire has inadvertently directed the pupils to the wrong division structure, she *realises* that this is so, and she resolves to find a way out:

> Máire: It costs three galleons. So if you share out your 3 galleons, you see how many packs of cards you're able to buy […] Megan you're already ahead of us. You've got 18 and what are you doing?

Máire is attempting to alter the direction of the discussion. Her use of the word 'share' to point to quotition is perhaps unfortunate (and, indeed, 'grouping' earlier when she had partition in mind). The child who responds has not altered course:

> Child: Splitting them up into three groups ...
> Máire: Ahh ...? Into groups of three [she nods]. And how many groups do you have?

Máire's response "Into groups of three" is a direct correction, and her language is now correctly aligned with quotition/grouping. The child replies:

> Child: Six.
> Máire: So how many packs of cards could Ron buy?
> Child: Six.
> Máire: He could buy six packs of cards. Can everybody follow that? What sentence would you write to explain what we just did?

This ability to change course as a result of reflection in action was not observed in the lessons that were the data for our original study. Schön's (1983) term 'reflective practitioner' conjures up the notion of teachers as professionals who learn from their own actions and those of others. Schön distinguished between two kinds of reflection. Reflection *on* action refers to thinking back on our actions after the event, whereas reflection *in* action is a kind of monitoring and self-regulation of our actions as we perform them. We see an instance of reflection-in-action in this episode, and in what we would call a 'contingent moment'. Máire could not have prepared (in her planning) for what she did at that moment, but what she did say and do brought about a significant and pedagogically important shift in the discourse and the cognitive content of the lesson. This was possible because Máire seems to have experienced an *insight* of some kind, an 'aha' of a pedagogical kind. This insight of Máire's was significant in terms of our conceptualisation of the Contingency dimension of the Knowledge Quartet. This dimension was rooted, as it arose from the data in our original study, in the teacher's response to *children's* insights and misconceptions. In this instance we seem to have a moment where Máire herself suddenly realises that the problem, the child's suggestion, and her approval, simply do not 'stack up'. In analysing Máire's lesson through the lens of the Knowledge Quartet, we apply a theory derived *from* practice back *to* practice. Máire's moment of insight is an instance where theoretical sampling has found the current theory wanting, and caused it to be rethought and enhanced. Consequently, we have added an additional code to the three previously associated with Contingency. Provisionally, this new code is 'teacher realisation' (TR). In principle, just one significant instance of TR, and the expectation that others might subsequently be identified, would justify its inclusion in the conceptualisation of the theory. In fact, once the notion of TR was raised and discussed within the research group, one of the team was able to point to further instances in the many lessons observed in her longitudinal study (Turner, 2007).

FINAL REMARKS

From Observation to Evaluation

In a paper presented to a meeting of teacher education researchers, Skott (2006) highlighted the changing nature of the relationship between theory and practice in teacher education. He observed that the theories brought to bear on the task of *improving* teaching increasingly derive from studies *of* teaching, and coined the term 'theoretical loop' to capture this dialectical relationship between theory and practice in teacher education. In the case of the research which has been the focus of this chapter, the Knowledge Quartet came about as the outcome of systematic analysis *of* mathematics teaching. Initially, we viewed it as a way of managing the complexity of describing the role of teachers' content knowledge in their teaching. In the spirit of Skott's theoretical loop, we subsequently developed ways of using the Knowledge Quartet as a framework to facilitate analysis and discussion of mathematics teaching among prospective teachers, their mentors and teacher educators (see Rowland & Turner, 2006).

The progression from observation of teaching to its description and analysis is clear, but, thus far, I have been less explicit about the *evaluation* of teaching. In the spirit of reflective practice, the most important evaluation must be that of the teacher him/herself. However, this self-evaluation is usefully provoked and assisted by a colleague or mentor. In a number of papers (e.g. Rowland et al., 2004; Rowland et al., 2004; Rowland & Turner, 2006) we have exemplified this provocation through the identification, using the Knowledge Quartet, of tightly-focused *discussion points* to be raised in a post-observation review. We have suggested that these points be framed in a relatively neutral way, such as "Could you tell me why you etc?" or "What were you thinking when etc?". It would be naïve, however, or a kind of self-delusion, to suggest that the mentor, or teacher educator, makes no evaluation of what they observe. Indeed, the observer's evaluation is likely to be a key factor in the identification and prioritisation of the discussion points. In post-observation review, it is expected that the 'more knowledgeable other' will indicate what the novice did well, what they did not do and might have, and what they might have done differently. The Knowledge Quartet is a framework to organise such evaluative comments, and to identify ways of learning from them.

Methodology

In his *China Lectures*, Hans Freudenthal (1991) ranted against the (then) new breed of professional methodologists. His words capture my own experience of research 'design' far better than I could express it myself:

> I don't remember when it happened but I do remember, as though it were yesterday, the bewilderment that struck me when I first heard that the training of future educationalists includes a course on "methodology". This is at any rate the custom in our country but, judging from the literature in general, this brain-washing policy is an international feature. Please imagine a student of mathematics, of physics, of - let me be cautious, as I am not sure how far this list extends - impregnated, in any other way than implicitly, with the methodology of the science that he sets out to study; in any other way than by having him act out the methodology that he has to learn! In no way do I object to a methodology as such - I have even stimulated the cultivation of it, but it should be the result of *a posteriori* reflecting on one's methods, rather than an *a priori* doctrine that has been imposed on the learner. (Freudenthal, 1991, pp. 150–151)

Many readers will have little sympathy for Freudenthal's suggestion that research methodology might be the outcome of reflecting on research action, arguing that educational research has reached new heights of scientific sophistication since Freudenthal composed this diatribe against "the pure methodologists, whose strength consists in knowing all about research and nothing about education" (pp. 150–151). At the same time, Freudenthal's version of events agrees reasonably well with my own experience. Much of the account that I have given of the research processes that the *SKIMA* team followed in arriving at what we came to call the Knowledge Quartet has been possible with the benefit of hindsight, "the result of *a posteriori* reflecting on one's methods". I have done my best to be true to our intellectual and practical experience, as documented and remembered, rather than to offer some idealised, even sanitised, version of events.

Applications and Next Steps

Research originally fuelled by curiosity about teacher knowledge and classroom practices led to the development of the Knowledge Quartet, a manageable framework within which to observe, analyse and discuss mathematics teaching from the perspective of teachers' mathematical content knowledge, both SMK and PCK. The framework is in use in teacher education programmes in Cambridge and elsewhere. Those who use it need to be acquainted with the details of its conceptualisation, because mere labels such as 'connection' may, for each individual, connote meanings other than those intended. Initial indications are that this development has been well-received by teacher-mentors, who appreciate the specific focus on mathematics content and pedagogy. They observe that it compares favourably with government guidance on mathematics lesson observation, which focuses on more generic issues such as "a crisp start, a well-planned middle and a rounded end. Time is used well. The teacher keeps up a suitable pace and spends very little time on class organisation, administration and control" (Department for Education and Employment, 2000, p. 11).

It is all too easy for analysis of a lesson taught by a novice teacher to be (or to be perceived to be) gratuitously critical, and it is important to emphasise that the Knowledge Quartet is intended as a tool to support teacher development, with a sharp and structured focus on the impact of their SMK and PCK on teaching. The post-observation review meeting usefully focuses on a lesson fragment, and on only one or two dimensions of the Knowledge Quartet, to avoid overloading the trainee-teacher with action points.

More recently, we have been analysing secondary mathematics lessons through the lens of the Knowledge Quartet. In a different development, colleagues working in English, science and modern foreign languages education found potential in the Knowledge Quartet for their own lesson observations and review meetings. What might the conceptualisations of the dimensions of the Knowledge Quartet look like in these and other disciplines? A more fundamental question would be: can a framework for knowledge-in-teaching developed in one subject discipline be legitimately adopted in another?

ACKNOWLEDGEMENTS

This research was supported by a grant from the University of Cambridge Faculty of Education Research Development Fund. Peter Huckstep, Anne Thwaites, Fay Turner and Jane Warwick were co-researchers in the project.

REFERENCES

Askew, M., Brown, M., Rhodes, V., Wiliam, D., & Johnson, D., (1997). *Effective teachers of numeracy.* London: King's College, University of London.

Ball, D. L. (1990). Prospective elementary and secondary teachers' understanding of division. *Journal for Research in Mathematics Education, 21*(2), 132–144.

Ball, D. L., & Bass, H. (2003). Toward a practice-based theory of mathematical knowledge for teaching. In B. Davis & E. Simmt (Eds.), *Proceedings of the 2002 Annual Meeting of the Canadian Mathematics Education Study Group* (pp. 3–14). Edmonton, Canada: Canadian Mathematics Education Study Group.

Ball, D. L., Thames, M. H., & Phelps, G. (submitted). Content knowledge for teaching: What makes it special?

Bishop, A. J. (2001). Educating student teachers about values in mathematics education. In F-L Lin & T. J. Cooney (Eds.), *Making sense of mathematics teacher education* (pp. 233–246). Dordrecht, the Netherlands: Kluwer Academic Publishers.

Brown, T., Mcnamara, O., Jones, L., & Hanley, U. (1999). Primary student teachers' understanding of mathematics and its teaching. *British Education Research Journal, 25*(3), 299–322.

BSRLM (2003). *Proceedings of the British Society for Research into Learning Mathematics, 23*(2).

Calderhead, J. (1981). Stimulated recall: a method for research on teaching. *British Journal of Educational Psychology, 51*(2), 211–217.

Carpenter, T. P., & Moser, J. M. (1983). The acquisition of addition and subtraction concepts. In R. Lesh & M. Landau (Eds.), *The acquisition of mathematical concepts and processes* (pp. 7–44). New York: Academic Press.

Corcoran, D. (2007, February). "You don't need a tables book when you have butter beans!" Is there a need for mathematics pedagogy here? Paper presented at the Fifth Congress of the European Society for Research in Mathematics Education. Larnaca, Cyprus.

Dey, I. (1999). *Grounding grounded theory: Guidelines for qualitative inquiry.* London: Academic Press.

Department for Education and Employment (1997). *Teaching: High status, high standards*: Circular 10/97. London: HMSO.

Department for Education and Employment (1998). *Teaching: High status, high standards*: Circular 4/98. London: HMSO.

Department for Education and Employment (1999). *The national numeracy strategy: Framework for teaching mathematics from Reception to Year 6.* Sudbury: Department for Education and Employment Publications.

Department for Education and Employment (2000). *Auditing mathematics in your school.* Sudbury: Department for Education and Employment Publications.

Dickson, L., Brown, M., & Gibson, O. (1984). *Children learning mathematics.* Eastbourne: Holt Education.

Freudenthal, H. (1991). *Revisiting mathematics education: The China lectures.* Dordrecht, the Netherlands: Kluwer Academic Publishers.

Glaser, B. G., & Strauss, A. L. (1967). *The discovery of grounded theory: Strategies for qualitative research.* New York: Aldine de Gruyter.

Goulding, M., & Suggate, J. (2001). Opening a can of worms: investigating primary teachers' subject knowledge in mathematics. *Mathematics Education Review 13*, 41–54.

Goulding, M., Rowland, T., & Barber, P. (2002). Does it matter? Primary teacher trainees' subject knowledge in mathematics. *British Educational Research Journal, 28*(5), 689–704.

Gray, E. M., & Tall, D. O. (1994). Duality, ambiguity and flexibility: A proceptual view of simple arithmetic. *Journal for Research in Mathematics Education, 26*, 115–141.

Huckstep, P., Rowland, T., & Thwaites, A. (2002). Primary teachers' mathematics content knowledge: what does it look like in the classroom? Symposium paper presented at the Annual Conference of the British Educational Research Association, University of Exeter, September.

Huckstep, P., Rowland, T., & Thwaites, A. (2003). Observing subject knowledge in primary mathematics teaching. *Proceedings of the British Society for Research into Learning Mathematics 23*(1), 37–42

Jones, K., & Mooney, C. (2002). Trainee primary teachers' knowledge of geometry for teaching. *Proceedings of the British Society for Research into Learning Mathematics, 22*(2), 95–100.

Lakatos, I. (1976). *Proofs and refutations*. Cambridge: Cambridge University Press.

Ma, L. (1999). *Knowing and teaching elementary mathematics: Teachers' understanding of fundamental mathematics in China and the United States*. London: Lawrence Erlbaum Associates.

Mason, J. (2002). *Qualitative researching* (2nd Ed). London: Sage.

McNamara, D. (1991). Subject knowledge and its application: problems and possibilities for teacher educators, *Journal of Education for Teaching, 17*(2), 113–128.

Morris H. J. (2001). Issues raised by testing trainee primary teachers' mathematical knowledge. *Mathematics Teacher Education and Development, 3*, 37–48.

Rowland, T. (2006). Subtraction – difference or comparison? *Mathematics in School, 35*(2), 32–35.

Rowland, T. (2007). Developing knowledge for mathematics teaching: a theoretical loop. In S. Close, D. Corcoran & T. Dooley (Eds.) *Proceedings of the second national conference on research in mathematics education* (pp. 13–26). Dublin: St Patrick's College.

Rowland, T., Huckstep, P., & Thwaites, A. (2003). The knowledge quartet. *Proceedings of the British Society for Research into Learning Mathematics, 23*(3), 97–102.

Rowland, T., Huckstep, P., & Thwaites, A. (2004). Reflecting on prospective elementary teachers' mathematics content knowledge: The case of Laura. In M. J. Høines & A. B. Fugelstad (Eds.) *Proceedings of the 28th Conference of the International Group for the Psychology of Mathematics Education* (Vol. 4, pp. 121–128). Bergen, Norway: Bergen University College.

Rowland, T., Huckstep, P., & Thwaites, A. (2005). Elementary teachers' mathematics subject knowledge: the knowledge quartet and the case of Naomi. *Journal of Mathematics Teacher Education, 8*, 255–281.

Rowland, T., Martyn, S., Barber, P., & Heal, C. (2000). Primary teacher trainees' mathematics subject knowledge and classroom performance. In T. Rowland & C. Morgan (Eds.) *Research in mathematics education* (Vol. 2, pp. 3–18). London: British Society for Research into Learning Mathematics.

Rowland, T., Martyn, S., Barber, P., & Heal, C. (2001). Investigating the mathematics subject matter knowledge of pre-service elementary school teachers. In M. van den Heuvel-Panhuizen (Ed.), *Proceedings of the 25th Conference of the International Group for the Psychology of Mathematics Education* (Vol. 4, pp. 121–128). Utrecht University, the Netherlands: Psychology of Mathematics Education.

Rowland, T., Thwaites, A., & Huckstep, P. (2003). Novices' choice of examples in the teaching of elementary mathematics. In A. Rogerson (Ed.), *Proceedings of the International Conference on the Decidable and the Undecidable in Mathematics Education* (pp. 242–245). Brno, Czech Republic: The Mathematics Education into the 21st Century Project.

Rowland, T., & Turner, F. (2006). A framework for the observation and review of mathematics teaching. *Mathematics Education Review, 18*, 3–17.

Sanders, S., & Morris, H. (2000). Exposing student teachers' content knowledge: empowerment or debilitation? *Educational Studies, 26*(4), 397–408.

Schön, D. (1983). *The reflective practitioner: How professionals think in action*. New York: Basic Books Inc.

Schwab, J. J. (1978). Education and the structure of the disciplines. In I. Westbury & N. J. Wilkof (Eds.), *Science, curriculum and liberal education* (pp. 229–272). Chicago: University of Chicago Press.

Shulman, L. (1986). Those who understand, knowledge growth in teaching. *Educational Researcher 15*(2), 4–14.

Shulman, L. S. (1987). Knowledge and teaching: Foundations of the new reform. *Harvard Educational Review, 57*(1), 1–22.

Skott, J. (2006). The role of the practice of theorising practice. In M. Bosch (Ed.) *Proceedings of the Fourth Congress of the European Society for Research in Mathematics Education* (pp. 1598–1608). Barcelona, Spain: FUNDEMI IQS, Universitat Ramon Llull. (Compact Disk: also retrieved 11.16.2007 from http://ermeweb.free.fr/CERME4/)

Strauss, A.L. & Corbin, J.M. (1998). *Basics of qualitative research: Techniques and procedures for developing grounded theory*. London: Sage.

Strong, M., & Baron, W. (2004). An analysis of mentoring conversations with beginning teachers: Suggestions and responses. *Teaching and Teacher Education, 20,* 47–57.

Thwaites, A., Huckstep, P., & Rowland, T. (2005). The knowledge quartet: Sonia's reflections. In D. Hewitt & A. Noyes (Eds.), *Proceedings of the Sixth British Congress of Mathematics Education* (pp. 168–175). London: British Society for Research into Learning Mathematics.

Teacher Training Agency (2002). *Qualifying to teach: Professional standards for the award of qualified teacher status. Handbook of guidance*. London: Teacher Training Agency.

Turner, F. (2007). Development in the mathematics teaching of beginning elementary school teachers: An approach based on focused reflections. In S. Close, D. Corcoran & T. Dooley (Eds.), *Proceedings of the Second National Conference on Research in Mathematics Education* (pp. 377–386). Dublin: St Patrick's College.

Vergnaud, G. (1983). Multiplicative structures. In R. Lesh & M. Landau (Eds.), *Acquisition of mathematics concepts and processes* (pp. 127–175). New York: Academic Press.

Winter, R. (1989). *Learning from experience: Principles and practice in action research*. London: Falmer Press.

Tim Rowland
Faculty of Education
University of Cambridge
U.K.

CRITICAL RESPONSE TO VOLUME CHAPTERS

JOHN MASON

13. PCK AND BEYOND

DEDICATED TO THE MEMORY OF LEONE BURTON (1936–2007)

Having been invited to join Leone Burton in reflecting on the chapters in this volume of the handbook, I dedicate my remarks to her memory. She was tireless in promoting social justice, gender equity, and above all, enquiry at every level of engagement, by students, teachers, and teacher educators. I hope that my attempts are worthy of her vision.

In this summary I look beyond the confines of PCK (pedagogic content knowledge) and its transformation into MfT (mathematics for teaching) and MiT (mathematics in teaching) in order to try to contact the essence of necessary and desirable preparation for effective mathematics teaching. I take an unreservedly eclectic and embracingly constructivist stance while at the same time being driven by an almost Aristotelian desire to probe the essence of what it is that informs and guides effective and efficient teaching involving mathematics at any level, aware that such essences say as much or more about my awareness as about teaching in general. At the same time I try to maintain a Heideggerian respect for 'being': in this case, being mathematical with and in front of learners. I suggest that there will be negative as well as positive consequences for trying to delineate and codify effective teaching acts, and make a plea for mathematics teaching to lead the way in promoting learning, teaching, and teaching teachers as essentially human activities which make integral use of the complexities of being human that cannot be set down in lists of attributes.

SUMMARISING THE VOLUME

I offer a brief summary of some of the points from the various chapters, as a foundation for suggesting directions of development of research and practice in professional development in mathematics education, and of PCK in particular.

Anna Graeber and Dina Tirosh give a fine summary of Lee Shulman's articulation of the notion of *pedagogic content knowledge* (PCK) and related constructs. They also track some of the forces which gave rise to this notion, to which might be added a significant political component. As well as contributing to making more precise a research agenda by re-articulating and developing Dewey's

P. Sullivan and T. Wood (eds.), Knowledge and Beliefs in Mathematics Teaching and Teaching Development, 301–322.

notion of *psychologising the subject matter* (Dewey, 1902/1971, p. 22), Shulman can also be seen as justifying the existence of education departments in the face of criticism from other academics. Unfortunately his paper, and the many subsequent ones drawing on it for inspiration and support, have failed to quell the voices of critics who proclaim that knowing the subject is sufficient for teaching it. This is despite the fact that as long ago as Aristotle the term *master* (probably the origin of current 'masters' degrees and the use of 'master' to refer to teachers in some schools in the past) was used to distinguish between someone who had learned and someone who had gone beyond the mere learning of subject matter so as to be equipped to teach it. Although Shulman does not mention it explicitly, in order to psychologise the subject matter it is necessary to be up to date both with the subject matter and the psychology of current learners, so the assumption that ongoing study of and engagement in mathematical thinking is unnecessary for alert and effective teaching is just as short-sighted and impoverished as overlooking the difference between studying content and being informed about teaching.

Paolo Boero and Elda Guala add to Shulman's categories the *cultural analysis of content*, which includes both awareness of how mathematics, being a cultural domain, can be arranged and presented according to epistemological, socio-cultural and psychological interests, and how it interacts with other cultural domains. Jill Adler and Danielle Huillet use discourses developed by Bernstein (1996, 2000) and Chevallard (1987, 1992) to provide a theoretical basis for re-formulating PCK and its related constructs in terms of an anthropological theory of individual and institutional relationships with practices and concepts, and contrasting types of discourse (hierarchical, strong and weak grammars).

PCK and its extensions attempt to bridge a gap between knowing for oneself and supporting others in coming to know as well. This fits nicely alongside the Vygotsky articulation of development as converting 'acting in oneself' (when triggered or cued) into 'acting for oneself' (initiating an action oneself) (Valsiner, 1988; van der Veer & Valsiner, 1991) which goes beyond Dewey's notion of making use of the current actions and concerns of children (Dewey 1913). What seems to be difficult, as the chapters in this volume show, is to put into words precisely what it is that guides and directs expert teacher behaviour, that is, how teachers come to act 'for themselves' rather than simply 'in themselves', expressed practically while remaining theoretically and philosophically well founded.

Doug Clarke reminds us of the many slips between cup and lip concerning teaching. At one end of the spectrum spanned by the institution of education there is an ideal education imagined by policy makers. This is transformed into an intended or planned curriculum, and then by textbook authors into a presented curriculum. This in turn is implemented and enacted by teachers, which in turn is experienced by learners. Learners are then tested both by teachers and by external agencies (an achieved curriculum), the results often being mistaken for evidence about attainment of the ideal, the implemented or the experienced curriculum. Since there can be so much more that happens for learners than is revealed by what they are tested on, there is also a maturing or interiorised curriculum which develops over time, visible more often than not only through narrated memories, because the more fully something is integrated into a person's functioning, the less visible it is likely to be, even when they are probed about the reasons for their choices.

Tim Rowland concentrates on methodological issues arising when a team of researchers probes novice teachers' use of their mathematical understanding. Using video records of novice teachers' teaching, researchers attempt to locate some of the kinds of mathematical choices being made, to trace some of their origins, and to uncover major influences on those choices. There is an increasing interest internationally in this kind of research in order to validate assumptions about effective teacher education and professional development and to inform further research, viz. ICMI 15th Study Conference (Ball & Even, 2005); Oberwolfach meeting (Ufer, 2007); ICMI Meeting (Ball & Grevholm, 2008) much of which is summarised by Graeber and Tirosh.

Helen Foragasz and Gilah Leder review research concerning beliefs as a significant attribute of the psyche which mediates practices and modulates what is attended to. Beliefs about the nature of mathematics; about its purpose in society, in the curriculum, and in students' lives; about how it is done, and learned; about what supports and fosters mathematical thinking; about what students are capable of; about the person's own competencies, dispositions, self-efficacy and identity; and about the opinions of others (particularly peers) all appear to play a role in influencing classroom and homework activity. When alignments and misalignments between parents, teachers and learners are included, the whole becomes a highly complex domain of interactions. What is certain is that whatever the construct 'beliefs' is taken to include, they are dynamic and evolving, sometimes in relatively stable configurations, and sometimes highly unstable.

Yeping Li, Yunpeng Ma and Jeonsgsuk Pang describe various practices in the preparation of prospective elementary teachers in China and Korea. This leads them to probe the nature of teacher PCK by comparing and contrasting both systems of teacher education and self-reports of sample participants in those systems. They highlight an ongoing divide between content courses and methods courses which is also a dominant feature of teacher education in North America and elsewhere, though not in England, Australia or New Zealand, among others (see Stacey this volume). They also reveal interesting self-reported weaknesses in teacher understanding of the published curriculum in both China and Korea, and in teacher knowledge about when and how topics are taught in earlier years. Their report distinguishes between teachers carrying out a mathematical calculation (comparing the result of dividing one fraction by two different fractions) and teachers articulating how they would explain to students by calling upon procedural or conceptual justification. They are led to challenge the assumption that most teachers in mainland China have a profound understanding of fundamental mathematics, at least as exposed in response to their probes. When combined with Rowland's chapter, fundamental problems arise in reliably researching the region between mathematical and didactical-pedagogical knowing.

Shiqi Li, Rongjin Huang, and Hyunyong Shin describe practices in the preparation of secondary teachers in China and Korea. They note that in Confucian

Cultures heavily influenced by Marxist elements of the Soviet Union the aim of education is "to transmit the most stable knowledge accumulated over the past thousands of years" to young generations. This is in line with the Chinese notion of teaching which is "to transmit, instruct, and disabuse". Recent political changes have brought about a transformation of education, with mathematics seen as contributing to economic progress as well as training the mind. Teacher education is dominated by the perceived need for a profound mathematical understanding, with pedagogy having a lower profile. In China, mathematics courses for teachers are being redesigned to integrate geometrical and algebraic thinking. In Korea, recent recognition of the value of integrating mathematics and pedagogy for prospective secondary teachers has been acknowledged.

Anne Cockburn compares the ways in which four different teacher education programmes, one in a Middle Eastern context, two in the U.K. and one in a continental European context, set about providing opportunities for novice teachers to demonstrate and develop the various types of knowing and 'being' associated with PCK. A range of devices are used, from stimulus to explore and research beyond the institutionalised course material, self-audits, presentations to and with peers, essays, examinations and government tests. Despite the claim that 'prospective teachers trade performance for grades' (Doyle, 1979), it seems that the assessment instruments did influence the perspectives if not the practices of some at least of the graduates of the programmes. Cockburn emphasises that the prospective teachers may sometimes exchange performance for grades, but that they are also driven by wanting to be successful as teachers. How prospective teachers can be suitably and reliably assessed for professionalism remains an on-going issue.

In his analysis of the usefulness of the distinction between CK and PCK, Mike Askew notes that research evidence for a strong correlation between the two, certainly at primary level, is difficult to find. What people have mostly focused on is based on a deficit model to try to account for perceived deficits in learning. His research has led him to a different way of conceptualising the basis for effective pedagogic choices made by primary teachers, to do with sensibility – for rather than knowledge – of mathematics. He builds on the argument that not only is teaching a profession concerning care of and for learners, but also care of and for mathematics as well. Effective teachers have a relationship of curiosity and enquiry. Instead of 'death by a thousand bullet points' induced by lists of 'things teachers need to know', teachers could be best supported by re-awakening their curiosity and natural disposition to enquire, and to engage them in mathematical exploration. Put another way, awareness is not the same as the aggregation of a lot of facts and procedural fluencies, which in turn is redolent of the 18th century observation that 'a succession of experiences does not add up to an experience of that succession'. A different level or type of awareness is required (Mason, 1998).

Kaye Stacey considers preparation of secondary teachers, noting that in common with the use of mathematics in other fields, what is required is a 'productive interplay between what the teacher knows about mathematics [and] what the teacher knows about students and curriculum'. This includes task analysis, example construction, student propensities and so on. She uses international data to compare and contrast different systems along many different dimensions. Four dimensions are distinguished: mathematical content and desirable qualities of this knowledge; experiencing mathematics in action, going back to Pólya (1962); knowing about mathematics through its history, changing epistemologies and philosophies; and knowing how to learn mathematics through pedagogic strategies. Through a comprehensive analysis, Stacey reveals problematic aspects of each dimension in attempts at implementation, especially when there are teacher shortages.

Ulla Runesson adopts Ference Marton's approach to the lived experience of learners, in which what is learned is the making of new distinctions by discerning variation, and becoming aware of new relationships and properties. So by clarifying precisely what it is that is to be learned, it is possible to provide learners with appropriate variation of significant features (dimensions of possible variation) within sufficient proximity in time and space so that the variation is likely to be detected. Runesson reports on comparison studies focusing on what is varied and in what ways, so that learners can detect variation and so assimilate the consequences. Her case studies provide evidence that where a feature is varied suitably, learners give evidence of assimilating that variation in their own behaviour subsequently.

The emerging picture of mathematics in and for teaching is of an immensely complex domain involving the interaction of multiple factors. Mathematics itself as a disciplined mode of enquiry and as a collection of techniques and concepts, didactical tactics, pedagogic strategies, historical-socio-cultural and personal-psychological forces all contribute both core sensitivities and obstacles which have epistemological, affective and behavioural components. Institutionalisation, in the form of privileged discourses and relationships forms an ecological environment. As with many concepts in education taken up by mathematics educators, and as demonstrated in each of the chapters in this volume, PCK as a technical term does not draw a clear and definitive distinction.

In the following sections I suggest that if the term *PCK* is used as a checklist of qualities, quantities and dimensions, it will only serve to obscure what is essential and central. It may even contribute to making the challenges of teacher education more difficult than they already are, by appearing to make things simpler, especially to policy makers.

REFLECTION AND TRANSFORMATION

Instead of seeing *PCK* or mathematics in and for teaching as a checklist, it can be used as a reminder, as a means of literally re-minding through bringing back to attention that knowing. Even knowing and doing mathematics does not in itself equip someone to teach effectively. Even knowing and doing mathematics and knowing about the pedagogic and historical-philosophical and socio-cultural influences is not enough to be an effective teacher. Just as learners need to be prompted to stand back from activity which arises from engaging in mathematical tasks if they are to become efficiently aware of the significance of that activity, so teachers similarly benefit in the effectiveness of their practices if they are prompted to draw back from the action of teaching and to reflect, contemplate, and analyse as part of preparing for the future.

Drawing back, or reflecting, as it is often labelled, is itself a complex action. If it is to be at all effective, it has to be much more than revisiting the highlights, much more than regretting the low points, and much more than resolving to 'do better'. It has to include trying to get a bigger picture, trying to see the wood instead of the individual trees. For example, specific incidents can be turned into phenomena by linking them to other incidents from the past and to possible similar incidents in the future. This hind and fore sight can usefully be linked to actions that it would be desirable to have come to mind, whether something that worked recently, or an alternative to something that did not 'work'. Reflection is most effective when it turns into 'pro-flection', that is, imagining something similar happening in the future and acting in some desirable or preferred way. This is how change and development is fostered and sustained. Effective professional development in whatever sphere of activity involves recognition of specific actions which could be undertaken in the future, and it is enhanced when the fundamental power of imagination is used to prepare the way (Mason, 2002). Theories and principles are all very well, but remain as abstractions until teachers can imagine themselves putting them into action.

Transformations

Each transformation from the imagined curriculum to the interiorised curriculum involves people making choices of what to stress or fore-ground, and what consequently to back-ground or even ignore. Usually carried out as a top-down process, each stage involves developing more detail in order to exemplify articulated generalities until reaching the specificities of classroom practice and learner experience. Once the learner has been inveigled into activity, it is necessary to learn from that experience, a process which seems to require explicit action more often than not. In order to foster and promote learning from experience, it is necessary that teachers are sensitive to, or aware of, what it is they are trying to achieve, the 'object(s) of learning'. This is in contrast to, for example, teachers who have been heard to say "the author's job is to teach; my job is to make it enjoyable for students".

Each stage of the transformation of curriculum also involves a problematic transformation not unlike the *didactic transposition* identified by Yves Chevallard (1985) in which expert awareness is transposed into instruction in behaviour (specifications of what to do). Nowhere is this more obvious than when teachers have enjoyed an experience of working on mathematics for themselves with colleagues. Because they want to share that experience with their learners, they construct worksheets which guide and direct learners through the 'exploration'. This is where a richly conceived *PCK* could come into play, but where a checklist perspective transposes the experience into something altogether different. For some reason it is difficult for teachers in these circumstances to bring themselves to relax constraints and trust their learners to get on with mathematical exploration using their natural sense-making powers; instead they feel a need to control and direct. In other words, it is easy to think that what you did is what others need to do in order to have the same experience, even if you also acknowledge that others cannot have 'the same experience'. And so worksheets are devised which drive learners through actions which previously arose spontaneously for the teacher. Sometimes, despite the transposition, learners get a taste of mathematical thinking and mathematics in the making, but often they do not.

The force of a collection of articulated requirements, such as in a curriculum, is to direct attention to checklists and away from being, from awareness. Instead of allowing themselves to 'be mathematical with and in front of their learners' teachers feel forced into controlling learner attention through short-term goals involving direct instruction and rehearsal of procedures.

SENSITIVITY AND AWARENESSES

My aim in this section is to try to probe beneath and beyond the PCK as a formulation of knowledge and beliefs, by adopting the language of sensitivities and awarenesses. I use the term 'awareness' in the sense of Caleb Gattegno (1987) to refer both to conscious and to unconscious actions integrated into psycho-somatic functioning. The section begins with an attempt to put this discourse in context, followed by some examples of what is being approached, and then some development of theoretical aspects arising from the other chapters in this volume.

Acknowledging Others

Many authors have tried to articulate the essence or core of topics, and the difficulty in doing so is reflected in the multitude of discourses which then arise. Different labels signal different foci of attention, stressing or foregrounding different aspects without denying others which are backgrounded.

Several authors have made use of metaphors involving a journey involving continuity, movement and terrain, in trying to describe how teachers might envisage their learners' growth of mathematical experience and appreciation. For example, Marty Simon (1995) used the term 'hypothetical learning trajectories' as a metaphor for how teachers imagine students developing as they encounter and move through a mathematical domain. James Greeno (1991) referred to learning number as more like getting to know a landscape than a linear journey, and Catharine Fosnot and Maarten Dolk (2002) refer to 'landscapes of learning' in preference to learning trajectories (see Clements, 2002 for a review of various ways that the construct has been interpreted). Marian Small (2004) refers to 'developmental continua' as a version of 'learning trajectories' which are used both to describe the process of development of mathematical ideas, and as hypothetical constructs to prompt teachers to plan sequences of lessons rather than working on a lesson by lesson basis. Using this metaphor, teachers need to be familiar with the landscape of each mathematical topic, being able, through listening to and watching learners in action, to recognise what aspects of the landscape might benefit from more attention.

It is not completely clear that learning can be either continuous, or a smooth ride. The 'staircase' metaphor of carefully planned steps whereby the learner ascends the mountain of knowledge surely belongs to past eras rather than the present. Even so, as a metaphor it is preserved in the images evoked in the language of knowledge being 'accumulated' or 'acquired', and in the specification of levels through which learners are supposed to progress. Rather, at various points there are shifts of perspective and attention to be made, somewhat akin to phase transition in physics: increase in energy usually results in rise in temperature but there are phase transitions where no increase takes place while the 'state' changes. Barbara Clarke (this handbook) uses the term 'growth points' to refer to times when learners are on the edge of making a shift in mathematical perspective or appreciation. Marty Simon (2006) refers to 'key developmental understanding' to refer to the underlying core awarenesses around which competence, fluency, facility, understanding and appreciation coagulate. He and his colleagues (Simon et al., 2004; Simon & Tzur, 2004) challenge the simplistic version of pedagogical sequencing in which learners are 'taught what they do not yet know', by pointing out that what is required is that learners become aware of the relationship between their actions (prompted by tasks) and the effects of those actions, so as to accommodate new concepts through modification of actions in order to meet fresh challenges.

In seeking to articulate the essence of a mathematical topic, Gattegno (1987) based his science of education on a complex notion of awareness (which need not be conscious). John Mason elaborated this into a three-fold framework based on the classical structure of the psyche (Mason, Volume 4) which was manifested in Griffin and Gates (1989) and re-articulated in Mason and Johnston-Wilder, 2004/2006) as 'the structure of a topic'. This was designed to augment and extend the notion of 'concept images' (Tall & Vinner, 1981). It focuses specifically on features of individual topics around which the language of technical terms, techniques and their associated incantations, generating problems and contexts in which the topic appears, concept images, examples and obstacles all cluster. In this perspective, teachers are engaged in an ongoing refinement of their articulation of the key elements of each and every topic they teach, though it is not often that systematic records are kept so as to inform preparation and planning in the future. This is one place where mathematics education seen as a disciplined mode of enquiry could support the development of prospective and serving teachers by supporting them in 'collecting data' in a structured format.

Dvora Peretz (2006) usefully distinguishes between latitudinal understanding which involves both contextualised and de-contextualised familiarity, and depth of understanding, which is commonly described in terms of levels. She also points out that understanding can be described as an ongoing process, and as an act, but she urges maintaining complexity rather than being drawn into ever more distinctions. Brent Davis and Elaine Simmt (2006) attempt to maintain the complexity of teaching mathematics, but nevertheless distinguish four embedded and recursively similar dynamical aspects: mathematical objects, curriculum structures, classroom collectivity and subjective understanding.

Liping Ma (1999) makes use of a simpler construct, namely 'knowledge packages': 'given a topic, a teacher tends to see other topics related to its learning' and such topics comprise the knowledge package for the topic to be taught constituting profound understanding of fundamental mathematics (Ma, 1999, p. 118). Using this articulation, teachers need a profound understanding of fundamental mathematical concepts in order to make informed choices when planning and when interacting with learners. Here the emphasis appears to be on the mathematics but it includes knowledge of both didactic tactics and pedagogical strategies.

Doug Clarke also draws attention to the notion of 'the big ideas' in various topics (Papert, 1980). These are the core or main ideas around which the topic is clustered. A related notion is that of 'mathematical habits of mind' (Cuoco, Goldenberg, & Mark, 1996) which meshes nicely with the five strands of understanding described by Kilpatrick et al. (2001). What these contribute to PCK is like an all embracing and sustaining 'field' of influence which can inform teacher choices both when planning and when interacting.

In an attempt to delineate various aspects so as to be able both to inform policy making and to enable more focused research, PCK has been approached as a bridge between mathematics and teaching by considering common content knowledge (CCK), specialised content knowledge (SCK), knowledge of content and students (KCS) and knowledge of content and teaching, with the addition of knowledge of the mathematics horizon and knowledge of the curriculum (Ball & Bass, 2006); Hill, Rowan, Ball, & Bass 2005), as in the diagram:

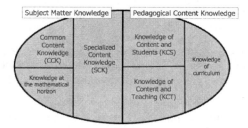

Figure 1. Taken from Bass et al. (2007).

Each technical term discerns and adds to the overall picture a subtle aspect which is marginalised or obscured by others. When PCK is perceived as dominantly psychological, it leads to a metaphor of teachers accumulating sufficient knowledge to have useful actions 'come to mind' when planning for and when running sessions with learners. When PCK is perceived as dominantly social, it leads to a metaphor of distributed cognition in which teachers draw upon knowledge distributed in the historical-cultural-social and institutional practices, in the texts, work-cards, apparatus and other materials available, and in the physical and affective milieu co-constructed with the learners. A more encompassing articulation may be more useful (Ruthven 2007). What comes to mind as possible actions is triggered by and resonated with a myriad of external factors in relation to personal sensitivities and awarenesses. These forces are not simply additive, but have complex interactions (Mason, Volume 4).

Each technical term introduced into the literature promotes the discernment of a subtle aspect which may be marginalised or obscured by other terms, and so adds to an overall picture of increasing complexity. It should not be surprising that it is difficult to pin down the essence and scope of a topic, because what is sought lies somewhere on or over the border between the explicit and conscious and the implicit, tacit and unconscious. It is precisely in this border territory that creativity is possible, through metaphoric resonances and idiosyncratic metonymic associations. If every topic could be completely articulated and captured, learning and living would be entirely mechanical, merely a matter of checklists. It is the presence in human beings with will and intentions, factored through complex psyche (see Mason, Volume 4) which makes education so important as well as so difficult.

Examples

Mathematics education, in common with mathematics, makes most progress when paradigmatic examples are provided through which it is possible to re-generalise for oneself. Here then are some examples which could be thought of as knowledge and beliefs, as awarenesses and sensitivities, and as assumptions and principles. In the sense of Boero and Guala, these arise from cultural analysis of content.

> In respect of counting on: awareness that a counting word is also the cardinality of a collection; sensitivity to the proceptual nature of this awareness (Gray & Tall, 1994).

> In respect of linear equations: equations are a statement of a constraint on the coordinates of sets of points; sensitivity to the need for multiple exposures to the dual presentation of equations as symbolic objects and as graphical objects.

> In respect of algebraic expressions: expressions can be seen as a rule or formula for calculating an answer, as the answer, as an expression of generality, and as an expression involving as-yet-unknown quantities; sensitivity to the need for continued exposure to these multiple ways of perceiving expressions, and to the value of learners expressing for themselves.

> In respect of decimals: each 'decimal place' has an associated value, so decimal notation is a short-form for a sum; sensitivity to the obstacle of inappropriate language use within and without the classroom (naming 0.12 simply as "oh point twelve").

In respect of multiplication: it arises from at least ten different types of actions (Davis & Simmt, 2006; see also Vergnaud, 1983).

In respect of mathematics generally: what learners say and do is rarely wilful and usually principled; sensitivity to 'buggy algorithms' (Brown & van Lehn, 1980; van Lehn, 1989).

These examples are necessarily summary and selective. It is the role of mathematics educators not just to elaborate and communicate expanded versions of these, but to work with teachers on how they can educate their awareness of these sorts of aspects of mathematical topics.

One common feature of these examples is that they do not involve technique, but rather are aimed at underlying awareness which may be manifested as 'theorems-in-action' (Vergnaud, 1981; 1997), may be succinctly articulated, or may be on some spectrum in between. But they can still be interpreted from several different stances. For example, a predominant stance currently sees teaching as about procedures and concepts which are believed to be learned by learners generalising from examples (worked examples of procedures, examples of concepts). One implication is that teachers need to have access to a range of examples and be aware of different obstacles to trying to learn from examples (for example, using variation theory, Runesson, this volume). They also need to be aware of successive processes of generalisation that need to take place for learners, and ways to provoke these. A different stance could be that learners actually learn by construing phenomena, and that practice to mastery is efficiently achieved by promoting explorations in which learners naturally construct examples and as a by-product of specialising for themselves, use procedures they need to rehearse, in order to re-generalise for themselves. Another stance could be based on shifts in epistemology and in the structure of attention required in order to appreciate the mathematical topic.

Although it is important for teachers to have a sense of what is available to be experienced and learned when they design, select, and present mathematical tasks, it is vital that they are aware that experience alone does not ensure learning, that learning is not like climbing a staircase step by step, as elaborated earlier. Furthermore, mathematics is most efficiently and effectively learned when students are provoked into using and developing their own powers of sense-making rather than having authors and teachers trying to do this for them. If teachers are aware that students often go through periods of mathematical 'babble' (Ainley, 1999; Malara, 2003; Berger, 2004) as they struggle to articulate and crystallise their experience, then they are more likely to arrange to 'keep the students immersed in the task long enough' (James & Mason, 1982) to enable them to reach some reasonably coherent articulation from which they can reconstruct the concepts and techniques when needed in the future.

JOHN MASON

Seeking an Essential Core of Mathematical Topics

In order to probe more deeply into the essential core of a mathematical topic, it is very tempting indeed to provide labels, to make distinctions and to add aspects. While aiding precision, it also contributes to the growth and profusion of discourses. An example of an often neglected aspect is raised by Doug Clarke who emphasises the need for realistic expectations of learners, both as individuals and as a group. Like many other awarenesses or sensitivities, this is a delicate matter. On the one hand there is no point in embarking on something that is going to alienate several or all of the group. On the other hand, the greatest obstacle to student learning is expectations, as manifested by teachers, by themselves and peers, and by their parents. If "didn't" (as in "I didn't get the answer") or 'won't' (as in "they won't be able to …") is allowed to turn into "can't", it can be a long road back (Dweck, 2000). If students are not challenged to reach beyond what they can do comfortably, they will not undertake the modification of familiar actions which is necessary in order to develop further. As Robert Browning put it in his poem *Andrea del Sarto* (L 97), "Ah, but a man's reach should exceed his grasp, or what's a heaven for?" Where teachers' expectations are challenged and extended, possibilities both for teaching and for learning are opened up. As Clarke reports, expectations can be higher at the end of a period of collaborative professional development than before.

Imagined actions influence articulation which reflects perception and orientation which privilege imaginable actions. For example, trying to 'ensure' or 'guarantee' learning is likely to draw upon a mechanistic metaphor involving goals and goal-seeking behaviour with an underlying assumption about rationality, reason, and consistency which is hard to credit to most human beings most of the time. This is compatible with checklists, levels, and staging points, and is nicely compatible with centralised control of teaching. Unfortunately there is a chasm between mechanistic delivery of curricula, and the lived experience of classrooms. The flip side is treating students and teachers as creative and trustworthy agents who will respond to opportunities to grow and develop, to meet challenges and to 'think outside the box' if they are respected and trusted. But the balance between these is delicate, and unstable: as soon as trust is abused, it is temptingly natural to impose control, and so to begin a slippery descent into more and more constraints; once control is established and power exercised, it is very hard to let go of, because letting go seems to lead to unstable conditions and so controls are re-imposed. The metaphor of a ball perched on an upturned salad bowl is apposite: any slight disturbance and the ball falls off, unable to return to its previous stability.

Approaching essence from the point of view of the mathematical topic, each mathematical topic (at school and early university) arises because a class of problems has been resolved, and the methods used are deemed teachable. Thus to bring the core sensitivities to mind is to reconstruct a route from

a collection of problems which prompted the original search for a solution;

through being aware of technical language especially where it uses otherwise familiar words but in possibly unfamiliar ways;

through concept images (Tall & Vinner, 1981), examples and ways of thinking associated with technical terms introduced;

through techniques and methods devised to resolve the class of problems;

through being aware of obstacles encountered by students, both epistemological obstacles requiring a shift of perspective and attention, and pedagogical obstacles arising from previous and current teaching;

to a sense of various other contexts in which the topic has arisen.

Justifications for and elaboration of these way-markers can be found in (Griffin & Gates, 1988; see also Mason & Johnston-Wilder, 2004/2006, 2005). Each contributes an aspect of the topic related to a prominent part of the human psyche (see Mason, Volume 4).

Approaching essence from the point of view of mathematical thinking, each task, interaction, and aspect of a topic can be related to the ways in which mathematical heuristics (Pólya, 1962; Schoenfeld, 1985), habits of mind (Cuoco, 1996), mathematical thinking (Mason et al., 1982) and mathematical themes (Mason & Johnston-Wilder, 2004) are brought to the surface and made use of by learners, not just by the teacher and text-author.

Approaching essence from the point of view of didactic tactics, the choice of tasks, modes of (re)presentation, and metaphor-analogies draws upon experience of teaching and of learning the particular topic, the particular concepts and the particular techniques (Rowland this volume).

Approaching essence from the point of view of mathematical pedagogy, various frameworks highlight useful distinctions which can be used to structure interactions with learners so as to enrich encounters with mathematical concepts and techniques as fully as possible (Mason & Johnston-Wilder, 2004/2006).

Approaching essence from the point of view of the lived experience of learners, attention is directed to what is being varied and in what ways, and how the consequent shifts of attention can be supported so as to be accommodated and integrated into learner functioning (Runesson, this volume). Attention is also directed to how learners' powers are being evoked and provoked so as to amplify their disposition to engage with mathematics productively.

Approaching essence from a historical-socio-cultural point of view, each topic is a manifestation of forces, investments and concerns (Boere & Guala, this volume).

Essence, then, depends on what is stressed or privileged. Essence is not an atomic 'thing', a pearl to be extracted from the shell of mathematical topics. Rather it is an amorphous conglomeration of all of the above approaches. The 'knowledge' and 'beliefs' referred to in the literature are, in my view at least, impoverished generalisations which, like the oyster shell, look innocuous and bland, whereas inside there is multi-coloured mother-of-pearl. The effects of basing behaviour on privileging mathematics, as in these approaches, which value and relate to the diversity of idiosyncratic variations of individuals, are in contrast

313

with effects of privileging cultural and social organisation and interaction. Of course effective behaviour will make use of the power of both collaborative and competitive interaction, but organisation of interaction follows and arises from the mathematical core, whereas mathematics often fails to arise or follow from organised social interaction which is not also centred in mathematics.

MECHANISM, ACTION AND CHOICE

One of the avowed purposes of trying to detail teacher knowledge and beliefs is to inform the search for mechanisms whereby teachers manage to influence learners. Teaching consists of acts in which actions involving learners are initiated. If control of those actions is retained by the teacher, there is less opportunity for those actions to involve learners sufficiently to produce any lasting transformation in their perspective, cognition, affect or future behaviour. The many-hued 'constructivist' discourse is centred on transformation of the individual and of the group, but if the teacher is unaware of the kinds of transformation which are possible, they may not even pursue or sustain actions, much less notice opportunities to initiate important actions. Thus Vygotskian discourse stresses the difference between scientific and natural knowledge, the former requiring specific teaching. Underpinning this 'knowledge' are shifts in the structure of attention and shifts in epistemological preferences. For example, shifting from basing validation of mathematics in experiences in the material world, to basing it on mathematical structural reasoning is non-trivial for many, especially when the material world is over-stressed for so long before the shift is initiated. These sorts of shifts, located through 'cultural analyses of content' (Boero & Guala, this volume) are likely to be central for the aim of teacher education and professional development.

It may easily be that the very notion of 'mechanism' with its associated sense of 'cause-and-effect' is completely inappropriate in the context of education, where the forces acting are products of human psyche, including will, attention, cognition, affect and behaviour, unlike machines. The metaphor of 'forces' which underpins much of the discourse in this area is itself open to question. Are social forces to be seen like forces in physics, adding up to some resultant force? If so, then what is needed is a delineation of the strength and direction of those forces so that the resultant can be predicted. But perhaps the 'forces' are more like chemical reagents. These actually transform and combine with each other to form new reagents. The combination is no simple addition but something much more complex; the final whole is not the sum of its original parts. Other metaphors are also possible, such as an environmental-biological one in which change is endemic and responses evolve over time.

A mechanistic view is amplified by and a product of an approach to assessment of teacher expertise in terms of knowledge (as manifested in essays and examinations). Anne Cockburn quotes Doyle (1979) as describing what happens when assessment is allowed to dominate instruction, as learners "exchange performance for grades". In other words, the learners' task is to work out the institutionalised responses to institutional probes (in the discourse of Chevallard from Adler & Huillet, this volume). Not only are learners impelled to develop facility in procedures, but novice teachers are impelled to gargle the discourse in the form of theoretical constructs privileged by their educators.

A mechanistic view supports training teachers in behaviours to be manifested in front of children; a holistic view supports fostering in teachers awareness of their own mental and physical states so that they are empowered to choose to be mathematical both with and in front of their learners. A mechanistic view presumes a degree of rationality and uniformity that simply does not match lived experience. Choices are rarely made rationally, especially when encountered in the flow of teaching. The very notion of 'choice' is complicated.

Choice Making

How and when are choices made? A rationalist position is that choices are made in every moment by the 'I' that dominates discourse. A phenomenological position observes that what look like choices or potential choices are either the working out of habits, that is, of choices made long in the past, or reactions triggered by associations and assumptions, most of which function below the level of consciousness.

Teachers are constantly evaluating the situation as they perceive it, both in planning and in engaging with learners. As anyone who has observed a lesson being taught knows only too well, there are numerous moments when the observer notices opportunities that the teacher does not exploit. This leads to the assumption that the teacher is making choices moment by moment. Attempts to probe those moments more closely led Kathleen McNair (1978a, 1978b) to use what came to be called 'stimulated recall' by showing teachers a video of a lesson soon after the lesson, and inviting them to comment on what strikes them, and to try to elaborate on what they were thinking at certain moments of interest to the researcher. This technique continues in use in many projects currently both with teachers and with learners.

In responding to these stimulated recall probes, teachers call upon various theories, abstractions, principles and discourses. For example, "they needed to spend more time manipulating" could be taken as a reference to three modes of representation (Bruner, 1966) and the principle that sufficient experience of physically manipulating objects is required before learners begin to internalise the action so that they can imagine it rather than doing it, before moving to symbols to (re)present that action. Taken at face value, the terms used and the principles invoked provide a rationale for their actions, and so indicate the basis for their choices.

However the situation is rather more complicated. As responsible people, it is considered culturally essential to be able to respond (literally, to justify) with explanations of our actions. The assumption that it is necessary to be able to justify and explain actions by reference to principles or theories presupposes that the explanations correspond to what actually happens. However, human beings are 'narrative animals' (Bruner, 1996): consciousness is an ongoing story told by individuals, drawing on narrative practices of communities in which they participate and are immersed. But the purpose of narratives is as much for self-calming and preservation of agency and identity (reaffirmation of the 'I') as anything else (Ouspensky, 1950). Thus it is felt to be essential to construct a story, especially when probed, yet that story may have little to do with the actual lived experience. Furthermore, continued pressure to tell stories to account for actions may actually lend credence to the mistaken assumption that such stories are actually descriptive.

Part of the narrative arising from being 'responsible' is that behavioural practices are initiated, sustained and completed by some guiding principles. If only the principles can be located, together with the mechanism(s) whereby these determine behaviour, professional development and behaviour modification would be straightforward. Close inspection of experience suggests that many of our actions are in fact habitual and automatic, triggered by metonymic associations and metaphoric resonances. Indeed, it has been proposed that consciousness itself as a generator of behaviour is an illusion (Nørretranders, 1998). Thus the search for mechanism only makes sense for situations in which people are acting mechanically, out of habit. Put another way, most of the time we are operating on automatic pilot, guided by pre-established patterns. In these circumstances, Skinner's stimulus-response theories and practices are both apposite and effective for making predictions. Of course it is necessary to function on automatic much of the time, as it is impossible to consider carefully multiple options and to make a reasoned choice at every moment. However, when will is factored in, acting as it does through dispositions with affective, enactive and cognitive dimensions, the metaphor of mechanism (presumably going back to Descartes' entrancement with the cuckoo clock), becomes at best suspect and at worst inappropriate for predicting the impulses acting when fresh choices are made, when a lesson switches from automatic working out of established patterns, to engagement with fundamental ideas, with ways of thinking and acting, and with core mathematical awarenesses.

An alternative to being 'responsible' is to transform it into 'being responsible', with emphasis on the 'being'. Boero and Guala move in this direction by stressing mathematics as a cultural domain which is entered and absorbed, like any culture, through participation. Not only are institutional practices acquired, whether through peripheral participation or direct instruction and training, but that extra human element that is so hard to articulate has a chance to emerge, manifested in the 'being' of the teachers. The more that educators can 'be mathematically-pedagogically-didactically aware, with and in front of novice teachers' the more likely it is that those novices will develop in wisdom as well as in knowledge, in 'being' as well as in expertise. To achieve this, it will be to their advantage to engage in 'cultural analysis of content'.

For these reasons, trying to trap choice-making, and to establish the grounds for those choices is exceedingly difficult. As a first approximation only, the theories, principles and discourses drawn upon in narratives in order to explain actions after the fact can be taken as at best an indicator of what comes to mind when a response is demanded, even if these may not be driving behaviour in the first place. Perhaps this goes some way to account for differences between the responses to probes recorded by Yeping Li and colleagues on the one hand, and Ma (1999) on the other. As consumers of research, educators also have theories and values which dispose them to accept or challenge the findings of colleagues.

An alternative, phenomenological approach to choice-making is to stimulate teachers to work on developing their mathematical being: how they respond to being stuck on a problem; how they respond to incomplete, inappropriate, or incoherent conjectures and guesses from learners; how they work with others to get them to conjecture and convince, to stimulate them to use their natural powers of mathematical sense making; how they are alive to possible avenues of enquiry through extending, varying and generalising; and how they connect mathematical topics together through the use of heuristics and mathematical themes. Then, as complex beings, they can manifest that being with and in front of learners, sensitive to the ways in which learners can be stimulated to make use of their own powers both individually and collectively.

Knowing

Another way of casting these observations about the mechanisms of choice is in terms of knowing. People can 'know-that' the pedagogic and didactic literature concerning a mathematical topic has found certain results through research; they can 'know-how' to act in a theoretical sort of way; they can 'know-why' certain tasks might be more effective than others, or know-why certain ways of organising the classroom or interacting with learners might be more effective than others. All of these constitute 'knowing-about' and can be tested by essay writing or multiple-guess probes of one sort or another. But as all teacher education programmes demonstrate through the importance of practicums (school-based practice), these are at best preliminaries to 'knowing-to' act in the moment, to having a suitable idea come to mind when it might be appropriate, to being mathematically sensitive as Mike Askew puts it.

One of the reasons that it is easier for someone observing a lesson to pick out possible 'choice-moments' than for the teacher is that observers are not under pressure to act. They do not have the tunnel vision which is integral to engaging in action, especially when in the role of initiating action. For example, it is easy to be aware of your breathing, of other people's postures, of reasons for acting in certain ways, of possible ways to proceed etc. when sitting watching or listening. It is much more difficult once you start talking, because the act of talking absorbs attention.

The aim of teacher education is to prepare the ground so that novice teachers will find themselves increasingly sensitised to noticing possibilities for initiating, sustaining or completing actions which they might not previously have had come to mind. This brings us back to the basis for those choices: mathematics, mathematical didactics (tactics pertinent to a particular topic) and mathematical pedagogy (strategies pertinent to many different topics and to fostering and sustaining mathematical thinking generally).

In order to support and sustain growth of mathematical being it is necessary that teachers develop as autonomous actors with sensitivity both to their own awarenesses and to the states of learners, mediated by such curricular forces as actually impinge on their practice. Guided by values and dispositions, it is vital to be neither so solipsistic as to treat everyone like themselves, nor so altruistic that they lose contact with their own appreciation of the structural necessities of mathematics.

Where classroom organisation and learner interaction has been stressed in preference to mathematics, attention is likely to remain there. When asked why they acted in some way at some moment, teachers will tend to refer at first to organisational matters, whether of a general pedagogic nature, or, when pressed, of a mathematical pedagogical nature. Typical discourses which might be employed include generating discussion, promoting conjecturing, and perhaps, provoking proving. Where mathematical being has been stressed and become the generator of actions, teacher attention is more likely to be centred on the development of learners' mathematical powers and habits of mind, and use of mathematical heuristics and themes. There will be explicit concern about the mathematical object of learning, rather than vague and generalised passing reference to the mathematical topic.

Put another way, where mathematical being is developing, attention will be on the specific didactical issues of specific topics, with pedagogical issues concerning classroom organisation and social interaction called upon to serve a greater aim.

PROBING

How can one probe beneath the surface of classroom practice to determine what influences the choices that appear to be being made? This is a non-trivial question. Although experienced teachers, as with experts in any field, are able to discern details and recognise relationships which are usually overlooked by less experienced observers, it is difficult to articulate what it is that is being noticed, even more difficult to describe the basis for that noticing, and even more difficult still to try to sensitise novices to make similar distinctions. The use of technical terms in any discipline, certainly in mathematics, and particularly in mathematics education, is a sign that the author makes distinctions which are considered to be significant. Whereas in mathematics the interplay between definition, examples and use in context is usually adequate to achieve consensus in the use of the technical term by a community, in mathematics education it is more difficult to achieve agreement as to the criteria for making distinctions. The notion of PCK is a case in point, as Graeber and Tirosh and other authors in this volume note. The 'discipline' of mathematics education has not developed to the point of agreed and established modes of making, labelling, and negotiating the meaning or use of technical terms. Instead we resort to verbal explanations and occasionally to examples, which often prove to be multiply interpretable and so less than definitive or paradigmatic.

Why Probe Deeper?

Apart from the political consideration of justifying the existence and enterprise of teacher education (both prospective and practising teacher professional development), another reason put forward for probing what it is that informs expert teacher behaviour is to improve research into teacher effectiveness, and consequently, teacher education itself. The thinking is that in order to study whether activities influence student learning, it is necessary to distinguish what it is that teachers might or might not be doing, and to correlate these with learner outcomes and performance. One immediate consequence of this would be to inform programmes of teacher development and enhancement. Naturally, one would expect teacher education and professional development not only to take into account the multiple layers of awareness and sensitivities being worked on, but to mirror that in not only be 'being mathematical with and in front of learners', but also 'being pedagogical and didactic with and in front of teachers'.

However, anything with positive potential also has negative possibilities. Anything which sounds like test items for teacher knowledge could be added to the list of competency tests. This in turn would amplify the stance which converts words into checklists and lists into competencies, and which in turn leads to mechanistic training of corresponding behaviour without requisite attention to educating awareness. The 'checklist' culture which pervades education fails to recognise that education is about human beings not machines, and that awareness and affect are intricately interwoven with behaviour. Furthermore, this compound psyche is driven not by rational reasoning (or checklists of procedures), but by intention and will. People are not good at 'doing what they are told', nor is what they do very effective if they are merely following orders. This applies just as well to learners of mathematics as to teachers and educators. Where individuals exercise personal and professional judgement, guided by articulated values and dispositions, as well as by taken-as-shared aims and goals, creativity and flair prosper.

Probing More Deeply Still

For progress to be made, I am confident that it is necessary for learners, teachers and educators all to take a reflective stance. This means interrogating personal experience in order to elaborate on personal concept images and example spaces associated with different topics, while at the same time building on the literature of observed and theoretical obstacles to form a rich picture of the core awarenesses, the key sensitivities teachers need in order to provoke learners appropriately and to respond creatively and effectively to what they say and do. I am sure that there will be ongoing empirical enquiry to observe teachers and to delineate the actions they initiate and engage in, and then to probe them for what brought those actions to mind, and for the basis for making choices, including choices not to act in certain ways. I hope that the two approaches work together, and that we suffer neither the potential negative consequences of more testing nor the effects of assuming that responses to test items are evidence of sensitivity and awareness.

REFERENCES

Ainley, J. (1999). Doing algebra-type stuff: emergent algebra in the primary school. In O. Zaslavsky (Ed.), *Proceedings of the Twenty Third Annual Conference of the International Group for the Psychology of Mathematics* (Vol. 2, p. 9–16), Haifa, Israel.

Ball, D. Bass, H., & Hill, H. (2003). Knowing and Using mathematical knowledge in teaching: learning what matters. In B. Davis & E. Simmt (Eds.), *Proceedings of the 2002 Annual Meeting of the Canadian Mathematics Education Study Group* (pp. 3–14). Edmonton, AB: CMESG/GCEDM.

Ball, D., & Bass, H. (2000). Interweaving content and pedagogy in teaching and learning to teach: Knowing and using mathematics. In J. Boaler (Ed.), *Multiple perspectives on the teaching and learning of mathematics* (pp. 83–104). Westport, CT: Ablex.

Ball, D., & Grevholm, B. (2008). Contributions to WG2 on teacher preparation and the role of ICMI. website: www.unige.ch/math/EnsMath/Rome2008/ (accessed Jan. 2008).

Ball, D., & Even, R. (2005). ICMI 15th Study Conference 15: The professional education and development of teachers of mathematics. website: http://stwww.weizmann.ac.il/G-math/ICMI/log_in.html (accessed Jan. 2008).

Bass, H., Ball, D., Sleep, L., Boerst, T., & Suzuka, K. (2007). Learning to use mathematics in practice. Presentation at Oberwolfach Nov. See www.mathematik.uni-muenchen.de/~didaktik/index.php?ordner=ufer&data=oberwolfach/workshop/Hyman_Bass.pdf

Berger, M. (2004). Heaps, complexes and concepts (part I). *For the Learning of Mathematics, 24*(2), 2–6.

Brown, J., & van Lehn, K. (1980). Repair theory: A generative theory of bugs in procedural skills, *Cognitive Science, 4*, 379–426.

Browning, R. (1850). *Andrea del Sarto.* Line 97. In R. Browning, *Men and women,* London.

Bruner, J (1966). *Towards a theory of instruction,* Cambridge: Harvard University Press.

Bruner, J. (1996). *The culture of education.* Cambridge: Harvard University Press.

Chevallard, Y. (1985). *La transposition didactique.* Grenoble: La Pensée Sauvage.

Chevallard, Y. (1992). 'Concepts fondamentaux de la didactique: Perspectives apportées par une approche anthropologique', *Recherches en Didactique des Mathématiques, 12*(1), 73–111. Translated as 'Fundamental concepts in didactics: Perspectives provided by an anthropological approach". In R. Douady and A. Mercier (Eds.), *Research in Didactique of Mathematics, Selected Papers, extra issue of Recherches en didactique des mathématiques* (pp. 131–167). La Pensée Sauvage, Grenoble,.

Clements, D. (2002). Linking Research and Curriculum Development. In L. English (Ed.), *Handbook of international research in mathematics education.* Mahwah: Lawrence Erlbaum p599–630.

Cuoco, A., Goldenburg, P., & Mark, J. (1996). Habits of mind: An organizing principle for mathematics curricula. *Journal of Mathematical Behavior, 15*, 375–402.

Davis, B., & Simmt, E. (2006). Mathematics-for-teaching: an ongoing investigation of the mathematics that teachers (need to) know. *Educational Studies in Mathematics, 61*(3), 293–319.

Dewey, J. (1913). *Interest and effort in education.* Boston: Houghton Mifflin. Reprinted by www.Kessinger.nert Kessinger

Dweck, C. (2000). *Self-theories: Their role in motivation, personality and development.* Philadelphia: Psychology Press.

Fosnot, C. T., & Dolk, M. (2002). *Young mathematicians at work: Constructing fractions, decimals, and percents.* Portsmouth: Heinemann.

Gattegno, C. (1987). *The science of education part I: Theoretical considerations.* New York: Educational Solutions.

Gray, E., & Tall, D. (1994). Duality, ambiguity, and flexibility: A proceptual view of simple arithmetic. *Journal for Research in Mathematics Education, 25*(2), 116–140.

Greeno, J. (1991). Number sense as situated knowing in a conceptual domain. *Journal for Research in Mathematics Education, 22*(3), 170–218.

Griffin, P., & Gates, P. (1989). *Project Mathematics UPDATE: PM753 A,B,C,D, Preparing to teach angle, equations, ratio and probability.* Milton Keynes: Open University.

Hill, H., Rowan, B., & Ball, D. (2005). Effects of teachers' mathematical knowledge for teaching on student achievement. *American Educational Research Journal, 42*(2), 371– 406.

James, N., & Mason, J. (1982). Towards recording. *Visible Language, 16*(3), 249–258.

Kilpatrick, J., Swafford, J., & Findell, B. (Eds.) (2001). *Adding it up: Helping children learn mathematics.* Mathematics Learning Study Committee. Washington DC, USA: National Academy Press.

Ma, L. (1999). *Knowing and teaching elementary mathematics: Teachers' understanding of fundamental mathematics in China and the United States.* Mahwah: Lawrence Erlbaum.

Malara, N., & Navarra, G. (2003). *ArAl: A project for an early approach to algebraic thinking.* Retrieved Jan 2007 from http://www.pitagoragroup.it/pited/ArAl.html

Mason, J. (1998). Enabling teachers to be real teachers: Necessary levels of awareness and structure of attention. *Journal of Mathematics Teacher Education, 1*(3), 243-267.

Mason, J. (2002). *Researching your own practice: The discipline of noticing,* London: Routledge Falmer.

Mason, J., Burton L., & Stacey K. (1982). *Thinking mathematically.* London: Addison Wesley.

Mason, J., & Johnston-Wilder, S. (2004). *Fundamental constructs in mathematics education.* London: Routledge Falmer.

Mason, J., & Johnston-Wilder, S. (2004/2006). *Designing and using mathematical tasks.* Milton Keynes: Open University, republished (2006). St. Albans: Tarquin.

McNair, K. (1978a). Capturing inflight decisions: Thoughts while teaching. *Educational Research Quarterly, 3* (4), 26–42.

McNair, K. (1978b). Thought and action: A frozen section. *Educational Research Quarterly, 3*(4), 16–25.

Norretranders, T. (1998). (J. Sydenham Trans.). *The user illusion: Cutting consciousness down to size.* London: Allen Lane.

Ouspensky, P. (1950). *In search of the miraculous: Fragments of an unknown teaching,* London: Routledge & Kegan Paul.

Papert, S (1980). *Mind storms,* New York: Basic Books.

Peretz, D. (2006). Teaching for understanding for teaching. *For the Learning of Mathematics, 26*(3), 24–29, 38).

Pólya, G. (1962). *Mathematical discovery: On understanding, learning, and teaching problem solving.* New York: Wiley.

Ruthven, K. (2007). Mathematical knowledge in teaching: a synthesis of presentations at a seminar in Cambridge, www.maths-ed.org.uk/mkit/Ruthven_synthesis.pdf (accessed Jan. 27, 2008).

Schoenfeld, A. (1985). *Mathematical problem solving.* New York: Academic Press.

Simon, M. (1995). Reconstructing mathematics pedagogy from a constructivist perspective. *Journal for Research in Mathematics Education, 26,* 114–145.

Simon, M. (2006). Key developmental understandings in mathematics: A direction for investigating and establishing learning goals. *Mathematical Thinking and Learning, 8*(4), 359–371.

Simon, M., & Tzur, R. (2004). Explicating the role of mathematical tasks in conceptual learning: An elaboration of the hypothetical learning trajectory. *Mathematical Thinking and Learning, 6,* 91–104.

Simon, M., Tzur, R., Heinz, K., & Kinzel, M (2004). Explicating a mechanism for conceptual Learning: Elaborating the construct of reflective abstraction. *Journal for Research in Mathematics Education, 35,* 305–329.

Small, M. (2004). *Navigating through problem solving and reasoning in Grade 2.* Reston, VA: National Council of Teachers of Mathematics.

Tall, D., & Vinner, S. (1981). Concept Image and concept definition in mathematics with particular reference to limits and continuity. *Educational Studies in Mathematics. 12*(2), 151–169.

Ufer, S. (2007). Oberwolfach Teacher Education website: www.mathematik.uni-muenchen.de/ ~didaktik/index.php?ordner=ufer&data=oberwolfach/workshop (accessed Jan. 2008)

Valsiner, J. (1988). *Developmental psychology in the Soviet Union.* Brighton: Harvester.

van der Veer, R., & Valsiner, J. (1991). *Understanding Vygotsky.* London: Blackwell.

van Lehn, K. (1989). *Mind bugs.* Cambridge, MA: MIT Press.

Vergnaud, G (1981). Quelques orientations théoriques et méthodologiques des recherches françaises en didactique des mathématiques. In *Actes du Vième Colloque de PME,* (vol 2, pp.7–17), Edition IMAG, Grenoble.

Vergnaud, G. (1997). The nature of mathematical concepts. In T. Nunes and P. Bryant (Eds.), *Learning and teaching mathematics: An international perspective.* London: Psychology Press.

Vergnaud, G. (1983). Multiplicative structures. In R. Lesh & M. Landau (Eds.), *Acquisition of Mathematics Concepts and Processes* (pp. 127–124). New York: Academic Press.

John Mason
Department of Mathematics
Open University
and
Department of Education,
University of Oxford
United Kingdom